Law in America's Crossroads

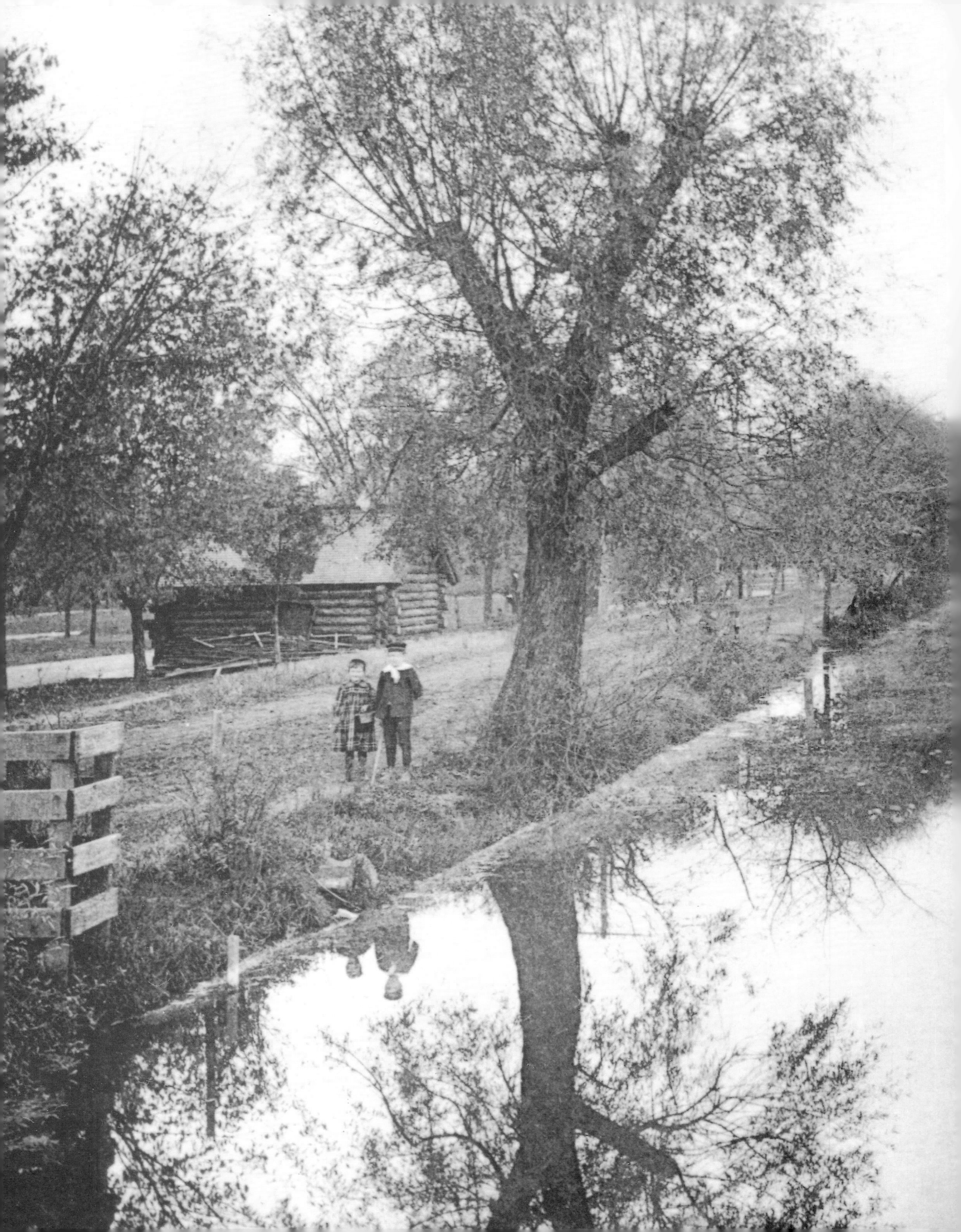

LAW IN AMERICA'S CROSSROADS

A HISTORY OF THE
INDIANAPOLIS LEGAL PROFESSION

ALICIA CARLSON and SANDRA CLINE

ASSOCIATION PUBLISHING COMPANY
BIRMINGHAM, ALABAMA

LAW IN AMERICA'S CROSSROADS

Published By
ASSOCIATION PUBLISHING COMPANY
100 Oxmoor Road, Suite 110, Birmingham, Alabama 35209
(205) 941-4623

JOHN COMPTON, *Publisher*

Published with the cooperation and assistance of the
INDIANAPOLIS BAR ASSOCIATION
JAMES DIMOS, *President*
JULIE ARMSTRONG, *Executive Director*

Written By
ALICIA CARLSON AND SANDRA CLINE

Book and Dust Jacket Design By
ROBIN MCDONALD

Editor
JAMES SUMMERVILLE

Photo Editor
DEBORAH MARKISON

COPYRIGHT ©2001 BY ASSOCIATION PUBLISHING COMPANY
All Rights Reserved
Published 2001

Printed in the United States of America by
TAYLOR PUBLISHING COMPANY, DALLAS, TEXAS

FIRST EDITION

ISBN 0-966-8380-2-5
Library of Congress Control Number: 2001094980

LAW IN AMERICA'S
CROSSROADS

TABLE OF CONTENTS

	FOREWORD	6
Chapter One	A CAPITAL PLAN	8
Chapter Two	WAR AND PROGRESS	24
Chapter Three	A NEW VITALITY	48
Chapter Four	A GREAT WAR AND THE EVE OF A GREAT DEPRESSION	64
Chapter Five	THE GREAT DEPRESSION, WAR AND PEACE	88
Chapter Six	AN ERA OF CHANGE	106
Chapter Seven	A CITY AT THE CROSSROADS	122
Chapter Eight	A CITY POISED FOR GREATNESS	138
	LAW FIRM HISTORIES	152
	FRIENDS OF THE BAR	211
	APPENDIX	220
	BIBLIOGRAPHY	222
	INDEX	224
	ACKNOWLEDGEMENTS	228

A History of the Indianapolis Legal Profession

LAW IN AMERICA'S
CROSSROADS

FOREWORD

As President of the Indianapolis Bar Association, let me extend our Association's hope that you will enjoy *Law in America's Crossroads: A History of the Indianapolis Legal Profession*. As with many other projects undertaken by our Association, the fact that we have published this book during my tenure has everything to do with fortunate timing. The vision, leadership, and effort contributed by my predecessors have much more to do with this project becoming a reality than anything that occurred during my term.

In addition to acknowledging the efforts of my more immediate predecessors Phil Isenbarger, Joe Russell and Karen Turner, I would like to thank those past presidents of the Association, Chic Born, Mary Marsh, Bo Hagemier, and John Houghton, who assisted with the preparation of this book. I would also like to thank our current Executive Director, Julie Armstrong, for keeping this project going over the terms of four successive presidencies.

I would also like to thank those members of the Association, in particular Hugh Reynolds, Virginia Dill McCarty, and the late Charlie Symmes, who helped provide historical perspective and insight to the creative process reflected in this book. Whether it was "correcting the record" or proofreading a chapter, each of these individuals made valuable contributions to this work. Of course, any project of this nature would have been incomplete without the irreplaceable assistance of our former Executive Director, Rosie Felton.

This project would not have been as successful without the contribution of The Indiana Historical Society, the staff and writers of Association Publishing, especially John Compton, and the countless individuals who shared with us their photographs, artifacts and stories. The most valuable contribution, however, came in the form of the cooperation, support and material provided by the law firms and individuals profiled in the book. Without their stories, the history of the profession in this community would have been incomplete.

As noted by the Rev. Dr. Martin Luther King, "we are not makers of history, we are made by history." As the following pages will reveal, history has made the legal profession in our community what it is today, with all its glory and flaws. As our profession enters a new era, we hope that this book not only entertains us but educates us as well as we face the challenges of the future.

James Dimos
123rd President
Indianapolis Bar Association

A History of the Indianapolis Legal Profession 7

CHAPTER ONE
(1820–1840)

A CAPITAL PLAN

In January, 1821, state legislators meeting in Corydon, Indiana began a debate over the future capital of Indiana. It was a lively debate, with nearly as much laughter as serious discussion.

The question was not about location. That much had been settled. The new capital would be located approximately 160 miles north of Corydon. It would be a planned city, built nearly from scratch, to serve as the seat of the government in the center of a fledgling state. But the bill creating the new seat of government had only a blank where the name of the proposed city should be. The name "Tecumseh" and other American Indian names were proposed. Another member proposed the name "Suwarrow." All were rejected.

In the end, Jefferson County Judge Jeremiah Sullivan—although other accounts would attribute also the idea to attorney and state treasurer Samuel Merrill—won the day with his suggestion: Indianapolis. Later, he would explain that the Greek word, "polis," meaning city, and the state name, Indiana, would "indicate to all the world the locality of the town." On January 6, 1821, the name and location were confirmed by the Indiana legislature.

Despite its designation as a state capital by birth, Indianapolis then could barely be described as a village.

In 1820—just a year after the first permanent white settlers arrived—only a dozen or so families were clearing the deep forest along the White River, scratching out a living by farming, fishing and hunting. The little settlement near the mouth of Fall Creek, where it emptied into the White River, attracted frontier people who had already experienced the hardships of life in the wilderness, hardships that 21st century Hoosiers can hardly imagine.

Those first years in Indianapolis were, as 19th century Indianapolis historian W. R. Holloway described them, "a period of isolation, and, for a time, of struggle for existence.

During these [first] years, no other village of the state had so much to resist, and so little to assist it. It was far from all navigable streams and all passable roads, and, for the first two years, was without clearing or adequate cultivations, without mills or means of subsistence, except what was brought in on horseback through 60 miles of forest. Sickness in the second year, which prostrated nearly everybody, made the isolation more dangerous, and sickness having prevented labor, an unpleasant approach to starvation followed the ague."

Yet it was this very fledgling community that commissioners of the new state of Indiana chose to be the capital for several good reasons, and one miscalculation.

When Indiana became a territory two decades earlier, Vincennes was its capital. As the territory's population grew both west and north, the capital was moved to Corydon. The way for settlement in central Indiana was opened further when the U.S. Congress authorized a state government for Indiana in 1816, and became inevitable with the signing of the Treaty of St. Mary's (Ohio), an agreement with the Miami and Delaware Indian tribes that stipulated Native Americans leave the region.

As the state's leaders began considering the future, Gov. Jonathon Jennings persuaded businessmen and land speculators that Indiana—unlike other states in the young country, which had capitals by accident, default or for purely political reasons—could actually create its own state capital to suit its present and future needs. As the population continued to settle in central and northern Indiana, Jennings argued, it only made sense to build a seat of government that would be centrally located.

Jennings appointed a commission to study possible sites. In 1820, he and several commissioners met at William Conner's farm near present-day Noblesville. From there, they rode to the Fall Creek settlement and spent several days studying the

Attorney and state treasurer Samuel Merrill directed the state capitol's move from Corydon to Indianapolis. The trip took two weeks by covered wagon.

A History of the Indianapolis Legal Profession

ABOVE: *Jeremiah Sullivan helped select the name Indianapolis for the new capitol city. He later served on the Indianapolis Supreme Court.*
RIGHT: *This Vincennes building served as the capitol when Indiana was still a territory.*
BELOW: *The first state capitol in Corydon, Indiana.*

possibilities. The Fall Creek site was eventually chosen as the state's new capital, owing in part to its level and fertile soil and its proximity to the advancing National Road.

The commissioners also reported that the land was on a navigable river, which was a key element at a time when travel by road was difficult and railroads were nonexistent. Too late, it would be discovered that the White River, in fact, was not navigable, except for flatboats and rafts.

While a lack of waterway was a miscalculation that kept Indianapolis isolated and slowed the development of settlement and business for years to come, the presence of the state capital would prove to be a more important factor for the future. It would also be an important factor in the development of a thriving legal community.

A member of Indiana's legal profession helped name Indianapolis, and lawyers were among the first citizens to settle the place.

LOG CABIN JUSTICE

CURIOUS ABOUT THIS NEW CAPITAL CITY, people began arriving in a steady stream in 1821. Lawyers Obed Foote and Calvin Fletcher were among them, and by the time they hung out

RIGHT: *Jonathan Jennings was elected Indiana's first governor in 1816.*
ABOVE: *An idealized view of Indianapolis in 1820.*

their separate shingles, Indianapolis could boast several stores and businesses, a sawmill, a gristmill, several taverns and a school. Indianapolis really took off with the sale of 315 lots over several days in October 1821, bringing the town's population to around 500 by the end of the year.

The governor and the state legislature did not immediately leave Corydon for Indianapolis. Instead, state legislators—especially those who hailed from southern Indiana and had a vested interest in keeping the capital in their vicinity—wanted to delay the move until there was an appropriate place to meet.

Indianapolis, also did not immediately have its own judicial jurisdiction. Instead, every serious criminal or civil case had to be tried at the county seat of Connersville, 60 miles away. In 1821, Gov. Jennings appointed James McIllvaine as the town's first justice of the peace, an office, it was said, that McIllvaine performed from the doorway of his dirt-floored log cabin at the corner of Ohio and Meridian streets. As McIllvaine puffed on his pipe and listened to complaints and evidence, his bailiff kept his eyes on the accused and

A History of the Indianapolis Legal Profession 11

the dense surrounding woods, which would have afforded easy escape.

Still, McIllvaine only had jurisdiction over petty crimes. Since Connersville was a long journey through the woods, it was to everyone's advantage to iron out conflicts without litigation. Criminal cases, too, were not filed lightly. After all, the trip to Connersville offered prisoners plenty of opportunity for escape, not to mention the cost and trouble involved in delivering offenders to the courtroom.

How citizens coped with the lack of immediate official justice became legendary. In one infamous case, four Kentucky boatmen came to Indianapolis for "a Christmas frolic." After getting quite drunk, they tore down a little shanty of a tavern owned by settler Daniel Larkins.

Although the perpetrators were driven off, Indianapolis residents, alarmed at the seriousness of the offense, later captured the men and brought them before McIllvaine. The justice of the peace fined the men heavily. When they could not pay, they were imprisoned until they could be taken to Connersville. During the first night of their captivity in Indianapolis, they escaped, to everyone's relief. No one, apparently, wanted to make the mid-winter trek to Connersville over a drunken brawl.

Meanwhile, the proposed future state capital was being organized. In 1821, the state legislature authorized formal organization of Marion County—named for the Revolutionary War General Francis "Swamp Fox" Marion—and appropriated $8,000 for the construction of a two-story brick courthouse that was completed in 1825. The legislature stipulated that the courthouse was to be used by the state for federal and state courts and for 50 years as a meeting place for the state legislature, if it so desired. In fact, the first courthouse was practically the only public building in town from 1825 until the first statehouse in Indianapolis was completed in 1835. At the same time, Marion County was made part of the Fifth Judicial Circuit, which, in 1822, included the counties of Marion, Monroe, Owen, Green, Morgan, Lawrence, Rush, Hendricks, Decatur, Bartholomew, Shelby and Jennings.

12   LAW IN AMERICA'S CROSSROADS

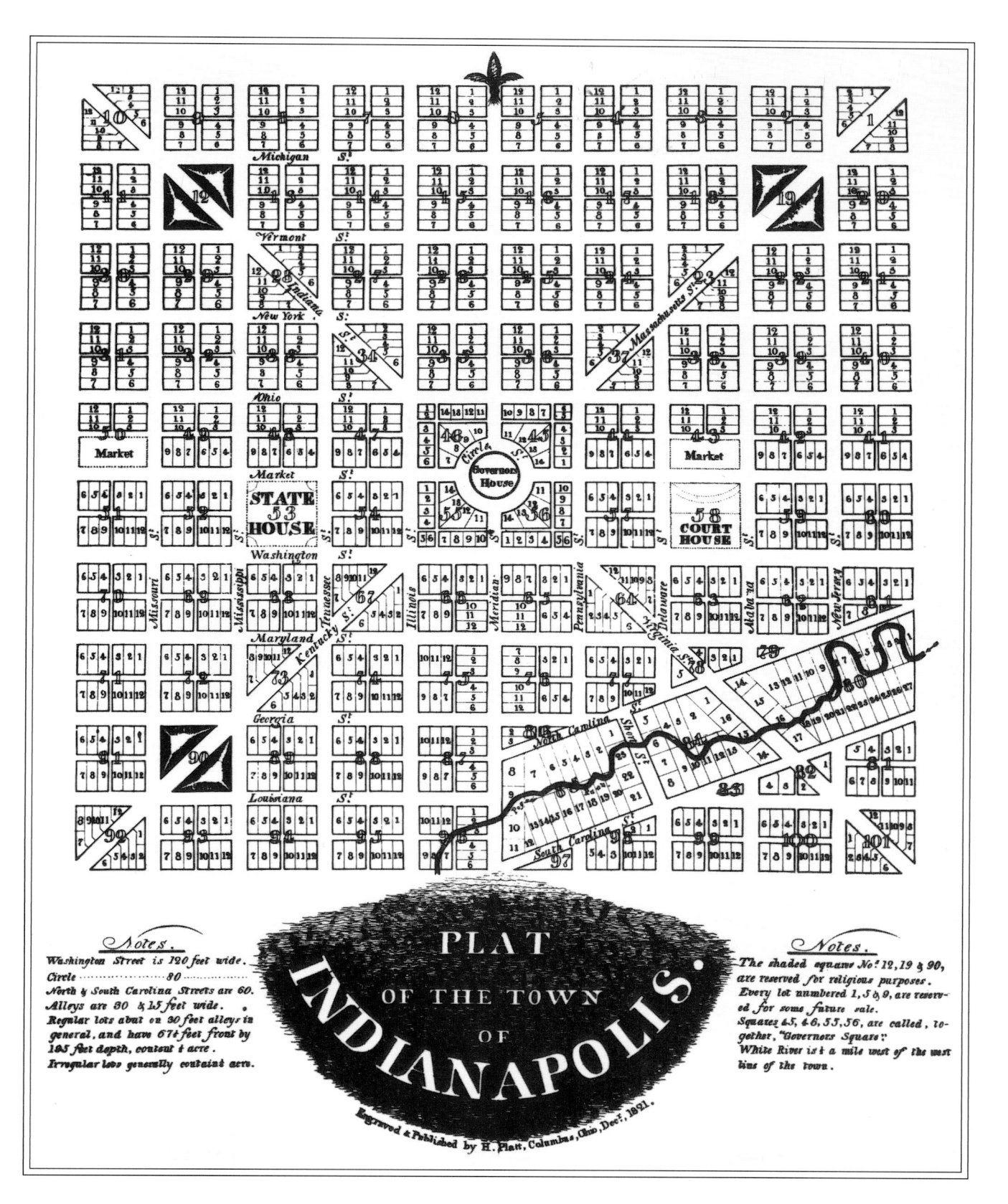

ABOVE: *This 1821 Plat of Indianapolis shows the city's distinctive layout.*
OPPOSITE PAGE: *Matthias R. Nowland's cabin on Washington Street was the site of an early real estate auction in October, 1821.*

A History of the Indianapolis Legal Profession

CALVIN FLETCHER: DIARY OF A FRONTIER LAWYER

NO HISTORY OF INDIANAPOLIS WOULD BE COMPLETE WITHOUT mention of Calvin Fletcher (1798-1866), not just because he was an early and prominent attorney and business leader, but also because of the unique record of his life that gives a glimpse into what life was like for the settlers of Indianapolis.

The Diary of Calvin Fletcher, edited by the late Indiana Historical Society librarian Gayle Thornbrough and published in nine volumes by the society in 1972, extends from 1817 to 1866. The volumes include Fletcher's diary entries, some personal papers, his legal licenses from Ohio and Indiana, selected newspaper clippings, and the journals of his wife, Sarah Hill Fletcher.

Fletcher was born in Ludlow, Vermont, on Feb. 4, 1798, the eleventh child of Jesse and Lucy Keyes Fletcher. He attended school in Vermont only sporadically, because he was needed as a laborer on his family's farm. When he was just 17 years old, Fletcher left home to work as a laborer on another Vermont farm, then attended school in Royalton and Randolph, Vermont, as well as in Westford, Mass.

In May 1817, Fletcher decided to seek his fortune by going west. He ended up in Urbana, Ohio, where he taught school and read law with a prominent attorney, James Cooley. In 1820, after a summer with his brother in Lynchburg, Va., he returned to Urbana to resume his law studies, and, a year later, was admitted to practice by the Supreme Court of Ohio. That same year, in May 1821, Fletcher married a young woman, Sarah Hill, in Urbana.

They didn't stay in Ohio long. In August, Fletcher visited Indianapolis and decided that he would have more opportunity in the fledgling capital than in Urbana, which already had a number of established lawyers.

On Oct. 1, 1821, the Fletchers arrived in Indianapolis to stay, despite the fact that, as Fletcher recorded in his diary, "I found the place very sickly." And it was. The summer and fall of 1821 had been especially bad in terms of rainy weather and illness, with 25 people losing their lives to what was then called "fever and ague."

Some newcomers became discouraged with the dampness and illness of Indianapolis and left, but not the Fletchers. He and Sarah built a life in Indianapolis, raising 11 children and Fletcher was active in the legal community, business and civic affairs.

Fletcher's active law practice in Indianapolis spanned about two decades. When the Marion County government was organized in 1822, he was appointed township overseer of the poor and prosecuting attorney. As prosecutor, Fletcher was paid anywhere from $20 and $50 during a given session of the court, which met each spring and fall. As an attorney for the Fifth Judicial Circuit, he traveled twice a year through up to 10 counties in central Indiana, practicing law. He prosecuted the accused in the infamous Fall Creek Massacre (1824-1825) and represented an African-American woman who sued for her freedom in 1829. From 1835 until 1843, Fletcher practiced law in a partnership with two other attor-

On September 26, 1822, the first session of the Marion County court assembled in one of the finest residences in town, a two-room log cabin that belonged to John Carr. With Judge William Wick presiding, 14 rules of practice were adopted, and 10 attorneys were admitted to practice: Fletcher, Hiram M. Curry, Foote, Daniel B. Wick, Oliver H. Smith, James Noble, James Rariden, James Whitcomb, Lot Bloomfield and Harvey Gregg.

After the admission of the lawyers, the first session of the court adjourned to meet in the afternoon at the house of Jacob R. Crumbaugh at the southwest corner of Market and Missouri streets. In the afternoon session, grand jurors were appointed, and Fletcher was named prosecuting attorney. Richard Good, an Irishman from County Cork, was naturalized.

The first liquor license in Marion County was issued for John Hawkins' hotel on the north side of Washington Street, midway between Meridian and Pennsylvania. In related business, 11 men were indicted for selling liquor without a license. Four millers were charged with obstructing the White River; their cases were tried later and two of the individuals were fined 1 cent, a punishment that was later suspended.

At the close of the first term, the court allowed Crumbaugh $7.50 for the use of his house. Subsequent sessions of the court rotated among several Indianapolis residents' cabins until the new courthouse—a two-story brick structure facing Washington Street, with an adjoining log jail whose walls were a foot thick—was built in 1825. But most lawyers and Judge Wick must have spent much of their time on horse-

Calvin Fletcher, shown with his wife Sarah, was a leading member of the community. His diary provides a rich resource for understanding what life was like in early Indianapolis.

neys, Ovid Butler and Simon Yandes. He also served as state senator, representing Boone, Hamilton, Hancock, Hendricks, Madison and Marion counties.

During 1820s and 1830s, Fletcher helped lay the groundwork of justice in Indianapolis, which attracted its share of roughnecks. Fletcher himself had something of a temper; he once punched fellow lawyer Obed Foote in the nose, but confessed the assault and battery to the court on his own and paid his $2 fine.

Fletcher arrived in Indianapolis a poor man but became one of the community's wealthier citizens. By the mid-1860s, he was among the largest landowners in Marion County, and he was director, then branch president, of the Indianapolis branch of the State Bank of Indiana. In 1857, he co-founded the Indianapolis Branch Banking Co. and developed other banking interests in the state. Fletcher promoted development of canal and railroad access to Indianapolis, and in 1855 was appointed director and president of the Indianapolis and Bellefontaine Railroad.

Committed to anti-slavery causes, Fletcher chaired the state's Free Soil Committee in 1848. He was a founder of both the Indiana Colonization Society, the Indiana Historical Society and was active in the Indiana Temperance Society and Indianapolis Benevolent Society. All of his life, Fletcher regretted his own lack of formal schooling and was active in establishing free, public schools in Indianapolis.

---

back. In addition to Marion County, Judge Wick had as many as 10 other counties in his jurisdiction in the Fifth Judicial Circuit, and most lawyers rode the circuit, too, visiting log cabin courtrooms throughout central Indiana.

In his *History of Indianapolis and Marion County, Indiana*, published in 1884, Berry R. Sulgrove writes, "We now have no idea of the hardships endured by the old bar in their practice, the circuit once extending from Bloomington to Fort Wayne, its whole extent a wilderness. Traveling it was a campaign often involving weeks of absence from home, manning swollen rivers, and sleeping in the woods. It was at all times tedious and laborious, and in some seasons difficult and dangerous. The fees were far less than they are now, and often remained mere promises to pay."

Most court business involved civil matters, and few cases were serious or involved much monetary damages. There wasn't much crime, and not much punishment, for that matter. In 1823, for example, a citizen named Robert Massey was charged with issuing a challenge to fight a duel, a serious crime in those days, close to a felony under the strict laws that had been enacted to stop the practice of dueling. Massey was fined one cent and costs and imprisoned for 60 days.

Yet log cabin justice could be swift and make powerful statements about what Indianapolis settlers were willing to tolerate, and what they would not.

In 1824, the capital city was stunned, and then alarmed, by murder. In February of that year, a party of nine American Indians, including two men, three women and four small children, camped northeast of Indianapolis at Lick Creek to hunt and fish. In early March, John Harper, a settler with a reputation for hatred toward Indians, saw the camp and made plans to raid it and seize the Indian's valuable furs. Harper recruited five other settlers, James Hudson, Andrew Sawyer, John T. Bridges and Bridge's 18-year-old son, John, Jr., to accompany him on his raid.

On the morning of March 22, the five men walked into the Indian camp and feigned friendship, asking for help in finding some lost horses. The Indian braves, a Shawnee named Ludlow and a Miami named Mingo, agreed to help. As they entered the woods, Harper and Hudson shot them in the back. Sawyer and the Bridges opened fire on the women and children. When the shooting stopped, all nine Indians were dead. Hoping to make the killings look like the work of other Indians, the men mutilated the bodies. They plundered the camp, loading their horses—which they had kept hidden in the woods—and rode away.

The next day, a trapper stumbled on the scene and reported the news in Pendleton. The murderers' plan to make it look as if other Indians had committed the killings didn't fool the experienced frontiersmen who investigated. White settlers were not willing to dismiss the killings, either. Instead, they were furious that the white killers would put everyone at risk of outraged Indians, who might decide to launch retaliatory attacks. Determined to make an example of the white men, a posse rounded up four of the perpetrators. Harper, the ring-

TOP: *Early lawyers endured many hardships while riding the circuit.*
ABOVE: *Christian Schraeder drew this view of Marion County's first jail, built in 1824 for a cost of $312. The ground floor had a one foot square window but no door. Access was gained through a trap door on the second floor.*

16   LAW IN AMERICA'S CROSSROADS

leader, was never apprehended and may have escaped to Ohio.

Local white leaders met with Indian chiefs and asked them not to take any action until the white government had a chance to bring the matter to justice. The Indian chiefs agreed to wait and see. Still, settlers in Indianapolis were nervous, worried that the Indians would retaliate regardless of what their chiefs said.

In April, the circuit court convened and the four alleged murderers were indicted. The following fall, one of the four, James Hudson, was tried first, gathering Indiana's then greatest—and not so great—legal talent in a two-room log cabin. Judge Wick was presiding judge, assisted by Samuel Holliday, a farmer, and Andrew Winchell, an illiterate blacksmith with no pretense of legal knowledge. General James Noble, then a U.S. senator, was employed by the secretary of war to prosecute, along with the local prosecutor, Fletcher. Attorneys Gregg, Bloomfield, Rariden, Wick and Charles H. Test were among those hired by the defense of all four men.

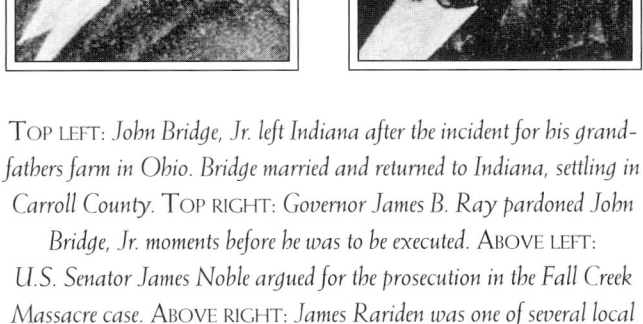

The argument by the prosecution was remarkable, according to the frontier lawyer Oliver Hampton Smith, who watched the proceedings. "General James Noble closed the argument for the State, in one of his forcible speeches, holding up to the jury the bloody clothes of the Indians, and appealing to the justice, patriotism and love of the laws of the jury, not forgetting

TOP LEFT: *John Bridge, Jr. left Indiana after the incident for his grandfathers farm in Ohio. Bridge married and returned to Indiana, settling in Carroll County.* TOP RIGHT: *Governor James B. Ray pardoned John Bridge, Jr. moments before he was to be executed.* ABOVE LEFT: *U.S. Senator James Noble argued for the prosecution in the Fall Creek Massacre case.* ABOVE RIGHT: *James Rariden was one of several local attorneys hired by the defense in the Fall Creek Massacre case.*

A History of the Indianapolis Legal Profession   17

that the safety of the settlers might depend upon the conviction of the prisoners, as the chiefs and warriors expected justice to be done. The speech had a marked effect upon the crowd, as well as the jury.

"Judge Wick charged the jury at some length, laying down the law of homicide in its different degrees, and distinctly impressing upon the jury that the law knew no distinction as to nation or color; that the murder of an Indian was equally as criminal in law as the murder of the white man."

During the spring court term, the three remaining defendants were tried and found guilty, and Judge Wick sentenced them to death by hanging. The cases were promptly appealed to the Indiana Supreme Court, but Judge Isaac Blackford upheld the verdicts and sentences.

Early sketch of the Marion County Courthouse.

Defendant Hudson was hanged before a large audience on January 25, 1825. The other defendants went to the gallows on June 3, 1825. Sawyer and the elder Bridge were hanged first, but, in what must have been an unimaginably dramatic scene to the crowd gathered for the executions, Indiana Gov. James Brown Ray rode up on horseback and pardoned the younger Bridge as the teenager stood on the scaffold.

The incident proved that while central Indiana was still mostly wilderness, a sense of justice and the rule of law had taken a firm hold. It wasn't perfect, but it was a start.

THE CAPITAL ARRIVES

With the construction of the Marion County Courthouse in 1824, plans could proceed to move the state capital to Indianapolis. Samuel Merrill, the state treasurer, directed the move, loading boxes of documents and silver from the state treasury into covered wagons to be moved overland from Corydon to Indianapolis. For Merrill, his wife and four daughters, it was an arduous two-week journey—on the best day of travel the caravan only managed 11 miles—on primitive roads, through virgin forests and across rivers.

Merrill, a native of Peacham, Vermont, attended Dartmouth College before leaving college to teach school and read law at York, Pennsylvania. In 1816, he moved to Vevay, Indiana, and was admitted to the bar there. A former state representative, Merrill was elected state treasurer in 1822 and served until 1834, eventually leaving state government to serve as president of the State Bank and as president of the Madison and Indianapolis railroad. Later, he founded the company that evolved into the Bobbs-Merrill Co., an Indianapolis publishing house.

Despite the serious impediments to travel that Merrill and his family experienced firsthand, Indianapolis was slowly opening up to the outside world. The first stagecoach lines came to Indianapolis in 1825–1826, and the National Road—the forerunner of U.S. 40—would come through Indianapolis in the 1830s from Ohio, through Richmond, and on to Illinois through Terre Haute. Construction on Michigan Road, which would provide north-south travel through Indiana from Madison, Ind. on the Ohio River to Lake Michigan, began in the spring of 1828. But plans to navigate the White River were finally abandoned. Although the river swelled during spring rains, steamboats would never be able to dock in Indianapolis.

As transportation improved, Indianapolis continued to grow. The population in 1826 was approximately 726 residents; four years later, the U.S. Census reported the population had swelled to 1,085.

According to historian George Geib, many of these early settlers came to Indianapolis from the neighboring states of Ohio and Kentucky, as well as the eastern United States, in part to win public offices in the community. These offices, including county positions such as recorder, clerk, judge, and commissioner, offered men (and they were all, without exception, white men) cash salaries that were welcome in a frontier society that was characterized by subsistence farming and barter.

In a similar fashion, the location of the state capital in Indianapolis boosted the entire town's prestige and economy.

RECOLLECTIONS OF EARLY INDIANA COURTROOM DRAMA

IF THE RECOLLECTIONS OF OLIVER H. Smith (1794-1859) are to be believed, today's television courtroom dramas have nothing on the central Indiana log cabin courtrooms of the 1820s.

Smith, one of the attorneys admitted at the first session of the Marion County Circuit Court in 1821, was a state legislator, U.S. congressman, Indiana senator and railroad entrepreneur. Based in Connersville, Indiana until about 1838, when he moved to Indianapolis, Smith was a circuit-riding lawyer, which meant he traveled throughout the Third Judicial District, including Indianapolis. In the book *Early Indiana Trials and Sketches: Reminiscences by Hon. O. H. Smith*, published in 1858, some 38 years after he began practicing law in Indiana, Smith recalls:

Oliver H. Smith was an early circuit-riding lawyer.

"The judiciary system at the time referred to was, like the country, in its infancy. The Circuit Court was composed of a president judge, elected by the legislature, who presided in all the courts in the circuit, and two associate judges, elected in each county by the people. These 'side judges,' as they were then called, made no pretensions to any particular knowledge of the law, but still they had the power to over-rule the presiding judge, and give the opinion of the court, and sometimes they even 'out-guessed' the president, giving the most preposterous reasons imaginable for their decisions.... The most important personages in the country, however, were the young lawyers, universally called 'squires' by old and young, male and female.

"The court-rooms in those days were prepared and furnished much simplicity, and yet they seemed to answer all the purposes absolutely necessary to the due administration of justice. The building, as I have stated, generally contained two rooms—the court-room being the largest—at one end of which there was a platform elevated some three feet for the judges, with a long bench to seat them. These benches were very substantial in general, sufficient to sustain the most weighty judges; yet on one occasion the bench gave way and down came three fat, aldermanly judges on the floor. One of them, quite a wag, seeing the 'squires' laughing, remarked, 'Gentlemen, this is a mighty weak bench.'

"The bar had their benches near the table of the clerk, and the crowd was kept back by a long pole fastened with withes at the ends. The crowds at that day thought the holding of court a great affair. The people came hundreds of miles to see the judges and hear the lawyers 'plead,' as they called it.

"On one occasion, there came to be tried before the jury an indictment for an assault and battery against a man for pulling the nose of another who had insulted him. The courtroom was filled to suffocation. The two associate judges were on the bench. The evidence had been heard, and public expectation was on tiptoe. All was silent as death, when my young friend, then 'squire,' afterward Judge Charles H. Test, rose and addressed the court: 'If the court please.' He was here interrupted by Judge Winchell from the bench. 'Yes, we do please; go to the bottom of the case, young man. The people have come in to hear the lawyers plead.' The young squire, encouraged by the kind response of the judge, proceeded to address the jury some three hours in excited eloquence upon the great provocation his client had received to induce his docile nature to bound over all legal barriers and take the prosecutor by the nose. All eyes were upon him, and as he closed, Judge Winchell roared out, 'Capital! I did not think it was in him!' The jury returned a verdict of not guilty amid the rapturous applause of the audience. Court adjourned, and the people returned home to tell their children that they had heard the lawyers 'plead.'"

A History of the Indianapolis Legal Profession

Indiana's first statehouse was a grand neo-classical building set amid rather rustic surroundings.

The legislators brought with them legislation and cash in their saddlebags, and taverns and merchants benefited from the former, if not the latter. Senators and representatives were paid two silver dollars a day during the sessions of the General Assembly and two dollars for every 25 miles they traveled through the Indiana wilderness.

On Feb. 10, 1831, the Indiana legislature authorized $56,000 for construction of the first statehouse. Construction was to be funded in part by the sale of lots that the state still owned in the original four-mile square area set aside by Congress for the state capital. It was a tough sell; in the final days of the sale, land agents reduced the price of prime downtown real estate for as little as $10 each. Almost all of the outlots remained unsold and were leased for cow pastures.

Morris Morris (1780–1864) was one of three building commissioners appointed to oversee construction of the statehouse. A native of Virginia, Morris moved to Kentucky as a youngster, where he read law and began a practice. He became a devout Christian, however, and decided to give up his law practice, after concluding that it was incompatible with his beliefs. He moved to Indianapolis with his family in 1821 and began acquiring land and building a political career.

Morris ran unsuccessfully for county clerk in 1822 and for sheriff in 1824. Two years later, he was elected to the Indiana House of Representatives, where he served for one year. In 1828, Morris became state auditor and served until 1844. Later, after leaving that position, Morris was elected to the Indianapolis City Council. He and his sons eventually operated a steam mill on south Meridian Street.

The statehouse was finished in December 1835, in time for the legislature to meet, at a final cost of around $60,000. At the time, the building was the pride of Indianapolis, which finally had a symbol for its place as the seat of government.

This idealized view of the state's first capitol looks rather different than the actual photograph.

Among the people who settled in Indianapolis with the state capital was Isaac Blackford (1786–1859), who was appointed to the Indiana Supreme Court by Gov. Jennings in 1817. Blackford was born in Boundbrook, New Jersey and graduated from Princeton University. He read and practiced law in New Jersey before moving west to Salem, Indiana, and then relocated to Indianapolis around the time that the seat of government moved from Corydon. He was considered something of a recluse, yet he lived in one of the community's most public places.

Blackford penned much of his eight-volume *Blackford Reports* in a house on the Circle that had originally been constructed as a governor's residence. No governor ever lived there, however, because of its location—no governor's wife wanted to hang her family's dirty laundry on the Circle, after all—and its lack of kitchen and general livability. The *Blackford Reports*, published between 1830 and 1850, were shortened versions of most decisions made by the Supreme Court and remain the primary source of the court's record during those years. The house on the Circle was torn down after Blackford's death.

James Scott and Jesse L. Holman were Blackford's colleagues on the Indiana Supreme Court. Scott, a native of Pennsylvania and a member of the judiciary committee that helped pen the Indiana Constitution, served from 1816 until 1830. Holman, who came to Indiana from Kentucky in 1810 with some of his family's slaves so that they could be freed under Indiana's anti-slavery provisions, sat on the Indiana Supreme Court during the same period. In 1835, upon the death of the first federal judge, Benjamin Parke, who had been appointed by President Thomas Jefferson, Holman became a federal district court judge, a post he held until his death.

During Marion County's founding decade, the Indiana Supreme Court shared the Marion County Courthouse with

A History of the Indianapolis Legal Profession

both the local trial court and the U.S. District Court, as well. As the state's population grew throughout the first decades of its existence, the legislature was forced to redistrict the circuit court jurisdictions several times. On January 14, 1824, the legislature redistricted the whole state into five judicial circuits, but left Marion County in the Fifth circuit with Morgan, Johnson, Shelby, Decatur, Rush, Madison, Bartholomew, Henry, Hamilton and Hendricks counties. In 1830, the legislature divided the state into seven judicial districts, with Marion County in the Fifth circuit with the counties of Hendricks, Morgan, Johnson, Bartholomew, Shelby, Hancock, Madison, Hamilton, and, the following year, Grant County.

Between 1833 and 1852, the legislature redistricted the state several more times, but Marion County remained part of the Fifth Judicial Circuit with the surrounding counties of Hancock, Shelby, Bartholomew, Johnson, Hendricks and Morgan. The 1816 Indiana constitution provided for a system of circuit courts, presided over by "president judges," elected by the legislature for seven-year terms. Each county elected "associates" who were to preside with the judges and who also could hold court in the president judge's absence. From 1822 until 1825, for example, James McIlvain, who had conducted his justice of the peace duties at the door of his log cabin and had no legal training other than that which he learned on the job, was an associate judge with Judge William Wick, who was a member of the bar.

CITY CHARTERS AND DEATH OF CANAL DREAMS

As steadily as Indianapolis was growing, it was still not officially a town until its municipal incorporation in 1832. The Indiana General Assembly adopted legislation on Feb. 2, 1832

Isaac Blackford served on the Indiana Supreme Court for 35 years. His Blackford Reports *chronicle decisions made by the Supreme Court between 1830 and 1850.*

that required two-thirds of eligible voters within the proposed town to sign a petition requesting county commissioners to approve incorporation and to call for public elections. Indianapolis voters prepared just such a petition on Sept. 3, 1832 and presented it to the commissioners, who called for the first election of trustees on Sept. 29.

Local attorney Obed Foote was elected president, and he and the newly elected town clerk divided the town into five districts, each with its own trustee. The trustees adopted the city's first charter, known as the Charter of 1832. Among its ordinances: a ban on kite flying, galloping a horse and shooting a gun within the town limits.

Four years later, the town adopted a special charter from the state legislature, which allowed Indianapolis to strengthen police powers. In 1838, the town reincorporated once again under yet another, stronger charter. That charter established a town council consisting of councilmen from six wards, and gave the town the right to prohibit gambling, regulate amusements, abolish nuisances, repair streets and control markets within the town's four square miles. The charter also required all adult males to work two days per year on street maintenance or pay a $1 tax.

By the mid-1830s, traffic in covered wagons, by horseback and on foot was bumper to bumper on the National Road through Indianapolis, but transportation was still Indianapolis' chief obstacle to progress. In hopes of remedying Indiana's isolation, "The Mammoth Improvement Bill" was signed into law in 1836. Under the legislation, Indianapolis would benefit directly from two proposed public works projects: the Central Canal, designed to link Muncie and Indianapolis with the Wabash and Erie canals; and the Madison Railroad, which would pass through Columbus, Indianapolis and Crawfordsville on its way to Lafayette.

Betting that Indianapolis was finally on its way, land speculators fueled real estate values. Contracting companies sprang up overnight, and bank notes traded hands. Meanwhile, construction began on the Central Canal at Broad Ripple during the summer of 1836, at the same time that work began on the Madison Railroad.

But the mammoth improvement bill proved to be a mammoth mistake. Financial collapse in 1839, accompanied by revelations of massive misconduct by state officials and private enterprise, halted all work on the canal. Only nine miles of canal were completed, at a cost of $800,000. The Mammoth Improvement Bill almost bankrupted the state, and hard times descended on Indianapolis.

The dream of a canal connecting Indianapolis with the outside world was history but town leaders—including prominent attorneys Oliver Hampton Smith and Calvin Fletcher—fixed their sights on railroads as the best bet for improving the city's fortunes. That dream would bear fruit, enabling Indianapolis to become a hub of transportation.

For the Indianapolis legal profession, the early years mostly meant settling and surviving. In his diaries from the first two decades in Indianapolis, Calvin Fletcher remarks on the weather, difficult travel, sickness and the struggle to educate his sons as much as his professional life. Despite the financial panic, life had begun to improve.

As life improved in the frontier town, the legal community began to mature.

Jacob Piatt Dunn, secretary of the Indiana Historical Society and author of *Greater Indianapolis: The History, the Industries, the Institutions and the People in a City of Homes*, published in 1910, summed up the training and practice of lawyers early in the city's history. "The tendency of the early period was to make ready lawyers, and 'all-round' lawyers. There were no specialists. As the country settled and railroads were built, the necessity for riding the circuit disappeared. Libraries increased; decided cases multiplied."

No one can dispute the importance of those early lawyers to Indianapolis' future. From its first settlement, members of the Indianapolis bar were instrumental in laying the groundwork for municipal government, a judicial circuit, better roads and civic improvements. It was a tradition that would continue into the future.

This 1833 Act from the Indiana Legislature requests additional funding for the National Road.

CHAPTER TWO
(1840–1870)

WAR AND PROGRESS

DESPITE THE COLLAPSE OF THE STATE'S INTERNAL IMPROVEMENTS project in 1839, Indianapolis was not a bad place for an attorney to begin a law practice in the decades before the Civil War.

Indianapolis was, without a doubt, on an upswing, the largest and most important city in the state of Indiana. The population grew by leaps and bounds, increasing from a modest 2,662 inhabitants in 1840 to 8,091 residents, including 30 lawyers, 25 doctors and 120 industrial establishments, a decade later. Between 1840 and 1860, the population had increased seven-fold; on the eve of the Civil War, in 1860, the population numbered 18,611. Three years later, Indianapolis was estimated to be a city of 25,000, the twenty-eighth largest city in the United States.

By most accounts, it was an energetic place. Gas works were constructed in 1851 and a few years later, the first street lamps lit Washington Street between Meridian and Pennsylvania streets. Along Washington Street, the city's primary commercial district, the streetlights were especially important, since merchants worked long hours. Most stores opened by 6 a.m., and few closed before 9 p.m. As new businesses multiplied, rents rose; in 1840 a merchant could rent prime Washington Street property for $400 per year, but by 1860, the Indianapolis branch of the State Bank of Indiana paid $1,200 for a Meridian Street corner. Walking to work or shop was dusty when it was dry, muddy or snowy when it was wet, since there were no sidewalks, except on Washington Street, which had brick walkways. The streets themselves were unimproved gravel.

Not that a young lawyer wouldn't have struggled. The city recovered from its initial economic disaster, only to suf-

An 1854 view of Indianapolis with a close-up of the buildings on Washington Street, the city's primary commercial district, below.

24 LAW IN AMERICA'S CROSSROADS

fer from the Panic of 1857 and the severe recession that followed. But while consecutive financial crises caused some concern, hard times were nothing new to settlers accustomed to scratching out a simple existence in a place that 19th century historian W. R. Holloway called "half village, half forest city." Life was simple and far from truly urban. According to a history by John Hampden Holliday, publisher of the *Indianapolis News* from 1869 until 1892, the majority of people in Indianapolis during 1840s and 1850s owned their own houses and at least a small plot of land on which they could keep a garden, pig, chickens and a cow. A workingman could comfortably support his family earning $500 annually; the president of the Indiana State Bank earned a "princely" income of $1,500 per year, according to Holliday.

Railroads, however, had already enriched Indianapolis and ensured its future. The Madison and Indianapolis Railroad reached Indianapolis on October 1, 1847, and a railroad boom followed. Within the next five years, seven separate lines would make Indianapolis a railroad hub, and city boosters hung the moniker, "Railroad City," on the formerly isolated burg. Union Station, one of the nation's first railroad stations in which several lines used the same building for passenger service, opened in 1854 and further aided communication and travel. Lawyers with broad business inter-

View of Indianapolis from the top of the Asylum for the Blind.

A History of the Indianapolis Legal Profession

These nineteenth-century homes, located on New York Street between West Street and the Central Canal, were well-kept and neatly fenced.

ests, including the ambitious settler Calvin Fletcher, president of the Indiana and Bellefontaine line, were promoters and investors in railroads.

Transportation also changed Indianapolis demographics. Easier access brought immigrants to the city in ever-increasing numbers. Attracted by economic opportunity brought about by canal and railroad jobs, Irish and German immigrants began arriving in the mid-1840s. By 1850, Indianapolis was 65 percent native-born Americans—most hailing from southern states—and 35 percent European immigrant. African-Americans accounted for about 6 percent of the population.

In 1847, Indianapolis at last became a full-fledged city with the adoption of an official charter and the election of its first city officials. Following the two-year term of Indianapolis's first mayor, Samuel Henderson, attorney Horatio Cooley Newcomb (December 20, 1821–May 23, 1882) was elected at the tender age of 27. He remains the youngest person to ever hold the office.

Newcomb, born in Wellsboro, Pennsylvania, moved with his widowed mother from New York to Jennings County, where he studied law in his uncle's law office. He moved to Indianapolis in 1846 and formed a partnership with a prominent attorney, Ovid Butler, then turned his attention to politics. Newcomb, a member of the powerful Whig party, was elected mayor in 1849, and was reelected in 1851. Just six months after his reelection, however, Newcomb resigned to return to his law practice. Still, his long career included a host of elected and appointed positions, including terms in the Indiana House of Representatives and state Senate, city council and as a Marion County Superior Court judge and Indiana Supreme Court commissioner.

"EVERY PERSON OF GOOD MORAL CHARACTER"

Newcomb's political success is just one example of the fluid mobility of Indianapolis culture during the first half of the

19th century. If a young man did wish to practice law, the doors of opportunity were wide open. During the early part of the century, being a lawyer usually meant "reading" law—often both English common law as well as U.S. laws and state and local ordinances—under the supervision of a judge or a seasoned lawyer. But not always.

During the mid-19th century, the young nation's egalitarian ideals stressed an individual's freedom to pursue any work he chose. Restrictions on admission to the bar, naturally, violated that principle. By 1850, there was outright hostility toward the idea that there should be some professional qualification for admission to the bar, and widespread resentment that the high salaries provided court officials were not attainable by men who were not members of the bar. According to *The Law in America*, a history of the legal profession by historian Bernard Schwartz, 15 of the 19 states and organized territories in the United States required a definite period of preparation for admission to the Bar in 1800. By 1840, only 11 out of 30 jurisdictions had some preparation requirement.

By mid-century, Indiana had joined that group of states with decidedly loose requirements for admission to the bar. The 1851 Indiana Constitution, Article 7, Section 21, included the provision that "Every person of good moral character who is a voter is entitled to practice law in any of the courts of this state." The state constitutional right—one that seems amazing to 21st century Hoosiers—remained in effect until 1932. It was not universally embraced. As far back as 1910, Indianapolis historian Jacob Piatt Dunn called the provision "absurd" and noted that: "In reality, this has been much more injurious to the public than to the lawyers, though the lawyers have made nearly all the complaint about it, and properly so, because it brings reproach on the profession. But at the same time, there has not been the sympathy with the profession in this matter that there might have been if the profession had shown more zeal in enforcing the provision for 'good moral character.'"

No doubt there were some standout lawyers who would have been successful in the practice of law even without that constitutional clause, but a lack of professionalism and scant education among members of the bar probably led to some unfavorable results for clients, as well as interesting courtroom exchanges. According to one account, an Indiana law-

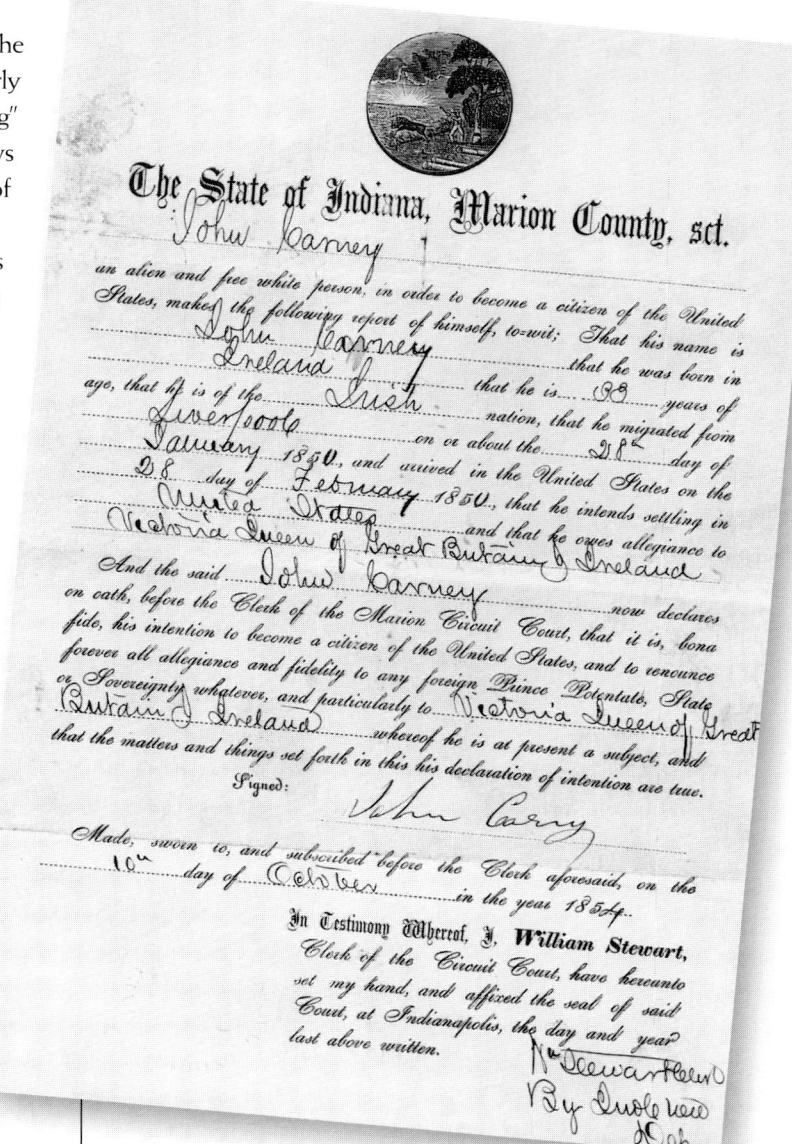

This 1854 Marion County Circuit Court certificate documents an Irish man's intention to become a United States citizen.

yer arguing his case to a jury referred several times to "The great English common law." His opponent scoffed: "If we are to be guided by English law, we want their best law, not their common law. We want as good a law as Queen Victoria herself makes use of."

Marion County remained part of the Fifth Judicial Circuit, which included 10 counties, until 1889. In 1849, the Indianapolis bar asked the General Assembly to pass an act creating a Common Pleas Court in Marion County, similar to one created in Tippecanoe County the previous year. The Indiana legislature gave the county the state's first criminal court in 1865, but a justice of the peace—an individual often

A History of the Indianapolis Legal Profession

untrained in legal matters and whose salary was dependent upon the fees and fines he assessed—held court to handle small claims and minor offenses.

Even with its court system in place, Indiana was still frontier, and different rules applied. Vigilantism was widespread throughout the 19th century. Andrew Jackson advocated vigilante justice, as did Theodore Roosevelt. As late as 1882, the U.S. Supreme Court even implied it might be justified, ruling "excuse may exist for the execution of lynch-law in savage or sparsely-settled districts, in order to oppose the ruffian elements which the ordinary administration of law is powerless to control." During the mid-1800s, Indiana vigilantes were known to march to an execution under the banner, "No expense to the country."

Yet there were signs that the Indianapolis legal profession understood the importance of preparing young lawyers. Men —and the profession was still, of course, exclusively male— still mostly studied as apprentices under a practicing lawyer. But in 1855, Indianapolis's first institution of higher education, North Western Christian University (now Butler University) opened its doors and offered law as a course of study, with Judge Samuel E. Perkins as professor of law.

Ovid Butler (February 7, 1801–July 12, 1881), a New York native who moved to Jennings County in 1817, was founder of the university. As a young man, Butler taught school and read law before moving to Indianapolis in 1836. He established a law practice and soon joined forces with Calvin

North Western Christian University began offering law classes in Indianapolis in 1855. (Courtesy Butler University Special Collections, Rare Books and University Archives)

Fletcher. Berry R. Sulgrove, a 19th century Indianapolis journalist and author of *A History of Indianapolis and Marion County, Indiana*, characterizes Butler's law career as "extensive and very lucrative." While Butler was far from being a great orator, Sulgrove recalls that "his style was strong and sententious, without ornament, without humor, without elegance, but logical and convincing. His clients always got his best ability in the preparation and trial of their cases."

Butler retired from his law practice in 1849 for health reasons, but stayed active in civic life and in the Christian (Disciples of Christ) Church. In 1850, he drafted a plan for a university and sold 20 acres of his land at the corner of 13th Street and College Avenue to be home to a Disciples of Christ school. Despite the fact that the fledgling law school graduated 21 men between 1856 and 1861, at a time when law school was not the most common way to enter the legal profession, "it was not much of a [law] school," Dunn noted. The university, which eventually moved from its first location to Irvington on the eastside, and then to its present northside location in Butler-Tarkington, continued to offer law courses until the mid-1870s. Most lawyers practicing in Indianapolis, however, were trained in law offices, reading legal texts and assisting their mentors with case preparation.

ISSUES, MORAL AND LEGAL

As the political epicenter for the state of Indiana, Indianapolis and its citizens struggled with some of the important issues of the day, including slavery and temperance.

While the nation stood on the brink of Civil War, African-Americans in Indianapolis represented less than 3 percent of the population. In a state of more than 1.3 million residents, the total African American population was less than 12,000. Under Title XIII of the 1851 Indiana Constitution, men and women of color were prohibited from even settling in the state. Marion County residents, considering the matter in an 1850 referendum, voted overwhelmingly in favor of the prohibition. Moreover, anyone who attempted to help an African-American settle in Indiana violated state law.

African-Americans could not vote, could not serve in the state militia, could not serve on a jury or testify against a white person. Intermarriage also was forbidden by law, and apparently carried stiff penalties by vigilantism, if not the state. Writing in 1870, Holloway describes this incident from 1838: "A young lady organist for the Episcopal church—the first, probably, who held that position—overcome by the fascinations of a handsome mulatto, married him. The news got abroad among the rowdies, and a crowd of them attacked the house where she and her husband were lodged, dragged them out, tarred and feathered him, rode him on a rail and ducked him in the river; and abused her, though not so severely. Both were driven out of the town."

Slavery, of course, had become a pivotal issue everywhere in the United States, and Indiana was no exception. Edward A. Leary, in *Indianapolis: The Story of a City*, states that, "Nowhere in America was a city or state more divided by the issues of freedom and slavery, union and disunion than Indianapolis and Indiana in the 1850s." The state was bordered by the slave state of Kentucky, and many Indiana settlers hailed from southern states. At the same time, Indiana was a free state with an ardent anti-slavery element that included members of the bar as outspoken critics of the institution and expansion of slavery. Attorney Ovid Butler, for example, was financial backer of a local antislavery newspaper, the *Free Soil Democrat*, a newspaper for "Free Soil, Free States and Free Men," and edited for a time by a young lawyer and son of an Indiana governor, Lewis "Lew" Wallace. Both Butler and Calvin Fletcher were supporters of the Free Territory party, organized in 1848, which opposed expansion of slavery into western territories and supported free-soil settlers in Kansas.

Ovid Butler. (Courtesy Butler University Special Collections, Rare Books and University Archives)

Not that African-Americans were welcome. Fletcher, who was firmly in the anti-slavery camp, had earlier also been a member of the Indiana Colonization Society, established in 1829 in Indianapolis. In addition to Fletcher, Indiana Supreme Court justices Jesse L. Holman and Issac Blackford and state treasurer Samuel Merrill gave the society clout in the Indianapolis white community. The society acknowledged that slavery was evil, but wanted to protect Indiana from a massive influx of African Americans who might migrate from slave states. The answer, society members believed, was to support colonization of free blacks in Africa. The idea was not well received in the small African-American community in Indianapolis, which organized a meeting in 1842 at the Bethel African Methodist Episcopal Church to declare its opposition. Still, colonization was advocated as a real solution into the 1850s.

Into this atmosphere of controversy and contradiction—a free state with a strong anti-slavery contingency, yet decidedly racist attitudes and laws—the John Freeman case emerged as one of the most celebrated illustrations of Indianapolis citizens' sympathy for antislavery causes.

The Fugitive Slave Law of 1850 gave the federal government sole jurisdiction over fugitive slave cases. Even in free states, special commissioners could issue warrants for the arrest of fugitive slaves and have them returned to their masters in the south. Commissioners were rewarded financially for their efforts to return slaves to their masters, yet alleged fugitives were not entitled to a jury trial and anyone who interfered with the Fugitive Slave Law could be fined and jailed.

John Freeman was born in Georgia, but came to Indianapolis in 1844 and started his own small but successful whitewashing business. By all accounts, Freeman was a respected member of the Indianapolis community, "an unusually quiet and deserving man," according to Holloway. So those who knew him were shocked when, on June 20, 1853, United States marshals arrested Freeman on an affidavit sworn by a Methodist minister, Pleasant Ellington of St. Louis, Missouri.

Ellington claimed that Freeman was, in fact, a slave named Sam who had escaped from Ellington in Kentucky 17 years before. While Freeman was held in jail, John L. Ketchum, Lucian Barbour and John Coburn, three prominent members of the legal community, came to his defense, and an excited crowd gathered in the streets. The attorneys—as well as the threat of mob violence if Freeman were sent South without a fair hearing—were able to convince the U.S. commissioner for additional time to prepare their case.

Freeman sat in jail while Coburn went to Georgia to find witnesses on his client's behalf. Indeed, Coburn did locate witnesses willing to testify that Freeman had lived in Georgia as a free person from 1831 until 1844. Furthermore, Freeman's lawyers located the real Sam in Canada, and also found witnesses who could testify to the physical differences between Freeman and Ellington's ex-slave. Meanwhile, Ellington produced his own witnesses to testify that Freeman was, in fact Sam, but his case fell apart when his own son could not identify Freeman as the former slave.

With the charges dismissed, anti-slavery factions celebrated with an abolitionist meeting at the Indianapolis Masonic Hall, yet all did not end well for Freeman. He was once again a free man, but during his nearly three months in jail, he had lost his business and savings. Ellington was charged with perjury and Freeman successfully filed a civil suit against him and the arresting federal marshal, John L. Robinson. Freeman never collected, however, because Ellington fled Indianapolis. The Indiana Supreme Court ruled in December 1855 that Freeman's case against the federal marshal had merit, but it had been improperly filed and, as a result, was dismissed. Freeman, who was free but impoverished by the ordeal, eventually sold his property in Indianapolis and moved to Canada.

Attorney John Coburn.

Coburn (October 27, 1825–January 28, 1908), it should be noted, went on to have an illustrious career in the Civil War and politics. A Whig at the time of the Freeman case, Coburn had already served one term in the Indiana House of Representatives from Marion County. In 1859, he was elected judge of the Marion County Common Pleas Court, but he resigned that judgeship to join the Union Army at the outbreak of the Civil War. He was serving as a colonel with the 33rd Indiana Volunteer Infantry when captured by Confederate forces, but Coburn was exchanged after a few months and returned to duty. He received the surrender of Atlanta from that city's mayor, and, upon the conclusion of the war, was promoted to brigadier general. Coburn went on to serve as a Marion County Circuit judge and, as a Republican, was elected in 1866 to the U.S. Congress for the first of four terms. Coburn served for one year as a supreme court justice for Montana Territory, but returned to Indianapolis in 1885 and resumed his law practice.

The John Freeman case was probably the most notable legal case to arise in Indiana regarding slavery, and it illustrates how strongly citizens in free states like Indiana were opposed to accommodating slave states with the Fugitive Slave Act. While the public seemed to flock to Freeman's support, race and racism remained complicated. Indianapolis would continue to struggle with the issues into the future.

Many of the same factions opposed to slavery were also in favor of temperance laws, and temperance became a key issue in the 1850s. Temperance had a long tradition in Indiana and its capital city, beginning with Sabbath observation laws. The first state legislature meeting in 1816–1817 passed "An Act to Prevent Certain Immoral Practices," which levied fines for anyone over age 14 found engaged in common labor, or activities such as hunting, fishing and "rioting," on Sunday. In 1837, Indianapolis town trustees imposed a maximum $5 fine on anyone convicted of playing cricket, bandy, pitching coins or pursuing any other public game or amusement on Sunday. In 1846, Calvin Fletcher spoke at a statewide convention in favor of strengthening Sunday observance laws and beginning court sessions on Tuesdays instead of Mondays, so that Sabbath observers could avoid traveling on Sunday to conduct their court business the next day.

At the same time, sentiment against drinking was growing. In 1828, Indianapolis residents organized the Temperance Society of Marion County, with its members taking the pledge to avoid alcohol, except for medicinal purposes. Predictably, among the community stalwarts in the temperance movement were attorneys like Fletcher, Butler and Samuel Merrill. While temperance advocated voluntary abstinence from alcohol, attempts at prohibition soon followed, and in 1855, the Indiana General Assembly enacted a law that prohibited the manufacture and sale of alcohol, except as medicine.

As a result, every tavern in the state of Indiana was closed, which had special ramifications in Indianapolis. For business and civic leaders like Fletcher, Merrill, Butler and others who supported temperance causes, temperance was a natural extension of a strict Protestant background that eschewed alcohol and drunkenness. Indianapolis, on the other hand, was experiencing an influx of German and Irish immigration that claimed a different tradition in which drinking was an accepted part of social life.

A clash was inevitable. Tavern owners in the German community openly defied the law, operating their beer gardens and saloons even as Indianapolis authorities began arresting the law's violators. On July 2, 1855, Indianapolis saloonkeeper Roderick Beebe was arrested and fined $50 in the mayor's court. When he refused to pay, Beebe was imprisoned. Meanwhile, a second saloonkeeper, William Hermann, also was arrested and imprisoned. Beebe appealed to the Indiana Supreme Court and his case was heard, although no ruling was handed down before the court's summer recess. During the court's recess, Hermann appealed for a writ of habeas corpus, which Justice Samuel E. Perkins issued, releasing Hermann from jail. Perkins, a Democrat, stated that the law was unconstitutional and that the state could not infringe on an individual's decision of what to eat or drink. During the Supreme Court's fall term, Justice Perkins' decision in the Hermann case was confirmed when the court sided with Beebe. The court ruled that prohibition violated the property rights of manufacturers, sellers and consumers and the guarantee against unreasonable search and seizure.

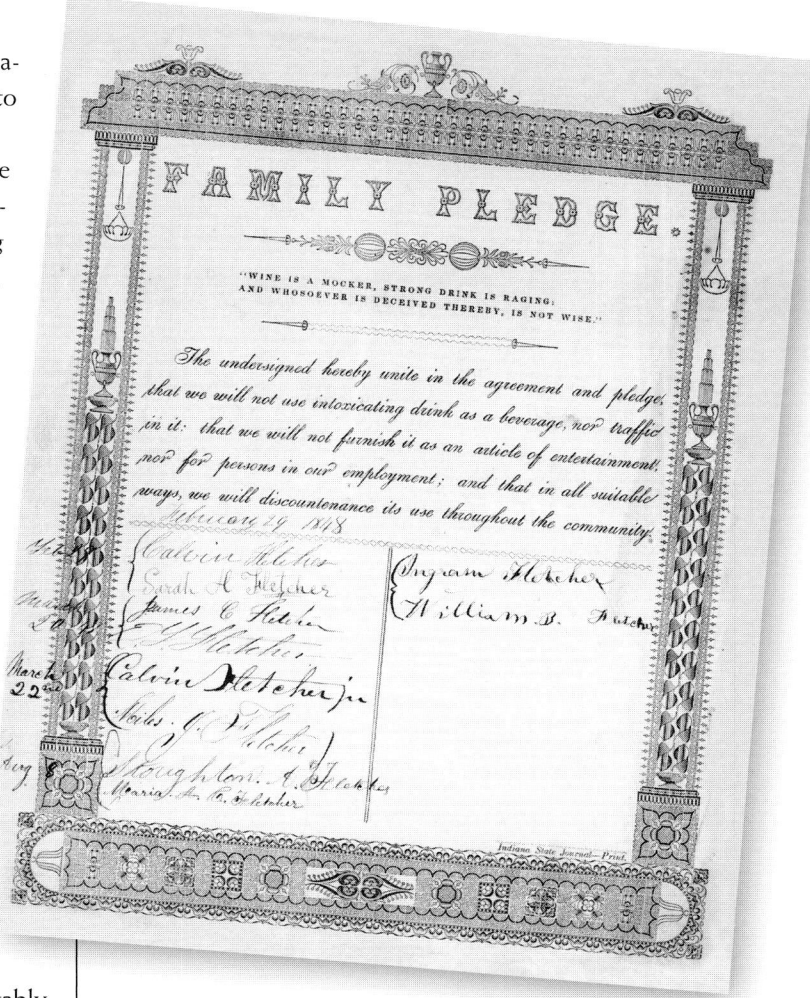

Calvin Fletcher was active in the Indiana Temperance Society. This pledge was signed by members of the Fletcher family in 1848.

Thus, the question of temperance and prohibition in Indianapolis was settled until the issue was revisited in the 20th century. Anyway, other issues facing Indianapolis and the country—including the future of the Union itself—vastly overshadowed the subject of drink. As in the past, members of the bar would play an important role in how Indianapolis coped with the challenges ahead.

INDIANAPOLIS AND THE CIVIL WAR

Voters in the fall of 1860 would help elect Abraham Lincoln to the presidency and a Republican governor, Henry Lane, on a platform of moderation, but there was plenty of behind-the-scenes maneuvering behind that Republican sweep.

Republican political operatives supported Lane as the nominee for governor with the idea that, upon election, the Republican-led legislature would name Lane to the U.S. Senate seat vacated by Graham Fitch and Lieutenant Governor Oliver P. Morton would be governor.

Democrats fielded their own candidate for governor of Indiana, Thomas A. Hendricks (September 7, 1819–November 25, 1885), a leading attorney and prominent politician. Hendricks was born in Ohio, but raised in Shelby County in Indiana. After graduation from Hanover College, he read law and opened a practice in Shelbyville, then moved to Indianapolis in 1860. By then, Hendricks had already served a term in the Indiana General Assembly and in the state constitutional convention of 1850–1851, the U.S. House of Representatives and as commissioner of the General Land Office under presidents Pierce and Buchanan. His unsuccessful bid in 1860 was one of three attempts to win the governor's office.

At the Republican national convention in Chicago that same year, the Indiana delegates agreed to support Lincoln with the understanding that one of their own, Hoosier attorney Caleb Blood Smith, would be named Lincoln's Secretary of the Interior.

The latter political alliance reflected Indiana Republican's agreement with Lincoln that preservation of the Union was paramount. Moreover, Lincoln was practically a Hoosier himself. He had spent much of his childhood on Pigeon Creek in Spencer County before leaving Indiana for the neighboring state of Illinois, where he built his law practice and political career.

Smith (April 16, 1808–January 7, 1864) was born in Boston, Massachusetts and moved with his parents to Ohio as a child. After studying at Miami University for two years, Smith began reading law in Connersville, Indiana in 1827 and was admitted to the bar the following year. He became active in the Whig political party, served as a railroad president and, from 1832 to 1833, edited the *Connersville Sentinel*. While at the *Sentinel*, Smith was able to articulate his Whig philosophy, and his political career soon took off. He was elected to the Indiana General Assembly, representing Fayette County, from 1833 until 1837 and again from 1840 to 1841. Smith was elected to the U.S. Congress in 1843, where he served until 1849. He left Washington for Cincinnati and a private law practice until 1858, when he returned to Indianapolis.

Lincoln needed Indiana's electoral votes to assure election in 1860, so Hoosier delegates had little difficulty in securing Lincoln's promise to appoint Smith to his cabinet. And in March 1861, after the inauguration, Lincoln named him Secretary of the Interior, making Smith the first citizen from Indiana appointed to a presidential cabinet post.

But in the meantime, Hoosiers, along with the entire country, were watching more important events unfold. Immediately after Lincoln's election, South Carolina followed through with its threat to leave the Union and seceded, fol-

President-elect Abraham Lincoln stopped in Indianapolis on February 11, 1861 while travelling to Washington, D.C. for his inauguration.

Oliver P. Morton was Indiana's governor during the Civil War. He was often referred to as "the soldier's friend."

lowed by six other states in the Lower South. While some politicians preached concession and conciliation, Indiana's lieutenant governor was not one of them. Morton spoke forcefully in favor of putting down the rebellion and that "if it was worth a bloody struggle to establish the nation, it is worth one to preserve it."

Who was this fiery figure? Morton (August 4, 1823–November 1, 1877) was a native of the tiny burg of Salisbury, in Wayne County. His mother died when he was very young, and Morton was raised by his grandparents and, later, two widowed aunts—women, it was said, who were tough on Morton, taught him how to shoot a gun and hit the target—in Springfield, Ohio.

With limited means, Morton was forced to apprentice himself to a hat maker and eventually earned enough money to attend Miami University in Oxford, Ohio, where he won a reputation as a powerful orator. After two years in college, Morton read law in Centerville, Indiana, and attended Cincinnati Law School. Early on, Morton was a Democrat who supported the Compromise of 1850, but he split with the party in 1854 over the Kansas-Nebraska Act. He aligned himself with the new Republican Party and was its first candidate for governor in 1856. Four years later, the rising star was elected lieutenant governor and then took over the governor's office when Lane went to the U.S. Senate.

From the start of his administration, Morton was a passionate defender of the Union and reacted with strong oratory to the secession crisis that embroiled the nation. According to Leary, Morton "regarded himself as the war's personal proprietor and the symbol of Union in Indiana, and he wielded raw, naked power with force, energy and determination for the winning of one and restoration of the other and, more often than not, for the greater glory of Oliver P. Morton and the Republican Party."

On February 11, 1861, President-elect Abraham Lincoln stopped in Indianapolis on his way to Washington, D.C. for his inauguration. Crowds jammed Illinois and Washington Street to hear Lincoln speak from the balcony of the Bates House hotel. Oratory turned to action in April 1861, with the attack on Fort Sumter, South Carolina. In Indianapolis, "sentiment crystallized in a flash. War had come unprovoked. The flag had been fired on and humiliated by defeat. There was but one voice—sustain the government and put down the rebellion. The 13th day of April was a great day in

A History of the Indianapolis Legal Profession 33

ABOVE: *Camp Morton, seen here in 1864, was located near today's 19th and Delaware streets.* OPPOPSITE PAGE: *A hand-drawn map of Camp Carrington, Indiana's largest military encampment.*

Indianapolis, the greatest it had yet seen; and it probably has never been surpassed in the intense interest, anxiety and enthusiasm exhibited. Never were its people so aroused," Holliday writes.

Within a week after Fort Sumter fell, Gov. Morton pledged 10,000 men from Indiana and within another week, 12,500 Hoosiers were in camp. The city was flooded with soldiers and would remain so throughout the duration of the war; before the end, 24 camps would be in operation, including Camp Morton, a Confederate prisoner of war camp and Camp Carrington, the state's largest military encampment, located between the Canal and Fall Creek, near 15th and Missouri streets. Eventually, three military hospitals, a federal arsenal and an artillery practice field would also be established in Indianapolis, the rallying point for central recruiting and the primary military depot for the state of Indiana.

The original six regiments were organized into the Indiana Brigade. Amazingly, the six regimental commanders included only one West Point graduate, but five lawyers, including Frederick Knefler and Ebenezer Dumont. Francis A. Shoup, a lawyer and West Point graduate, led an Indianapolis-based militia until the war started. He left Indianapolis for the south, where he became a brigadier general in the Confederate army.

Lew Wallace, a veteran of the Mexican War, received command of the 11th Zouave Regiment, which included four companies of city volunteers, and before leaving for the front, he marched his men to the State House, where they swore to avenge the alleged cowardice of Indiana troops at the Battle of Buena Vista in the Mexican War. Within the first months of the war, the regiment would distinguish itself by marching 46 miles in less than 24 hours to stage a raid on Romney, Virginia. Other Indianapolis regiments soon organized; an all-German regiment, an all-Irish regiment (which was later consolidated with a second all-Irish regiment), and the 28th Colored Regiment, U.S. Colored Troops. In addition to the troops made up primarily of Indianapolis men, Indianapolis was the starting point for most Union soldiers from Indiana. Altogether, 104 of 169 Indiana regiments began their military service in the city.

As the conflict turned bloodier, those soldiers who lost their lives had to be replaced. Like other Union cities, Indianapolis had to meet troop quotas, a challenge it met every time by appealing to patriotism, paying bounties, and helping to support families left in hardship by their departing men. But Indiana was a crucial cog in the Union war machine, and not just because it produced soldiers. Indiana's farms were a source of food needed to feed soldiers and civilians alike, and its railroads provided the crucial transportation of troops and supplies.

Morton was tireless in promoting Indiana's war effort, especially when it came to the well being of Indiana troops. He was given special war powers by the General Assembly, but he went even beyond those to ensure that Indiana troops were fed, clothed and armed. He raised money, drafted volunteers to make uniforms and once sent 29,000 overcoats to cold Hoosier soldiers in the mountains of West Virginia when the military failed to provide what Morton thought Indiana men needed. Appreciative troops forever after called him "the soldier's friend."

The Civil War would make Morton famous as "the soldier's friend," but an enemy of wartime civil rights and political dissent. While Morton led the state's war machine and Indiana was overwhelmingly pro-Union, Indiana also was home to people who were originally from the South and still had strong ties to that part of the country. There also were people who were critical of Lincoln and the emancipation of slaves. Morton and his Republican cohorts labeled all dissenters—Democrats and members of loosely organized groups like the Sons of Liberty and the Order of American Knights—as treasonous.

In 1863, shortly after Lincoln issued the Emancipation Proclamation, some 10,000 Democrats met at the State House on May 20 for the state Democratic convention. Soldiers home on furlough, angry Democrats and spectators clashed as convention delegates were leaving town by train. Union supporters began searching Democratic delegates for weapons and a number of—no one is sure how many—knives, pistols and rifles were thrown out the train windows into Pogue's Run, a small stream that runs through the Mile Square.

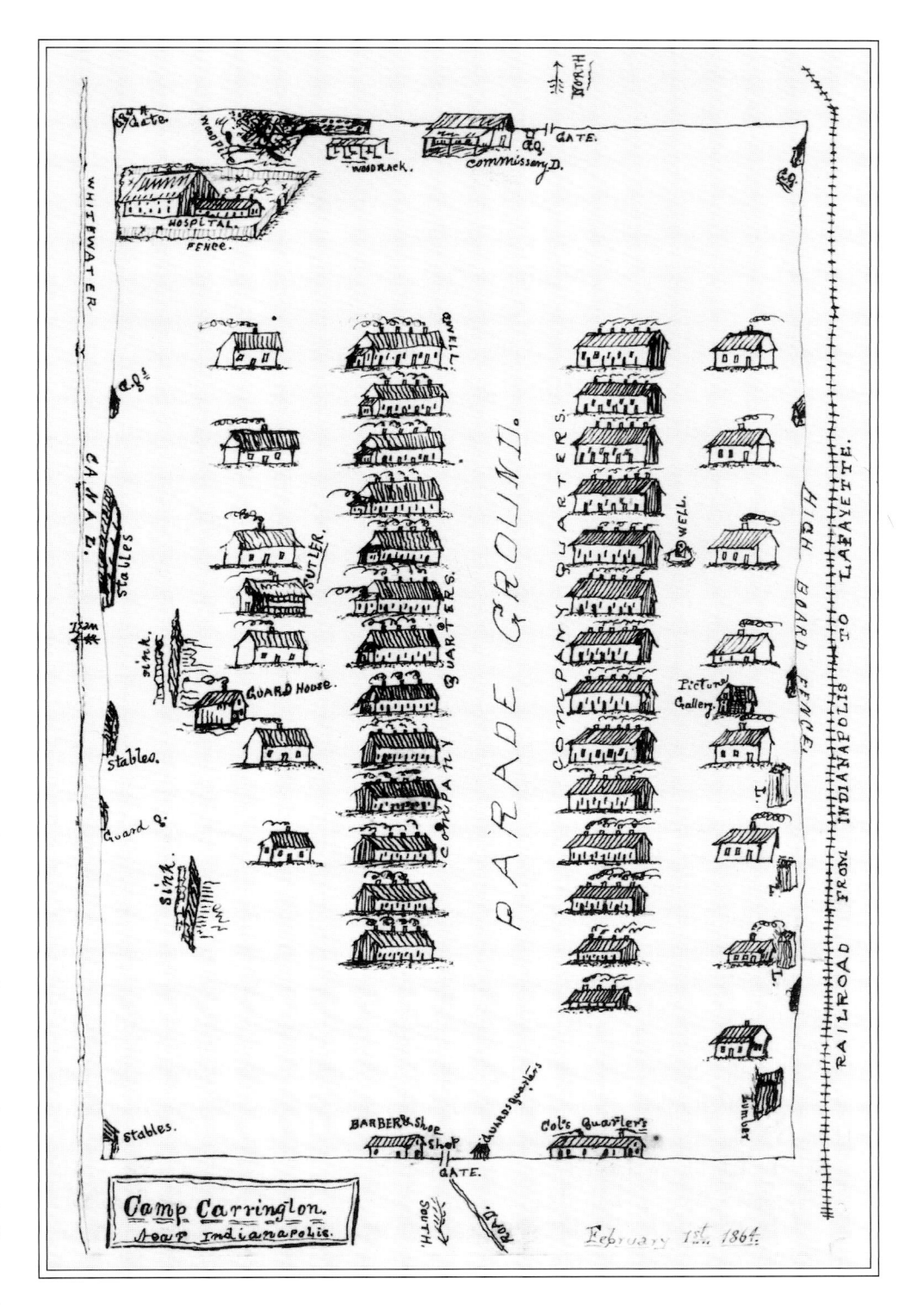

ABOVE: *Caleb Blood Smith became the first Hoosier to be appointed to a cabinet position, serving as Secretary of the Interior from 1861 until 1863.*
LEFT: *Thomas A. Hendricks, a Democrat, was elected to the U.S. Senate in 1863. He ran three times for governor, and was elected in 1872.*

the United States in 1849 and soon found his way to Indianapolis, where he began reading law in the office of the court clerk. After the war, Knefler began practicing law with John Hanna, former U.S. District Attorney, and was appointed pension agent by President Hayes. Knefler went on to become president of the board of regents of the Soldiers and Sailors Monument.

Gov. Morton won a second term as governor in 1864, and three years later was elected U.S. senator. Once a moderate who opposed suffrage for former slaves, Morton reversed himself and became a Radical Reconstructionist and champion of African Americans in the South. As powerful as ever in Indiana, Morton engineered the state's ratification of the Fourteenth and Fifteenth Amendments to the U.S. Constitution in 1869. African-Americans, who were now free in the rest of the country, as well as Indiana, would be given the right to vote, but would still suffer from discrimination in every public venue including Indiana courts.

Morton's political rival, Thomas Hendricks, was elected to the U.S. Senate in 1863, where he was one of a small group of Democrats who opposed the Radical Republicans. He was nominated again as the Democratic candidate for governor in 1872, and this time won the election and even greater national prominence among Democrats.

During the war, in 1863, a lawyer named John Caven (April 12, 1824–March 9, 1905) was elected mayor of Indianapolis. Caven, a Republican, would go on to serve as mayor for a record five terms, from 1863 until 1867 and from 1875 until 1881. And a lawyer named Benjamin Harrison would return from the Civil War to restart his law practice and a political career, and would eventually make lasting contributions to the legal profession in Indianapolis and the state of Indiana.

THE CIVIL WAR TREASON TRIALS

WHILE NO CIVIL WAR BATTLES WERE FOUGHT IN INDIANA, Indianapolis was the setting for a landmark legal struggle.

In remarks to an Indiana University Law School-Bloomington audience on "Civil Liberty and the Civil War: The Indianapolis Treason Trials" in 1996,[1] U.S. Chief Justice William Rehnquist talked about the lasting impact on American justice. The following is an excerpt of that speech:[2]

"The Civil War was the first time that the United States government mobilized for a major war effort, and a major war effort necessarily results in the curtailment of some civil liberties. The Civil War era produced the first important civil liberties decision from the Supreme Court of the United States—the case of *Ex parte Milligan*[3] decided in 1866.

"The ramifications of the *Milligan* case are with us to this day. And, the case is of particular interest here in Indiana, because it arose out of what historians call the Indianapolis treason trials, which took place in your state capital in the fall of 1864.

"[It] is probably easier to discuss the limits of civil liberties during war time when there is no war, rather than when conflict is raging. There is an oft-quoted Latin maxim: *silent leges inter arma*, which has been loosely translated to mean that in time of war the laws are silent and the guns speak. Peacetime offers an opportunity for detached reflection on these important governmental questions which are not so calmly discussed in the midst of a war.

"Even those of you who didn't major in American history will recall that Abraham Lincoln was inaugurated as President on March 4, 1861. At this time the seven states of what was called the "Lower South"—South Carolina, Georgia, Florida, Alabama, Mississippi, Louisiana, and Texas—had seceded from the Union. But the four states of the "Upper South"—Virginia, North Carolina, Tennessee, and Arkansas—had not yet joined the original seven. The next tier of states—both working northward geographically, and considering their likelihood of secession—were the three so-called "border states"—Missouri, Kentucky, and Maryland. Lincoln thought it essential to keep the border states in the Union.

"For six weeks after Lincoln's inauguration, the situation remained precariously balanced while the Administration tried to make up its mind whether to attempt to reprovision Fort Sumter, a Union fort located in the harbor of Charleston, South Carolina. When the federal government did finally make the attempt, it was turned back, and the batteries in Charleston Harbor began firing on Fort Sumter. On April 14, the Union garrison in the fort surrendered. The next day, Abraham Lincoln issued a proclamation calling for 75,000 volunteers to put down the rebellion.

"Soon after Lincoln issued his proclamation, the four states of the "Upper South" seceded and joined the Confederacy. They had been playing a waiting game, but each was determined that if the Union attempted to "coerce" the Confederacy, they would secede. Their secession dramatically changed the military status of the nation's capital in Washington. When only the states of the "Lower South" had seceded, the border between the Confederate states and the United States was the southern border of North Carolina. But after Fort Sumter, that border was the Potomac River which separates Maryland from Virginia. Washington went from being an interior capital to a capital on the very frontier of the Union, raising the definite possibility of raids and even investment and capture by the Confederate forces.

"Lincoln, fully aware of this danger, was most anxious that the 75,000 volunteers for whom he had called would arrive in Washington and defend the city against a possible Confederate attack. The North, as a whole, had rallied to Lincoln's call to arms, and new volunteer regiments and brigades were oversubscribed. But the only rail connections from the North into Washington ran through the city of Baltimore, forty miles to the northeast.

"Herein lay a problem: there were numerous Confederate sympathizers in Baltimore, and the city itself, at that time, had a reputation for unruliness—it was known as "Mob City." Three rail lines—one from Philadelphia and the northeast, another from Harrisburg and the northwest, and the B&O from the west, converged in the city or close to it. To complicate matters further, it was necessary for passengers en route from Philadelphia to Washington to change depots. Shortly after troops from the northeast arrived in Baltimore, a riot broke out while troops were in transit from one depot

A History of the Indianapolis Legal Profession

to another. Some of the troops were riding in railroad cars drawn by horses through the downtown streets of the city, while others were marching in military formation through those same streets. A hostile crowd pelted the troops with stones, who in turn fired shots into the crowd. Several soldiers and several bystanders were killed.

"That night, the chief of police in Baltimore, who was a Confederate sympathizer, and the Mayor of Baltimore, who was a less open one, spearheaded a group of Confederate sympathizers who blew up the railroad bridges leading into Baltimore from the north.

"Troop movements through Baltimore were temporarily suspended, so troops bound for Washington were sent by ship from a point on Chesapeake Bay above Baltimore to Annapolis, from which point they traveled to Washington over land. But this alternative route was not a satisfactory substitute for the main lines of the railroads, and Lincoln believed that the loss of the rail connection through Baltimore seriously threatened the safety of Washington. Urged on by Secretary Seward, he took the first step to curtail a civil liberty. He authorized General Winfield Scott, commander-in-chief of the Army, to suspend the writ of habeas corpus at any point he deemed necessary along the rail line from Philadelphia to Washington.

"Several weeks later, federal troops arrested a man named Merryman, whom authorities suspected of being a major actor in the dynamiting of the railroad bridges. No sooner was he confined in Fort McHenry than he sued out a writ of habeas corpus. The following day, Chief Justice Roger Taney, sitting as a circuit judge in Baltimore, ordered the government to show cause why Merryman should not be released. A representative of the commandant appeared in court for the government to advise Taney that the writ of habeas corpus had been suspended, and asked for time to consult with the government in Washington. Taney refused, and issued an attachment—a form of arrest—for the commandant of Fort McHenry. The next day, the marshal reported that in his effort to serve the writ he had been denied admission to the fort. Taney then issued an opinion in the case declaring that the President alone did not have the authority to suspend the writ of habeas corpus—only Congress could do that—and holding that Merryman's confinement was illegal. The Chief Justice, knowing that he could not enforce his order, sent a copy of it to Lincoln.

"Lincoln ignored the order, but in his address to the special session of Congress which he had called to meet on July 4, 1861, he adverted to it in these words: 'Must [the laws] be allowed to finally fail of execution even had it been perfectly clear that by the use of the means necessary to their execution some single law, made in such extreme tenderness of the citizens' liberty that practically it relieves more of the guilty than of the innocent, should to a very limited extent be violated? To state the question more directly, are all the laws *but one* to go unexecuted, and the government itself go to pieces less that one be violated?'[4]

"Lincoln, with his usual incisiveness, put his finger on the debate that inevitably surrounds issues of civil liberties in war time.

"The provision of the Constitution dealing with habeas corpus is found in Article I, dealing with the legislative power vested in Congress, and provides that the writ of habeas corpus shall not be suspended unless in time of war or rebellion the public safety shall require it. The question of whether only Congress may suspend it has never been authoritatively answered to this day, but the Lincoln Administration proceeded to arrest and detain persons suspected of disloyal activities. People so detained, including the mayor of Baltimore and the chief of police, were first imprisoned at Fort Lafayette in New York harbor—a hardship post as prisons went. They were later transferred to less harsh facilities at Fort Warren in Boston. All of the arrests and detentions in 1861 were initiated by Secretary of State William Seward—a rather unusual official in whom to repose such duties, but one who apparently welcomed them.

"Newspaper publishers did not escape the government's watchful eye either. The Administration was especially concerned about the New York press, which had a disproportionate impact on the rest of the country. In that era before press wire services, newspapers in smaller cities frequently simply reprinted stories which had been run earlier in the metropolitan press. In New York, the *Tribune*, the *Herald*, and the *Times* generally supported the Northern war effort, but several other papers did not. In August 1861, a Grand Jury sitting in New York was outraged by an article in the New York *Journal of Commerce*—a paper which opposed the war—that listed over one hundred Northern newspapers opposed to "the present unholy war." The *Journal of Commerce* frequently editorialized in no uncertain words about the malfeasance of the Administration.

"The grand jurors inquired of the presiding judge whether such vituperative criticism was subject to indictment. Because the Grand Jury was about to be discharged, the judge did not oblige. Nevertheless, the jurors simply requested that a list of several New York newspapers, including the *Journal of*

In early 1862, Edwin Stanton succeeded the incompetent Simon Cameron as Secretary of War.

Commerce, be called to the attention of the next Grand Jury. They had heard no evidence, and received no legal instructions from the judge; they simply made a "presentment"—a written notice taken by a Grand Jury of what it believes to be an indictable offense.

"On this thin reed, the Administration proceeded to act. Postmaster General Montgomery Blair directed the Postmaster in New York to exclude from the mails the five newspapers named by the Grand Jury. This was significant because the newspapers of that day were almost entirely dependent upon the mails for their circulation. Gerald Hallock, the part owner and editor of the *Journal of Commerce*, was obliged to negotiate with the Post Office Department to see what the paper would have to do to regain its right to use of the mails. The Post Office Department told him that he must sell his ownership in the newspaper. Hallock reluctantly agreed, and retired, thereby depriving the paper of its principal editorialist opposing the war. The *New York News*, owned by Benjamin Wood, brother of New York Mayor Fernando Wood, decided to fight the ban against his paper. He sought to send its edition south and west by private express, and hired newsboys to deliver the paper locally. The government ordered U.S. Marshals to seize all copies of the paper. In fact one newsboy in Connecticut was arrested for having hawked it. Eventually Wood, too, gave up.

"Remarkably, other New York newspapers did not rally round the sheets that the government was suppressing. Instead of crying out that the First Amendment rights of these papers had been abridged—as they would surely do today—their rivals simply gloated. James Gordon Bennett's *Herald* was *"gratified"* to report the death of the *News*, and the *Times* observed that Ben Wood should be thankful he could 'walk the streets.'

"Even clergy were subject to detention for perceived disloyalty. Perhaps the most egregious example was that of the Reverend J. R. Stewart, the Episcopal rector at St. Paul's Church in Alexandria, Virginia, who was undoubtedly a southern sympathizer. For two Sundays in a row, he had omitted the customary Episcopal prayer for the President of the United States in the course of the service. On the second of these occasions, he was arrested in the pulpit of the church, and briefly detained until cooler heads prevailed.

"In early 1862, Edwin Stanton succeeded the incompetent Simon Cameron as Secretary of War. He persuaded Lincoln to transfer the security functions to his Department, and to issue a general amnesty for those imprisoned if they would swear loyalty to the Union. But under Stanton, arrests and detentions continued. It turned out that he did not so much disapprove of the earlier arrests in principle; rather he disapproved of them as having been made by the *Secretary of State* rather than the *Secretary of War*.

"In the summer of 1862, Congress enacted the first draft law, and Lincoln and Stanton issued executive proclamations suspending the writ of habeas corpus for those accused of various crimes. These proclamations not only authorized detention, but also authorized trials of the miscreants before military commissions instead of civil courts.

"These proclamations introduced an entirely new element into the civil liberties equation. Suspension of habeas corpus permitted detention, but release usually followed in a few months. But if a defendant was actually tried and sentenced by a military commission, not merely temporary detention but a long prison term might well await him. Thus came the second question debated during the Civil War—could civilians outside of the war zone be tried before a military commission, or could they insist on being tried in the civil courts?

"Before a military commission, a defendant was denied many of the procedural rights guaranteed by the Bill of Rights to the Constitution. There was no right of jury trial—with

A History of the Indianapolis Legal Profession **41**

its attendant guarantees of a jury composed of local citizenry and of a unanimous verdict requirement. A military commission could be composed of officers from anywhere in the country, and could convict by a majority vote in non-capital cases. To impose the death sentence, however, required a two-thirds vote.

"But it was not just procedural rights that might be denied by a military commission. What law was the commission to apply? Was it limited to defendants who were charged with having violated the federal criminal code, or could it apply the much more general and vague notions of martial law?

"The Indianapolis treason trials, held in the fall of 1864, starkly posed these questions. Immediately after Fort Sumter, the states of the old Northwest—Ohio, Indiana, and Illinois—had loyally supported Lincoln's call for volunteers. Subsequent events, however, disillusioned a good number of the citizens of these states. Traditionally, farmers there had shipped their farm produce to market down the Mississippi River to New Orleans, where it was transshipped to the east coast or to Europe. But the secession of the southern states closed this route, and the farmers were forced to ship their produce by rail to the east coast. The railroads were owned by easterners, and Midwestern farmers felt they were gouged by excessively high rates.

"In September 1862, Lincoln issued his Emancipation Proclamation, freeing slaves in Confederate territory. What had started out as a war to preserve the Union now seemed to become a war to end slavery. Most of the Midwesterners who had voted for Lincoln in 1860 had agreed with his platform plank that said slavery would not be disturbed where it already existed, but it should not be allowed to spread further into the territories. But there were not many abolitionists—people who believed that slavery should be simply forbidden nationwide—in this part of the country. This distinction was particularly true in Indiana, which was described as the most southern of the northern states.

"In the election of 1862, which came shortly after the Emancipation Proclamation, this sentiment was reflected as Democrats gained control of state legislatures in both Illinois and Indiana. The electoral result here in Indiana produced a complete standoff between Governor Oliver P. Morton, a strong-willed Republican, and the Democratic legislature.

"Eighteen sixty-three and 1864 were years of bloody conflict on the battlefield. After the battle of Gettysburg in July 1863, it became clear that the South could not win the war and by force of arms establish a separate nation. But enormous battlefield casualties continued, and even increased as U.S. Grant and Robert E. Lee slugged it out in Virginia. A war weariness began to be felt in the North, caused not by fear of military defeat but by concern that military victory would not be worth the price. The Democratic party split into two camps on this issue—the "war Democrats" supported the northern war effort, while the "peace Democrats" (called "copperheads" by their Union opponents) favored a negotiated peace. Among their other activities, the copperheads formed secret societies, and it was the activities of these societies which led to the Indianapolis treason trials.

"In August 1864, military authorities raided the offices of an Indianapolis man named Harrison H. Dodd and found guns, ammunition, and incriminating documents. Based on this evidence, Dodd, Lambdin P. Milligan, a lawyer from Huntington, Indiana, and three others were charged with conspiracy against the government of the United States, conspiracy to aid the rebellion, and conspiracy to overthrow the government of the United States. The federal government decided to try these defendants before a military commission, rather than a civil court, and the trial began in the federal courthouse in Indianapolis in September 1864.

"The defendants were an oddly assorted lot. Harrison H. Dodd, the ringleader, on whose premises the guns and ammunition had been found, was born and raised in upstate New York. As a youth, he had moved to Toledo where he became treasurer of a local trade association. In 1856, he joined his brother in Indianapolis, where they formed a partnership in a printing business. Concerned with what he regarded as excesses on the part of the military authorities in Indiana during the Civil War, Dodd became active in the Democratic party. In the summer of 1863, he assumed the leadership in Indiana of a secret society known as the Order of American Knights.

"Lambdin P. Milligan was a lawyer in Huntington, Indiana, where his legal abilities were well recognized. He had been born in Ohio, but moved to Indiana and had, like Dodd, become active in Democratic politics. Milligan had a firm belief in the correctness of his own opinions, and vehemently insisted that he could only be tried in a civil court and not before a military commission.

"Horace Heffren was also active in Democratic politics. Although early on he had served in the Union forces, he left the service and won a seat as a Democrat in the Indiana legislature. He was described by one of his political opponents

---

OPPOSITE PAGE: *These five men were defendants before an Indianapolis military commission in 1864.*

A History of the Indianapolis Legal Profession

These men served on the Indianapolis military commission that tried five men for treason in 1864.

as "a disgusting compound of whiskey, grease, vulgarity, and cowardice."

"The oldest of the defendants was William Bowles, who was in his eighties. He had been a captain in the Mexican War, but his sympathies with the South in the Civil War were well known. His wife was from New Orleans, and after their marriage, they brought a number of slaves with them to Indiana. An Indiana law forbidding slavery, however, eventually required them to send their slaves back to Louisiana. Bowles was by now one of the wealthiest men in Indiana; he was a physician, and a large landowner in the area of French Lick Springs.

"Andrew Humphreys and Stephen Horsey had none of the prominence of the other defendants. Humphreys was active in local politics in his part of the state, while Horsey engaged in farming and other odd jobs.

"Much of the evidence was circumstantial, hearsay, and not overly persuasive, especially in regard to Milligan's culpability. But some of the evidence revealed contacts between some members of the charged conspiracy and Confederate agents in Canada as well as an aborted plan to seize a federal arsenal and free Confederate prisoners held in a military camp near Chicago. Concealed guns and ammunition had been delivered to Dodd, who escaped and fled to Canada before his trial was completed. The evidence as to another conspirator, William Bowles, would very likely have been sufficient to convict him in a civil court. The same cannot be said of the other defendants. One of them turned state's evidence during the trial, and the military commission found all four of the remaining defendants guilty and sentenced three of them to hang.

"They had been tried in the fall of 1864, before the presidential election of that year. However, by the time the military commission rendered its decision at the end of 1864, Lincoln had won re-election by a substantial margin, Atlanta had fallen to the Union troops, and Sherman was on his way to Savannah. The end of the war appeared much closer. Public sentiment began to change from a desire for harsh penalties to a desire for leniency. Lawyers for the convicted defendants pleaded their case before Lincoln, who had to approve all death sentences imposed by military courts, and he gave them reason to think that he would in due time set aside the sentence. But in April 1865, Lincoln was assassinated by John

Wilkes Booth at Ford's Theater in Washington, and Andrew Johnson succeeded to the Presidency. Johnson was at first determined to treat the Confederate leaders harshly, and ordered that the sentence be carried out. The defendants then sued out a writ of habeas corpus in federal court in Indianapolis, and under the procedures which then prevailed, the case went to the Supreme Court under the name of Ex parte Milligan.

"In January 1866, the Supreme Court granted a motion to advance the Milligan case on its docket, thus indicating that it regarded the case as one of great importance. Argument was set for the beginning of March, and several counsel for each side argued the case before the Court for six days. The government was singularly unfortunate in its representation before the Court. The burden of its case was carried by James Speed, one of the least competent Attorneys General in the history of that office, and Benjamin Butler, who combined a sharp legal mind with a reputation for self-promotion and dubious ethical practices. One of the principal arguments made by the government was that the Bill of Rights to the Constitution—the first ten amendments which guarantee free speech, free press, and numerous rights to those criminally charged—had no application in time of war. The Milligan petitioners were ably represented by the young James A. Garfield, a future President of the United States, and David Dudley Field, a leader of the New York bar. The basic argument of the petitioners was that, even in time of war, civilians could not be tried before a military commission so long as the civil courts were open for business.

"Five of the nine Justices of the Court at this time had been appointed by Abraham Lincoln: Chief Justice Salmon P. Chase, and Justices Noah Swayne of Ohio, Samuel Freeman Miller of Iowa, David Davis of Illinois, and Stephen Field of California. The other four had been appointed by one or the other of Lincoln's Democratic predecessors— James Wayne of Georgia, nearly thirty years earlier had been appointed by Andrew Jackson; Samuel Nelson of New York, by John Tyler; Robert Grier of Pennsylvania, by James K. Polk; and Nathan Clifford of Maine, by James Buchanan. Court watchers were naturally interested to see how this interesting mix of Justices would react to the important questions presented to them by this case.

"A few weeks after the argument, at the close of its term in April, the Court entered an order that the writ of habeas corpus sought by Milligan and the others should be granted, but that opinions in the case would not be filed until the beginning of the next term in December 1866.

"At that time, two opinions were filed: an opinion for the majority of the Court by Justice David Davis, and an opinion for four concurring Justices by Chief Justice Salmon P. Chase. All the Justices agreed that the trial of these defendants by a military commission was invalid. But they divided five to four on their reasoning. The five Justice majority basically adopted the position of the petitioners and held that a United States citizen not in the armed forces could not be tried before a military commission even in time of war if the civil courts were open for business. According to the majority, as the federal court in Indianapolis had been open for business throughout the war, these defendants should have been tried there, rather than before a military commission. The majority opinion relied on the definition of judicial power in Article III of the Constitution, and on the Sixth Amendment guarantee of the right to jury trial.

"The concurring Justices held that a law passed by Congress in 1863 allowed those suspected of disloyal activity to be detained, but only until a Grand Jury had an opportunity to indict them. If the Grand Jury indicted, they were to be tried in the civil courts; if it did not, they were to be released. Thus, in effect, these Justices said Congress itself had ruled out trials of civilians by a military commission.

"All members of the Court joined in rejecting the government's argument that the Bill of Rights simply did not apply in wartime. The majority opinion contains a somewhat rhetorical passage for which it is justly famous:

The Constitution of the United States is a law for rulers and people, equally in war and in peace, and covers with the shield of its protection all classes of men, at all times, and under all circumstances. No doctrine, involving more pernicious consequences, was ever invented by the wit of man than that any of its provisions can be suspended during any of the great exigencies of government. Such a doctrine leads directly to anarchy or despotism; but the theory of necessity on which it is based is false; for the government, within the Constitution, has all the powers granted to it, which are necessary to preserve its existence; as has been happily proved by the result of the great effort to throw off its just authority.[5]

"The majority opinion went on to say that neither the President nor Congress could authorize trial of civilians before military commissions in territory where the civil courts were open. This was the baldest sort of dicta—a statement made which is not necessary to decide the case—and it was at this point that the concurring Justices parted company with the majority. Nobody contended that Congress had

A History of the Indianapolis Legal Profession   **45**

affirmatively authorized trials of civilians by military commission, and therefore it was totally unnecessary for the Court to express any opinion on that subject. It was the President who had sought to authorize such trials and therefore the majority had legitimately dealt with that question and should have confined itself to it.

"The four concurring Justices took the majority to task for indulging in this *dicta*, and went on to express their own opinion that Congress, had it chosen to do so, could have authorized trials of certain civilians by military commission in a state such as Indiana, which had been invaded by Confederate forces and subjected to a widespread conspiracy.

"Predictably, the decision angered many in the North, and was hailed by many in the South. A respected law review of the time expressed a moderately critical view in this language:

"[H]ad [the Court], in truth, simply adhered to their plain duty as judges,—they could have united in one opinion on this most important case, we deem the course they saw fit to adopt matter for great regret. Instead of approaching the subject of the powers of the co-ordinate branches of the government as one of great delicacy, which they were loath to consider . . . they have seemed eager to go beyond the record, and not only to state the reason of their present judgment, but to lay down the principles on which they would decide other questions, not now before them, involving the gravest and highest powers of Congress. They have seemed to forget how all-important it is for the preservation of their influence that they should confine themselves to their duties as judges between the parties in a particular case; how certainly the jealousy of the co-ordinate departments of the government and of the people would be excited by any attempt on their part to exceed their constitutional functions; and how, the more a case before the Supreme Court assumes a political aspect, the more cautious should the judges be to confine themselves within their proper limits."[6]

"The primary reason for the Supreme Court's practice of refraining from deciding a constitutional question unless it is necessary to reach a decision is the "delicacy" involved when one branch of government declares the action of a co-ordinate branch of that government invalid. But an additional reason for caution is that unnecessary *obiter dicta* come back to haunt the Court in future cases. Some of the *dicta* in the *Milligan* opinion did just that in *Ex parte Quirin*,"[7] a case that arose during the Second World War.

"While the United States and Germany were at war in 1942, Richard Quirin and seven other German soldiers were

Chief Justice Salmon P. Chase had been appointed to the United States Supreme Court by President Abraham Lincoln.

trained in the use of explosives and secret writing at a sabotage school near Berlin and set on a mission to destroy war industries in the United States. Four of them were transported by German submarine to Amagansett Beach on Long Island. They landed under cover of darkness in June 1942, carrying a supply of explosives and incendiary devices. At the moment of landing they wore German uniforms, but they immediately buried their uniforms on the beach and went in civilian dress to New York City.

"The remaining four who had been trained at the sabotage school were taken by another German submarine to Ponte Vedra Beach, Florida. They too landed in German uniform, but proceeded to Jacksonville in civilian dress. All eight saboteurs were ultimately arrested by the FBI in New York or Chicago.

"President Franklin Roosevelt appointed a military commission to try Quirin and his cohorts for offenses against the laws of war and the Articles of War enacted by Congress, and he directed that the defendants have no access to civil courts. While they were being tried by the military commission, which sentenced all of them to death, they petitioned the Supreme Court of the United States for review of the procedures under which they were being tried. The Supreme Court convened in a special term on July 29, 1942, to hear arguments in their case.

"One of the principal arguments made by able counsel for the petitioners was that, at the time of their trial, the civil courts throughout the United States were open and there had been no invasion of any part of the country. Therefore, relying on the *Milligan* case, the petitioners argued that the government could not resort to trial by a military commission. Counsel noted that one of the petitioners, Herbert Haupt, had been born in the United States and was a United States citizen. At the conclusion of the arguments in the case, and after deliberation, the Court on July 31st announced its ruling upholding the government's position, but its full opinion did not come down until October 1942. In that opinion the Court stated:

"Petitioners, and especially petitioner Haupt, stress the pronouncement of this Court in the *Milligan* case, . . . that the law of war "can never be applied to citizens and states which have upheld the authority of the government, and where the courts are open and their process unobstructed."
. . . We construe the Court's statement as to the inapplicability of the law of war to Milligan's case as having particular reference to the facts before it. From them the Court concluded that Milligan, not being a part of or associated with the armed forces of the enemy, was a non-belligerent, not subject to the law of war save as . . . martial law might be constitutionally established.

'The Court's opinion is inapplicable to the case presented by the present record. We have no occasion now to define with meticulous care the ultimate boundaries of the jurisdiction of military tribunals to try persons according to the law of war. It is enough that petitioners here, upon the conceded facts, were plainly within those boundaries . . . ."[8]

"Thus, the Court had to retreat from the *dicta* of *Milligan*. The *Milligan* decision is justly celebrated for its rejection of the government's position that the Bill of Rights has no application in wartime. It would have been a sounder decision, and much more widely approved at the time, had it not gone out of its way to declare that Congress had no authority to do what it never tried to do.

"What can we learn from all of this? The least defensible of the Administration's actions was the suppression of dissent in the press or from the pulpit. As for trials of civilians by military commissions, the answer is less clear. Did the fact that the *Milligan* case was decided more than a year after the end of the Civil War affect the way in which it was decided? Did the fact that the *Quirin* case was decided in the truly dark days for America of World War II—the summer of 1942—affect the way it was decided? Perhaps even landmark decisions such as the *Quirin* and *Milligan* cases cannot totally gainsay the Latin maxim *silent leges inter arma*.

"As for Abraham Lincoln, he himself did not approve in advance most of the arrests, detentions, and trials before military commissions which took place during the Civil War. His cabinet secretaries and other advisors did that, but Lincoln acquiesced in almost all of their decisions. In this respect, he seems to me to have acted similarly to the way President Franklin Roosevelt did during the Second World War. Lincoln felt that the great task of his Administration was to preserve the Union. If he could do it by following the Constitution, he would; but if he had to choose between preserving the Union and obeying the Constitution, he would quite willingly choose the former course.

"To an audience consisting of many law students, lawyers and judges, this may seem a condemnation, but it is not intended to be so. Neither Abraham Lincoln during the Civil War, Woodrow Wilson during the First World War, nor Franklin Roosevelt during the Second World War, could by any manner or means be described as strong supporters of civil liberties. It may be that during wartime emergencies it is in the nature of the presidency to focus on accomplishing political and strategic ends without too much regard for any resulting breaches in the shield which the Constitution gives to civil liberties. Perhaps it may be best that the courts reserve their serious consideration of questions of civil liberties which arise during wartime until after the war is over. At any rate, these are questions worth thinking about not only in wartime but in peacetime as well."

FOOTNOTES

1. © 1997 by William H. Rehnquist.
2. These remarks were delivered at the Indiana University School of Law-Bloomington on Monday, October 28, 1996.
3. 71 U.S. (4 Wall.) 2 (1866).
4. Address by Abraham Lincoln to Special Session of Congress (July 4, 1861), in *The Collected Works of Abraham Lincoln* 430 (Roy B. Basler ed., 1953).
5. *Ex parte* Milligan, 71 U.S. (4 Wall.) 2, 120-21 (1866).
6. *Summary of Events*, 1 Am. L. Rev. 37, 38 (1867).
7. 317 U.S. 1 (1942).
8. *Id.* at 45-46.

CHAPTER THREE
(1870–1900)

A NEW VITALITY

FADED AND GRAINY BLACK AND WHITE PHOTOS OF INDIANAPOLIS from the latter half of the 19th century reveal a city that, to modern eyes, looks rustic. Horse-drawn wagons and carriages line the still unpaved streets. Streetcar tracks for the "mule cars" also can be faintly seen (electric streetcars would not appear on Indianapolis streets until 1890). An 1872 photo of Washington Street shows a crowded street—still the busiest commercial district—attracting both businessmen and shoppers, perhaps to one of the city's six national banks, or venerable retail institutions like The New York Store. In 1870, there was no monument on the Circle; in fact, stately Christ Church overlooked a bare and neglected circular "park." Construction on the Soldiers and Sailors Monument began in 1888, and from that point until it was completed in 1901, a tall wooden fence encircled the area.

Yet to the Indianapolis lawyers and their families who lived in the city before and after the Civil War, the growing and—to their eyes, at least—modern metropolis was anything but old fashioned. Gas lamps lit miles of streets and by the 1870s, new houses were equipped with gaslines for lighting. The Indianapolis Water Works Co. began supplying piped water in 1871, and a new—albeit rudimentary—underground sewer system was a welcome change from the wooden gutters and culverts that had previously discharged their smelly contents into the White River.

Suburbs like Irvington, where former U.S. Congressman George Washington Julian lived and practiced law, as well as fashionable Woodruff Place and working class Haughville were springing up. The surging city population made housing denser within the original Mile Square. The old Marion

This was the corner of Illinois Street and Washington Avenue looking east in 1891.

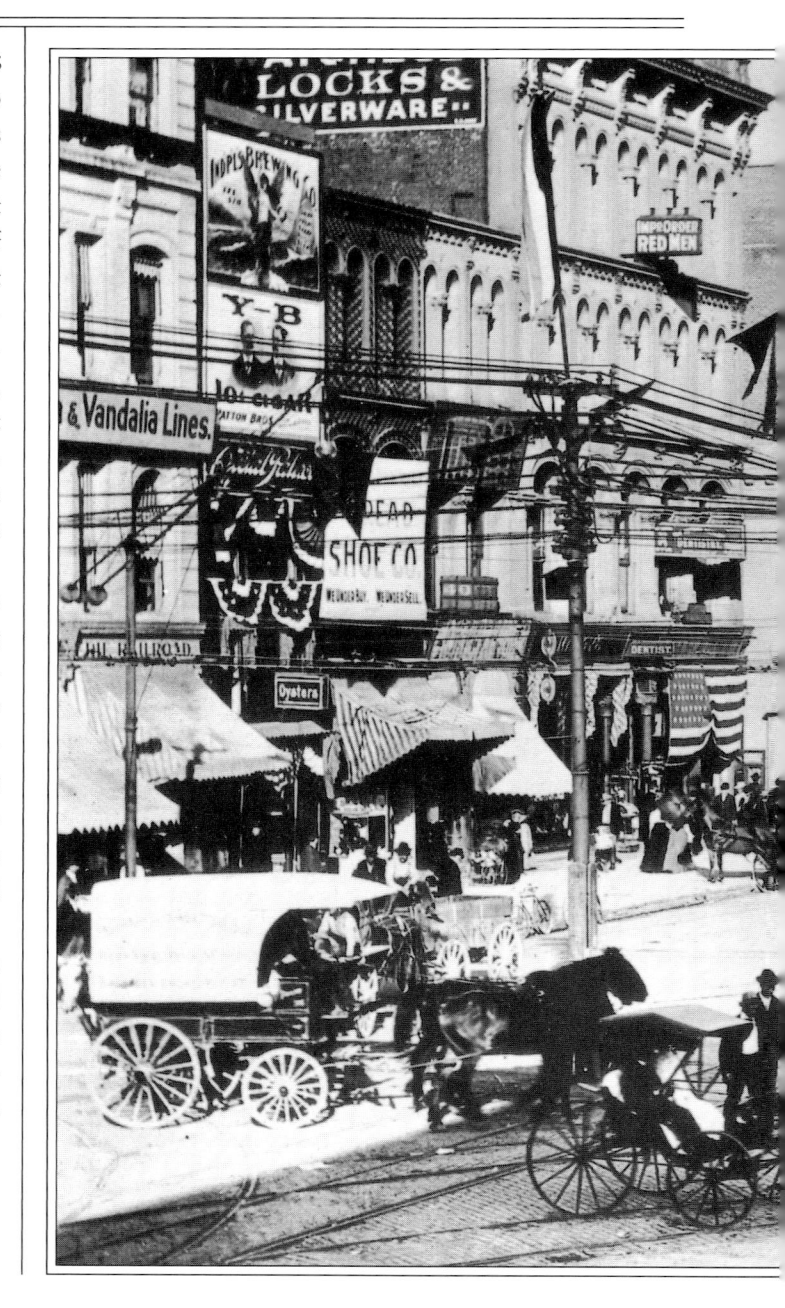

48   LAW IN AMERICA'S CROSSROADS

County Courthouse was torn down in 1870, and a new, much larger structure took its place in 1876. A new, 250-acre cemetery, Crown Hill, was *the* place to be buried.

In 1860, the population of Indianapolis was 18,611, but by 1870, U.S. census figures showed that city had ballooned to 48,244. Twenty years later, the population would top 100,000 and by 1900, the population of Indianapolis stood at 169,164. According to the 1880 census, 86 percent of Indianapolis's residents had been born in the United States. Germans and Irish still made up most of the remaining 14 percent of the foreign-born population, although the first Chinese immigrants appeared in the city in 1880.

Many of the Germans who settled in the city were educated professionals, including Bavarian-born Phillip Rappaport (March, 1845–Dec. 7, 1913) who studied law in Cincinnati before arriving in Indianapolis in 1873 to practice law. He went on to serve as editor and publisher of the *German Daily Tribune*, one of two German-language newspapers and seven daily newspapers in Indianapolis.

Indianapolis's black population was growing as well. Former slaves from the South settled in Indiana throughout the later half of the century, and by 1900 accounted for 10 percent of the population, or 15,931 individuals. Formal legal barriers were removed by the 14th and 15th Amend-

A History of the Indianapolis Legal Profession

ABOVE: *Today's Monument Circle looked quite different in the late 19th century. The Governor's Mansion that once occupied the site had been torn down. An unkempt park replaced it.* RIGHT: *Construction of the Soldiers and Sailors Monument, built to honor Indiana's Civil War veterans, lasted from 1888 until 1901. Here, soldiers guard the cornerstone for a dedication ceremony in August 1889.* OPPOSITE PAGE: *Woodruff Place was noted for its tree-lined boulevards and beautiful landscaping.*

50   LAW IN AMERICA'S CROSSROADS

ments to the U.S. Constitution—ratified by Indiana only thanks to the brash political maneuverings of U.S. Senator Oliver P. Morton—and in 1869 the state legislature provided for separate schools for blacks. By 1877, the legislature amended the law to give local schools the option of segregating blacks or allowing them to attend the same schools as whites. Indianapolis opted to segregate. Widespread white prejudice negated an 1885 Indiana civil rights law that prohibited racial discrimination in public places.

Attorney James T. V. Hill (Oct. 27, 1854–Feb. 20, 1928) was the first black man to break the color barrier in the Indianapolis legal community. Born in Chillicothe, Ohio, Hill arrived in Indianapolis in 1874 and worked as a barber and postal clerk. Hill had greater ambitions, apparently, and enrolled as the first African-American at Central Law School. After graduation in 1882, he immediately opened a legal practice and was the first African-American lawyer in Marion County, and later the first black member of a grand jury in Indiana. He later served as deputy prosecutor in Marion County, and was an active Democrat and civic leader, practicing law until his death.

Women still did not have the right to vote, and many members of the bar in the 19th century assumed this meant that they could not become lawyers. The assumption that there were no women lawyers, however, is unfounded. Order Book Number 24 of the Vigo County Circuit Court shows that on September 8, 1875, Bessie Eaglesfield—a graduate of the University of Michigan School of Law—was admitted to the bar. Eaglesfield did go on to practice law in Indianapolis, Terre Haute and Grand Rapids, Michigan.

Eighteen years later, Antoinette Dakin Leach asked to be admitted to the bar in Greene County Circuit Court. When her petition was rejected, Leach took the matter to the Indiana Supreme Court, which ruled in her favor in 1893. In her brief—one of the first typewritten briefs to be submitted to the Indiana Supreme Court—Leach argued that the provision in the 1851 Indiana Constitution that "Every person of good moral character, being a voter, shall be entitled to admission to practice law in all courts of justice," was not intended to exclude women from the practice of law. While Leach practiced law in Sullivan, Indiana, for 25 years, her admission to the bar was not greeted

A History of the Indianapolis Legal Profession   **51**

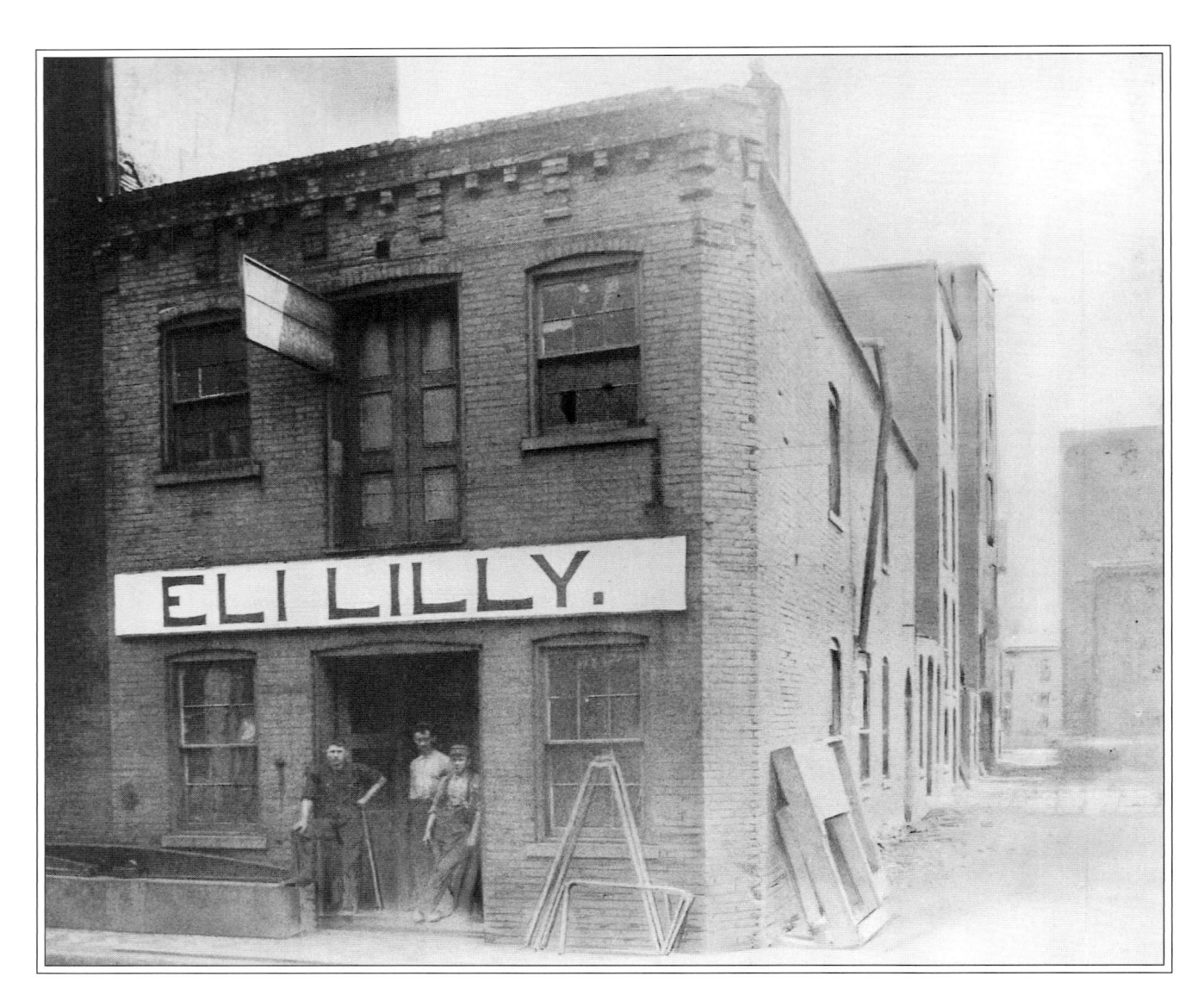

Eli Lilly opened his company's first plant on Pearl Street in 1876. (Courtesy Eli Lilly and Company)

favorably by most of her fellow lawyers. An Indianapolis attorney wrote in *The Bench and Bar of Indiana* in 1895 that the decision "has not been accepted by the Bar." Because "only voters" could be admitted, it was understood that admitting women was "impossible."

While suffragists were busy on behalf of women's rights, the temperance movement also experienced a revival. While there was no outright prohibition on the sale or consumption of liquor, the Baxter Law in 1873 imposed strict guidelines for new liquor licenses and required saloonkeepers to post a $3,000 bond. The city's German immigrants protested, the law was repealed, and in 1875 the legislature gave county commissioners sole authority over liquor sales.

Indiana continued to try to keep up with the increasing caseloads of its county court system, especially in Marion County. The legislative act of February 15, 1871, provided for a Superior Court for Marion County, to be presided over by three separate judges, Frederick Rand, Solomon Blair and Horatio C. Newcomb.

BUSINESS LAW BOOM

Behind the swelling numbers of residents, municipal improvements and social movements was a vast increase in industrial and commercial activity. Indianapolis was a "railroad city" and boosters advertised the advantages the "Crossroads of America" offered to industry.

Much of what civic leaders said about the city was simple boosterism, but there was a lot of truth in the fact that Indianapolis had diversified and industrialized. The city supported a rolling mill that produced iron for rails until the Civil War, when the economy and demand for iron made the mill self-sufficient. There also were a dozen flour mills, 500 grocery stores, blacksmith shops, machine shops and the world's most modern meat-packing plants, Kingan Brothers. In 1876, Colonel Eli Lilly opened a pharmaceutical company on Pearl Street; the next year, American United Life Insurance is founded, and in 1878, the state's first telephone firm, Indiana District Telephone Co. is organized. Indiana University historian James Madison, writing in the *Encyclopedia of Indianapolis*, noted that by 1880, nearly 10,000 industrial workers produced more than $27 million worth of goods, "making the city the leading industrial center in Indiana." By 1900, the city's manufacturing output had more than doubled.

According to legal historian Bernard Schwartz, the Fourteenth Amendment did more than protect the freed slaves after the Civil War; it also ushered in the "years of laissez faire." The amendment, stating that "No state shall make or enforce any law which shall abridge the privileges or immunities of citizens of the United States, nor shall any state deprive any person of life, liberty or property, without due process of law; nor deny to any person within its jurisdiction the equal protection of the laws," was the basis for the legal ideology supporting laissez-faire capitalism of the post-Civil War era. "Concern with the vindication of civil rights, which had dominated the Reconstruction era, now receded. In its place, legal stress was placed almost exclusively upon property rights—especially those possessed by corporations," Schwartz writes.

The legal system was changing, and business was at the heart of change. In a speech at the Indiana University School of Law-Indianapolis in 1994, Lawrence M. Friedman, Marion Rice Kirkwood Professor of Law at Stanford University, noted that the industrial revolution had an enormous impact on relationships between corporations and individuals, corporations and government, and, finally, law in America. "It would hardly be an exaggeration, for example, to say that the railroad created tort law," he said. While states still regulated much of business, the federal government was becoming involved, too, with the passage of the Interstate Commerce Commission Act, which was passed in 1887, and the 1890 Sherman Antitrust Act.

What did all of these changes mean to Indianapolis and its lawyers? Not only were Indianapolis lawyers not riding the circuit for court business—those days were long gone—but they also were more deeply involved in the city's commercial activity.

Lawyers were mostly still general practitioners, but rising attorneys like Benjamin Harrison—partner in a successful Indianapolis law firm grossed as much as $25,000 in 1873—found themselves protecting clients' business concerns as well as arguing on behalf of a defendant in a murder trial. And men like William H. English (August 27, 1822–Feb. 7, 1896), who practiced law only briefly, no doubt found their reading, training and legal community contacts helpful. English, who helped found the First National Bank of Indianapolis before the Civil War, went on to make his fortune in the Indianapolis Railway Co. and real estate, as developer of the landmark English Hotel and Opera House in 1880. His son, William Eastin English (Nov. 3, 1850–April 29, 1926), who also practiced law briefly in Indianapolis, chose politics over business.

William H. English's real estate investments led him to construct the English Hotel and Opera House, a noted city landmark on the northwest quadrant of Monument Circle for many years.

The boom in legal business was tested by the Panic of 1873, a severe economic depression that suddenly brought an end to postwar prosperity. The panic was brought about

A History of the Indianapolis Legal Profession 53

EDUCATING LAWYERS, IN AND OUT OF INDIANA'S FIRST LAW SCHOOLS

DURING THE FIRST HALF OF THE 19TH CENTURY, MOST INDIANA lawyers were trained as unpaid apprentices in law firms. "Reading law" meant reading books on subjects such as Anglo-American law, pleading and evidence, wills, property law, criminal law, contracts and municipal law, as well as reports on Indiana statutes and trials written by respected Hoosier jurists.

Some lawyers commenced their law studies after attending college, but many were educated only in small frontier schools and worked as laborers or as apprentices to some other trade before setting their sights on a law career. In law offices, they were often assigned to copy, as neatly as possible, endless legal papers, and gain by observation the practical aspects of law practice.

While a few Indiana lawyers were educated at law schools in the East—where law schools were established as early as 1784—there was no formal law school in the state until the 1840s. Pioneering legal educators like David McDonald (May 4, 1803–August 25, 1869) must have felt their lack of formal education keenly and tried to improve legal education in Indiana by teaching in one of the state's earliest law programs.

A Kentucky native who was admitted to the bar after completing grammar school and reading law for two years, McDonald was a member of the Indiana General Assembly from Davies County, a prosecuting attorney and circuit court judge before 1842, when he was appointed professor of law at the founding of the Indiana University Law School in Bloomington. He served as that school's only faculty member for five years, and later moved to Indianapolis to practice in the federal courts. In 1856, he published what became known as *McDonald's Treatise*, a volume designed to help justices of the peace and other officers of the court, but which became valuable to Indiana lawyers as well.

Civil war—which took most eligible young men out of school—economic depressions and low enrollment all contributed to early law schools' uneven fortunes. Despite McDonald's early interest, the law school in Bloomington suffered from interruptions, once closing for a 13-year period from 1876 until 1889. In 1856, North Western Christian University (now Butler University) began its law department, which operated until the mid-1870s, when it became an independent program called the Central Law School. DePauw University, too, operated a law department, but only sporadically, from 1853 until it closed permanently in 1894.

David McDonald was an early proponent for improving legal education in Indiana.

Both the Central Law School and DePauw University are probably forerunners of what would eventually become known as the Indiana Law School, organized in 1893. Four prominent Indiana lawyers—William Fishback, Byron K. Elliott and his son, William F. Elliot, and John L. Griffiths—were faculty members in the DePauw law department and then became the nucleus of the Indiana Law School. Other prominent citizens were associated with the Indiana Law School. Former President Benjamin Harrison was a trustee, as was pharmaceutical industrialist Eli Lilly, and Charles W. Fairbanks was a founding faculty member.

It was, in many ways, an amazing group that organized the law school. "These five faculty members could probably claim as much distinction in their field as any comparable group in any law school in the United States," wrote a faculty member from the IU School of Law-Indianapolis in a 1995 history of the law school.

William Fishback (Nov. 11, 1831–Jan. 15, 1901), an Ohio native who graduated from Farmers College in Cincinnati, studied law with his father, an attorney. In 1857, he moved to Indianapolis and opened a law practice and served as Marion County prosecutor from 1858 until 1861. In 1862, he went into practice with Benjamin Harrison, forming the firm of Fishback and Harrison. Fishback left the practice in 1870 to join his cousin in the newspaper business as co-owner and editor of the *Indiana Journal*. He later sold that paper and bought another in St. Louis, but that paper failed and Fishback returned to Indianapolis in 1874 and the practice of law. Fishback was appointed clerk and master of chancery of the United States courts for the district of Indiana in 1877, a position he held until his death. Fishback became the law school's dean in 1894, and also founded a privately owned publication in 1895 called the *Indiana Law Journal*, which contained both short articles on legal subjects and news of the legal profession.

Bryon K. Elliott (Sept. 4, 1835–April 19, 1913) was another Ohio resident who moved to Indianapolis to practice law. Elected city attorney in 1859, Elliott's legal career was interrupted by the Civil War. After serving as an adjutant general during the war, Elliott was again elected city attorney from 1865 until 1869, and judge of the Marion County Criminal Court in 1870. He was elected judge of the Marion County Superior Court in 1876, and five years later was elected to the Indiana Supreme Court. Elliott served as a justice until 1893, but failed to win re-election. Elliott later practiced law with his son, William F. Elliot, and together they co-authored important legal works including *The Law of Roads and Streets*, *Elliott on Evidence*, *The Law of Railroads* and *The Work of The Advocate*. On his own, the younger Elliott wrote *Commentaries on the Law of Contracts* and *The Law of Bailments* and co-authored *Indiana Criminal Law*.

Fairbanks, who eventually became a U.S. senator and vice president, was on his way to a promising political career when he began teaching at the school.

Byron K. Elliott, along with his son William F. Elliott, authored numerous important legal volumes.

The Indiana Law School first offered a two-year course of lectures to students already working in Indianapolis law offices, but soon switched to a traditional format of textbook and case method. For a time, from 1896 until the early part of the 20th century, the Indiana Law School was affiliated with an ill-fated University of Indianapolis movement that included the Indiana Dental College and the Medical College of Indiana and Butler College, as it was called then.

Although they were rare indeed, the Indiana Law School did allow women in its ranks. Helen G. Parry graduated in 1896, and Elizabeth Myers graduated the following year from the school. It is unclear whether these women ever practiced law in Indianapolis—there was no central registry of lawyers in Indiana in the 1890s—but their inclusion is remarkable. After all, they began their studies only a few years after the 1893 Leach decision by the Indiana Supreme Court, which rejected the idea that only men could be admitted to the practice of law.

While the Indiana Law School offered a full-time day program, two other schools at the turn of the century started evening programs. In 1898, the Indianapolis College of Law organized, and a few years later, a second evening school, the American Central Law School began operations. Those schools would eventually merge to form the Benjamin Harrison Law School, another forerunner of Indianapolis's only modern-day law school, the Indiana University School of Law–Indianapolis.

Stanford law professor Lawrence Friedman calls the 1890s a "boom time" for law schools. With the advent of the typewriter—an amazing technology at the end of the century—there was no longer a need for the legal apprentices who laboriously copied legal documents in law offices. There was, however, a need for people who could file and type, but those jobs began going to secretaries as opposed to would-be lawyers.

By the end of the century, the fledgling law schools in Indianapolis were among 100 law schools in the nation, and the old tradition of "reading law" would soon become a thing of the past.

Federal District Judge Walter Q. Gresham.

by the failure of a New York banking house, Jay Cooke & Co., but the ramifications were quickly felt in Indianapolis. Banks closed their doors, companies went bankrupt, and people went hungry. The fact, however, that small and large businesses suffered setbacks and failure meant more work for Indianapolis lawyers, who were flooded with bankruptcies, foreclosures and other legal tangles.

The Panic of 1873, which brought about widespread unemployment for years, fed the frustration of workers. When companies, confronted with low cash flows, slashed their payrolls and reduced wages, working people responded by striking. Labor unrest was a common occurrence.

Concern for the rights of the individual did not apply equally to workers and corporations. In 1877, when railroads announced wage cuts, workers on the East Coast began striking. The strike action quickly spread to the Midwest, including Indianapolis, where union workers gathered on July 21, 1877 to rally support. Railway transportation was frozen, and while state and local governments tried to persuade workers to return to work, railroad operators turned to Federal District Judge Walter Q. Gresham (March 17, 1832–May 28, 1895), a native of Harrison County.

Gresham, who practiced law in Corydon before the Civil War (he ended his service as a brigadier general in the Union army) was appointed federal district judge for Indiana by President Ulysses S. Grant. Gresham was unsympathetic with the strikers. He deemed the situation in Indianapolis both critical and dangerous, and organized a citizen militia. President Rutherford B. Hayes sent federal troops—the first time U.S. forces were marshaled for a labor dispute—and eventually workers, under order of Judge Quintin, returned to work. Governor James D. Williams formed an arbitration committee to help settle the strike, which finally ended on August 1, 1877.

On July 27, before the strike ended, however, 15 strikers were arrested and charged with contempt for interfering with the operation of railroad lines. Judge Thomas Drummond tried the men without a jury in federal court and found 13 guilty. Drummond handed down sentences to the men ranging from one to six months in jail, but under pressure from a public that saw the punishments as largely unfair, he later ordered the strikers each released on $500 recognizance.

POLITICAL PEOPLE

Political life in Indianapolis and the state of Indiana continued to be dominated by men who, to a greater or lesser extent, were trained in and practiced law. Some of these individuals went on to make a name on the national stage as well, most notably Benjamin Harrison, 23rd president of the United States (see sidebar: "Benjamin Harrison: From Indianapolis to the White House")

Thomas Hendricks, who formed a legal firm in 1860 in Indianapolis, was one of the city's leading attorneys and active Democrats for 25 years. After serving in the Indiana General Assembly, the U.S. House of Representatives and the U.S. Senate, Hendricks went on to be nominated three times for governor. It was his misfortune, however, to finally be elected governor in 1872, only to be faced with the Panic of 1873 and subsequent years of his term were mired in labor and financial upheaval. Democrats nominated Hendricks three times as a presidential candidate, and he came within a hairbreadth of being vice president under Democratic presidential hopeful Samuel Tilden in the closely contested election against Rutherford B. Hayes in 1876. Finally, in 1884, Hendricks won the vice presidency with President Grover Cleveland, but alas, died at his home in Indianapolis just nine months into his term.

In 1874, Charles E. Fairbanks arrived in Indianapolis as an attorney for the Indianapolis, Bloomington and Western

Railroads. Not content with the fortune he made in the railroad business, Fairbanks became involved in Republican politics through his support of Judge Gresham over then-Senator Benjamin Harrison for the 1888 presidential nomination. Although Harrison would be victorious—and no Indiana lawyer or politician of the 19th century would surpass Benjamin Harrison in the national political arena—Fairbanks parlayed his power into chairmanship of the Indiana Republican Convention and later to a seat in the U.S. Senate. At the turn of the century, Fairbanks was still a powerful political figure and would later serve as vice president of the United States under President Theodore Roosevelt.

Closer to home, Indianapolis was served by a series of lawyers-turned-mayors, and of the five mayors elected between 1881 and 1901, four were attorneys. James L. Mitchell (Sept. 29, 1834–Feb. 22, 1894) was a native of Kentucky who moved to Indianapolis in 1859, served as an officer in the 70th Regiment of the Indiana Volunteer Infantry and came home to Democratic politics. In 1873, he became the first Democratic mayor of Indianapolis in two decades, but he served only two years before returning to his law practice. Mitchell didn't completely retire from public life, however, and was elected prosecutor for Marion and Hendricks counties in 1886 and 1888.

No mayor in the 19th century probably had more of an impact on the city, however, than a lawyer named John Caven. Born in Pennsylvania on April 12, 1824, Caven was educated in a log cabin school, worked in his father's salt works and in coal mining before leaving home at age 21. He found his way

Charles E. Fairbanks served as vice president of the United States under Theodore Roosevelt.

to Indianapolis in 1845 and took a job in a shoe store. Two years later, he began to read law at the law office of Smith and Yandes, and eventually opened his own practice with Berry R. Sulgrove, who published a history of Indianapolis.

First elected mayor as a Republican during the Civil War, Caven returned to his law practice in 1867, but only briefly left politics. He served three terms in the state legislature, where he supported progressive political action: schools for black children, a city library for Indianapolis and the establishment of a bipartisan election board.

THE INDIANAPOLIS BAR ASSOCIATION: MINUTES FROM A FIRST MEETING

On November 30, 1878, Benjamin Harrison was among 40 lawyers gathered in the law offices of Dye & Harris to form the Indianapolis Bar Association.

It was always be a matter of pride that Harrison, later 23rd president of the United States, and Charles W. Fairbanks, who would go onto serve as vice president of the United States under Theodore Roosevelt, were among the association's first members.

The bar association organized in 1878 was actually a successor to an earlier group formed in the early 1870s. Apparently it was fairly active—attorney Harrison was asked by the group to head a committee to investigate the inadequacies of the Indianapolis court system—but its success was short-lived. The Indianapolis Bar Association that was founded in 1878 absorbed the earlier group's library and treasury.

The following purposes were adopted, and stand today in Article II of the Association's Articles of Incorporation:

PURPOSES

Section I. In General. The purposes for which the corporation is organized are as followes:

a. To uphold and defend the Constitution of the United States of America and the State of Indiana;

b. To develop and maintain the integrity and impartiality of the administration of justice;

c. To promote reforms in the law and modernization of the judicial system;

d. To cultivate jurisprudence;

e. To encourage and provide for continued education of the practicing lawyer and cultivation of professional excellence and maintenance of high ethical standards;

f. To uphold the honor of the profession of law;

g. To apply knowledge and experience in the field of law to the promotion of public good;

Caven was re-elected mayor in 1875 and served until 1881. Those years—marked by an economic depression—were perhaps his finest as an activist mayor. He was a voice of calm when a riot broke out in the election of 1876, and again during the Railroad Strike of 1877.

That same year, Caven prevented another riot when hundreds of hungry, jobless men assembled on the Statehouse lawn. Caven asked them to keep the peace, and to follow him to Simpson's bakery, where he handed out loaves of bread, until all the bread was gone. Caven then took the hungry crowd on to Bryce's bakery, where he passed out more bread, all at his own expense. Caven also promised jobs; the year before, he had presented his plan for economic revitalization in Indianapolis, including construction of a Belt Line Railroad that would connect with all the rail lines entering Indianapolis and encircle the city. Caven invited the jobless mob to report to

John Craven was mayor of Indianapolis from 1863–1867 and again from 1875–1881.

h. To carry out the foregoing purposes in concert and cooperation with other agencies or organizations when deemed appropriate to do so; and

i. To engage in such other activities as are incidental or related to the foregoing purposes or in the public interests.

At its founding, admission to the Indianapolis Bar Association was open to "any member of the bar in good standing who has been admitted to practice in the U.S. Circuit Court for the District of Indiana, or having an office in the city of Indianapolis may become a member by vote of the association or recommendation of members." Members had to pay $2 to join, and then were expected to remit $5 in annual dues. In 1879, the amount was raised to $20, but the association quickly settled on annual dues of $10.

Meetings at first were short and without much pressing business. By 1897, however, the association had formed committees to investigate court practices—one such committee responded to complaints about two criminal court judges, including one justice who apparently used some offensive language from the bench—and other issues facing members, including the pressing need for a more complete law library.

Formation of the Indianapolis Bar Association coincided with a revival of bar associations in Indiana and other states across the country. The revival culminated in the founding of the American Bar Association. Legal historian Bernard Schwartz gives credit for the ABA's founding to Simeon E. Baldwin, a professor at Yale Law School and later chief justice and governor of Connecticut. After an informal two-day meeting in Saratoga, N.Y., 100 lawyers adopted a constitution and by-laws drafted by Baldwin.

"Some of the nation's best-known lawyers participated in the first ABA meeting," wrote Schwartz in *The American Heritage History of the Law in America*. "They set the tone for the association's early years, during which it was a select group of lawyers, almost a club of intimates." Over liquid refreshments, they would decide on officers for the next year, and Southerners were almost always well represented, since Saratoga was a popular destination for Southern tourists.

By the end of 1878, 284 members from 27 states and territories were members of the ABA. The first published membership rolls in 1879 reveal that Harrison was among 35 members from Indiana.

The ABA maintained restricted membership rolls for decades, refusing to admit women until 1918. In 1912, members engaged in a bitter battle over the accidental election of three black lawyers by the Executive Committee, which had been unaware of their race, according to Schwartz. A statement of race was required on ABA application cards until the 1940s, when African Americans were finally admitted.

---

work the next day; when he visited the jobsite the next day, 300 men were employed, the Belt Line Railroad "had thus providentially come to the rescue," he later wrote.

Caven went on to become president and a director of the Indianapolis Brush Electric Light and Power Co., which eventually merged with other electric companies to become the Indianapolis Power and Light Co. He died in 1905.

John L. McMaster (Feb. 9, 1843–May 29, 1914) was born and educated in Ohio, but opened a law practice in Indianapolis in 1870. Regarded as an "able lawyer," who practiced law until the end of his life, McMaster didn't fare as well in politics. He lost his bid for superior court judge, and when he was elected mayor of Indianapolis in 1884, he only served one term before losing the Republican Party's nomination to Caleb S. Denny. McMaster went on to be elected superior court judge three times, serving 16 years on the bench, and remained active in civic affairs.

Denny (Jan. 1, 1886–Jan. 1, 1890), on the other hand, enjoyed popularity as Indianapolis mayor, from 1886 until 1890, and again from 1893 until 1895. Born in Monroe County, Denny moved from the family farm to Boonville, Indiana, as an apprentice to a tinsmith after the death of his father. He abandoned the trade, however, to attend school at Indiana Asbury (DePauw) University in 1866. Short of funds, Denny was forced to leave college and turned instead to teaching. He also began to read law. Denny was named assistant state librarian in 1870 and moved to Indianapolis, where he continued to read law. Admitted to the bar in 1872, Denny was appointed assistant attorney general of Indiana the next year and remained in office until 1875, when he returned to his law office. From 1881 until 1885, Denny was elected and re-elected city attorney for Indianapolis, then beat McMaster for the Republican nomination for mayor.

Denny was considered the law-and-order candidate, supporting strict enforcement of Sunday closing laws, and curbing gambling and prostitution. He also fought two laws passed in 1889 by the Indiana General Assembly giving control of

Caleb S. Denny served as Indianapolis' mayor from 1886–1890 and again from 1893–1895.

the public works of the city, police and fire departments to boards appointed by the legislature. Both laws were later held to be unconstitutional by the Indiana Supreme Court. He successfully saw the city through a Pullman Railroad Strike of 1894 and, during Denny's administration, Indianapolis had its first asphalt-paved streets and electric trolleys. No doubt his success fed that of his son, George L. Denny, who also served as an Indianapolis mayor during the 20th century.

Sandwiched in between Denny's administrations was Thomas L. Sullivan (October 6, 1846–July 9, 1936), mayor from 1890 until 1893. A Democrat and the first mayor to be born and raised in Indianapolis, Sullivan was a lifelong resident of Downtown Indianapolis and had politics in his blood. On his mother's side, Sullivan was the grandson of Judge Oliver H. Smith, a U.S. senator. His paternal grandfather was Jeremiah Sullivan of Madison, Indiana and is credited with naming the city of Indianapolis. He also helped found a dynasty of sorts; his son, Reginald H. Sullivan, also served as mayor in the 1930s and '40s.

Sullivan graduated from Racine College in Wisconsin in 1869 and returned to Indianapolis to read law and attend the Indiana Law School. He opened his own practice in 1872 and in 1888 was appointed to a vacancy on the Marion-Hendricks County circuit court. He did not win the election to keep the seat, but the close contest attracted the admiration of Democrats, who nominated him for mayor the following year

As mayor, Sullivan helped draft a new city charter and led the city through extensive modernization. His administration initiated a systematic approach to the planning and construction of streets and concrete sewers; street signs were installed and the Virginia Avenue viaduct was built. When the Panic of 1893 hit, Sullivan and the Democrats fell out of favor, restoring Denny to office.

TOP: *Thomas L. Sullivan was the first mayor born in the city of Indianapolis. His administration was marked by extensive public improvements.* ABOVE: *Poet James Whitcomb Riley had once studied law.* LEFT: *The Virginia Avenue viaduct, built over rail lines, improved traffic flow in the city. The old Marion County Courthouse is visible in the background of this photo.*

Despite the political upheaval, however, Indianapolis was looking forward, no longer a simple country town. The city had produced politicians, including a U.S. president, and a best-selling author, Lew Wallace. Hoosier poet James Whitcomb Riley, who had once studied to become a lawyer in his hometown, was becoming famous with his writings from his Victorian home in Lockerbie Square. City boosters William Fortune, a newspaper publisher, and pharmaceutical entrepreneur Eli Lilly founded the Commercial Club, a predecessor of the Chamber of Commerce. By the 1890s, it had attracted more than 1,000 members and built an eight-story building on Meridian Street.

Indianapolis had a new county courthouse and a new state capitol, a Neo-Roman structure built of Indiana limestone with a huge copper-covered dome, completed in 1888. Construction continued on a monument honoring Indiana's soldiers and sailors on the Circle. With gaslights, electric trolleys, thriving retail businesses and a diverse industrial base that included the manufacturing of a new, "horseless carriage," Indianapolis would emerge from the 19th century nearly a full-fledged city.

A History of the Indianapolis Legal Profession

BENJAMIN HARRISON: FROM INDIANAPOLIS TO THE WHITE HOUSE

BENJAMIN HARRISON (AUGUST 20, 1833–March 13, 1901) was the grandson of President William Henry Harrison, ninth president of the United States and the first governor of Indiana Territory, and namesake of his great-grandfather, Benjamin Harrison, a signer of the Declaration of Independence.

An impressive lineage, but Harrison, 23rd president of the United States and the only Hoosier to win the White House, was no crowned prince of American politics. His political career was aided by his famous name, certainly, but his success also was largely the result of hard work, beginning as a struggling young lawyer in Indianapolis.

Born in North Bend, Ohio, Harrison was educated at home by tutors until age 14, when he went off to Farmer's College near Cincinnati. At age 17, Harrison went off to Miami University in Ohio—not the "Yankee" ivy-league university his poverty-stricken father had once hoped for—and graduated two years later. While reading law in Cincinnati, Harrison married Caroline Scott and finished his two years of study before passing the bar. He considered moving on to Chicago to make his fortune, but after visiting Indianapolis in 1854, Harrison instead decided to move to the capital city.

Indianapolis attorney Benjamin Harrison was the twenty-third president of the United States. (Courtesy President Benjamin Harrison Home)

In an age of freelance lawyers and no large law firms in Indianapolis with which to associate, Harrison was a practically penniless, clientless, attorney when he arrived. He had to work hard to earn clients and fees—a case netting $5 was a welcome occasion—for representation in petty suits and routine legal matters such as foreclosures and wills. Legend has it that Harrison once was hired to prosecute a man who had obtained money under false pretenses. The future president had to hire a horse and ride 10 miles through the country to Clermont, where he tried his case before a justice of the peace whose backyard was an open-air courtroom.

Yet Harrison proved to be an opportunist when it came to politics. The Whig Party was collapsing in Indiana, and Harrison aligned himself with the Republicans. He served as city attorney—a post paying all of $400 a year—in 1857 and three years later was elected reporter of the Indiana Supreme Court.

By 1861, Harrison's legal career and reputation in politics were both on the rise. He and William Pinkney Fishback opened a law office at 62 E. Washington Street. Fishback later said that Harrison "worked like a slave" both at the office and at his new home, at the corner of Alabama and North streets.

Harrison's career was interrupted, however, when he left Indianapolis to fight in the Civil War, as a second lieutenant in the 70th Indiana Infantry. Within a month, Harrison was made colonel, despite his ignorance of military drill and discipline. The 70th Indiana, however, went on to contribute to Union victories, and Harrison finished his wartime service as a brevet brigadier general.

After the war, Harrison returned home to his Supreme Court reporter post and, later, his law practice. His reputation as a lawyer grew with each case, including one of the most famous murder trials of the 19th century.

The Cold Spring Murders, as they became known, involved the discovery of the bloody corpse of Jacob Young, an Indianapolis businessman, and the half-burned body of Mrs. Young on September 13, 1868 at Cold Spring, north of Indianapolis. A woman's shoeprint led to the arrest of three suspects, including William Abrams, Silas Hartman and Nancy Clem.

The law firm of Harrison and Fishback was hired on behalf of the state of Indiana to assist in the prosecution of Clem, who, it was discovered, had engaged in some questionable financial transactions with Jacob Young and then planned his murder. His wife was killed because she had the bad fortune to accompany her husband that day.

Harrison's passionate arguments before the jury helped convict Clem in the second of two separate trials—the first ending with a hung jury—although between hung juries and appeals to the Indiana Supreme Court, she never served a sentence for the murder. The trial, covered in sensational detail by every newspaper in the state, secured Harrison's reputation and helped him build statewide popularity.

He moved quickly up through the Republican Party ranks, too. In 1876, the party's gubernatorial nominee quit the race due to allegations of financial misconduct, Harrison accepted the Republican nomination for governor. Harrison lost the race, but won further political popularity.

The next year, his reputation as a leader grew with his handling of the Railroad Strike of 1877. Harrison, who argued that the strikers' grievances should be addressed when they returned to work, also took command of a citizens militia company to maintain order, reinforcing his reputation as a law-and-order candidate and cementing labor leaders' suspicions. Later that year, former Gov. Oliver P. Morton died, Harrison was the state's new Republican Party leader.

Harrison was elected to the U.S. Senate in 1881, bringing him national attention. In 1888, the Republicans nominated him for president in a race with Grover Cleveland. The campaign was a front-porch affair, largely waged from Indianapolis, and ended with a Harrison victory in the Electoral College, although he trailed Cleveland by more than 90,000 votes in the popular election.

Historian Charles W. Calhoun characterizes Harrison's presidency as "one of the 19th century's most activist administrations," with passage of the McKinley Tariff Act, the Sherman Anti-Trust Act and the Meat Inspection Act. It was a presidency also marked with personal sorrow: his wife, Carrie, died in the White House in 1892.

Harrison did, not, however, win re-election in a re-match with Cleveland in 1892. Leaving the White House, he returned to Indianapolis, where he practiced law, re-married and became a father again. His last years were busy and established Harrison as a renowned lawyer of international reputation and a distinguished elder statesman.

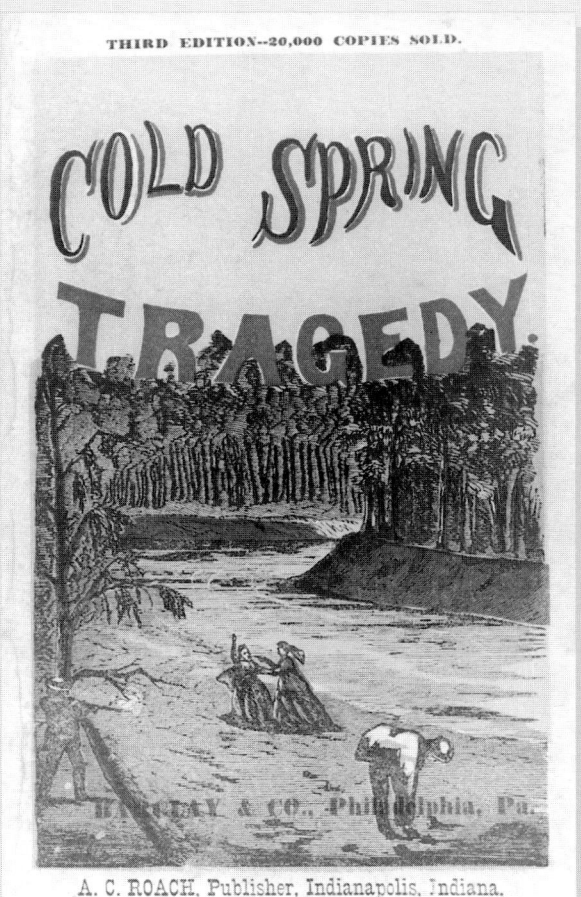

Benjamin Harrison's involvement with the prosecution for the Cold Springs Murders trial increased his public stature. This popular account of the incident was published in 1869.

CHAPTER FOUR
(1900–1930)

A GREAT WAR AND THE EVE OF A GREAT DEPRESSION

DURING THE EARLY 1900S IN INDIANAPOLIS, THE LANDSCAPE WAS changing dramatically again. Horse-drawn wagon and carriages began to gradually disappear from city streets. In their place, automobiles emerged and forever changed the way the city looked and how citizens lived. A sepia-toned photograph from 1915 of the corner of Meridian and Maryland streets suggests what the transition must have been like for Indianapolis. New-fangled automobiles, electric streetcars and horse and wagons all crowd the intersection at the same time. Ten years later, horses would practically disappear from city streets altogether.

"In one brief decade, traffic leaped from obscurity to municipal limelight, electric and gas engines replaced the plodding mule and an era of brick and asphalt relegated dirt and macadam streets to the urban Dark Ages," one historian observed.

All over Indianapolis and Indiana, the automotive dream grabbed businessmen, engineers and marketers. Between 1898 and 1937, there were 250 makes of autos built in Indiana, including 64 in Indianapolis alone. The city ranked fourth in auto production in 1907, and ranked second only to Detroit in 1913.

The elite of the automotive industry came from Hoosier hands, including Stutz, Duesenberg, Auburn, Cole and Marmon. Most of the autos built in Indianapolis were expensive, unlike the plain black cars Henry Ford produced in Michigan. Indianapolis cars were generally custom-made by craftsmen, using wood, leather, and metal. A 1929 Dusenberg roadster—one of America's most famous luxury vehicles—cost $8,500. But you also could buy a Model T Ford for less than $400 in 1918. Dealerships dotted Meridian Street.

With the advent of cars came the need for better roads. There was less than a mile of paved roads in 1890; by 1907, about 125 miles were paved in the city. With better roads, the number of cars increased, resulting in traffic laws, taxes, speed limits, license plates and police. The state board of health began tallying auto deaths in 1906, when three people were killed. The number grew to 100 deaths in 1915 and to more than 1,000 in 1928.

Auto registration was first required in 1903, when owners had to list their name, address and description of the car with the state. In return, they were issued a three-letter code that was painted on the car. The first license plates went on cars in 1911. In 1907, there were about 900 cars in Indianapolis. By 1920, there were 333,067 cars owned by Hoosiers throughout

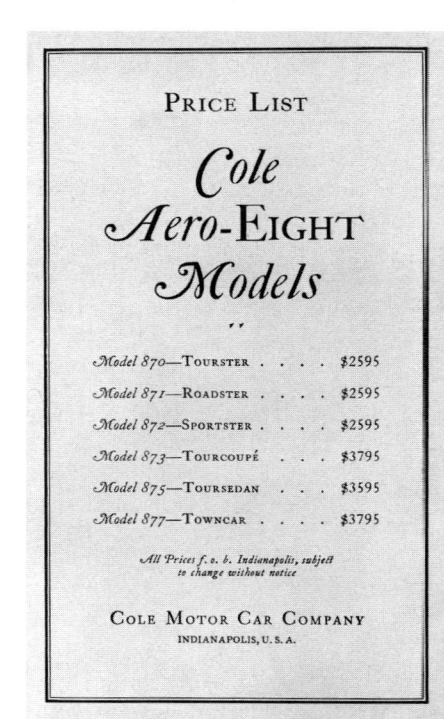

> PRICE LIST
> *Cole*
> *Aero-*EIGHT
> *Models*
>
> Model 870—TOURSTER $2595
> Model 871—ROADSTER $2595
> Model 872—SPORTSTER $2595
> Model 873—TOURCOUPÉ . . . $3795
> Model 875—TOURSEDAN . . . $3795
> Model 877—TOWNCAR $3795
>
> *All Prices f. o. b. Indianapolis, subject to change without notice*
>
> COLE MOTOR CAR COMPANY
> INDIANAPOLIS, U.S.A.

64   LAW IN AMERICA'S CROSSROADS

ABOVE: *Increased downtown traffic necessitated police officers directing traffic at busy intersections such as this one on Virginia Avenue in 1918.*
OPPOSITE PAGE: *The Cole Motor Car Company produced automobiles from 1909 to 1925.*

ABOVE: *Duesenburgs were true luxury automobiles.* RIGHT: *The Flat Tire Club, later known as the Hoosier Motor Club, was formed in 1902 to help early automobile drivers deal with car trouble.* OPPOSITE PAGE: *A downtown streetcar platform, ca. 1909.*

66   LAW IN AMERICA'S CROSSROADS

the state. To help motorists with car trouble, the Flat Tire Club—later known as the Hoosier Motor Club—was founded in 1902.

Lawmakers in 1925 tried to put the brakes on drunk driving with the Motor Vehicle Statute and the Intoxicating Liquor Statute, but in many ways only confused the matter, according to Indianapolis attorney W. W. Thornton.

"The legislature of 1925 enacted two statutes, each making it an offense to operate a motor vehicle 'upon any public highway of this state while under the influence of intoxicating liquor,' as Thornton wrote.

"It is observed that the Act of March 14, 1925, contains no definition of 'intoxicating liquor or narcotic drugs;' while the definition of 'intoxicating liquor,' and other definitions in the Act of March 4, 1925, are confined to the provision of that Act. They do not apply to the Act of March 14.

"The question arises in prosecutions (under the Intoxicating Liquor Statute), what condition must a driver of a motor vehicle on a highway be in to be 'under the influence of intoxicating liquor or narcotic drugs?'

"A fluid or liquor that does not fall within this meaning of 'intoxicating liquor' or 'narcotic drugs' is not covered by (the statute). Tea and coffee have a stimulating effect, yet no one worthy of consideration can claim they are intoxicating liquors."

Thornton found some resolution in a Pennsylvania case, where a judge charged a jury: "There are degrees of intoxication or drunkenness, as every one knows. A man is said to be dead drunk when he is perfectly unconscious – powerless... Whenever a man is under the influence of liquor so as not to be entirely at himself, he is intoxicated; although he can walk straight; although he may attend to his business, and may not give any outward and visible signs to the casual observer that he is drunk, yet if he is under the influence of liquor so as not to be at himself, so as to be excited from it, and not to possess that clearness of intellect and that control of himself that he otherwise would have, he is intoxicated." (*Elkin v. Buschner*, 16 Atl.102.)

DECADES OF GROWTH AND CHANGE

Indianapolis streets were transformed not only by automobiles, but also by sheer growth. In 1900, there were 169,164 residents, including 15,931 African-Americans. Twenty years later, the population had nearly doubled, to 314,194, including 34,678 African-Americans. Indianapolis' population continued to reflect its roots as a mixture of southern American, Irish and German stock, but many other immigrant groups began arriving in greater numbers by the early 20th century. Jews from Russia and Poland brought the city's Jewish population to 2.5 percent of the total population by the end of World War I. Still, the city's immigrant population—totaling 20,000 in 1910—was still low compared to other northern urban areas.

The low number of immigrants was a point of pride for city boosters, who extolled Indianapolis as a "100 percent American town," a concept that would be celebrated in the 1920s by the Ku Klux Klan.

A building boom, too, would bring about some of the landmark structures modern Indianapolis knows today: the Marott apartments on north Meridian Street, the Columbia Club on Monument Circle, the Chamber of Commerce building, Tabernacle Presbyterian Church, the Scottish Rite Cathedral and, over on Butler University's new campus, Jordan Hall and Hinkle Fieldhouse.

Despite the growth of Indianapolis at the turn of the century, city offices continued to operate out of the courthouse on Washington Street, between Alabama and Delaware streets, which was built in 1876. But by 1906, the need for a new home for city government became apparent. In 1909, a new City Hall was constructed at 202 North Alabama Street with a cornerstone inscribed with "I am myself a citizen of no mean city." The building, which was

BELOW: *The Scottish Rite Cathedral, located at 650 North Meridian Street, features a Gothic carillon tower.* OPPOSITE PAGE ABOVE: *Indianapolis City Hall, seen here in 1920, has been listed on the National Register of Historic Places since 1974.* OPPOSITE PAGE BELOW: *An 1888 interior view of the Marion County Courthouse.*

a point of local pride for decades, served as headquarters for city government from 1910 until a new City-County Building was constructed in 1962.

Judges and lawyers, their clients and others with legal matters continued to conduct legal business in the Marion County Court House. The Judge John Lewis Niblack (Aug. 14, 1897–June 16, 1986), in his autobiography *The Life and Times of a Hoosier Judge* fondly described the Court House as a "four story limestone building built in 1870 to hold five courts and not paid for until 1928. It was situated on the south half of the block surrounded by Washington, Market, Delaware and Alabama streets, with the main entrance on Washington.

"There was a large tunnel under Washington Street connecting the basement floor with the jail, one block south. The Court House was too hot in the summer and too cold in the winter. It was plenty dirty and harbored more rats and cockroaches than any place in town except the City Market just across the street. Occasionally, a janitor would put out some rat poison, and if you have never smelled 50 dead rats

A History of the Indianapolis Legal Profession **69**

decaying deep within walls, you have a treat coming. Winos also slept in the basement in winter."

The old courthouse is gone, but the basement of the current City-County building is still sometimes referred to as the "bum room," a legacy from the unofficial guests of the county who sought refuge from the cold decades ago.

JUVENILE JUSTICE

Indianapolis attorney George W. Stubbs (Sept. 1837–March 3, 1911), who was elected police court judge in 1901, quickly became concerned about the number of children brought before him to be tried as adults. At the time, "Regardless of age, anyone taken into custody was considered a criminal. Punishment often in severe extremes, rather than rehabilitation of a child was the guiding principle," according to the *Indianapolis Star Magazine*, April 4, 1964.

Vendors sold a variety of produce at this market day held on the grounds of the Marion County Courthouse in 1926

"To Judge Stubbs, a kindly, understanding and compassionate man, the very idea of lumping erring children into the judicial Mixmaster with known and hardened criminals was nothing short of soul-searing."

Stubbs traveled to Chicago to study the country's only juvenile court system and came back full of ideas and enthusiasm. Along with Indianapolis Police Chief G. A. Taft and other judges, Stubbs drafted legislation for the 1903 Indiana General Assembly.

On March 10, 1903, the legislature gave circuit courts jurisdiction over juveniles, except in Marion County, home of Indiana's first juvenile court. It was created as "a special court, to be known as the Juvenile court, which shall have jurisdiction of all cases relating to children, including juvenile delinquents, truants, children petitioned for by boards of children's guardians, and of all other cases where the custody of legal punishment of children is in question," according to *Courts and Lawyers of Indiana* Vol. II 1916.

Buoyed by the success of the new juvenile system, the legislature expanded the court's powers on March 6, 1905 to include "all cases against parents and all other adults for contributing to the delinquency of children."

By Feb. 23, 1907, the legislature expanded the juvenile court to be more of a family court, adding "the exclusive jurisdiction of all cases against parents and other adults for the abandonment, nonsupport, or neglect of children in their custody, together with power to enforce the proper support of children by parents, or to take children away from drunken, depraved or vicious parents, if necessary. In case parents were separated, the court was granted the power to decide which parent, if either, should be given the custody of the children. The act of 1907 also gave the court jurisdiction over all homeless, abandoned, destitute and dependent children, as well as those taken from vicious parents. The court was given the power to take children from parents in private homes or in public or private children's institutions at the expense of the county."

Indianapolis was only the second American city to develop such a juvenile justice system, and much of the credit goes to Stubbs, the founding judge of the Marion County Juvenile and Domestic Relations Court.

"This kindly, genial man, by his wholesome advice and admonition, started hundreds of wayward and delinquent boys and girls on the road to upright and useful manhood and womanhood. His appeals to drunken and dissolute fathers and others brought happiness to many a home in Indianapolis.

"Yet, if the milk of human kindness failed to bring about the proper results, he did not shirk from sending miscreant fathers to the workhouse or vicious mothers to a place where they would not have the opportunity to injure their children. He was always looking out for the welfare of the child, and many children now living in the city have been rescued from vicious, immoral and drunken parents and placed in surroundings where they might have a fair chance to become useful citizens. He returned to their homes many runaway or vagrant children each year, sending them either to their own homes or intrusting them to the care of some children's institutions. Sick and afflicted children were given needed medical attention (and) abandoned children were properly cared for. In fact it is impossible to estimate the

George W. Stubbs was instrumental in developing Indianapolis' juvenile justice system.

good which this man did for the children of the city," according to *Courts and Lawyers of Indiana* Vol. II 1916.

Indianapolis' juvenile court drew the attention of dignitaries from throughout the country and world. In 1906, Harold Salemon, a judge from Stockholm, Sweden, visited Stubbs to learn about the system. Salemon implemented many of Indianapolis' practices in Sweden and influenced similar changes in Italy and other European countries. Salemon also wrote a 280-page report of his Indianapolis study, which Stubbs translated into a pamphlet.

Although the attention from his peers near and far pleased Stubbs, he remained focused on his young charges. "He felt, as many of today's Juvenile Court judges and probation workers, that many children 'became delinquent because of their environment and through the criminal neglect of their parents,'" *Star* Magazine reported in 1964.

Stubbs, born in 1837 in Shelby County, was studying law when he enlisted in the Civil War. He served as a private with the 16th Indiana Volunteer Regiment and the Signal Corps. After the war, he returned to Shelby County to continue his law studies and opened an office in Shelbyville. In

Unbeknownst to strict prohibitionist Charles W. Fairbanks, alcohol was served at this lawn party he hosted for President Theodore Roosevelt in 1906.

1871, he moved his practice to Indianapolis and became active in Republican politics.

In 1899, Stubbs lost his left arm in a rabbit hunting accident in the fields north of Irvington. In the early 1900s, he was severely injured while trying to board a streetcar, an event that foreshadowed his untimely death in 1911. When trying to board the streetcar, Stubbs got caught up in a rope and was thrown to the ground. The injuries were serious and his recovery slow.

On March 3, 1911. Stubbs was on his way home when he was struck by an Indianapolis & Cincinnati interurban car as he crossed Delaware Street in front of the courthouse. Knocked unconscious, Stubbs was moved to the courthouse lawn, where he regained consciousness and asked to be taken to his home at 2460 Bellefontaine St., where he died later that night.

Among Stubbs' effects was found this note entitled "My Thought":

"I have struggled happily. I have done my best. Whatever comes to me I know that nothing can take from me the consciousness that my life has been largely spent trying to help others. Have I done any good in the world: I do not know. More than 60 years ago, while I was yet a boy, I gave breath to a thought that has since become common property. It was that I hoped to live so that the world might be better because of my having lived in it. Has the world been bettered, even in some small degree, by my life: I hope so, but I do not know."

POLITICAL AND BUSINESS DEALINGS

The early part of the new century saw the spotlight on Indianapolis in national politics when the Republican Party nominated Indianapolis attorney and U.S. Sen. Charles Warren Fairbanks as Teddy Roosevelt's running mate.

Fairbanks was born in 1852 in Ohio, where he was reared a strict Methodist. He graduated from Ohio Weslyan University in 1872, and became an attorney for the Indianapolis, Bloomington and Western Railroad, which brought him to the city in 1874. He supported Walter Q. Gresham instead of Sen. Benjamin Harrison for the presidential nomination for the Republican Party. His ability to organize grassroots support earned him the chairmanship of the Republican Party in Indiana from 1892 to 1896.

Fairbanks lost his bid for the Republican presidential nomination in 1908, supposedly because of a lawn party he held in 1906 for President Roosevelt. Known as a strict prohibitionist, he did not know that alcoholic beverages were served at the party. Dubbed "Cocktail Charlie" in subsequent news reports, Fairbanks was mortified. He was defeated again in a run as the vice presidential candidate on the ticket with Charles Evans Hughes in 1916, as they lost to Woodrow

A History of the Indianapolis Legal Profession

John Worth Kern, Sr.

Wilson and Hoosier Thomas R. Marshall. Fairbanks returned to Indianapolis, where he died in 1918.

Indianapolis attorney John Worth Kern Sr. (December 20, 1849–August 17, 1917), was nominated in 1908 to be the vice presidential candidate on the ticket with William Jennings Bryan, primarily because of his pro-union stance and progressive views. He favored civil service, a graduated income tax and lower tariffs. Nonetheless, the ticket was defeated by Republican William Howard Taft.

Kern was born in Howard County, taught school in Indiana and studied law at the University of Michigan. He opened a law office in Kokomo and started his political career in 1870 with an unsuccessful bid to the Indiana General Assembly. In 1884, he was elected reporter of the Indiana Supreme Court and moved to Indianapolis. Defeated four years later, he was elected to the Indiana Senate in 1892, where he made a name for himself defending labor and promoting child labor legislation.

Indianapolis Mayor Thomas Taggart named Kern city attorney in 1900. Kern ran for governor in 1904, but lost. Kern was elected to the U.S. Senate in 1911, and was named majority leader in 1912. He was an expert at crafting successful legislation that reflected the Democratic Party's goals and is credited with helping Wilson's New Freedom program pass the Senate. He died in 1917.

Labor unrest became violent with strike-related bombings first occurred at sites in Indianapolis in September 1909 during a construction workers strike. In 1911, the secretary-treasure of the Bridge and Structural Iron Workers Union was arrested in his Monument Circle office in connection with the bombing of the Los Angeles Times building in California. Another 51 ironworkers were indicted for transporting dynamite. The arrests resulted in a federal trial in Indianapolis. Although defended by John W. Kern Sr., 38 of 40 were found guilty, including union president Frank W. Ryan. The convictions, subsequently upheld by the U.S. Supreme Court, bolster the area's anti-labor movement and damaged unions.

Madame C. J. Walker, one of the country's first female millionaires, moved her million-dollar African-American hair care products company to Indianapolis in 1910. The African-American woman became a leader in the civic and business communities. In 1916, she moved to New York and left the management of the business to Indianapolis attorneys Freeman B. Ransom (July 7,1884–August 6,1947) and Robert L. Brokenburr (November 16, 1886–March 24,1974). They continued to promote Madame Walker's philosophy of independence for the former maids, laborers, housewives and teachers that were employed in the company's factories, offices and as sales staff.

Both Ransom and Brokenburr had active law practices in addition to their work for Madame Walker. Brokenburr successfully pled landmark civil rights cases challenging segregation in housing and theaters. From 1919 to 1931, Brokenburr served as a deputy prosecuting attorney for the 19th Circuit Court of Indiana, and went on to serve as the first African-American senator in the Indiana legislature from 1940 until 1960. Ransom, a graduate of the law department at Walden University in Tennessee, represented several Indianapolis businesses, served as a city councilman, and was heavily involved in civic life.

The seven-day Street Railway Strike beginning October 31, 1913 drew 800 streetcar operators away from their jobs to gain recognition for the Teamsters, support for higher wages and better working conditions. Three people were killed during street mob scenes and Gov. Samuel Ralston called in 1,800 National Guard troops to restore order. Another violent Teamster's strike in November damaged further the area's support for labor unions. The work of the

Associated Employees, the strikes and a 1919 national steel strike convinced the Indianapolis City Council to enact anti-picketing legislation, which stayed on the books until the mid-1930s.

In 1914, lawyer Joseph E. Bell (November 28, 1865–September 1, 1923) was elected mayor after several years of working his way up from precinct committeeman to the national conventions in the Democratic Party. Bell's race had a Republican and Progressive opponent and four minor ones. He garnered 37 percent of the votes, however irregularities resulted in the indictment of Bell, Taggart and others, who were charged with conspiracy to commit a felony. The mayor was acquitted after a jury deliberated for two hours, and he went on to establish the city's first vice squad and make other public improvements, including levees along White River, covering the Pogue's Run ditch and took steps to create the boulevard system.

LEFT: *Madam C. J. Walker became a millionaire by producing African-American hair care products.*
BELOW: *Attorney Freeman B. Ransom in his office at the C. J. Walker Manufacturing Company.*

A History of the Indianapolis Legal Profession

WAR AND THE INDIANAPOLIS HOMEFRONT

As the century reached its second decade, Hoosiers were mindful of the war raging in Europe.

Indianapolis attorney and businessman John M. Judah was chairman of the Marion County Council of Defense, which helped coordinate support for the war effort on the homefront. More than 70,000 yards and vacant lots were turned into gardens for food crops by the Patriotic Gardeners Association of Indianapolis. The city chamber opened an office to help businesses with war contracts, and many local manufacturers geared up to make weapons, airplane engines, uniforms and explosives.

Loyalty clauses were demanded of Indianapolis public school teachers and in June 1918, more than 40,000 school children marched in 65 parades to sell War Savings Stamps. Those not working or in the military were labeled "war loafers," and the free speech rights of the First Amendment seemed to be set aside as "city officials encouraged citizens to report neighbors who demonstrated any sort of disloyalty or pacifism," according to the Encyclopedia of Indianapolis.

Before the United States entered the war, many German-American residents supported their homeland. Many had not been in the U.S. for very many years, and still had strong family ties to Germany. Support shifted to the United States once it entered the war. However, "patriots" regularly berated German-Americans who continued to engage in cultural activities or associate with German organizations. German property was vandalized and the *Indianapolis Star* listed the names and addresses of 800 unnaturalized Germans. Germans ceased publishing their German language newspapers and changed many names, including *Das Deutsche Haus* to the *Athenaeum*. Teaching German in the schools was banned in January 1918.

The Indianapolis Bar Association met on May 2, 1917 to discuss the war and its impact on the local legal profession. The membership voted to convene a war committee, excuse members from payment of their dues upon their enlistment in the war effort and to post a "roll call of honor" which listed members of the Indianapolis bar serving in the war in each courtroom of the Marion County Courthouse. The preliminary list included 57 names, but by the end of the war, the roll call of honor had 133 attorneys, including Robert E. Kennington, who was killed in action at Chateau Thierry in France.

On December 5, 1917, the war committee issued a report. "The attention of the committee has been called to the fact that the absence of many attorneys in the military ser-

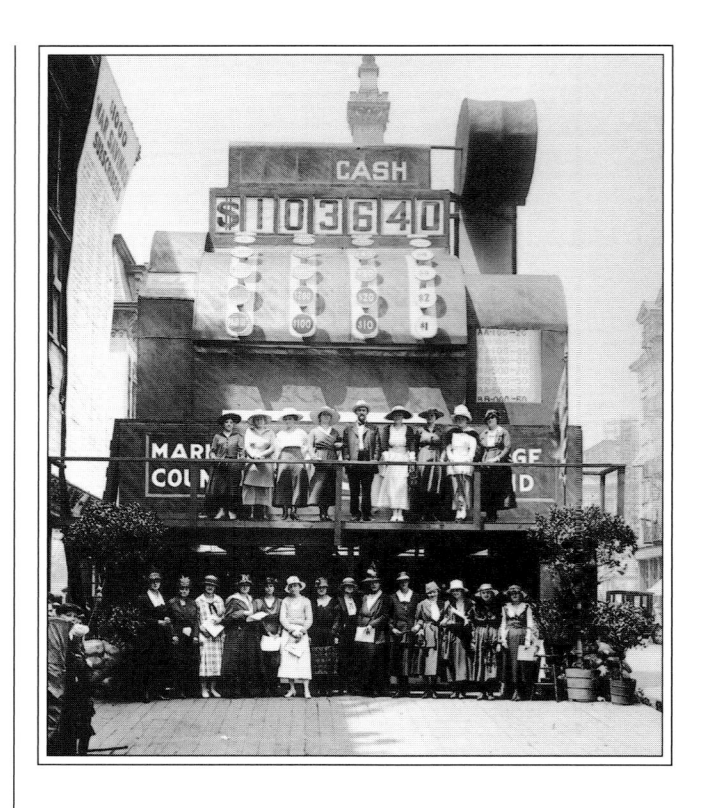

ABOVE: *This large cash register was part of Indianapolis' patriotic effort during World War I. It stood on the northwest corner of Meridian and Washington Streets.* OPPOSITE PAGE: *Returning soldiers paraded through Monument Circle under this massive victory arch on Welcome Home Day, May 7, 1919.*

vice will delay and perhaps render inefficient the administration of estates, guardianships and trusts in the probate and other courts. Members of this committee, without any authority, but of their own responsibility, have recommended to the judge of each count that he ask such attorneys to resign, and failing to receive their resignation that he remove them, with honor, to the attorneys so removed and appoint an administrator, or guardian, receiver or trustee to complete the execution of the trust. Of course, administrators, guardians and trustees thus removed should be liberally treated in the apportionment of such allowances as the court may make for the administration of the trust in question.

"The committee has assumed that when the list of attorneys who represent attorneys in the military service has been completed, it may become necessary to see that the absentees who are underrepresented be the special care of the committee, and that upon the request of the judges of the proper court, the committee arrange to assign to members of the Bar the care of such litigation, to the end that avoidable defaults not be taken, and that justice be done to all parties concerned."

Finally, the committee issued a stern concurring opinion in the matter of disloyalty or pacifism. "In the opinion of this committee, the Bar Association, through its proper representation, should organize to co-operate with the various defense leagues and relief associations in Indianapolis, to the end that disloyalty to the United States at this time be speedily discovered and punished, and that the arm of the government be strengthened in its efforts not only to crush out disloyalty, but to render effective the various military and civil agencies involved in the prosecution of the war."

The war committee's report in 1918 also detailed the committee's work on behalf of the American cause. "Various questions incident to the solving of problems of the administration of justice growing out of the war emergency were referred to the war committee," the report read. "and advice and opinions were given by that committee before courts, to soldiers and to the families of soldiers, without compensation. A single instance of the character of service rendered may be mentioned. An officer in command of a regiment in the U.S. military camp at Hattiesburg, Mississippi, wrote to the president of the [Indianapolis Bar] Association, asking if relief could be secured for a sergeant, who, during the stay of the regiment at Fort Benjamin Harrison, had married an Indianapolis girl, only to discover afterwards that she had another husband who was asserting prior claim to her affections and marital relations. The solution of this sergeant's difficulty was referred to the president of this association to the war committee. Suit was brought to annul the marriage, in which a hearing was had before Judge Hay in Room 2 of our Superior Court, which resulted in a decree of annulment. It is needless to say that this service was rendered without compensation."

Peace came Nov. 7, 1918 and a celebration was held on Monument Circle on May 7, 1919. The same year, the American Legion selected Indianapolis as its national headquarters and plans were struck to build the Indiana World War Memorial Plaza.

A CHANGING PROFESSION

Meanwhile, the Indianapolis Bar Association grew to 300 members by the 1920s.

One of the bar association members was attorney Robert L. Bailey (June 29, 1885–March 4, 1940) who served on the Legal Aid Committee, the only African-American member of the association in the 1920s.

During Bailey's tenure as an attorney, there were fewer than 100 African-American lawyers in the state. Most of them were in Indianapolis, but most were excluded by the local bar. Instead, many formed their own group, the Marion County Lawyers Club, now called the Marion County Bar Association, in 1921.

In Indianapolis, an exception was Bailey, who also was a member of the Illinois Bar Association. He was active in the National Association for the Advancement of Colored People, serving as president and counsel of the Indiana chapter, and a member of its Redress Committee.

Bailey started his work life as a federal railway postal clerk. In 1913, he was one of the founders of the National Alliance of Postal Employees, where he also served as counsel. In 1921, Bailey temporarily served as an assistant attorney general for Indiana in a trial involving neighbors, fences and spite. Bailey represented Dr. Lucien Meriweather, a black man whose white neighbors built high fences around their properties to isolate his. After a one-week trial, the fences were ruled illegal.

Bailey held a permanent post as assistant attorney general from 1929 to 1933. After leaving the state office, he resumed private practice law. "'Brilliant' is the word of praise selected by members of the bar to describe Bailey's defense and argument in an estate case only months before his death," wrote Stanley Warren in a biography of Bailey in the *Black History News and Notes*, February 1994. "For working as a housekeeper and in the restaurant of a deceased city resident, a woman filed a claim of $16,580 against the decedent's estate. Bailey chose to build his case with analogies by illustrating how the habits of criminals had led to their capture in several cases. He proved that the decedent was in the habit of forming partnerships in his business dealings. Eventually, he convinced the jury that the claimant was listed as an owner of the restaurant rather than an employee of the decedent, thereby rendering her ineligible to receive back pay from the estate."

Another lawyer, James Bingham, opened his own law firm in the Odd Fellows building in 1914. Bingham had started working at the tender age of 12 as a "printer's devil" for the *Veedersburg News* in Veedersburg, Indiana in 1900. After

ABOVE: *Hoagy Carmichael graduated IU Law School in 1926. He worked at the law firm Bingham Mendenhall & Bingham before turning to music.* OPPOSITE PAGE ABOVE: *A June 1917 interior view of the Marion County Superior Court, Room 3. Pictured at the far left is Will Remy who later prosecuted Klan leader D. C. Stephenson.* OPPOSITE PAGE BELOW: *James Donadio. (Courtesy Indianapolis Bar Association)*

graduating from Wabash College in 1911, Bingham studied law in Indianapolis under his stern uncle—another James Bingham, who had been an Indiana attorney general—in what was known as the Law Building on East Market Street.

Bingham was soon joined by his father, George F. Bingham, and the practice moved to the Merchants Bank building. From 1918 until his father's death in 1947, the father-and-son practiced together. In 1925, they were joined by Maurice L. Mendenhall, Indiana's first securities commissioner. A graduate of the Indiana Law School, Mendenhall had also served as Hamilton County prosecutor while still a student there.

In 1926, a new associate joined Bingham Mendenhall & Bingham. Howard Hoagland "Hoagy" Carmichael came to work at the firm after receiving his law degree at Indiana University in January of that year. The composer of "Stardust," "Georgia on My Mind," "Lazy River" and "In the Cool, Cool, Cool of the Evening," worked mainly in collections for the automobile company which the law firm represented, going throughout the state to settle damage claims for 10 cents on the dollar.

Hoagy often started a project in the morning, but by afternoon could often be found at the piano at the Columbia Club. He later told people that although he liked the Binghams very much, he believed that the decision to leave the firm for music had been a good one. Music lovers would agree.

Meanwhile, the Indiana Law School and the Benjamin Harrison School of Law were turning out a new generation of attorneys, including James Donadio, who graduated from the Indiana Law School in the class of 1928.

Prior to his graduation, Donadio went to school from 8 a.m. until 1 p.m. and worked during the afternoon in the Marion County Superior Court. In a 1993 interview with William F. Harvey, professor of law at the IU School of Law-Indianapolis, Donadio—by then a senior partner with the

A History of the Indianapolis Legal Profession 79

firm Ice Miller Donadio & Ryan with more than 60 years of law practice—recalled that Indiana Law School Dean James Rohbach provided leadership for the part-time faculty and law school classes of 30 or so aspiring attorneys. Faculty included men like John Kern, Jr., who eventually became mayor of Indianapolis, and William Forney, one of the first municipal judges in Indianapolis. Fred McCallister, who was in partnership with the well-known criminal lawyers Ira Holmes and Ephraim Inman, also taught at the school.

The law school allowed Donadio and others the opportunity to attend law school without having first earned a college degree, and provided practical instruction from standout lawyers, Donadio said. "The law school gave a good many common boys the opportunity to become lawyers and, me excluded, to become prominent," he told Harvey.

Meanwhile, the Benjamin Harrison School of Law offered classes in the evening. John Niblack enrolled in the Benjamin Harrison School of Law in September 1923 when the law school offered a two-year course, with classes held ten months a year, five nights a week from 6 to 8 p.m.

The schedule Niblack maintained in order to earn his law degree was demanding, but probably not unusual for the law students who worked during the day and attended classes at night. "I arose each week day at 6:00 a.m. and was at work by 7:00 a.m. and I don't mean 7:01. I got off at 5:00 p.m. and had supper somewhere, and attended class from 6:00 to 8:00. I studied in a lawyer's office until 9:30 or 10:00 and went to bed 11:00, slept seven hours and started all over again," Niblack wrote. After this rigorous routine, Niblack apparently was eager to embark on his career. On Jan. 1, 1926, he was sworn in as deputy prosecutor under William H. Remy, at a salary of $200 a month.

Judge John Lewis Niblack, author of The Life and Times of a Hoosier Judge. *As a reporter, he covered the trial of Klan leader D. C. Stephenson for rape and murder.*

With the passage of the 19th Amendment, which gave women the right to vote, the Indianapolis branch of the Women's Franchise League of Indiana was disbanded on April 16 and re-established itself as the League of Women Voters.

On Aug. 28, 1920, Mary Bostwick, a reporter at the *Indianapolis Star*, was the first woman summoned to serve on a jury in Indiana. She was assigned to an all-woman jury to hear a case involving Lane Robertson and Philip Sachs in a dispute about a talking machine. Justice of the Peace T. Ernest Maholm, who presided over the case, said that "…because it is the first time a woman jury has served, the Rev. C. C. Gohn, pastor of the First United Brethren Church, will invoke the divine blessing upon the jurors after they have been sworn. The service of women on juries was made possible by the ratification of the suffrage amendment," reported the *Indianapolis Star*.

The Indianapolis Bar Association voted unanimously in 1925 to raise the standards for admission. The question of how one could become a lawyer in Indiana had bedeviled the profession since the turn of the century, when an increasing number of lawyers apparently became concerned with the quality of men presenting themselves for admission to Indiana's courts, owing to Article VII, Section 21 of the 1851 Indiana Constitution allowing anyone with "good moral character, being a voter, shall be entitled to admission to practice law in all courts of justice."

Previously, the General Assembly had attempted to amend that provision, and indeed, voters did approve an amendment, but not by a constitutional majority. In 1900, George L. Denny declared himself to be of good moral character and a voter in Marion County, and declined to submit to Marion County's bar examination. When Marion County officials refused to admit him to the bar, he sued. The Indiana Supreme Court ruled in Denny's favor. In 1906 and 1910, the same attempts were made to amend Article VII, Section 21, with the same result.

There would be no bar examination to determine a lawyer's professional fitness until 1931, and even then, strenuous debate occasionally erupted over whether a bar exam was appropriate. After all, Abraham Lincoln, it was frequently argued, never attended law school or passed such an exam.

Other issues came to the fore of legal discussion during the 1920s. At a bar association meeting Oct. 20, 1926, Raymond F. Murray, a candidate for Marion County prosecuting attorney, said the "fee system" associated with liquor cases was "ineffective and exceedingly burdensome to the taxpayers. Marion County Prosecutor William H. Remy said he had begun to require a $5,000 bond to be posted in appeals of conviction of liquor law violations, something he said would "deter the present practice of bootleggers, by which they often remain at liberty, although they have been convicted of three or four violations of legislative laws and appeals in these cases are then pending," according to the 1926–27 Indiana Law Journal.

The bar association continued to promote reform of criminal law and procedure in Indiana by meeting with newspapers and other influential leaders throughout the community. The *Indianapolis Star* editorialized in favor of the local bar's support of procedural reform recommended by the American Bar Association. The Indiana General Assembly approved increasing the salary for Marion County judges to $10,000 a year.

Congress approved a bill that provided two federal district courts for Indiana. "Under this plan, there would be two federal district judges in Indiana rather than one as at present. One of the judges would preside over a federal court at Indianapolis and the other at South Bend There would be separate district attorneys and legal staffs for each court," reported the 1927–28 *Indiana Law Journal*. On Feb. 27, 1928, the *Indianapolis News* editorialized that "while the shyster was universally condemned by bar associations and leading lawyers, there was no similar condemnation visited upon those prominent members of the legal profession who had been guilty of occasional breaches of honorable methods in their profession. The editorial advocated increased teaching of legal ethics and inculcating of morals as a means toward raising the standards of the bar."

The Indianapolis Bar Association appointed William L. Taylor chairman of a committee to select a home for the organization on Nov. 10, 1929. The search for a home base was aided greatly by a gift of more than $100,000 from Susan W. Butler, Margaret Butler Snow, the widow and daughter of the late John W. Butler, an Indianapolis attorney who was a member of the bar.

The Indiana Ku Klux Klan was the country's largest, with as many as 40 percent of the white native-born men in Indianapolis paying $10 to join. This photograph of a Klan rally in June 1924 was commissioned by a local fireworks company. Note the words "DUTY" and "HONOR" along with the three crosses.

A History of the Indianapolis Legal Profession

"I AM THE LAW IN INDIANA"

There was little in the 1920s' legal activity, however, that could overshadow the flames of racial and religious hatred that had ignited young white men in the city, and a sensational trial that brought about an end to one of Indianapolis' darkest chapters.

David Curtis Stephenson, a self-described lawyer who called himself "a nobody from nowhere," moved to Indianapolis in the early 1920s to become Grand Dragon of the Ku Klux Klan for Indiana and 22 other northern states. Stephenson's goal was no less than the White House, and at the time he was arrested in connection with the rape and death of a young female clerk, he was working on a plan to be named to fill a vacant seat in the United States Senate.

Known to Klan members as "the old man," he was 34 years old when he was sent to prison. But before the cell door slammed shut, Stephenson headed up the Indiana Klan, the country's largest, with as many as 40 percent of the white native-born men in Indianapolis paying $10 to join and hear white supremacist messages against blacks, Catholics, Jews and many immigrants. Stephenson was known to brazenly tell people not to worry about breaking the law. "I am the law in Indiana," he'd say.

By 1923, the Klan had begun to gain control of the Indiana Republican Party and some county Republican and Democratic organizations. Within the next two years, candidates supported by the Klan gained a Marion County congressional seat, the mayor's office, and posts on the city council and school board.

Clinton H. Givan was one of those elected officials targeted by Stephenson and the Klan. Elected to the Marion County Superior Court in 1924, the elder Givan was one of only a few local judges who would allow Catholic, Jewish and African-American lawyers to practice in the court without white, Protestant co-counsel, according to his son, retired Indiana Supreme Court Justice Supreme Court Chief Justice Richard Givan. D.C. Stephenson came to see him to suggest that was not the way things should be done. Givan thanked him for his time and continued doing as before. Stephenson returned a few months later with the keys to a new Buick. He tossed them on Givan's desk and told him the car was his, if he would start running his court Stephenson's way. Givan threw the keys back and escorted Stephenson out. Stephenson mounted a campaign against Givan in the next primary and he was defeated, returning to private practice.

Niblack had a front row seat in the Marion County Courthouse during those years, and witnessed the corruption of the Klan firsthand. "I was there three and half years as a reporter and then I served as deputy to the elected prosecuting attorney of Marion County, Mr. William H. Remy, from Jan. 1, 1926 to December 31, 1928, having graduated from night Law School in 1925," Niblack recalled in *The Life and Times of a Hoosier Judge*. "As a reporter I covered Klan activities, politics and Stephenson's trial for the rape-murder of a young woman; and as Deputy I assisted in all the Grand Jury investigations and trials caused by Stephenson's 'squealing' on his former Klan and political allies when they would not come to his aid after his conviction.

"In those six years I got a good education on political and Ku Klux Klan activities in the Hoosier State, and I believe there has never been another era in Indiana like that of the "Roaring Twenties" for political corruption and skull-duggery in all the 153 years of its statehood."

TOP: *Klan support helped elect Edward Jackson as Indiana's governor in 1924.*
ABOVE: *Indianapolis mayor Lew Shank opposed the Ku Klux Klan.*

D. C. Stephenson's prison mug shot. Notations on the card are based upon the Bertillan criminal identification system. Invented by a Frenchman in 1883, the Bertillan system relied upon a series of twelve body measurements that were supposedly unique for each adult. Criminals were photographed and measured by this system until around 1903 when it generally became discredited. Criminals then began to be fingerprinted. Inmates at the Indiana State Prison in Michigan City were measured according to the Bertillan System from 1897 until 1932. (Courtesy Indiana State Archives)

A History of the Indianapolis Legal Profession

The Klan did not go unchallenged, however. A group led by Catholic Indianapolis policemen broke into Klan headquarters and stole the membership list. The *Tolerance*, an anti-Klan newspaper in Chicago published the list, embarrassing many local members, including Secretary of State Edward Jackson, who went on to be elected governor in 1924. Republican Mayor Samuel Lewis Shank also opposed Klan activity by banning masked parades and use of Tomlinson Hall (a civic auditorium and produce market located on Market Street, just east of Monument Circle) for a rally by the Women of the Ku Klux Klan, and enforcing a ban on cross burnings under public safety laws.

In 1924, Jackson was elected governor on a statewide slate of Klan-endorsed candidates. The next year, Klansman John Duvall, an Indianapolis attorney and a Republican, succeeded Shank. As the Klan's strength grew, it had a hand in where schools were built and whom they served. Crispus Attucks High School was built during this time to serve only African-American students.

ABOVE: *Crispus Attucks High School opened in 1927 to serve the city's black high school students. It remained segregated into the 1970s.*
OPPOSITE PAGE: *Due to a change in venue, D. C. Stephenson's trial was held at the Hamilton County Courthouse in Noblesville. This photo is from the 1920s, taken about the time of the trial.*

Nearly every white, Protestant man in Indianapolis at some point was approached to join the Klan. Niblack said that he was asked to join one day as he worked his reporter's beat at the Court House in the clerk's office. "... and a big Klansman Deputy Clerk, a veteran of World War I, and a Republican, took me to one side and asked me, 'How would you like to be naturalized tomorrow night?'

"I said, 'what do you mean, naturalized?'

'Well,' he said, 'You know, you pay $10 and you get naturalized. We are going to have a meeting out at Bridgeport in a grove.'

"I said, 'Well, I don't have to be naturalized as I was born down by Vincennes, Indiana, and I am an American citizen

84   LAW IN AMERICA'S CROSSROADS

and I have no reason for being naturalized, let alone paying $10. I suppose you are talking about the Ku Klux Klan?'

"He said, 'Yeah, that is about it, you ought to join, everybody else is joining.'

"I said, 'Well, tell me, friend, what is it with you fellows in the Klan, what do stand for?'

" 'We are against the Negroes, the Catholics, the Jews and the foreigners,' he said.

Niblack went on, 'The consequence was that I didn't join, although I had many Protestant friends who did join. Quite a few politicians around the town and the state, major and minor, both Democrat and Republican, joined the Klan to obtain political preferment."

By the mid-1920s, however, the Klan was beginning to lose its influence. Part of its demise can be attributed to the second-degree murder conviction of Stephenson, in a trial that was moved from Indianapolis to Noblesville, in Hamilton County. The change of venue came at the request of Ephraim Inman, a former prosecutor who was one of Stephenson's defense attorneys. The case had been set before Marion County Criminal Court Judge James A. Collins, a known Klan sympathizer. Stephenson was convicted in the death of Madge Oberholtzer, whom he kidnapped and raped (see sidebar). After 31 years in the Indiana State Prison at Michigan City, Stephenson was released. He stayed in Indiana for several years, eventually moving to Tennessee, where he died in 1966.

Indianapolis Mayor Duvall, who came into office with support from the Klan, was accused of promising jobs for votes during the campaign. Convicted of violating the state's corrupt practices act, he was sentenced to 30 days in jail. He resigned in October 1927 at the insistence of the City Council. The *Indianapolis Times* won the Pulitzer Prize for its coverage of Klan activities in Indiana.

The decade ended with the city and the nation facing long lines of hungry, unemployed, homeless people looking for relief from the Great Depression.

A History of the Indianapolis Legal Profession

TWO HEROES

IF THERE ARE ANY HEROES IN THE D. C. STEPHENSON CASE, Marion County Prosecutor William H. Remy and Indianapolis attorney Asa. J. Smith would be at the top of the list. Remy was prosecutor in the case, and Smith, a friend of Madge Oberholtzer's family, is credited with gathering the most compelling evidence in the sensational trial.

Remy was born on Dec. 18, 1892 in Columbus, Indiana, but graduated from Manual High School in Indianapolis in 1910. Remy went on to study at the Indiana Law School and, after graduating in 1915, practiced law in Indianapolis until the start of World War I. He enlisted as a private, and at the end of the war returned to his law practice.

In 1921, Remy went to work in the Marion County Prosecutor's office as deputy prosecutor. When the prosecutor resigned, Remy served out the term and ran for re-election in 1924 and won a surprising victory, since he campaigned on an anti-Klan platform.

Newspaper reporters referred to Remy as the "boy prosecutor" for his youthful looks, but there was nothing boyish about his stand against the Klan. The late Judge John Lewis Niblack, who covered the 1925 Stephenson trial as a reporter and later served as deputy prosecutor, credits Remy with the downfall of the Klan in Indiana. Remy was only "one of the two County officials not in 'the Old Man's' pocket. Remy was intensely anti-crime, anti-Klan, and anti-Stephenson.

"Once he had taken hold of a case, he pursued it relentlessly through thick and thin, like a bloodhound on a warm trail," Niblack wrote. "He had a keen, logical mind, a world of determination, and he was an ideal prosecutor to represent the public. He hated organized or premeditated crime like the Devil hates Holy water. He had high ideals for public office, and for crooked politicians and cheating public officials he had only the highest disdain. He was a masterful trial lawyer before a jury. There was none better in the state of Indiana."

After winning Stephenson's conviction, Remy remained Marion County prosecutor until 1928 before returning to private practice. He later served as president of the city's board of public safety. In the early 1950s, Remy left Indianapolis and died in 1968 in Marissa, Illinois.

Smith was born Jan. 20, 1994 in Wabash. His father was a Civil War surgeon and his mother was among the first women to graduate from medical school. Smith graduated from DePauw University in 1915 and the Indiana University School of Law in 1917.

During World War I, he served with the Fourth Marine Brigade in France, where he was wounded in Belleau Wood and given a medical discharge. In 1923, Smith was elected a state representative and is credited with developing the law that gave the State Board of Accounts the authority to inspect completed public construction projects, such as highways.

Marion County prosecutor Will Remy led the case against Ku Klux Klan leader D. C. Stephenson.

In 1925, as the Oberholtzer's family attorney, he was pulled into one of the country's most sensational trials involving rape, suicide, kidnapping, the Klan, corrupt politicians and the victim's riveting deathbed statement. During several visits in March and April of 1925, Smith wrote a first person, 14-page manuscript of his conversations with the young woman, who was dying of self-induced mercury poisoning. On March 15, 1925, the 28-year-old Madge Oberholtzer was forced to drink alcoholic beverages, kidnapped from Indianapolis and taken aboard a Pullman train car to Hammond, Ind.

Throughout the trip she was repeatedly raped and brutalized by Stephenson. She took several tablets of mercury bichloride in an attempt to make herself sick enough that Stephenson would let her go. The poison eventually killed her April 14, 1925.

"I did not wish to take a statement of this kind from the girl because it was a rather brutal thing to do, unless there was absolutely no hope of her recovery," Smith said. He knew the deathbed statement would not hold up in court unless it could be proved through other witnesses that the woman knew she was dying.

On March 28, her physician, Dr. John K. Kingsbury, "went upstairs to talk with Madge. Shortly afterward, he came back downstairs and said, "I have told Miss Oberholtzer that she cannot possibly get well and she understands it and is willing to make her statement. Then Smith, Dean Moore and Kingsbury went upstairs. The Oberholtzers waited downstairs with the notary public.

"In the bedroom Dr. Kingsbury took his position near the head of Madge's bed. Asa Smith knelt at one side of the bed, beside the dying woman. Griffith Dean sat on the left side of the bed, near the foot. Ermina Moore sat on the opposite side of the bed.

"Madge was pale and weak but still conscious. Kingsbury said, "I have explained to Miss Oberholtzer that she cannot get well and she understands and is reconciled."

"Smith asked her if this was true. Madge nodded and said, "It is. I understand."

"Smith told her, "Madge, it is necessary to feel in making a statement of this kind that you cannot get well and that you are going to die." Again, she indicated that she understood. Then Smith read the opening section of the dying declaration, the part that stated she knew she was near death. He asked her if this was accurate, and she said that it was.

"Madge, I have had typewritten very carefully what you have told us about your condition, and it is necessary for me to read it to you very slowly and very carefully," said Smith. "I will not be tiresome anymore than is necessary, but you must say whether or not what I read to you is true.:

"When Smith finished reading this part, he asked her, "Do you feel that you are going to die or live?"

"To die," she said.

"Do you affirm what I have just read?" he asked.

"I do," she replied.

"Then Smith gave her a pen. He took a magazine and used it to support the statement, propping it in front of her with a pillow. Kingsbury and Moore helped raise Madge up in bed. Smith held the pen in her hand, guiding it toward the page. "Madge, the pen is now at the end of the statement that I have read to you, and if it is true you may sign it," Smith said. As they all watched, Madge slowly signed her name."

The signature sealed a second-degree murder conviction and a 20-year prison sentence for Stephenson, who bragged throughout his reign that he was the law in Indiana. Oberholtzer's deathbed statement was ruled admissible at trial, and even today, the ruling on dying declarations as an exception to the hearsay rule remains a fixture in law school evidence classes.

Smith, who was nicknamed "the colonel," also handled civil cases. In 1928, he successfully represented customers of the Indianapolis Water Company in their petition to have the utility pay for the installation of meters instead of themselves. He was an unsuccessful Republican candidate for Congress in 1930, and during World War II, served again with the Marines as commander of the barracks at Auckland, New Zealand.

In 1947, he was appointed a commissioner of the Federal District Court for Southern Indiana, a post he served until 1950, when he was named special master of the court. In 1954, Marion County Prosecutor John G. Tinder named Smith chief deputy prosecutor, and he remained in that office until 1958. While in office, he investigated and prosecuted state highway department officials for bribery. A rare wit and considered an expert on Shakespeare, Smith died Feb. 12, 1973.

As the Oberholzer's family attorney, Asa J. Smith played a pivotal role in D. C. Stephenson's 1925 trial.

CHAPTER FIVE
(1930–1945)

THE GREAT DEPRESSION, WAR AND PEACE

A DIVERSIFIED ECONOMY BOLSTERED BY A SOLID MIDWESTERN ethic of personal responsibility was the principal asset Indianapolis carried into the Great Depression that began in October, 1929. Insulated by that advantage from some of the worst misery of the economic collapse, the city and its people nonetheless tasted the deprivation and gloom that gripped the nation.

Between 1927 and 1933, ten local banks closed, and unemployment skyrocketed. In early 1930, fewer than ten percent of the Indianapolis workforce was out of work; by 1933 the number peaked at 37 percent. Industrial production slid from $427 million in 1929 to $168 million in 1933.

The city's automotive industry was hit first and hardest, with every manufacturer and many dealerships closing. Other sectors followed the downward spiral. Construction slowed, neighborhood business centers disappeared, and many enterprises that stayed open did so with a drastically reduced workforce, often on a part-time schedule.

Before the city's recovery was complete, the electric interurban system, already financially fragile because of competition from the automobile, would fold, and neighborhoods close to the city center would deteriorate into the community's first true slums.

City leaders grasped the magnitude of the situation early, with local business leaders and the Chamber of Commerce forming a commission in February, 1930 "to study and act for the stabilization of employment in Indianapolis." The Emergency Work Committee focused its efforts on getting families safely through the Indiana winter. And, true to the city's bootstrap attitude, the goal was to provide not simply relief, but work for benefits.

The effort was funded by the charitable conscience of the community, and recipients of its programs were recommended by civic and religious welfare organizations as well as the public schools' social service department. A benefit football game between Shortridge and Cathedral high schools kicked off the fund-raising effort in fall, 1930, with the $10,500 earned that evening supplemented in January, 1931, by a $42,500 grant from the Indianapolis Community Fund. Many of those fortunate enough to be employed kicked in one percent of their salaries to the Emergency Work Committee, and the local chapter of the American Red Cross diverted funds originally designated for World War I veterans.

Those who received the Committee's assistance were required to work for their benefits, repairing streets and sidewalks, painting, mowing grass and cleaning up trash. For their efforts, they initially received cash for three days' work. But as the numbers of unemployed grew and economic conditions worsened, compensation was adjusted: food and cash for three days' work; then food for two days' work; and, finally, a basket of groceries valued at $2 or $5, depending on family size, in return for 16 hours of work.

In 1932 and 1933, the Indianapolis economy bottomed out. Charities such as the Sunshine Mission reported feeding 300 people each day, with others waiting unfed when the food ran out and the doors closed.

Even in independent Indianapolis, it fell to government to lend a hand and turn the tide. The governor's Commis-

In 1932, the year this photo was taken, many city residents received aid. People often worked in exchange for groceries. By 1933 unemployment in Indianapolis had climbed to 37 percent.

A History of the Indianapolis Legal Profession

sion on Unemployment Relief (GCUR) was created by the General Assembly in early 1933, with a Women's Work Division organized under the federal Civil Works Administration. By November, 1933, employment on Civil Works Administration projects had picked up the slack and more new jobs were created by the government than were eliminated by private employers. Jobs were created building the Lockefield Gardens public housing project and the Naval Armory. Others were put to work constructing Indianapolis Metropolitan Airport (now Indianapolis International), the Indiana State Library and Historical Building, and the State Fairgrounds Coliseum.

Following the bank holiday called by President Franklin D. Roosevelt on March 5, 1933, the Chicago office of the Federal Reserve Bank allowed three national banks to re-open in Indianapolis on March 15. Two days later, Indiana Governor Paul V. McNutt ordered all solvent state banks reopened,

ABOVE: *Crowded street scene outside the Hotel Washington in downtown Indianapolis, 1930. Note the "selling out" signs in the window of the French Apparel Shop.* OPPOSITE PAGE ABOVE: *Stokely-Van Camp, known for its Pork and Beans, originated in the depression when the two firms merged.* OPPOSITE PAGE BELOW: *Rising automobile travel, coupled with financial hardships of the 1930s, spelled the end of interurban travel in the city.*

as well. The upward trend continued throughout 1934 and 1935. By March, 1936, only six percent of Marion County residents reported receiving public relief, down from 19 percent a year earlier.

Despite the struggles and failures, not all the news in Indianapolis was bleak. During the entire period, Eli Lilly and Company kept its workforce intact, retaining every employee. Local sausage makers Erwin Wetzel and George Stark enlarged their business, creating Stark, Wetzel & Company.

William B. Stokely acquired the financially strapped Van Camp Packing Company, keeping it open and merging into the Stokely-Van Camp Company headquartered in the city. Indiana University expanded its Indianapolis-based Medical Center, and the four-year Catholic liberal arts school Marian College opened on the former estate of James A. Allison.

Another business that managed to stay open throughout the Depression was the Columbia Conserve Company. But while the radical experiment in industrial democracy weathered the financial crisis, it was so weakened financially and philosophically that it was unable to survive the prosperity that followed.

William Hapgood's wealthy father purchased the small canning plant and turned its management over to his Harvard graduate son, who converted its operation into what he described as "a laboratory to test relations of workers with owners and technicians." A Plant Council of ten employees elected by the workers ran the business, with sole responsibility for all business functions and decisions, including worker discipline and discharge. Eventually, the Council was enlarged to include all employees, with decisions determined by majority vote at weekly meetings. The Council cut the workweek from 55 to 50 hours, eliminated time clocks, and instituted now-common but then unheard-of benefits such as free medical coverage, pension and profit-sharing plans and on-site training classes. They established annual salaries based on worker need, with scales for unmarried and married employees and additional compensation for each child supported by the employee. The experiment, considered by many in the local business community to be extreme and reckless, succeeded through the 1920s, with profits growing through 1930. By then, 61 percent of the com-

ABOVE: *These ramshackle houses were replaced by the Lockfield Gardens public housing project.* RIGHT: *Funded by the federal Public Works Administration, Lockfield Gardens provided low income housing in a spacious, low density setting with many amenities for residents.*

pany stock was owned by an employee trust, and the company functioned as a producer cooperative.

The beginning of the Depression coincided with the arrival at Columbia Conserve of William Hapgood's only son Powers and his militant labor unionist friends John Brophy, Dan Donovan and Leo Tearney. With the company losing money for the first time since the experiment began, the Plant Council sliced wages in half rather than lay-off employees. The announcement of a plan to spend money on a national advertising campaign to encourage sales was the final straw for employees, who wanted the money used instead to restore wages to 1930 levels. Management and workers deadlocked over the issue and production stopped. Beginning "to doubt the wisdom of letting workers decide issues by a majority," William Hapgood fired Brophy, Donovan

92   LAW IN AMERICA'S CROSSROADS

ABOVE: *Columbia Conserve Company employees took substantial paycuts during the Depression rather than face lay-offs.* LEFT: *Columbia Conserve Company's Worker's Council was responsible for business decisions as well as company policies and operational matters.*

and Tearney, and Powers walked out in sympathy with his friends. A Board of Directors was established to augment and assist the Plant Council in determining policy.

By 1942, with prosperity restored, Hapgood was working on a new guaranteed annual wage plan when workers struck the plant. Although the strike lasted only a week, employee discontent was so endemic that workers filed a lawsuit for receivership against the company and management. Trustees who held the company's stock for the workers filed a countersuit asking the Marion County Superior Court to dissolve the trust. The court ruled for the company in 1943, ordering the trust dissolved and the stock distributed to all employees who had worked at the company since January 1, 1925. The experiment had ended, and the now-public company entered into a labor agreement with the C.I.O.

A History of the Indianapolis Legal Profession

PRACTICING LAW IN THE GREAT DEPRESSION

Like other businesses in Indianapolis, law practices suffered the Great Depression to different degrees. Some major firms came through the period intact (Baker & Daniels; Bamberger & Feibleman). Others disappeared (Pickens, Davidson, Gause & Pickens; Elliott Weyl & Jewett). Still others reorganized (Miller, Dailey and Thompson, the largest and one of the most prestigious firms in 1929, split into three smaller firms in 1930). All faced hard management decisions.

Harry T. Ice in his history of the Ice Miller firm, *History of a Hoosier Law Firm*, told of pay cuts that kept the support staff employed through the worst of the Depression. Secretarial salaries at the firm then known as Matson Ross McCord & Clifford were cut from $35 a week to $29, and the workweek was cut from six days to five in November, 1931. Three months later, the secretaries were asked to return to work on the sixth day, but at the reduced, five-day salary. In January, 1933, salaries were finally restored to $35.

The firm's income, which had climbed to almost $146,000 in 1929, dropped to $64,000 by 1933, and only returned to six-figure levels in 1941. "At least one fee was taken in kind," Ice reported. "As attorneys for the receiver of a cemetery in Shelbyville, (the firm) received six crypts in the mausoleum for part of (its) pay."

Senior partner Frederick E. Matson's foresight carried the firm's employees through the 1933 banking crisis in perhaps better shape than many Indianapolis residents. The week before Roosevelt's March 5 announcement, Matson hand-carried the firm's statement for services to Chicago and presented it to client Walgreen Drug Company. He took the company's check to a Chicago bank and exchanged it for a briefcase full of small bills, returned to Indianapolis and placed the cash in the firm's safe.

On Monday, March 6, Matson called the firm's employees into his office and told them he would advance daily sums to those who needed money for food or transportation until the banks reopened. When word of the money stash spread throughout the building, others stopped by the law firm office to ask for help. The firm was able to lend carfare and grocery money to all who requested it during the 11-day bank holiday.

While the Matson firm refrained from taking on new lawyers during the Depression (Ice, hired in 1929, remained the youngest associate until 1937), Matson himself saw that none of the partners and professional staff suffered financially more than necessary. In sole control of the annual partnership agreement, he demonstrated his selflessness by consistently reducing his partnership draw as firm income sank. At the lowest point, in 1933, his draw was just 40 percent of its 1929 level; in his last full year of practice, 1940, it had recovered only to 83 percent. Associate Ice reported that he had been granted a salary increase every year during the 30s. "The increases were all at Mr. Matson's expense in hard dollars," Ice gratefully wrote.

For the sole practitioner without a generous employer, Depression practice was more severe. John L. Niblack remembered in *The Life and Times of a Hoosier Judge* how he scrambled to earn a living in the early 1930s. He recited a litany of the tribulations facing an independent Republican lawyer: "I opened my law office in 1928; the stock market crashed in 1929; Marion County elected a Courthouse full of Democratic Judges in 1930 who wouldn't allow a Republican attorney in the Court room unless he had a

TOP: *Harry T. Ice. (Courtesy Indianapolis Bar Association)* ABOVE: *Frederick E. Matson was senior partner at the Matson Ross McCord and Clifford law firm during the Great Depression. (Courtesy Indiana State Library)*

Democrat co-counsel; I got married in 1931, and my new wife quit her job; and men sold apples in the streets."

The Matson firm took advantage of depressed demand for downtown office space to relocate into new space and dramatically improve its facilities. Klein & Kuhn, managers of the Consolidated Building offered free remodeling and redecorating to tenants who would sign a five year lease in 1933. The initial low rental would be stepped up each year in anticipation of a growing economy. Office equipment vendors were similarly desperate for sales and made impressive price concessions, including interest-free installment payments, in return for the right to use photographs of the finished space in advertisements.

Office rentals remained a burden for many lawyers and the Indianapolis Bar Association attempted to intervene on their behalf in 1932. Rents in better buildings were "exorbitant," and owners were not making "material reduction of rents," attorneys complained. Efforts by individual lawyers to "procure relief from the burden of excessive rents have availed little or nothing," a Bar Association resolution noted, despite lowered rents for other kinds of real estate in Indianapolis. As a result, a committee of five was appointed "to use all honorable means to bring about a reasonable reduction of office rents."

Government's response to the Depression—new laws and regulations aimed at solving the economic crisis—created new opportunities for lawyers, and both large and small firms benefited. From challenging the constitutionality of state laws such as the 1933 gross income tax act to helping clients navigate the maze of New Deal agencies and regulations, Indianapolis lawyers rose to the task.

By the late 1930s, those lawyers and firms who had survived the Depression were again prospering and hiring. But full recovery and financial comfort were still in the future. Harold R. Woodard tells of returning to Indianapolis to practice law after receiving his legal education at Harvard University in 1936. He was employed as an associate, the third lawyer in a two-man partnership. Woodard "felt lucky" to be offered a $50 per month salary. He lived with his parents in the family home near 36th and Delaware streets, and walked two blocks to catch the trolley to work. Four tokens were just 25 cents, he remembers, while the bus that ran along Delaware was 10 cents each way.

The Indianapolis legal profession was still predominantly male in the 1940s. Office conveniences for female staff were minimal. Female office staff in the Fletcher Trust Building, where Harold R. Woodard's practice was located, had the use of only one restroom, and it was located on the fourth floor.

A History of the Indianapolis Legal Profession   95

THE LAST HANGING

BY ORDER OF THE UNITED STATES DISTRICT COURT FOR THE Southern District of Indiana, George Barrett was hanged in the Marion County Jail yard in 1938. He was the last person to suffer that punishment in Indianapolis.

Barrett was convicted of the murder of two agents of the Federal Bureau of Investigation. According to Judge William E. Steckler in an interview given in 1987, there was some question as to exactly which United States District Court had jurisdiction over the crime because it happened virtually at the line separating the Northern and Southern districts of Indiana. The agents, Steckler said, were on one side of that line; Barrett fired his weapon from the other side. Ultimately, it was decided the crime occurred in the Southern District and Barrett was tried before Judge Robert C. Baltzell. The defendant was in a wheel chair during the trial because of bullet wounds to both legs suffered during his apprehension. But he had fully recovered by the time of his execution and walked to the gallows.

Records provided by the Marion County Sheriff's Department describe a local citizen hired to erect a portable scaffold under a tent at the north end of the old jail. The scaffold was open for public viewing the day before the execution, and thousands of citizens mustered to file through the tent and observe the apparatus.

The execution was scheduled for midnight, with just a few people authorized to witness Barrett's hanging. Among them were the Marion County sheriff, two U.S. marshals, a doctor, a number of sheriff's deputies assigned to the detail, and the professional executioner hired specifically for the event. By 10 p.m. officers began rerouting traffic around Delaware, Alabama and Maryland streets to avoid crowds. By 11:30, though, some 200 people who had wrangled passes to the execution crowded into the tent to watch.

Walter "Smokey" Davis who had joined the Sheriff's Department on December 15, 1935, was one of the deputies assigned to the execution. He later described it:

"A few minutes before midnight, Barrett was escorted past Bum Row and outside through the coal chute door beside the boiler room on the northwest corner of the basement. Without delay, he was walked to the 13 steps that went to the platform. He never looked back.

"Almost exactly at midnight, he was standing beside the closed trap door, hands cuffed behind his back. He stood there in a pair of borrowed pajamas, about seven feet above ground level. A hole two feet square and two feet deep had been dug directly beneath the trap door.

'The marshal asked Barrett if he had any last words. His only reply was a head shake, meaning 'no.' Barrett was gently nudged to his place on the trap door. A black hood was draped over his head and fell loosely across his shoulders. His legs were strapped together. The noose was carefully lifted over his head and lowered into position by the executioner. The

---

The practice was more leisurely than at the turn of the millennium in 2000, Woodard recalls, with "a great deal more civility among lawyers." In fact, the county courts went on vacation schedules, with only one court remaining open during summer months; the courts rotated the duty so all judges and staff could take part of the summer off.

Like most young attorneys of the era, Woodard entered a legal fraternity that was largely white and male and formal. Lawyers wore suits, he remembers, "and the suit coat remained on throughout the day." Both men and women wore hats to work, and offices were open for business six days a week. Office conveniences for female staff were minimal; even when Woodard returned from World War II in 1946, the Fletcher Trust Building where his practice was located had just one restroom for women, and it was located on the fourth floor.

THE BAR EXAMINATION

In late 1926, Harrison White refused to pay the Indianapolis Bar Association $10 and submit to the judgment of its three-person committee on his fitness to practice law. When his application to practice in the Circuit Court of Marion County on January 6, 1927, was denied, he headed to the U.S. District Court of Indiana and sued the Bar Association, demanding $1 million as compensation for denying him the right to practice law. White's complaint referred to the Bar

knot was drawn to Barrett's left ear, and the slack of the rope was fed back through the guide hole in the heavy beam above his head. Federal physician Robert Dwyer had taken his place beneath the platform to officiate in determining when Barrett would be dead. There was absolute silence in the tent.

"The marshal's head nodded, the executioner's hand tightened on the lever and jerked. The 'CLUNK' of the lever slamming against the stop, the quick groan of the trap door swinging down and away, and the 'SNAP' of the rope running instantly to its measured length were almost the same sound. Barrett's head was tilted unnaturally at an angle through the noose toward his right shoulder. The drop had left him suspended with his shoulders at about eye level to the men who were closest to the scaffold. His sudden stop at the end of the rope made his borrowed pajamas slide down over his ... er, buttocks. The doctor put them back in place right away and pressed his stethoscope to listen until the heartbeat stopped. In a few minutes, he ordered the body taken down.

"It was embalmed on the spot, as soon as the on-lookers had gone. His remains were displayed in an open casket in the garage area until relatives arrived to pick it up. Compared to the hanging, there was very little interest in his remains.

Robert C. Baltzell served twenty-five years as U.S. District Court judge. He presided over the trial of George Barrett, the last man in Indiana to be sentenced to hang.

"The next day, the scaffold and tent were taken away."

They were never again erected in Indianapolis.

But the memory of that day, and who had ordered it stayed forever with Judge Baltzell. As he prepared to turn over his courtroom to Steckler, Baltzell spoke of the unpleasant things a United States District Judge is required to do.

"Tears came to his eyes," Steckler remembered, "and he made the remark that he hoped I would never, ever have to do what he had to do—sentence a man to die. He looked at me with the tears in his eyes, and said, 'I often wonder whether I will reach heaven as a result of having to pronounce a death sentence.'"

Steckler tried to reassure the retiring judge that he had but done his duty, following the oath of his office.

"Then I said, 'I agree, I hope I never ever have to do that,'" Steckler continued. "But I said, 'I'm sure the Good Lord will forgive you and accept you for what you really are, the good man that you have been.' I was hard pressed to know what to say."

Steckler became judge of the U.S. District Court for the Southern District of Indiana on January 19, 1950, and Baltzell assumed senior judge status. Ten months later, on October 18, 1950, the elder man died. His health, Steckler said, had been overtaxed by 25 years on the bench.

Association's fee as a "vicious and unlawful (rule) of extortion and submission by and to a government other than the United States and the State of Indiana." The $1 million demand, he admitted to news reporters, was an arbitrary figure chosen simply to impress the court and the Bar Association with the gravity of his action.

White did not succeed, but efforts by the Bar Association and its counterparts throughout the state to reform legal education and regulate the practice of law finally did succeed in the early 1930s. Under the Indiana Constitution of 1851, any Indiana resident at least 21 years of age and of good moral character could be admitted to practice. A 1931 amendment granted authority to govern admissions to practice to the Supreme Court, and the first rules were handed down on November 15, 1933. A state board was created to write, administer and grade bar examinations, and anyone who wanted to practice law in Indiana would be required to sit for and pass the exam. The only exceptions were made for those who were admitted prior to July 1, 1931.

Still, would-be lawyers tried to circumvent the new requirements. After the 1931 constitutional amendment had been ratified, Lemuel S. Todd petitioned the Indiana Supreme Court for admission to the bar without taking the bar examination. He claimed the amendment had not, in fact, been ratified since it had not received a majority of votes from all those who voted in the election, but only a majority of those who voted on the amendment itself. The court quickly dismissed his argument and overruled an earlier decision on which it was based. Henceforth, amendments to Indiana's Constitution would require only a majority of those votes cast for or against the amendment, rather than a majority of all votes cast in the general election. (*In Re Todd*, 208 Indiana Reports 168 (1935))

The Democratic General Assembly and governor attacked the decision, as did the *Indianapolis News*, calling it "disquieting" and warning that it "may have opened the floodgates to a deluge of visionary amendment proposals of no merit." Todd's challenge to the bar examination requirement was not to be the last in Indiana. Bills introduced before both the House and Senate chambers of the General Assembly in 1937 would have tampered with the system. The Senate bill called for transferring supervision of the bar examination to the Judicial Council instead of the Supreme Court and passed overwhelmingly. It did not, however, survive in the House. Rather, a bill introduced in and passed by the House attempted to repeal the 1931 act entirely; it did not pass, although there was significant public pressure in its favor. The pressure came from the many people without law school training who had been unable to pass the bar examination.

S. Hugh Dillin, writing in the *Indiana Law Review*, told of a junior in the Indiana University School of Law at Bloomington who also was a freshman representative. Although the bill would have eliminated the need for the student-representative to take the bar examination, he rose to speak against its passage. "He stated that he was willing to take the examination and thought that it was in the public interest to require all applicants to do so," Dillin wrote. "The bill was killed. I was that student-representative. (When I was confronted with the exam the following year, I questioned my chutzpah.)"

Again in 1939, bills were introduced in both houses of the General Assembly attempting to abolish the State Board of Bar Examiners. Both bills were defeated, and aspiring lawyers have since been tested before gaining admission to practice in Indiana. The initial examination consisted of 50 essay questions answered over two days. Indiana remains one of only four states with bar examinations comprised solely of essay questions, although the number of questions has been reduced by almost half. Contemporary graduates also are required to pass the Multistate Professional Responsibility Examination.

S. Hugh Dillin was a freshman legislator in the 1937 Indiana House of Representatives.

LEGAL EDUCATION IN THE 1930s

Though passing the bar examination had become a prerequisite to entering the practice of law, a degree from law school was not yet essential in the Depression era. Still, the custom of "reading" law—gaining a legal education through an apprenticeship to a practicing lawyer—was "not very popular" in those days according to William E. Steckler, who was to become the last jurist to sit as the sole judge of the U.S. District Court for the Southern District of Indiana. The need to pass the bar examination further reduced the number of would-be lawyers who chose that path. "The bar examination was difficult to pass," Steckler said. "A large percentage of the applicants who did not have a formal legal education could not pass the bar."

William F. Harvey, retired professor and former dean of the Indiana University School of Law at Indianapolis, expands on that theory. "Excellent legal education developed long before and independent of the bar examination," he says, "and 'reading law' could provide excellent legal education independent of a law school curriculum. If reading law became unpopular, it was because a law school offered legal education in a shorter period of time, and some form of certification when one was finished."

Nowhere, Harvey insists, provides a clearer example of American legal education than Indianapolis and Indiana. Benjamin Harrison Law School was established in 1916 when two evening schools—the Indianapolis College of Law and the American Central Law School—merged. It was one of two law schools in Indianapolis. The other, Indiana Law School, had offered full-time day classes since 1894 as part of the newly-formed Indiana University that included Butler University, the Medical College of Indiana and the Indiana Dental School. Its initial faculty included many who were on the teaching staff of the DePauw University School of Law when it closed in 1893. The two schools collaborated closely and, in 1936 the Benjamin Harrison Law School became the evening division of the Indiana Law School.

"The Indiana Law School," Harvey says, "was an outstanding 'blue-collar law school,' (while) the Indiana University School of Law in Bloomington was an equally good college campus law school. The former provided legal education for persons who did not have sufficient funds to attend a college campus law school. Additionally, those students might not have met the admission criteria of a college campus law school. In those days, those criteria were used mainly because they sustained other campus colleges or programs in the university with which the law school was associated."

He points out that the Indiana Law School admitted minorities and women before 1900 and women constituted as much as 25 percent of the enrollment in some classes after World War I. "When one considers these lives and these classes," Harvey says, "an initial appreciation for a 'blue-collar law school' begins to develop. Indiana Law School offered a splendid academic, personal and intellectual development that was very different from the routine and bureaucracy of a college campus legal education. It was different, and very, very good."

During the World War II years, none of the schools had large enrollments, however and the Indiana Law School, unlike the public universities, did not have the state's treasury to sustain it. It also had another disadvantage in the history, conduct and policies of the American Bar Association. "In a nutshell," Harvey says, "the ABA targeted independent and 'private or corporate' law schools for closing and extinction. In this very clearly the ABA had the assistance of the college campus law schools, deans and administrators. This combination, invoked at a critical moment, ended the independence of the Indiana Law School."

In 1945, the Indiana Law School was absorbed into Indiana University, becoming the Indianapolis Division of the Indiana University School of Law, where it operated as an evening school until 1968. At that point, it became the Indiana University School of Law—Indianapolis, with a complete range of full- and part-time study plans and classes for both day and evening students. Harvey became the law school's dean in 1973, but still grieves the loss of the Indiana Law School as a "profound tragedy" to the development of law in Indiana.

William E. Steckler.
(Courtesy Indianapolis Bar Association)

Fortunately for Steckler, those events had not yet come to pass when he faced decisions about his academic future in the early 1930s. After high school, he was offered a scholarship to DePauw University but was unable to accept because his family could not afford the attendant costs of the college. Steckler investigated the law curriculum at Indiana University in Bloomington, but found it required at least two years of collegiate pre-law study. On the advice of a trusted family friend in his Posey County hometown, he turned to the Benjamin Harrison School of Law in Indianapolis, and entered in 1933 without benefit of an undergraduate degree. He earned an LL.B in three years of evening classes and continued on to obtain a J.D. degree after an additional year's study. Only the top 10 percent of the class was accepted into the fourth-year program.

It was a difficult program. Tuition for each of three terms per year was $33, and Steckler had his living expenses to pay, as well. He worked full-time at Methodist Hospital—first mopping floors, then working as a bellman, bell captain, and eventually in the accounting department—and "studied every hour of the day that I could find available for study." The effort paid off. He was graduated second in his class and admitted to the J.D. program. First in the class was Statehouse employee Barbara Miscevich. The two were among only 61 of the original 120 who enrolled in 1933 to be graduated.

A long list of attorneys who wielded great influence upon the practice of law in Indianapolis shared the distinction of having been graduated from either the Indiana Law School or the Benjamin Harrison School of Law. Among them were James V. Donadio, Federal Judge Cale J. Holder, Karl J. Stipher, Thomas M. Scanlon, Julian Bamberger, Judge Joseph W. Laudermilk, William B. Miller and Dr. John Morton-Finney.

A History of the Indianapolis Legal Profession

THE EXPANDING JUDICIARY

From the county courthouse to the statehouse to the federal courthouse, the judiciary, like the practice of law, was changing and evolving during the era. The regular meeting of the Indianapolis Bar Association on November 19, 1924, considered the problems of the overburdened City Court that had been established by the General Assembly in 1905. The single judge had concurrent jurisdiction with the Circuit Court on some matters and exclusive jurisdiction over matters involving city ordinances. The Bar Association's judiciary committee urged reform that would eliminate four of the five Justice of the Peace courts in Center Township along with the City Court.

In their place would be a Municipal Court with four judges appointed by the governor to four-year terms. As envisioned, the court would have concurrent civil jurisdiction in matters not exceeding $500 with the circuit and Superior courts, and the same criminal jurisdiction vested in the City Court. The last City Court judge, Delbert O. Wilmuth, was a vocal proponent of the change, which also would grant the new Municipal Court judges salaries double the existing $2,500 per year paid to the City Court judge.

During the 1925 session of the General Assembly, Sen. Thomas A. Daily actively championed the bill introduced as Senate Bill No. 179 to create a municipal court in any Indiana county with an incorporated city of at least 300,000 population. Only Marion County qualified. Daily was a member of the Indianapolis Bar Association's judicial committee that had drafted and advocated the change. A Conference Committee report added language providing that no more than half the judges appointed to the Municipal Court could be from the same political party; otherwise, S.B. 179 passed substantially as drafted.

"This bill met the needs of the growing Capitol City by providing it with additional judges with required training and experience, and with a salary twice that provided for the replaced City Judge," wrote William T. Sharp, who later sat on that bench. "It was the hope that these changes would attract and retain more capable and reliable judges."

The first four appointments to the newly created Municipal Court—Edward Webster Felt, Dan White, Fred McCallister, and Paul Wetter—were for staggered terms. Felt, a 66-year-old Democrat who had been on the Indiana Appellate Court from 1911 to 1919, served just five months before he died from injuries suffered in a fall from a ladder at his home. McCallister, also a Democrat, was a 50-year-old native of Montgomery County who had lived in Indianapo-

The Federal Courthouse, seen here in 1918, occupies a full city block in downtown Indianapolis. It is bounded by Meridian, Ohio, Pennsylvania and New York Streets.

100 LAW IN AMERICA'S CROSSROADS

LEWIS A. COLEMAN
(1873–1940)

Lewis A. Coleman may have personified the dignity, industry and generosity of Indianapolis lawyers during the first half of the 20th Century.

Born in a log cabin near Sharpsville in Tipton County, Indiana, on August 8, 1873, Coleman attended public schools and read law in the office of Tipton attorney Robert D. Beauchamp. While there, he taught himself typewriting and the Pitman shorthand method. When he came to Indianapolis in 1895 to enter the Indiana School of Law, he also sought and gained employment as clerk to former Indianapolis Mayor John W. Holtzman and continued reading law under Augustus L. Mason. He found time to court Margaret Alice Davis, and the couple was married on June 23, 1897, a year before Coleman completed his legal education.

He entered into a law practice with Holtzman (Holtzman & Coleman), and the two remained partners until 1923. Coleman's son Robert was graduated from Harvard Law School that year, and joined his father in a law practice for the remainder of the senior Coleman's career.

In addition to being an active member of the Indianapolis Bar Association, Lawyer's Club and the American Bar Association, Coleman left his mark on the city's business and social communities. He helped organize the Indianapolis Athletic Club and Meridian Hills Country Club, and was a charter member of each.

He played an important part in the organization of Continental National Bank, Aetna Trust Company, Sterling Fire Insurance Company, American Mortgage Guaranty Company and Bankers Trust Company. He also was an active part-owner of Riverside Amusement Park.

Although Coleman never sought or served in public office, his impact on the legislative history of Indiana was remarkable. He wrote and helped shepherd through the General Assembly a law to protect insurance companies from predatory receiverships and to cause control over the institution of lawsuits to be placed with the State Insurance Commissioner.

He wrote the law authorizing Indiana corporations to issue no par value stock, and also wrote the law permitting the organization of mortgage guaranty companies. That act was later incorporated in Indiana's trust company laws.

He also helped write the first Indiana law providing safeguards around the issuance and sale to the public of corporate securities.

Indeed, Coleman was so dedicated and diligent in his efforts for his clients and community, that many believed the illness that forced his retirement and kept him largely an invalid for 15 years before his death was attributable solely to the grueling pace he maintained throughout his legal practice.

When the Indianapolis Bar Association met to memorialize Lewis A. Coleman in early April, 1940, the depth of his peers' respect and admiration was extraordinary.

"Mr. Coleman had a clean mind," one said. "Vulgar or profane language embarrassed him, and he never found it necessary to use either." One termed him, "always friendly, always kindly, and always a gentleman." And one praised him for helping so many young lawyers get a foothold in the profession.

Another offered the observation that perhaps every lawyer would hope to claim as his or her own legacy:

"He prepared his cases well. He was fair, he was honest. He had the confidence of the court, and the jury was soon with him. When he advised his clients, if he found they were in the wrong, the told them to settle their cases, to compromise their cases. He rarely went into the courtroom unless he believed firmly in the cause of his client; and he had just cause to believe in that because he had made a thorough investigation."

Lewis A. Coleman was president of the Indianapolis Bar Association in 1922. He occasionally entertained members of the Bar at a large farm he owned on the city's north side.

A History of the Indianapolis Legal Profession

lis for 25 years. He had been chief deputy prosecutor and was a criminal law instructor at the Indiana Law School and Benjamin Harrison School of Law. He committed suicide three days before the end of his two-year term in December, 1927, and many believed he was despondent because he thought he would not be reappointed to the bench. He had met with the governor shortly before taking his own life.

White's appointment was for a three-year term. A 41-year-old Republican, he had been born in a log cabin on a farm in Tipton County and, as a youth, had driven stage coaches loaded with gold through the Rocky Mountains in Colorado. He was reappointed for four additional four-year terms, twice by Republican governors and twice by Democrats. The fourth judge, Wetter, was initially appointed for one year, and reappointed at the end of that term. A 33-year-old Republican, he had been a deputy prosecutor and pauper attorney. He later served as Magistrate of the Beech Grove Court, despite having become totally blind.

The four judges immediately drafted rules for the Municipal Court. Among them were two that evidenced a clear understanding of the practical problems faced by defendants, their families and friends:

XXII—Attorneys who make it a practice of loitering at the Police Station at unusual hours of the day or night for the purpose of soliciting business, or who divide fees with Bondsmen, will not be permitted to practice in the Criminal Division of the Municipal Court of Marion County.

XXV—Bondsmen who make it a practice to loiter in the corridors of the Police Station or the Turnkey's office at unusual hours of the day or night for the purpose of soliciting business, or who divide fees with attorneys, will be denied the right to sign bonds in this Court.

At the statehouse, the General Assembly continued tinkering with the appellate court system. In the late 19th century, the legislature had initiated a simple amendment to the 1851 constitution that made it possible for lawmakers to add the appellate court to Indiana's judicial system. The original language of the constitution read: "The Judicial power of the State shall be vested in a Supreme Court, in Circuit Courts, and in such inferior Courts as the General Assembly may establish." By substituting the word "other" for the word "inferior," they opened the door for a judiciary placed between the Supreme and Circuit courts. In response to the overwhelming caseload of the Supreme Court in 1891, the legislature took advantage of the amendment to create the Appellate Court of Indiana.

In 1929, the General Assembly granted the Appellate Court of Indiana temporary jurisdiction over all criminal appeals other than those involving imprisonment or the death penalty. The jurisdiction was to expire on January 1, 1931. In the interim, the Appellate Court's decisions were "final and conclusive," with appeal to the Supreme Court prohibited. Further action by the legislature in 1933 solidified the Appellate Court's jurisdiction until 1970. It established two grounds for transfer of cases from the Appellate Court to the Supreme Court: that the opinion of the Appellate Court contravened a ruling precedent of the Supreme Court, and that a new question of law was directly involved and had been erroneously decided.

Changes also were being made at the federal court level during the mid-1920s. When Judge Albert B. Anderson was appointed to the Circuit Court of Appeals in Chicago in 1924, President Calvin Coolidge appointed Princeton, Ind., lawyer and Gibson County Circuit Court Judge Robert C. Baltzell to replace Anderson as the sole judge of the United States District Court for Indiana. Nominated on January 2, 1925, he was confirmed by the Senate and commissioned on January 13, 1925. He was alone on the District Court bench for only five weeks. A second judge had been approved for the District of Indiana and, on February 6, 1925, President Coolidge appointed South Bend, Ind., lawyer and former prosecutor Thomas Whitten Slick. He was confirmed by the Senate and commissioned on February 17.

Although only one U.S. District Court served Indiana, the two judges conferred and agreed to divide the state geographically. Slick would cover the northern half, and Baltzell would handle the southern half. His primary court would be in Indianapolis, and he also held sessions in Terre Haute and Evansville.

In 1928, the agreed separation was made official. Two district courts were mandated—a northern district and a southern district—and each sitting judge was terminated from the District of Indiana and reassigned to the district where he had been effectively presiding. The division took place on April 21, 1928.

Baltzell was a hard-working, dedicated jurist who enjoyed a good reputation and strong personal opinions throughout his 25 years as U.S. District Court judge. He was 54 years old when he ascended to the federal bench, and he brought with him the solid religious and personal ethic he honed as a World War I veteran and a Circuit Court judge. Among the papers he left in the care of the Indiana State Library upon his death, was an August 8, 1925 clipping from *The Truth Seeker*, identified only as a "New York publication." The judge had suspended the sentence of a 17-year-old defendant convicted of robbing the mails. The condition: that the youth-

Patriotic Hoosiers rallied to collect this scrap aluminum for a war-time drive

ful offender attend church and Sunday school each week. The offended publication editorialized: "Robert C. Baltzell of Indianapolis, Indiana, is a good Christian and, consequently, a bad judge."

Later that same year, reporting on Baltzell's temporary assignment to a Chicago courtroom, the *Indianapolis Star* described him as "a quiet, thin-faced little man (who) was striking terror into the hearts of those facing him reminiscent of the fear inspired by Judge K. M. Landis when he was on the Federal bench." The article continued to quote one Chicago criminal sentenced by Baltzell referring to the judge as "that hard-boiled little fellow."

In 1935, the Treasury Relief Art Project sponsored a competition to design and paint murals in the Federal courthouse. Grant Christian, a 24-year-old Herron School of Art graduate won and the murals he produced remain an important part of the historic building at the northeast corner of Meridian and Ohio streets.

On the south wall is a series of panels titled "Mail, Transportation and Delivery," and featuring "The Capital's First Railroad, "Transportation and Communication," and "Industry and Legislation." Indiana Governor Paul V. McNutt and Indianapolis Mayor John W. Kern, who were in office when the mural was painted, are featured figures. Other images include a sleek, modern train, the Indiana State House dome, the city and a rural letter carrier.

On the northwest and northeast corners are murals tracing "Early and Present Day Indianapolis Life," showing the history of the city's development from the frontier to urban development. The panels include "Marion County Pioneers," "Clearing and Building," and "Backwoods Indiana." The murals also show contemporary, mid-1930s Indianapolis, featuring "Culture and Education," "Safety Patrol," and "To Those Who Served." The Indianapolis-Marion County Public Library Central Branch is depicted, along with the World War Memorial.

WAR AND PEACE

When the first rumblings of another war began to be taken seriously in Indianapolis, the city's population was nearly 400,000, and the Great Depression was hanging on by the flimsiest thread. By the time World War II officially ended, $3 billion in defense contracts would have been awarded to Indianapolis companies, 40 percent of the city's wages would be paid by wartime contracts, and fully one-third of the workforce would be female.

Perhaps no city in America was as well prepared in 1941 to provide the industrial might needed by the armed forces as was Indianapolis. In 1939, business leaders had begun nudging the local economy toward defense production, and that preparation quickly earned the city the wartime name "Toolmaker to the Nation." Dozens of industries were converted to enable production of war materials—parts, engines and weapons. In May, 1942, the Naval Ordnance Plant opened a $13.5 million facility that had more than 14 acres under roof on the east side of Indianapolis. It was there that Carl Norden, at one time protected by 350 security guards, would supervise the manufacture of the Norden bombsight. Real Silk Hosiery Mills employed more than 1500 people turning out silk parachutes. Curtiss-Wright Corporation's Curtiss Propeller Division became the nation's largest propeller factory. Allison Division of General Motors had 23,000 employees working around the clock seven days a week to build more than 70,000 V-1710 aircraft engines. In January, 1945, the J33, America's first jet engine, came off the line at Allison Division. The Marmon-Herrington Company produced tanks. Hundreds of plants, large and small, employed skilled labor at high wages. Factory employment more than doubled, with 30,000 people at work manufacturing transportation equipment alone. Plants staggered shift times to ease the strain on local streets and public transportation. Many of the assembly line workers were women; others moved from farms to the city to join the labor force; yet others were immigrants from the American South. Within a two-year period, 9,000 new homes were built to accommodate the influx of people.

The recovery brought on by the war would last more than a decade. Industrial production in 1939 was $140 million; 15 years later it was $940 million. But during the war itself, much of the income flowing into workers' pockets found its way into Savings Bonds and accounts. Rationing was in effect, consumer goods were scarce, and the money earned was tucked away to power postwar growth.

WARTIME PRACTICE

The effect of World War II on Indianapolis lawyers was twofold: there was an increased demand for lawyers' services helping business deal with material and employment priorities, wage and price controls and other wartime regulations and agencies; and, there were far fewer lawyers available to provide that assistance.

Earl B. Barnes, Hubert Hickam, Kurt F. Pantzer and Alan W. Boyd had in 1940 formed the partnership that would evolve into Indianapolis' largest law firm, Barnes & Thornburg. The firm developed an ambitious recruiting program that limited selection to the top students from the best law schools. But most of those who began to practice there in 1941 and 1942 had, at most, months to settle in before being called to one or another branch of the service. By the time John Woodburn Houghton joined Barnes, Hickam, Pantzer & Boyd after com-

City residents celebrated V-J Day on August 14, 1945 as large, excited crowds gathered on Monument Circle.

A TRIBUTE TO THE LAWYER-SOLDIER

When Harvey A. Grabill took the gavel as president of the Indianapolis Bar Association in early 1943, he was leading a group whose numbers had been dramatically reduced by the call to service in World War II.

Grabill's first address to his fellow lawyers remaining behind in Indianapolis included an emotional summons to remember those who had left the city to serve in the armed forces. A portion of that address read:

"These lawyer soldiers are the sons, the brothers and the bosom friends of each and all of us. Aside from the medical profession, the Bar of the country is contributing more manpower to the War Effort than any other profession.

"This Association has a representative on every battlefield where the American Forces are making a stand. Tonight in England, Iceland, Australia, North Africa and Guadalcanal some member of this Association is standing guard. Many of these lawyers have taken down their shingles, and they will never go up again. Many of them have closed their office doors, and they will never reopen. The law of averages makes it a certainty that some of these men will make the supreme sacrifice.

"I know lawyers and know their thinking processes. We lawyers are prone to look upon any show of sentiment toward our fellowmen as a fundamental sign of weakness, to treat any and all public demonstrations of loyalty to our country as patriotic pretense. This is due, no doubt, to the particular nature of our business. We, ourselves, are all more or less actors in the game of life and therefore, cynical. But tonight we are not kidding.

"These sons, these brothers, these bosom friends of ours are sitting in at a deadly game, and they are playing for 'keeps.' They are putting everything they have in this world on the line. They are 'shooting the works,' and there can be no 'bunk' about dying for one's country.

"So, with your permission, I would like tonight to commit this Association to the proposition of doing anything and everything in our power during the coming year to support and stand back of these lawyer soldiers, and to win the war."

---

pleting his J.D. degree at the Indiana University School of Law in 1943, 10 older attorneys had already left the firm for military service. Thomas M. Scanlon, in his *Early History of the Firm*, acknowledged that, "the firm probably had more of its members in the armed forces than there were lawyers in any other law firm in the state." A pierced eardrum rendered Houghton unacceptable for military service, but he gave the law firm a much-needed extra hand during the war years.

Like many other lawyers who remained in Indianapolis during the early 1940s, Houghton "was asked to assume responsibilities which would normally not have been asked of lawyers after many years of experience," Scanlon wrote. "But John methodically worked his way through this mountain of work and survived the war period, emerging as an experienced lawyer."

Harry Ice's history tells of a revolving door at the Matson firm, with young law school graduates coming on board for periods often lasting only months before they were drafted or volunteered for service. The lawyers left behind, he wrote, worked long days made longer by the need to wait for other members of the carpools they were forced to utilize because of gasoline rationing, or jostling on crowded streetcars between homes and offices.

Business travel was similarly difficult, with civilians often bumped from planes by servicemen and hotel rooms nearly impossible to find. The Matson firm eventually rented an apartment in Washington so attorneys traveling on urgent client business had a place to sleep in the city.

"It was a difficult period," Ice wrote. "The load of work in the office was heavy, the pressure was great. Government contracts meant the survival or demise of a client. Priorities on materials and labor were essential to their daily operation. The lawyer carried the burden of securing the essential governmental approvals. The documentation required was voluminous. The work was tedious. Time was of the essence in every matter. Every day brought new regulations, restrictions and orders posing new problems to be solved. The tyranny of the immediate had taken over."

CHAPTER SIX
(1945–1965)

AN ERA OF CHANGE

LOW-INTEREST MORTGAGES MADE POSSIBLE BY THE ENFORCED savings of the war years helped fuel the post-war housing boom that foretold the suburban sprawl of Indianapolis in the late 20th Century. The construction would be necessary to house a population that grew from less than 400,000 in 1940 to 427,173 in 1950, and 476,258 in 1960 as the city expanded faster than any other in the state.

Land costs remained low as farmers competed to sell large tracts to developers, who applied new building techniques to maintain a housing price point affordable to the working class families moving into the city. Those families came from the small towns and farming communities throughout the state, and from southern states, seeking employment at the many new and expanding factories and retail centers in Indianapolis.

The face and focus of the city was altered dramatically during the post-war period. Perhaps nothing so exemplified that change as the disappearance of the English Hotel and English's Opera House, replaced on the northwest quadrant of the Circle by a sleek modern building housing the J.C. Penney chain store. Ownership of the historic property had passed to the William E. English Foundation, which sold it to Equitable Life Assurance Society. That company took the brunt of public protest over plans to raze the building and erect the department store, but persevered in spite of the objections. Conforming to the English will, a new English Foundation Building was constructed on North Alabama Street to house charitable and social service organizations.

Although J.C. Penney occupied the new space, the next 20 years would not be kind to downtown retailing. As retail construction followed home construction to the new suburbs, downtown stores declined and often failed, losing customers and business to the convenience and free parking offered by strip centers and malls in far-flung neighborhoods.

The flight from the central city mirrored the loss of industries that had long been an important part of the city's economy. Food processing, stockyards and railroads declined and all but disappeared in Indianapolis. Union Station, which handled more than 100 passenger trains each day during World War II, saw ridership dwindle to almost nothing as both passenger and freight trains disappeared and tracks were abandoned. Finding an appropriate, viable and permanent use for the Romanesque station would be an unmet challenge to city leaders through the remainder of the 20th Century.

Inner-city neighborhoods were similarly stressed as suburban living was enthusiastically embraced by both blue-collar immigrants to the city who snapped up energy-efficient, inexpensive ranch-style homes lining subdivision streets, and the well-to-do who deserted their gracious near-downtown residences in search of the lawns, gardens and security of the outlying townships. Too often the large homes they left behind were chopped into apartments and entire neighborhoods seemed to be transformed almost overnight from the stability of middle-class, single-family communities into declining areas crowded with low-income renters paying absentee landlords.

But, while the inner-city experienced some of the decay common in cities throughout the nation during the post-war period, Indianapolis thrived and the positive changes far outweighed the negative. Home ownership soared, median family income was impressive, and employment rates were high. New schools—both public and private—were built, and entertainment and recreation sites were developed. Marian College expanded into the William B. Stokely estate and the former home of Park School. The private boys' school, founded in 1914, merged with private Tudor Hall School for Girls, established in 1902, and the resulting Park

The modern City-County Building rises above the nineteenth-century Marion County Courthouse to provide a sharp contrast in this 1961 photograph.

Tudor was relocated to a new campus at 7200 North College Avenue. Clowes Hall opened on the Butler University campus in 1963, and the Christian Theological Seminary moved into a splendid new facility adjacent to Butler in 1966. The city opened its first zoo in 1964, and later moved and expanded the facility into a White River Park project that would eventually include a variety of family entertainment sites. Flood control efforts on Eagle Creek on the northwest side created the largest city park in the nation.

A new State Office Building was constructed across from the Statehouse in 1963, and the Indianapolis City Hall and Marion County Courthouse buildings were replaced with the 28-story City-County Building in 1963.

Much of the growth of the city hinged on its attractiveness to industry. Throughout the period, Indianapolis business boomed. Established firms such as Allison Division, Ford and Western Electric added onto existing facilities, and the federal government located the Army Finance Center at Fort Benjamin Harrison on the city's east side. RCA built nine plants in Indianapolis during the 1960s, and more than 23 million square feet of new industrial space was constructed in a single four-year period. Hundreds of new companies were started or moved to the city and, by the end of the 1960s, unemployment lingered in the two- to three percent range.

The J. C. Penney building, seen here in 1952, replaced the English Hotel and Opera House after it was demolished in 1948.

Travel around and through the city was automobile-dependent. The trolley system had expired and buses ran only within limited districts near and through downtown. Indianapolis residents loved their private cars. The city responded by welcoming the interstate system, and although it displaced housing in many areas, the result was the largest system of limited access federal highways in the nation with a circular belt around the county. Even before completion, the outer belt (I-465) was peppered with industrial parks, apartment construction and new subdivisions adding even more jobs and housing opportunities for a growing city.

The Indianapolis Motor Speedway was purchased by Anton (Tony) Hulman Jr. in 1945, setting the stage for the resurgence in popularity of the 500 Mile Race. Hulman poured millions of dollars into the racing facility, adding thousands of additional seats for spectators, and new garages and pits. In 1955, he spearheaded the formation of the United States Auto Club, which would sanction the race for decades. His deft management and generous investment turned the track and the race into an institution that helped give Indianapolis an international reputation, and city leaders latched onto the opportunity as a showcase event. The 500 Festival was established in 1957 as the city cleared the decks in May and added a parade, golf tournament, formal ball and other activities to the Memorial Day race, stretching the affair to a month-long occasion for tourism and hype.

THE INDIANAPOLIS BAR ASSOCIATION EXPANDS

The Bar Association made its own contributions to the quality of life in Indianapolis during the postwar period, and they were not insignificant. In November 1945, the group partnered with the law school deans to initiate a refresher course for attorneys returning from the war, helping reintroduce them to the practice of law and update them on changes in the law during the past four years. The *Indiana Law Journal* began publishing the following March a series of articles, broken down into the various fields of law, to further assist returning lawyers. In 1949, Bar Association President Herbert E. Wilson announced an ambitious program of seminars to be conducted in conjunction with association meetings to continue the educational process for practicing lawyers.

Following on the heels of its successful launch of the Legal Aid Society in 1941 (Jerry Cadick was the first chairman of the committee developed to plan, initiate and oversee the society), the Indianapolis Bar Association began in 1953 to pave the way for a system of lawyer referrals. By March 1954, Lawyers' Referral Committee chairman Ben Weaver and committee members Robert D. Armstrong, Charles B. Feibleman, James C. Jay and William M. Evans had developed the system and an application was sent to all association members inviting them to participate. A $10 fee was charged for registration and, within a month, more

Once the hub of a busy rail system, traffic at Union Station had dwindled considerably by the late 1950s and early 1960s.

A History of the Indianapolis Legal Profession **109**

ROBERT LEE BROKENBURR
(1886–1974)

"I BELIEVE IN THE FATHERHOOD OF GOD AND THE brotherhood of man," Robert Lee Brokenburr wrote in an inspirational piece published by the Indianapolis *Star Magazine* on July 15, 1951. "Beneath their color and other superficial physical features, there is in all men a spark of divinity. ... All men long to be respected. All men hate to be looked down upon. From all races, creeds and countries come great souls who express themselves in the loftiest manner and who benefit the entire human race."

Brokenburr was such a man. Born in Phoebus, Virginia, to Benjamin and Mary Elizabeth Baker Brokenburr, he was the oldest of nine children and learned the value of work early, selling newspapers to earn money. His first real job—shaking out laundry—netted him $2.50 a week. But he was born to parents who valued education and encouraged him to expand his. He worked his way through Hampton Institute in Virginia and was graduated in 1906. The school's motto, "Live to Serve," became his personal mantra. After earning a law degree from Howard University, he came to Indianapolis in 1909 on the advice of George L. Knox, publisher of the *Freeman*. He later said that he arrived in the city with "a stylish panama hat on his head and $125 in his pocket." He was admitted to the bar in 1910.

Shortly after Brokenburr's arrival in Indianapolis, Madam C. J. Walker also moved to the city. Knox introduced the two and, in 1911, Brokenburr incorporated the Madam C. J. Walker Manufacturing Company. He served as general manager and counsel to it for many years.

Brokenburr built his practice and the respect of city leaders, serving as deputy prosecuting attorney and as pro-tempore judge in local courts. He also ran, albeit unsuccessfully, for the Indiana House of Representatives in 1912, 1932 and 1934. In 1940, he changed his strategy and ran for the Indi-

In 1953, Robert Lee Brokenburr became the first African-American attorney admitted to the Indianapolis Bar Association.

ana Senate, winning the seat he would hold for 20 years. He was the first African-American elected in the state.

One of his early involvements in community activism was serving as chairman of the Better Indianapolis League. The group protested attempts to build a segregated high school in Indianapolis. Although they were unsuccessful—Crispus Attucks High School was the resulting institution—Brokenburr gained widespread respect for the role he played in the opposition.

Throughout his public and private life, Brokenburr maintained his unflinching belief in civil rights and the value of all people. He was a successful advocate in cases challenging segregation in housing and theaters. But perhaps his greatest contribution to ending discrimination was as a legislator, where he authored bills that made significant changes to Indiana's laws on the treatment of African-Americans.

Shortly after taking his seat in the Senate, he pushed a bill in 1941 to force the Indiana High School Athletic Association to admit segregated black schools to the organization. The bill didn't pass, but the IHSAA leadership was so astonished by the degree of support Brokenburr had mustered that it promised it would eliminate its exclusivity without legislative action. In 1943, it did. Later that year, he authored a bill to remove Marion County officials from the system whereby elected officials retained a portion of the fees their agencies collected and compensate them by salary.

Brokenburr also was active in community and charitable affairs. He served on the board of directors of Flanner House, was a trustee of the Jones Tabernacle AME Zion Church, and was a 33rd degree Mason and senior grand warden. In 1950, he was honored by the Indianapolis Community Chest for his work on behalf of others in the city; and, in 1955, he received the Stephen Wise Award of the American Jewish Congress. He was the second president of the Indianapolis chapter of the NAACP. He was active in Kappa Alpha Psi fraternity, served as a board member of the United Negro College Fund, and worked for the Boy Scouts of America and the Young Men's Christian Association.

The Indianapolis Bar Association voted unanimously to admit him to membership in 1953, breaking the color barrier that had kept white and black lawyers in separate organizations. Within months, other African-American lawyers had been accepted as members, as well.

A conservative Republican, Brokenburr became the first Hoosier to serve as an alternate representative to the United Nations when President Dwight D. Eisenhower appointed him in 1955.

Brokenburr and his wife, Alice, of Cherokee Springs, SC, were married on June 28, 1911, and had two children, daughters Nerissa Lee Stickney and Alice O. Ray. After Alice's death, Brokenburr married Nettie. She, too, preceded him in death.

Robert Lee Brokenburr earned the respect and admiration of lawyers, business people and voters, living as an example of the kind of person he expected all men—black or white—to be. Asked late in his life if he thought he occasionally had been too strident or pushed too hard in seeking an end to racial discrimination, he demurred, replying, "Can you move too fast in getting that which is really yours?"

than 50 attorneys had sent their completed applications and payments. Individuals seeking referral to an attorney were charged one dollar. Within a year, more than 60 people had asked for help. Some, upon interview by the referral officer, were determined not to have a legal problem at all. Others were indigent and were referred, instead to the Legal Aid Society. But 30 had been put in touch with a Bar Association member for possible representation.

That same year, the association approved a placement committee to assist young lawyers seeking to begin their practices in Indianapolis.

Quietly and without public fanfare, the Indianapolis Bar Association in 1953 took another step to significantly change the way law was practiced in Indianapolis. It accepted into membership Robert Lee Brokenburr and opened the door for full participation by African-American lawyers in the Indianapolis Bar Association. The selection of Brokenburr to break the color barrier was not random. Lawyers Alan T. Nolan and John Houghton confirm that a small group of members believed it was time to erase the color line and carefully considered the best candidate to place before the membership. Members would be hard-pressed to object to the distinguished State Senator and conservative Republican, the group believed. Still, they did their homework, meeting privately with other lawyers to marshal support for the nomination before bringing Brokenburr's name before the May 1953 meeting. He was accepted unanimously. Within months, Nolan recalls, half a dozen other African Americans would be admitted to membership, including Mercer M. Mance, the first African-American elected as a judge in Indiana, and Rufus Kuykendall, who also would serve on the Marion County bench.

In 1960 the Indianapolis Bar Association faced another challenge to its long-held policies; but this one could not be handled in such a quiet and gentlemanly fashion. It was forced into the public eye by the Indianapolis *Star's* publication of a series of articles described by the Board as "attacking certain members of the Indianapolis Bar Association and the Association's fee schedule in divorce cases." The association had long published minimum fees it believed to be appropriate for members to charge clients in various matters, courts or situations. The *Star* objected to the practice (particularly the suggestion that, in divorce cases, the husband's attorney should always be paid as much as the wife's attorney) and the association was particularly distressed by the tone of the articles that ensued in February—so much so that a libel action was considered and a committee appointed to study that possibility.

ABOVE: *Mercer Mance's swearing-in ceremony. Mance was elected Marion County Superior Court judge in 1958, becoming the first African-American judge elected in Indiana.* LEFT: *Alan T. Nolan.* RIGHT: *Judge Rufus C. Kuykendall. (Courtesy Indianapolis Bar Association)*

The committee, headed by James V. Donadio with the assistance of Howard S. Young Jr., David M. Lewis, Elbert R. Gilliom and John K. Rickles recommended against instituting suit. "It is the unanimous considered opinion of your Special Committee," they reported, "that, under the existing weight of authority, the Indianapolis Bar Association cannot, for itself or on behalf of its members, successfully maintain a libel action against The *Indianapolis Star*."

Instead, the Minimum Fee Committee reworked the fee schedule and the Board of Managers approved a new document in September intended to avoid another public relations disaster. The recitation of recommended fees was prefaced with the disclaimer:

"A fee schedule for the service of a lawyer cannot cover every situation in which the determination of a fee is involved. This schedule is designed to express generally the minimum fee which should be charged in the circumstances indicated. A minimum fee is not necessarily a proper fee in many instances. The lawyers should recognize that there are cases where a proper charge should be less or greater than the minimum fees suggested herein.

"The practicing lawyer is free to contract with his client with regard to compensation in any manner satisfactory to both; no two cases are alike and in determining a proper fee the lawyer is bound by Canon No. 12 of the Canons of Professional Ethics as enunciated by the American Bar Association and heretofore adopted by the Indianapolis Bar Association."

By the early 1960s, the pace of the practice of law mirrored the acceleration of business activity in Indianapolis. The leisurely profession Harold R. Woodard recalled from his first assignment in 1936 and upon his return from World War II had been replaced by one of increasing pressure on attorneys. The Bar Association urged the Marion County courts to recognize the urgency felt by clients and adjust its long-held practice of holding a "vacation term" during July and August of each year. The "vacation term" limited transactions during the two summer months to emergency matters and administrative chores within the courts. But with the population of Indianapolis in excess of 500,000, lawyers noted, case loads were mounting and clients were impatient. In an effort to "assist the citizens of this County by expediting completion of ... litigation," a resolution of the Bar Association read, its members were willing to volunteer their time as pro-tempore judges during July and August so that courts could remain open and functioning. The judges responded with their own suggestions for keeping more courts open during the summer months, and so began the ultimate end of an era when the Indianapolis legal system clung to its genteel roots.

RIGHT: *John J. Dillon served as attorney general in 1965.*
BELOW: *Virginia Dill McCarty, who ran for attorney general in 1976, was appointed U.S. Attorney in 1977. (Courtesy Virginia Dill McCarty with special thanks to MediaWright, Inc.)*

PRACTICING LAW—OR NOT—IN AN ERA OF CHANGE

The admission of Robert Lee Brokenburr to membership in the Indianapolis Bar Association had little impact upon the few women who were graduated from law schools in the early 1950s or upon those already practicing law. There had been no similar unwillingness to grant women admission to the association. But there was a very real reluctance to admit them into the firms that were making legal history in the city. Virginia Dill McCarty remembers job seeking in Indianapolis after earning her law degree from Indiana University School of Law at Indianapolis in 1950. Only one law firm offered her a job, and that was as supervisor of the secretarial pool. "There was a sign out," she says, "'No Women Allowed.'" In fact, she says, she overheard a young woman in a ladies' room conversation expounding on her Circuit Court judge father's opinion that women didn't belong in the practice of law. Such views were widely held and stymied the career aspirations of many female attorneys of the era.

A History of the Indianapolis Legal Profession **113**

McCarty finally obtained a position at the H. P. Wasson department store as a wage and price controller, and later worked in the Office of Price Stabilization during the Korean War. In frustration, she quit working when her first child was born in 1955. She maintained a small, independent practice in real estate and wills, she recalls. She was a "Thursday lawyer," retreating to her home office on the day when the housekeeper came and she could claim a little time for herself. It was not until 1965, when John J. Dillon was elected attorney general of Indiana that McCarty's considerable skills were put to use in the legal field. She had been in law school with Dillon and called him seeking a job in his department. He hired her, starting her on a course that would eventually lead her to make her own bid for attorney general in 1976 (though unsuccessful, she led the statewide Democratic ticket) and to an appointment as U.S. Attorney in 1977. That, she says, was the best job any lawyer could have—prosecuting both civil and criminal cases, with investigators pulled from the FBI, DEA and ATF.

ABOVE: *Harriette Bailey Conn was a prominent member of the Marion County Bar Association.* OPPOSITE PAGE ABOVE: *In 1930, Henry J. Richardson, Jr. was appointed as temporary judge in Marion County Superior Court. Much of Richardson's career championed civil rights.* OPPOSITE PAGE BELOW: *Henry J. Richardson presided as special judge in a 1948 second-degree murder trial. This courtroom scene shows Special Judge Richardson on the bench along with, left to right, Deputy Prosecutors George Kissler and Charles Clark, Defense Counsel Willard B. Ransom and Robert L. Brokenburr and the defendant.*

McCarty recalls with some amusement how she and other pioneering women lawyers would lunch at the Indianapolis Bar Association's club rooms, frequently debating whether it was better to dine as a group at a single table or to disperse and invite themselves to join men at their tables. It was not an insignificant question. Lunches in the club rooms were extraordinary networking opportunities, and most Indianapolis attorneys took advantage of the exposure at least occasionally.

The club rooms were opened at 33 North Pennsylvania Street above Loew's Theatre in Spring 1956, at a cost to the Bar Association of more than $165,000. They were open from 11 a.m. until 7 p.m., Monday through Friday, with rooms available for conferences, depositions and dictation. The rules were brief: guests were permitted with members only, everyone paid cash for meals with no checks or tabs permitted, there were no reserved tables and no games—the club rooms were for serious business. Despite early "substantial operating losses," the rooms remained open and functioning until the building was torn down in the late 1960s.

THE MARION COUNTY BAR ASSOCIATION

From the day in 1882 when James T. V. Hill was the first African-American admitted to the bar in Indianapolis, black lawyers have been a minority determined to distinguish themselves in the local legal community. It was not always easy.

Robert Lee Brokenburr was the first of them elected to membership in the Indianapolis Bar Association, but he was not the only one who earned the respect of white lawyers through his professionalism and dignity. Henry Johnson Richardson Jr. was graduated from Shortridge High School in 1921 and from the Indiana Law School in 1928. Almost immediately, he became active in politics. His appointment as temporary judge in Superior Court was said to be the first time an African-American served on an Indiana bench. Two years later, he and Robert Stanton were elected to the Indiana General Assembly. During his six years in the legislature, Richardson wrote the first fair employment practices in the law and helped end discrimination in Indiana University dormitories. He also is credited with helping change the Indiana Constitution so that African-Americans could serve in the Indiana National Guard. Despite his impressive record, Richardson, too, was denied membership in his hometown Bar Association.

Partially from the frustration of exclusion and partially from a positive determination to support and advance their mutual careers, black attorneys formed the Marion County Lawyers' Club in 1925. The organization was incorporated and its name changed to the Marion County Bar Association on October 27, 1942. As an affiliate of the National Bar Association, the MCBA first hosted the NBA in Indianapolis in 1949. An invitation to the Indianapolis Bar Association to participate in hosting a dinner during the convention was rebuffed, "for the reason that the (Indianapolis Bar) Association did not have budgeted funds for such a purpose," minutes recorded.

Writing in response to questions about the continuing value of the Marion County Bar Association in 1999, then-President Derek S. Burrell said,

"As early as 1932, Dr. J. Clay Smith Jr. noted that Segregation retarded the Afro-American lawyer's growth and development to diversify his practice in specialized civil law

A History of the Indianapolis Legal Profession **115**

areas, to diversify his client base, to break into corporate law firms, corporate and government legal offices and to diversify the courts of our nation at every level.

"The Lawyers' Club was created, in part, in response to those concerns. While our government has led the way in the march for progress in this regard, other important institutions, including our courts and law firms, have lagged far behind. ...

"Thus the concerns of 1932 are still salient in 1999. Until a majority of the professional, social and economic barriers that plague the minority attorney are eliminated, there will be a continual need for the Marion County Bar Association." ("Is there still a need for the Marion County Bar Association?" *The Indiana Lawyer*, February 17, 1999)

So the organization continues to be active in Indianapolis, following the tradition of such respected members as Willard B. Ransom, Rufus C. Kuykendall, Harriette Bailey Conn and Robert L. Bailey. An MCBA publication identified the group's guiding principle as "to seek, find and secure justice for all people and to break down the barriers of injustice and callousness which have restricted the equal opportunity of Black Americans. Today, the Marion County Bar Association continues to lend its advocacy to remove the barriers of injustice. The MCBA helps minority lawyers accomplish career goals and make significant contributions to the legal profession and the Indianapolis community."

FIXING THE "FIX"

The Municipal Court system in Marion County was established in 1925 (see Chapter 5) and remained largely unchanged until 1971—plenty of time, some say, for corruption and bribery to gain a foothold. Just how serious the problem became is the subject of disagreement. According to former Circuit Court judge and retired U.S. Magistrate J. Patrick Endsley, there's "no doubt" there were problems with the Municipal Courts in the 1950s and '60s, but they never reached the level of abuse suggested.

Because they heard traffic offenses, the courts were the only judicial experience for the average person, Endsley says. They were "blue collar, dirty knuckle" courts that were transformed into a collection machine for a system that saw speeding tickets as an opportunity to raise money. When judges balked at the wholesale effort to squeeze dollars from people ticketed for minor offenses, more elite lawyers and judges decided the Municipal Court judiciary was dishonest. Endsley acknowledges that judges often withheld judgment on those cases or suspended fines and costs, but believes that was a

TOP: *Judge J. Patrick Endsley. (Courtesy Indianapolis Bar Association)* ABOVE: *Judge Paul H. Buchanan, Jr. (Courtesy Indianapolis Bar Association)*

JOHN BIRCH SOCIETY REFLECTS INDIANAPOLIS CONSERVATISM

THE NEW DEAL WAS AN ANATHEMA IN INDIANAPOLIS, INDEED, throughout Indiana. In the mid-1940s, the General Assembly had taken the unusual step of formally passing a resolution denouncing on principle the concept of federal aid and urging Indiana's representatives in the United States Congress to "fetch our county courthouses and city halls back from Pennsylvania Avenue."

It was in this context that an east coast candy manufacturer named Robert Welch invited 11 friends to meet with him at the Indianapolis home of Marguerite Dice in December 1958. Welch was a North Carolina native who had spent two years at Harvard Law School before entering the business world. By 1957, he had become a virulent anti-communist and retired to devote his time and energy to that cause. At the conclusion of a two-day roundtable discussion on December 9, 1958, the group assembled in Indianapolis bought into Welch's dream to create an organization they described as "anti-collectivist (and) anti-communist."

The organization would take the name of an obscure U.S. soldier, John Birch. It was an honor Birch's family and friends did not fully appreciate, fearing the memory of the deceased young man was being exploited by an extremist group. The Society's biography of Birch describes him as a Baptist missionary to China who heroically led Col. James H. Doolittle and members of his raiding party of 12 American bombers to safety in free China after their legendary bombing raid on Tokyo. He then performed high-risk intelligence gathering missions on the ground as the "eyes of the 14th Air Force" as a member of Gen. Claire Chennault's legendary "Flying Tigers," the Society says, adding that "Chennault credited Birch with the fact that 90 percent of his downed flyers were rescued."

He died under mysterious circumstances on August 25, 1945, 11 days after the end of World War II. But the Society that adopted his name believes there was no mystery. He was part of an official military mission that was illegally detained by Chinese Communists, they say, when he was separated from the group and shot in the leg. Hands tied behind his back, Birch was executed with a bullet to the back of the head and his dead body was desecrated. The U.S. Government, the Society says, "in its desire to depict the Red Chinese as innocuous 'agrarian reformers,' ... suppressed the news of the unprovoked murder of Captain Birch."

---

reasonable response. "What has collecting money got to do with justice?" he asks. "You don't stop traffic deaths by extorting dollars from people."

To former Court of Appeals Judge Paul H. Buchanan Jr., what was going on in the Municipal Courts was far more sinister. "The citizen was exploited," he believes. "Exorbitant fees were charged for 'the fix' or what might be represented to be a fix." He describes a shadow bar peopled by "side men" who courted judges in return for preferential treatment for clients. Questionable loans to judges, campaign donations and conveniently lost "bets" were the payoff, he says, for judgments withheld or never handed down. And the "side man" lawyers collected large fees for the connections that guaranteed favorable outcomes.

Endsley, though, cautions that "they never proved anything against any of them."

Whether the system was merely friendly, sensitive or incurably sinister, it was destined to change, and the Indianapolis Bar Association took the lead in making that happen. In 1968, the association prevailed upon Governor Edgar Whitcomb to refuse reappointment to three sitting judges. An American Bar Association Traffic Court Division study team was enlisted to make recommendations for revamping the system, and Circuit Court Judge John Niblack headed the group that wrote a mini-Missouri Plan merit System for the selection and retention of Marion County Municipal Court judges. With support from former Presiding Judge William Sharp and then-Presiding Judge D. William Cramer, the law passed in 1971. A nominating commission was established to evaluate candidates for the Municipal Court bench and pass those names to the governor for appointment.

A History of the Indianapolis Legal Profession

LAWYERS INSTRUMENTAL IN FORMATION OF INDIANA CIVIL LIBERTIES UNION

Because of a fire that destroyed records of the Indiana Civil Liberties Union in the early 1970s, no one is quite certain who all the founding members of the organization were. Certainly, though, lawyers were deeply involved in the effort. Among them were Joseph O'Meara, dean of the Law School at Notre Dame, Ralph Fuchs, a law professor at Indiana University School of Law, the first president of the ICLU.

Two members of one of the largest firms in the city, Ross McCord Ice & Miller (now Ice Miller), were active in the organizational effort. When Merle Miller and Alan T. Nolan participated in founding the Indiana affiliate of the (at least in Indianapolis) controversial American Civil Liberties Union, questions were raised both within the firm and among the firm's clients. "Some of the firm's clients let their views be known to various partners. Some business was taken elsewhere," Harry T. Ice wrote in his book about the firm, *History of a Hoosier Law Firm*. Feelings among the lawyers were intense, and Nolan later told Ice:

"Some members of the Firm felt that those who were attempting to found the Indiana Civil Liberties Union were correct on the merits and defended them. Others felt that, correct on the merits or not, the lawyers in question had a right to act out their judgment in the matter. Still others felt that it was inappropriate for members of the Firm to engage in such activities. Their feelings were affected by various considerations, including their own concern about the problem of communism and their belief that, regardless of the extent of that problem, the Firm would suffer significantly in terms of client relationships. It is certainly true that a number of clients were aware of the issue and that some of them reacted negatively to the involvement of the lawyers from this office."

The involvement of Miller and Nolan had come to the attention of other members of the firm and its clients because of extraordinary publicity surrounding the initial meet-

---

Wishing to hold its organizational meeting in the Indiana World War Memorial, the Indiana Civil Liberties Union was denied access after the Indiana Department of the American Legion objected. After a 20 year struggle, the Indiana Supreme Court decided the issue in 1973 by ordering the facilty opened to the ICLU.

118 LAW IN AMERICA'S CROSSROADS

ing of the ICLU on November 20, 1953. The organizing committee had applied for permission to hold the meeting at the Indiana War Memorial in Indianapolis; but, after the Indiana Department of the American Legion objected, permission was denied.

CBS newsman Edward R. Murrow learned of the denial and sent two camera crews to Indianapolis to cover events of that Friday night in November. One crew filmed the ICLU's meeting at St. Mary's Catholic Church; the other filmed the American Legion meeting. On the following Tuesday, Murrow devoted much of his half-hour *See It Now* broadcast to coverage of the controversy and the two meetings. Although no Indianapolis television station regularly carried *See It Now*, one did arrange to air that particular episode.

The ICLU continued making application to the Indiana War Memorial Commission which managed the facility. Its members, political appointees of the governor, continued denying the requests for various reasons grounded in their own rules. When the ICLU adjusted its request to conform to the rules, the rules were changed. Finally, in the early 1960s, the first of a series of lawsuits was filed, by an individual who objected to the possibility that the ICLU might finally be allowed to meet at the War Memorial. The ICLU sued in 1968, seeking its right to meet in a public building. The issue was finally settled by the Indiana Supreme Court in 1973, and the ICLU's 20-year struggle for access to the Indiana War Memorial was won.

INDIANAPOLIS GAMBLING CASES REACH STATE SUPREME COURT

The 1851 Constitution's prohibition on lotteries has sent a variety of gambling cases to the Indiana Supreme Court. Two of those that arose during the 1950s were initiated in Indianapolis. The first involved a statute enacted by the General Assembly that exempted religious, patriotic, charitable and fraternal groups from a laundry list of gambling-related activities outlawed in the state. When one of those exempt organizations attempted to have gambling tickets printed in Indianapolis, a Marion County judge issued an injunction against the printer. The Supreme Court in 1953 declared the law class legislation, ruling there was no valid reason for the distinction between which organizations were and were not permitted to engage in gambling-related entertainment. The law, they said, was "unreasonable, artificial and arbitrary and not founded upon a reasonable basis." (*Fairchild v. Schanke*, 232 Indiana Reports 480 (1953))

Marion County Prosecutor John Tinder, Sr.
(Courtesy Indianapolis Bar Association)

A few years later, Marion County Prosecutor John Tinder, Sr. decided popular pinball machines violated the constitutional ban on lotteries and began seizing machines that gave free replays based on the player's score. A trial court judge's injunction against further seizures brought the matter before the Supreme Court, where the justices were faced with the decision of whether pinball machines were games of chance or skill. They determined that there was a necessary degree of skill involved in manipulating the flippers of the machines and upheld the injunction. Tinder was prohibited from seizing more machines or otherwise interfering with the operating company's business. The Court warned, though, that the ability to exchange free replays for any other valuable compensation would convert the games to illegal gambling. (*Tinder v. Music Operating Co.*, 237 Indiana Reports 33 (1957))

During the same period, the federal judiciary was expanding in Indianapolis. On February 10, 1954, one additional judgeship was authorized for the U.S. District Court for the Southern District of Indiana. The appointment of

Cale James Holder was among the most controversial in state history. The *Indianapolis Star* snidely reported that the reception honoring Holder when he was sworn in was more interesting in noting who had boycotted the event than who was present.

The court was expanded again when S. Hugh Dillin was appointed in 1961, and once more when James Ellsworth Noland was appointed in 1966.

MULTI-PARTY LITIGATION AND THE FAIRGROUNDS COLISEUM

What may have been the worst mass tragedy in Indianapolis history exploded on Halloween night, October 31, 1963.

The orchestra had just begun the playing the finale of the Holiday on Ice show at the State Fairgrounds Coliseum when leaking propane gas detonated under a section of seats where some of the audience of 4,327 were watching the skaters glide onto the ice. A concessionaire had stored popcorn under the concrete section, keeping it dry with a heater fueled by propane gas. More than 350 people were injured, 74 were dead. Because Holiday on Ice was a family entertainment, the victims included men, women and children.

This view of the Indiana State Fairgrounds Coliseum was taken several days after the 1963 explosion on Halloween night. The damage to the seating section on the left in the photo is clearly visible. The tragedy killed 74 people and injured more than 350 others.

A CHILD'S DEATH SHOCKS CITY

On October 26, 1965, Indianapolis police discovered the body of 16-year-old Sylvia Marie Likens lying on a soiled mattress on the floor of an upstairs bedroom in a home on East New York Street. She had been systematically abused, starved and tortured by a band of children led by a 37-year-old divorced mother of seven, Gertrude Baniszewski. The story unfolded when Sylvia's younger sister, Jenny, 15, volunteered to tell police what had happened if they promised to remove her immediately from the Baniszewski home.

Sylvia and Jenny were the children of Lester and Betty Likens, who worked as traveling fair concessionaires. They had left their daughters as borders in Baniszewski's home in July, 1965, and the torture games began soon after. Sylvia had been cut, beaten, scalded, branded and burned with cigarettes more than 100 times. During the last weeks of her life, she had been confined to the basement and denied food and water. As the story unfolded, the city was horrified to learn that neighbors had been aware of Sylvia's condition but didn't intervene.

Four children ages 11 to 13 were initially charged with injury to person and later released as state witnesses. Four of Baniszewski's children, ranging in age from 1 to 11, were separated and placed in foster homes. Her three remaining children, Paula, 17, Stephanie, 15, and John Jr., 12, were charged with first-degree murder, as were two neighbors, Coy Hubbard and Richard Hobbs, both 15. Baniszewski, too, was indicted for first-degree murder.

Gertrude Baniszewski pleaded not guilty by reason of insanity, but the jury returned a guilty verdict and she was sentenced to life in prison. The verdict was reversed on appeal in 1970 and a new trial was ordered with a change of venue. She was again found guilty. More than 40,000 signatures protested her 1985 parole.

Paula Baniszewski was found guilty of second-degree murder. At a new trial in 1970, she pleaded guilty to involuntary manslaughter and was sentenced to 2 to 21 years in prison. Despite two prison escapes, she was paroled two years later. The three teen-aged boys were convicted of manslaughter and served 18 months of their 2 to 21 year sentences. They were released on parole in 1967.

Because she agreed to testify for the prosecution, Stephanie Baniszewski was granted a separate trial, and found not guilty.

The first of many lawsuits was filed almost immediately, with the Coliseum Corporation, the concessionaire, the bottled gas companies and other individuals and businesses named as defendants. Attorney Stan Lawton of Ice Miller Donadio & Ryan quickly recognized that "there was not only a race to the courthouse, but a race to judgment which would quickly exhaust the limited insurance," Harry Ice wrote. His concern was that those cases heard first would collect on the policies, leaving later plaintiffs with uncollectible judgments. To avoid that likelihood, and the necessity for his insurance clients to defend later suits even though there was no obligation to pay any judgments, Lawton filed in the U.S. District Court for the Southern District of Indiana, seeking to join all parties to the 129 lawsuits already filed and all potential claimants in a single action.

Judge S. Hugh Dillin sustained his jurisdiction and relieved the insurers of liability after they filed a bond to pay the principal of the policies into the court. The court would then determine the equitable distribution of the funds among all possible claimants. Explaining the importance of the decision, Ice wrote:

"Indiana was a no action state—i.e., no direct action was permitted against insurers by claimants, their rights being only against the insured. Further, in only one other action had a court sought to control the allocation of funds between claimants as against allocation of funds between successful claimants. Judge Dillin proceeded to require submission to a panel of the question of the right to and amount of all possible claims and to allocate the fund on the basis of the relative size of all claims found valid.

"The case was destined to be much cited, discussed, followed and distinguished in subsequent decisions."

In addition to the civil actions, a Marion County grand jury investigated the cause of the explosion and returned seven indictments. None resulted in conviction.

A History of the Indianapolis Legal Profession

CHAPTER SEVEN
(1965–1990)

A CITY AT THE CROSSROADS

ENERGY CRISES AND INFLATION WOES IN THE 1970S THREATENED the economic and cultural boom that had energized Indianapolis throughout the post-war period. But a combination of dynamic leadership, determined citizens and a shared vision kept the city on a steady course of growth and prosperity.

A record voter turnout elected John J. Barton mayor of Indianapolis in 1963 and, although he would be the last Democrat to hold the office in the 20th Century, he initiated a series of bold and innovative policies that would be carried forward and expanded by the three Republicans who followed him. Among the social programs he championed were the city's participation in Head Start, the reactivation of the Indianapolis Housing Authority, and the establishment of the Community Action Against Poverty program. Perhaps the most far-reaching of Barton's legacies, though, were starting in 1964 and 1965 respectively the Greater Indianapolis Progress Committee (GIPC) and the Capital Improvement Board (CIB). Originally an advisory committee of corporate and civic leaders, GIPC grew into a powerful and resourceful coalition of representatives from virtually all sectors of the community to develop solutions, guide projects, and provide the focus that makes things happen in a diverse city. From government reforms to capital improvements, little happened in Indianapolis during the last third of the century that GIPC did not in at least some way influence.

One place where GIPC cast an especially long shadow was in the revitalization of downtown Indianapolis, and there the landscape—and the skyline—made dramatic changes. Reflecting the city's new emphasis on tourism and sports, the $26 million Indiana Convention Center opened in 1972 and was expanded in 1984 with the addition of the 60,500-seat Hoosier Dome (now RCA Dome) stadium and two exhibit halls. Market Square Arena added another venue in 1974, and both arenas were quickly rewarded with professional teams. The American Basketball Association Pacers were one of only three teams from the league to make the move into the National Basketball Association when the ABA folded in 1976, and the Baltimore Colts' midnight flight to Indianapolis made national news just two months before their new Hoosier Dome home was completed.

The commitment to make Indianapolis the Amateur Sports Capital of the World resulted in even more world-class facilities coming on line during the era: the Indianapolis Sports Center tennis complex in 1979; in the 1980s, the Indiana University Natatorium, Major Taylor Velodrome, Lake Sullivan BMX Track, William Kuntz Soccer complex, Indiana/World Skating Academy and Research Center, Eagle Creek Archery Range, Eagle Creek Regatta Course, and the National Institute for Fitness and Sport; and, in 1991, the Little League Baseball Central Regional Headquarters.

New office buildings and skyscrapers were the evidence of the business community's commitment to downtown Indianapolis. Blue Cross and Blue Shield's new 17-story Indiana headquarters, the Indiana National Bank Tower and the renovation of Jefferson Plaza ushered in the '70s. By 1990 they would be joined by Market Square Center (the Gold Building), the AUL Tower, Capital Center, Bank One Tower/Center, and others. Meanwhile historic downtown buildings disappeared, including the Lincoln Hotel, where Merchants Plaza would be erected in 1978, and the Claypool Hotel,

Lewis C. Bose (1917-2001) was integrally involved in the creation of Uni-Gov. He represented the nine Marion County school corporations in the landmark case, United States v. Board of School Commissioners. (Courtesy Bose McKinney & Evans, LLP)

A History of the Indianapolis Legal Profession 123

where the Embassy Suites would rise in 1985. In March, 1990, a major demolition project cleared the way for the long-planned Circle Center Mall.

New residential construction and gentrification of existing downtown and near-downtown neighborhoods strengthened the population base as young professionals snapped up condominiums in Lockerbie-area adaptations of the Indianapolis Glove and Real Silk factories. New townhouse construction and restoration of existing single-family homes helped the turn-around story there and in other near-downtown neighborhoods such as the Old Northside and Chatham Arch.

But the excitement building downtown couldn't silence the siren call of the suburbs. Retail continued the exodus begun more than a decade earlier, shifting focus to new shopping centers off the I-465 beltway. Castleton Square and Keystone at the Crossing both opened on the far north side in 1973, the former a sprawling enclosed mall and the latter an innovative, two-building Bazaar and Fashion Mall concept. Washington Square brought local and national chain retailers to the far east side in 1974. Outlots soon blossomed with other retail and dining opportunities, expanding suburban shopping opportunities.

Two other construction projects in the early 1970s were major indicators of the emerging focus of suburban living. In 1972 St. Vincent Hospital abandoned its near-downtown location and moved to a new home on West 86th Street, soon drawing medical and supporting businesses into the area. And, in the same year, three unique glass-and-concrete structures sprouted from a cornfield at Michigan Road and I-465. The Pyramids were to be the anchor for the expansive mixed-use development of College Park that eventually would include apartments and condominiums, low- and high-rise office buildings, and retail outlets.

That such widespread development continued in the 1970s was a tribute to the city's can-do attitude and determination. Rates of inflation, which averaged four percent at the end of the 1960s, and long-term interest, which had been around eight percent, soared. President Richard M. Nixon re-instituted limited wage and price controls to help cope, but by the end of the decade, interest rates danced around 20 percent. Mortgage interest rates were prohibitive and commercial construction slowed.

Richard Lugar was mayor of Indianapolis when Uni-Gov was adopted.

Still, Indianapolis was a good and popular place to live. 1960's population of 476,258 grew to 741,952 by 1990. Of course, some of that growth was attributable to the new Uni-Gov boundaries of the city, *infra*, but all of Marion County added 100,000 souls during the same period, growing from 697,567 to 797,159. The city lost a bit of its family orientation: almost 70 percent of the population lived in traditional, married, two-parent households in 1970, compared with fewer than 50 percent in 1990. But it became much more ethnically diverse, as the African-American and Hispanic communities grew and made their presence known. Indiana Black Expo, a nonprofit organization to celebrate African-American achievement, was founded in 1971 and began its annual summer festival now billed as the largest such event in the nation. The week-long celebration includes trade and employment fairs, religious and educational opportunities, and a variety of entertainment events. Members of the growing Hispanic community formed the Hispano-American Society in 1968 and, with the support of the city, established the Hispano-American Center (now El Centro Hispano) in 1971. Fiesta Indianapolis was organized in 1981, offering a festival of Hispanic food, entertainment and cultural activities, and the Greater Indianapolis Hispanic Chamber of Commerce followed in 1984.

Unemployment in the city, which reached 11 percent in 1983, declined to less than six percent in 1990. Minority and female employment rates climbed dramatically between 1970 and 1990, as well. Although African-American males experienced an increase in joblessness in the middle of the period, their employment rates had climbed past 40 percent by 1990. Like so much of the city's success, the strong employment could be attributed to the powerful partnership between government and business, seeking new responses to old problems.

UNI-GOV REDESIGNS INDIANAPOLIS

The model was called "Uni-Gov," short for "unified government." But from the beginning, political response was anything but unified. Republicans touted it as "Your Government: Blueprint for the Future." Democrats called it "Uni-Grab" and said it would dilute the minority vote. In a taped interview several years later, James W. Beatty, Marion County Democratic leader when Uni-Gov became law, said, "It was a design in impact, if not in intent—and I believe it was in intent as well—to dilute black voting power.... That's what Uni-Gov was. It was a shift of political power. It was nothing else." Then Marion County Republican Party Chairman L. Keith Bulen saw it differently. Uni-Gov came into being, he said, because the city could not function effectively as an urban center with the government in place at the time. In 1969, he said, "the feeling was right, the need was there, and the people were right."

Uni-Gov was the first major consolidation of city and county governments in the United States to take place without a referendum in modern times. And it was designed, written and shepherded through the legislative process by Indianapolis lawyers. One of the most heavily involved was Lewis C. Bose, who later described the part attorneys played:

"This was the special function of a lawyer ... people who understood the goal of centralized management in essential functions, and what you could give up without giving that goal up, dealing with the structures that existed, understanding what the powers were and what the relationships were, because these are people who are going to question the proposal with great clarity, or great noise, great affect, determining whether or not it can be really approved. ...

"So I would say the lawyers were an essential part of Uni-Gov. Not the whole part of course, but ... one without which it really couldn't have been effective."

The attorneys, perhaps 50 to 60 of them over the course of the work, unselfishly devoted thousands of hours of professional time to the quest. Whatever the motivation of the politicians, the lawyers, Bose said, operated from a sense of responsibility. "Those of us who were interested," Bose recalled, "were interested because we were interested in our city."

The parochial government structure in place in the mid-1960s no longer served the growing urban city. Separate city, county and township governments with overlapping responsibilities and oversight were bulky and inefficient. And if the initial concepts for Uni-Gov were developed by the Marion County Republican Action Committee, the formal commission for working out the details fell to a 40-member GIPC Governmental Reorganization Task Force named by Mayor Richard G. Lugar and an 11-member Lawyer's Task Force appointed by Bose and committee head Charles Whistler.

The final design of Uni-Gov is a clearly political document tempered by the expertise of the many lawyers involved and, although hardly less complicated than the government it replaced, it ultimately satisfied most of the concerns that spurred the initial planners. The thorny questions police and fire protection were avoided simply by leaving them out of the reorganization. As a result, law enforcement is under the auspices of the Indianapolis police within the old city limits and the Marion County Sheriff's Department outside those boundaries. In a decision that would haunt the city into the 21st century, school districts also were excluded, and eight metropolitan township school districts and the school systems of Indianapolis, Beech Grove and Speedway remain intact. The Health and Hospital Corporation of Marion County also remained independent because, according to Bulen, of "compassion" and the feeling that the City-County Council shouldn't be running a hospital. Five other independent municipal corporations were excluded, including the Capital Improvement Board, the City-County Building Authority, the Indianapolis Airport Authority, the Indianapolis Public Transportation Corporation and the Indianapolis-Marion County Public Library. All six of the corporations, though, have at least a measure of accountability to the Uni-

Gov legislative and executive branches through budget reviews and governing board appointments.

The nine townships retain elected trustees and responsibility for poor relief services, and four excluded cities within Marion County—Beech Grove, Lawrence, Speedway and Southport—maintain their own governments in addition to the right to participate in Uni-Gov elections. Marion County, too, retains some elected officials and functions. The constitutional offices of auditor, clerk, coroner, prosecutor, recorder, surveyor and treasurer are separate from Uni-Gov, as is voter registration. Seventeen municipalities incorporated within the county prior to Uni-Gov were designated "included towns" with the right to maintain governments, levy property taxes and provide services. Although a few continue, most no longer bother. In another important limitation—the refusal to permit the city of Indianapolis to annex territory outside Marion County—was brokered to maintain support from legislators in the surrounding, donut counties who entertained some justifiable worries that the strengthened and enlarged Uni-Gov would in turn and gobble up outlying suburbs, as well.

Important elements of government, however, were consolidated under Uni-Gov to provide countywide service delivery and management. The legislative City-County Council replaced the Indianapolis Common Council and the Marion County Council and the executive power is vested in a mayor elected countywide. The mayor supervises six administrative departments, with responsibility for planning and development, parks and recreation, public safety, public works and transportation. The city's property tax base expanded to include the entire county except for the four excluded cities.

As complicated as it was, Bose remained convinced that the lawyers had done their jobs well. Pre Uni-Gov, he said, Indianapolis and Marion County were ruled by an antiquated tapestry of entities developed over 100 years that could not adequately serve a growing urban society. The system may have worked well in the 1800s, he said, but was ineffective after World War II, and resulted in disputes, inaction and corruption. Uni-Gov, Bose believed, amounted to a complete reorganization of civil structure into something that more closely reflected private organizations.

Immediately upon passage of the Uni-Gov bill in March 1970, Bose fashioned a "friendly" lawsuit, with Indianapolis Chamber of Commerce executive Carl Dortch as plaintiff challenging the legal status of the consolidation effort. The point was to test the legislation against the likely claims of prospective future litigation. Just over a year after the consolidation occurred on January 1, 1970 the Indiana Supreme Court unanimously upheld the Uni-Gov law (*Dortch v. Lugar*, 266 N.E.2d 25 (1971)).

UNITED STATES V. BOARD OF SCHOOL COMMISSIONERS

Carefully crafted and negotiated as it was, no one foresaw the pivotal role the Uni-Gov legislation would ultimately play in a lawsuit filed a year before the General Assembly acted to consolidate the Indianapolis government. That act and a little noticed piece of legislation that passed just 16 days earlier proved crucial in the lawsuit brought by the U.S. Justice Department against the Indianapolis Board of School Commissioners in 1968.

To place the case in context, it's important to begin with the 1949 General Assembly which passed a law prohibiting segregated schools in Indiana and requiring that all pupils be enrolled in the school in the district where they lived. Although Indianapolis school authorities had lobbied against such legislation, they set about to comply and, in 1953—a full year before *Brown v. Board of Education* was decided by the U.S. Supreme Court—announced that the city's schools were to be fully integrated. The reality was somewhat different, though, and by 1968 the Justice Department had initiated a full-scale investigation of the system based on the complaint of an Indianapolis parent. When negotiations with the school board mired, the Justice Department filed suit against the Indianapolis Public Schools (IPS) on May 31, 1968, alleging violations of the 1964 Civil Rights Act. That original lawsuit and its many permutations adding plaintiffs and defendants and reflecting the shifting political views in Washington D.C., eventually involved, as Emma Lou Thornbrough noted, "a large part of the legal talent in Indianapolis."

On August 18, 1971, Judge S. Hugh Dillin of the U.S. District Court for the Southern District of Indiana issued his ruling: IPS was guilty of *de jure* segregation. School district boundary changes, optional attendance zones and discriminatory construction policies were among the practices he cited. Seeking a long-term solution, he also added the State of Indiana and more than 20 metropolitan school corporations as defendants. And he singled out the Uni-Gov law as overwhelming evidence that segregation was, in fact, the intention of IPS and the suburban school districts excluded from government consolidation. By a narrow four-to-three vote, the IPS school board ordered an appeal of the decision.

LAWYERS AT THE CENTER OF CONTROVERSY

THEY COULD HARDLY HAVE BEEN MORE DISSIMILAR.

One a patrician Indianapolis native who was graduated from Swathmore College before earning a law degree at Yale University; a Navy veteran of World War II who began his legal career at one of the largest and most prestigious firms in Indianapolis and left to found another that would become similarly respected.

The other a bootstrapping African American born in Fairfield, Alabama; the first of his race to clerk at the Indiana Court of Appeals, but unable to garner even an interview with any of the city's prominent all-white firms upon his graduation from Indiana University School of Law at Indianapolis in 1961.

They were adversaries in the landmark *United States v. Board of School Commissioners*, John Moss representing the class of black children who wanted a unified central Indiana school plan and a declaration that Uni-Gov was unconstitutional, and Lewis C. Bose representing the nine Marion County school corporations on the opposite side. Neither won everything he hoped to gain for his clients, but each grew and increased in stature within the legal community and the city for the skill and professionalism with which he pressed his clients' case.

Bose had long been involved in education law. He was author of much of contemporary Indiana law on education and had been actively involved in working out details of the 1959 school corporation reorganization act and the 1965 school powers act. He also was one of the handful of individuals most directly responsible for the Uni-Gov legislation.

Moss's campaigns in education and law were a bit different. He had represented Shortridge High School students arrested at a sit-in protest in the late 1960s and, in a similar case, represented Indiana State University students.

But there were strong similarities between Bose and Moss, as well. After Bose died on February 5, 2001, Daniel C. Emerson, a partner at the firm Bose founded, wrote of his mentor: "What truly set Lew apart from other lawyers, and other people, were his patience, his kindness and his gentleness. He rarely lost his temper and never raised his voice. Lew taught generations of young lawyers that, in both the first and the final analysis, good lawyers are problem solvers. He insisted that no problem was insoluble, but that some just needed more thought than others." (*Indianapolis Star*, February 22, 2001)

Attorney John O. Moss, Jr. represented a class of African-American school-children who wanted a unified central Indiana school plan. (Courtesy John O. Moss, Jr.)

Moss shares those qualities. Interviewed recently at his office, he declined to speculate on the impact of racial discrimination upon his law career. He preferred to discuss the "we can" attitude nurtured by his environment, family and education, an attitude that motivated him to follow in the respected footsteps of the Indianapolis black attorneys who preceded him in Indianapolis—"men with good legal education and talent," he said. He preferred to speak, instead, of his enormous respect for the Indiana judiciary, where he has been treated in courthouses from rural counties to cities with deference and courtesy. While he has not always emerged with victory, he has always been confident that Indiana judges have made their decisions based on their understanding of the law, rather than any prejudice against Moss or his clients.

He mourned what he perceives as a lack of trustworthiness among some lawyers today. "When I started," he said, "your word was your bond. You should be able to rely on statements another lawyer makes." Now, he said, too many lawyers are not speaking as clearly—or listening as well—to each other.

When Bose died, he left a legacy that included a firm of almost 100 lawyers and a name engraved on many of the most important cases of the last 50 years.

Moss practices in the firm that bears his name, his son and two other attorneys sharing the offices and the work. He continues to serve as an example of skill, integrity and diligence that defined the best of Indianapolis lawyers for generations. It is an example that Bose, too, personified.

A History of the Indianapolis Legal Profession

But they were to find no more success with the Seventh Circuit Court of Appeals, which upheld Dillin's decision in February 1973, or with the U.S. Supreme Court, which denied *certiorari* in June 1973. The case was sent back to Dillin for determination of the state's responsibility and whether the suburban school districts should be included in the remedy.

By that time, a new set of plaintiffs had joined the action. Lawyers John Moss and John Preston Ward, who would take a lead role in pressing the action from then on, filed a motion to intervene on behalf of a class of African-American school children. These plaintiffs sought to have parts of Uni-Gov declared unconstitutional and asked for a unified central Indiana school plan.

A second four-week trial resulted in Dillin's July 20, 1973, ruling that the state was partially responsible for the remedy and that no permanent solution to the problem could be effected without the inclusion of the suburban schools. They were ordered to accept minority students from IPS beginning with the 1973–74 school year. Another appeal delayed the implementation of that order, but busing within IPS began in September 1973. In 1974, the Seventh Circuit again upheld Dillin, but eliminated the suburban schools outside Marion County from the busing remedy.

On August 1, 1975, Dillin ordered 15 percent of minority IPS students bused to the Marion County suburban schools. That order, too, was appealed; but the Seventh Circuit and U.S. Supreme courts again affirmed the District Court judge, remanding the case to Dillin on several occasions. Again and again, the Indianapolis case was distinguished from other cities where the federal courts had limited or eliminated busing, largely on the basis of Uni-Gov. A law passed just 16 days before the Uni-Gov legislation in 1968 was cited by the Seventh Circuit Court as evidence of "significant segregative effect." That act repealed a 1961 law requiring that school boundaries match civil boundaries. Its repeal in 1968, the Seventh Circuit Court said, was a "fail safe" guarantee for legislators who would otherwise have been reluctant to pass Uni-Gov lest the school districts, too, be consolidated.

Changes in the make-up of the IPS school board led to another twist in the case, when a new board petitioned to switch from defendant to plaintiff. Because they disagreed with the former board's position on busing, they claimed, they were more properly plaintiffs. Dillon refused their request, but did allow them to present their own two-way busing alternatives. It was unfair, the new board said in asking for leave to design such a plan, to place the entire burden of the segregation remedy on the African-American children who had been harmed by it.

In 1979 Dillin approved "Plan A" which called for the busing of African-American students at the elementary school and freshman high school levels to the suburban township schools. Beech Grove and Speedway school districts were exempted since the two cities were excluded from Uni-Gov. On October 6, 1980, the case ended with the U.S. Supreme Court's refusal to hear yet another appeal, although it was reopened at the District Court level several times in the 1980s and 1990s. One-way busing of IPS students to the suburbs began in September 1981.

Thirty years after it began, the case came to a conclusion in June 1998 when Judge Dillin approved an agreement between the Justice Department, seven school districts and state officials terminating the desegregation order. The settlement permitted IPS to phase out the transfer of students to suburban schools. Suburban schools with a minority population of more than 20 percent were allowed to stop receiving new IPS students in the fall of 1999. School districts with a smaller minority population were permitted to stop receiving the students in 2004.

In a separate but related agreement, the Indianapolis Housing Agency agreed to work with state assistance toward increasing affordable housing opportunities throughout Marion County. Acting Assistant Attorney General for Civil Rights Bill Lann Lee called the companion agreement "a unique remedy for a unique school desegregation case. By requiring that steps be taken to further integrate the surrounding suburbs, this agreement will help to achieve diversity in schools and communities throughout Marion County."

In approving the agreement, Dillin released IPS from court supervision.

REDEFINING THE SUPREME AND APPELLATE COURTS

The elections of 1970 were the last to list candidates for the Supreme and Appellate courts of Indiana under partisan political banners. In 1964, Governor Roger D. Branigan, himself a lawyer, had urged the General Assembly to eliminate party politics from the judiciary and replace it with a system "which will offer to the judges of our Appellate and Supreme courts the promise of reasonable tenure if they perform well, and which will insure them, to the fullest extent possible, freedom from political pressures." On November 3, 1970, Indiana voters in the highest turnout in the history of constitutional amendment referenda, ratified an amendment making judges of the Supreme and Appellate courts subject to a merit system of selection and a periodic non-partisan retention vote. Since that time, a seven-member, non-partisan judicial nominating commission forwards to the governor a list of three nominees for each new judgeship or vacancy on the state's two highest courts. The governor appoints from that list and new appointees serve a minimum of two years before facing a yes-no retention vote in the next general election.

At the same time, the Appellate Court was renamed the Court of Appeals and gained, for the first time, constitutional status. It was granted no original jurisdiction other than, if authorized by the rules of the Supreme Court, to review all decisions of administrative agencies. Also for the first time, all litigants in Indiana—criminal and civil—were granted an absolute right to one appeal.

Over the next several years, jurisdictional changes mandated by the expanding criminal docket would test both courts. In 1959, the number of judges on the Appellate Court was increased to eight, where it remained until the 1970 amendment which added a ninth. But an increasing population and exploding backlog of cases had extended the average waiting period for an appeal to be heard to nearly two years by 1978. Although nearly 800 cases made their way through the court each year, another 800 remained backlogged. The legislature added three judges to the Court of Appeals that year, and three more were added in 1991. The last addition was in response to a 1988 amendment to the state constitution which dramatically increased the number of criminal appeals heard in the Court of Appeals. The amendment provided that criminal cases would be appealed directly to the Supreme Court only if a sentence of more than 50 years for a single offense had been meted out. The change from the previous 10-year sentence limit added another 300 criminal cases to the Court of Appeals docket.

The Supreme Court took another step in 1973 to limit its caseload, telling aspiring attorneys they could not turn directly to the high court if they failed the bar examination on their first attempt. The rules were changed in response to a 1970 controversy involving a student who worked as a law clerk for an Appellate Court judge. The student failed his examination and appealed to the Supreme Court. To bolster his plea, he filed a detailed brief addressing one particular question on which he had been granted only four of a possible ten points. On a 3-2 vote, the Court accepted the applicant's reasoning and overruled the Board of Law Examiners. When eight members of the Board resigned in protest, the Court refused to back down on the appeal and appointed replacements for the eight. But that was to be the last time an applicant was afforded such an opportunity. Admission and Discipline Rule 14 was adopted on March 5, 1973.

In 1984, Judge Sarah Evans Barker became the first woman to serve on the U.S. District Court in Indiana. (Courtesy Indianapolis Bar Association)

Members of the Board of Law Examiners were not the only officials to resign in protest of Supreme Court actions during the 1970s. In January 1976, Marion Superior Court Judge Andrew Jacobs Sr. handed in the first of three resignations protesting a Supreme Court trial rule. The judge refused to grant a criminal defendant's request for a new judge, although he was required by the Rules of Criminal Procedure to do so. When the Supreme Court ordered him to comply with the rule, Jacobs resigned. Two weeks later, he returned to the bench at the request of Governor Otis R. Bowen.

But Jacobs continued to chafe under the rule and, in January 1977 went public with his dissatisfaction, calling the rule "the greatest obstacle in law enforcement." Not every Marion County judge agreed, and one even publicly suggested that Jacobs' difficulties were of his own making. The judge's public

A History of the Indianapolis Legal Profession   129

A SUPREME COURT JUSTICE, THE STATE AUDITOR, THE SHERIFF AND $12.8 MILLION

INDIANAPOLIS EMBRACED THE CONCEPT OF THE interstate highway system early and built the largest system of limited access federal highways in the nation during the 1960s. But the construction of the superhighways and the increased traffic flow created unanticipated problems with the surface access streets. It seemed only fair, the Mass Transportation Authority (MTA) decided, that the state should contribute to the upgrading and maintenance of those streets. The General Assembly agreed and, just two days before the end of its 1967 session, passed House Enrolled Act No. 1818, providing for the distribution of inheritance tax funds on the basis of 10 percent to the state and 90 percent to the MTA of Marion County to help pay those costs.

Governor Roger Branigan opposed the measure and, therefore, took none of the steps outlined in the State Constitution to either veto or approve the bill. His "pocket veto" dashed the city's hopes, and set up a confrontation that would see the Appellate Court order State Auditor Trudy Slaby Etherton taken into custody by the Marion County Sheriff.

The MTA, represented by attorney Richard M. Given, filed suit in Marion Superior Court asking the court to order the Indiana Revenue Board to administer and enforce the inheritance tax laws as contained in House Enrolled Act 1818, and enjoin them from continuing to apply the prior law. The court acted quickly, issuing a temporary restraining order against the Revenue Board.

Indiana Attorney General John Dillon moved just as quickly, filing a petition to transfer the case to the Indiana Appellate Court. The court, sitting *en banc*, assumed jurisdiction and transferred the case, dissolving the Superior Court's restraining order. Judge Charles W. Cook participated in the argument and

ABOVE: *Indiana Supreme Court Judge Richard M. Givan. (Courtesy Indianapolis Bar Association)* OPPOSITE PAGE ABOVE: *Governor Richard Branigin's opposition to a 1967 bill led to a stalemate before officials finally issued payment to the Mass Transportation authority.* OPPOSITE PAGE BELOW: *Indiana Court of Appeals Judge Patrick D. Sullivan. (Courtesy Indianapolis Bar Association)*

conferences on the case and concurred in the majority opinion. Though he died before the final draft of the opinion was completed and delivered, he was listed as one of the five members of the court voting to grant judgment for the MTA.

130   LAW IN AMERICA'S CROSSROADS

The opinion was a scathing one, excoriating both the General Assembly for ignoring the Constitutional prohibition against delivering bills to the governor in the final two days of the session and the governor for effecting an illegal pocket veto:

"When we, as Judges of an appeal court, have before us a case such as this, in which it appears that those in power, after having sworn to uphold and defend the Constitution have openly and flagrantly violated its provisions, we must not ignore such illegal actions and remain silent, for to do so would thereby condone such behavior and we would be betraying the citizens whose rights and privileges under the Constituion we have sworn to protect.

"If the Courts as the guardians of the rights guaranteed to the people by the constitution should ever relax their vigilance in enforcing the provisions of the constitution and yield to the pressures of any groups having special interests, including officeholders in the legislative and executive branches of government, our present system of constitutional government would collapse." (242 N.E.2d 642, 645 (Ind., 1968))

The State promptly appealed to the Indiana Supreme Court, where by now Givan served as one of five justices. Because he had been one of the attorneys representing the MTA, he did not participate in the decision. Without Givan's vote, the court split, 2-2, and transfer was denied. The Appellate Court's decision stood.

Givan recalls that Dillon appealed to the U.S. Supreme Court, accusing Givan of unethical conduct for recusing himself from the decision and causing the split decision that gave victory to his former client. It truly would have been unethical, Givan says today, for him to have participated in a decision appealing a case on which he had been one of the original attorneys.

But Givan's conflict was only one of several that arose during the case. When the U.S. Supreme Court refused to hear the case, it returned to the Appellate Court which, in a per curiam opinion held that retroactive repeal of the legislation did not apply to the judgment in force prior to the repeal. The court ordered payment of some $12.8 million to the MTA from state inheritance tax funds. The newest member of the Appellate Court, who had replaced the deceased Judge Cook, did not participate. He was Charles White, who had served as Dillon's Chief Deputy during the original 1968 case.

Two months later, the MTA still did not have its money. State Auditor Trudy Slaby Etherton, in agreement with Governor Branigan, State Treasurer John Snyder and now Attorney General Theodore Sendak, objecting to the attorney fees to be distributed from the money to Givan and other lawyers representing the MTA, refused to release the funds.

On February 26, 1970, the Appellate Court again sat *en banc* in a contempt proceeding against Etherton. Again White recused himself. Judge Patrick D. Sullivan remembers that the members of the court were nervous as they entered the courtroom. This was a trial, but no rules of procedure had been agreed upon, and no one knew exactly what would happen if one judge upheld an objection that another, simultaneously, overruled.

The judges had ordered Marion County Sheriff Lee Eads to be on hand and prepared to take Etherton into custody if the court so ordered. But rumors that the State Police had been ordered by the governor to prevent such an outcome had circulated, and no one knew how far the confrontation might escalate.

Etherton was found in contempt and quietly left the statehouse courtroom in the custody of the sheriff. But, either by pre-arrangement or foolishness on the sheriff's part, Etherton apparently asked to stop in the governor's office to retrieve some personal items before being carted off to the Marion County Jail. She remained behind locked doors with the governor, state Treasurer John Snyder and then Attorney General Theodore Sendak in an apparent stalemate which the sheriff was unable or unwilling to forcibly break. Several hours passed before Etherton and the other state government officials emerged, agreeing to follow the Appellate Court's order and issue payment to the MTA.

Even now, Givan scoffs at suggestions that his potential fee had any real impact on the dispute. By the time all the attorneys involved had received their share, he says, the amount paid to him was insignificant.

A History of the Indianapolis Legal Profession 131

In 1964 Vivian Sue Shields became the first woman judge elected in Indiana. Thirty years later she made history again when she was the first woman appointed as a U.S. Magistrate Judge for the U.S. District Court for the Southern District of Indiana.

portrayal of his stance as a "hanging judge" invited defendants to seek a replacement, Jacobs' fellow judge said. Jacobs then decided to enforce a strict interpretation of the rule which required a petition "by the defendant." He would no longer accept any request for a change of judge unless it was personally signed by the defendant. It took little time for one of those defendants to challenge the judge and, once again, the Supreme Court ordered Jacobs to accept and grant petitions signed by either the defendant personally or the defendant's attorney. Jacobs submitted his second resignation. At Governor Bowen's request, he once again returned to the bench.

Jacobs' third resignation came in April 1977. The controversy had escalated to include an angry public statement by the judge claiming that the Supreme Court endorsed a system that favored criminals and that he would not participate in it. The Supreme Court remained silent and, this time, so did the governor. Bowen did not intervene and Jacobs was gone from the Marion Superior Court bench.

The rule he found so offensive, though, eventually was changed. A 1981 modification required that criminal defendants must show cause for the removal of a judge, and now the request is to be granted only if there is "a rational inference of bias or prejudice." (Rules of Criminal Procedure, Rule 12 B)

As the Indiana Supreme Court and Court of Appeals were growing and changing, so, too, was the U.S. District Court for the Southern District of Indiana. James Ellsworth Noland was appointed to the new fourth judgeship in 1966, and Gene Edward Brooks was appointed to the new fifth judgeship in 1978. Judge Cale Holder died on August 23, 1983, and in 1984 President Ronald Reagan appointed Sarah Evans Barker to take his place. She became the first woman to serve on the U.S. District Court in Indiana.

PRACTICING LAW IN A CITY AT A CROSSROADS

Judge Barker's appointment to the U.S. District Court bench reflected the growing acceptance and influence of women throughout the Indianapolis legal community during the 1970s and 1980s. Almost a century after Bessie Eaglesfield of Vigo County became the first woman admitted to practice law in Indiana in 1875, Vivian Sue Shields became Indiana's first woman judge when she was elected to the Superior Court bench in Hamilton County. It was 1964 and Shields was 25 years old. Her bid for the newly created bench was intended to bring attention to the law practice she shared with her attorney husband; lawyer advertising wasn't yet permitted in the state and the couple saw the campaign as an opportunity to promote their fledgling practice. Shields never joined her husband in the new law office. She defeated her male opponent in the primary election and was unopposed in the November general election, setting in motion a lengthy and distinguished judicial career.

In 1977, she was the first woman nominated to the Indiana Supreme Court and, although she did not win the appointment, Governor Otis R. Bowen named her to the Indiana Court of Appeals in 1978—another first for Indiana. In 1994, she became the first woman appointed as a U.S. Magistrate Judge for the U.S. District Court for the Southern District of Indiana. One of her former colleagues on the Court of Appeals praised her as among the most influential people in the Indianapolis legal community. "She works hard, loves the law, does quality work, and earned respect quickly," he said. The Indianapolis Bar Association agreed, granting her both the first Antoinette Dakin Leach Award and the Paul Buchanan Award of Excellence.

But it was 11 years after Shields ascended to the bench in Hamilton County before Indianapolis would elect a woman judge. Betty Scales Barteau claimed her place as Marion Superior Court Judge on January 1, 1975. She is credited with establishing an alternative dispute resolution program in the Marion County Domestic Relations Counseling Bureau in the late 1970s—long before the state officially adopted ADR rules. When Barteau followed Shields to the Indiana Court of Appeals in 1991, she became the third woman to serve there.

Patricia L. Gifford became the second woman on the Marion Superior Court and the first to serve in the Criminal Division in January, 1979. Just a few months later, in August 1979, Antoinette Anonellis Cordingly became the first woman judge on the Marion Municipal Court.

During the 1970s and '80s, women entered Indiana law schools in increasing numbers—four percent of graduates in 1970 were women, 30 percent in 1980, and 40 percent in 1991. And as the number of graduates grew, so did the presence and influence of women in Indianapolis law firms, courtrooms and legal fraternities. The Indianapolis Bar Association elected its first female president, Mary Y. Marsh, in 1989.

The problems faced by women in the early part of the era gradually diminished; but the prejudice they initially confronted still rankles many. In a dissertation on "Indiana's Women Judges" (30 Ind.L.Rev. 43), Barteau recites responses she received from many of the women she interviewed:

"These future judges had many different experiences when they left law school and sought jobs. During an interview with a private firm, a 1961 graduate was told that the firm would not consider hiring her because it had inadequate restroom facilities for a female associate. A 1965 graduate said, 'One judge interviewed me for a part-time commissioner job and then said he couldn't hire me because I was a woman, but he wasn't too prejudiced to interview me.' A 1969 law school graduate said, 'Getting interviews with law firms after law school was nearly impossible, never mind landing any offers.' Another 1969 graduate of law school was assigned to a major law office to be an intern. When she arrived, she was shown to her office, which was a typing pool. One attorney offered a 1971 graduate the job of law librarian, stating that the county was not ready for women lawyers. Another 1971 graduate did not get a job with a law firm because the partner's wife did not want any women attorneys in the firm. A 1976 graduate returned to her home town to practice law and at one of her first interviews with a law firm she was asked, 'Do you have a boyfriend? Are you intending to get married? Are you intending to have children? If you have children, will you practice law or stay home with them?' As late as 1980, one future judge applied for a position as a manager of a Chamber of Commerce, but was advised that they were looking for a man."

Judge Patricia J. Gifford became the second woman to serve on the Marion Superior Court and the first woman to serve in the Criminal Division in 1979. (Courtesy Indianapolis Bar Association)

Despite a litany of discriminatory treatment, women persevered and became a valuable part of the legal community. Virginia Dill McCarty dates the beginning of the change to 1971 and the founding of the Women's Political Caucus. It, like Business and Professional Women and other similar organizations, she says, "helped redirect women's aspirations." Now, with the geometric progression pushing women into the majority at Indiana law schools as the 21st century begins, McCarty believes it is the excellence of women in the profession that has turned the tide. Judge Z. Mae Jimison told Barteau she didn't know exactly what kind of discrimination she faced in her quest for legal success. "I never stopped to consider whether a denial of a job opportunity was because of race, gender, or both," she said. "I just kept right on stepping."

'REMNANTS OF THINGS THAT HAVE PASSED AWAY'[1]

The story began in a village on a small island in the Mediterranean Sea in the early sixth century, A.D.

It ended in an Indianapolis courtroom in 1989.

And in between it featured war and intrigue, deception and greed, beauty and prejudice.

More than 1400 years ago, an unknown artist created a large mosaic of jewel-like colored glass, marble and stone depicting the Virgin Mary on a throne, holding in her lap her child, Jesus Christ. In the piece, the two were attended by two archangels and surrounded by the 12 apostles. The mosaic was displayed in the apse of the Church of the Panagia Kanakaria in the small village of Lythrankonu, Cyprus and eventually was sanctified as a holy relic by the Greek Orthodox Church. As more and more such relics were destroyed, this mosaic became increasingly precious.

When Cyprus gained independence from British rule in 1960, tensions between the Greek-Orthodox Cypriots of Greek descent and the Muslim Cypriots of Turkish descent increased. The former were largely concentrated in the southern part of the island and the latter in the north, with United Nations peacekeeping forces between. In 1974, Turkey invaded Cyprus and occupied the northern third of the island. Lythrankomi is located within that region, and most of the Greek Cypriots, including priests from the Kanakaria Church, were forced out in 1974. A pseudo-government, the Turkish Republic of Northern Cyprus, was established in 1983, recognized only by Turkey.

By then, Greek Cypriots had learned that the church in Lythrankomi had been vandalized and plundered—the mosaics, broken into parts, had disappeared. The Republic of Cyprus moved quickly to recover them, contacting and requesting assistance from a long list of international art organizations, governments and auction houses.

But it was not until 1988 that the Kanakaria mosaics resurfaced in the hands of Peg Goldberg, an art dealer in the Indianapolis suburb of Carmel. She told of being con-

INDIANAPOLIS BAR ASSOCIATION EXPANDS SERVICES

As women wielded their influence before the bar in Indianapolis, another woman—one without a law degree—was making a significant contribution to the practice of law in Indianapolis, as well. In 1971, a young employee of the Houston Bar Association followed her transferred husband to Indianapolis. Rosie Felton had been associate director of the Houston Bar, increasing public relations and membership. Through her work there and with the American Bar Association, she had met Indianapolis Bar Association President Kenneth Foster and President-Elect William J. Wood. She went to them seeking a job with the Indianapolis Bar and was hired as the librarian; the only other employee in the association's single-room office was an executive secretary. A year later, Felton was named executive director and began a 24-year career building, promoting and marketing the Indianapolis Bar Association. She worked closely with association presidents and boards of managers, developing and implementing programming. "It was," she says, "a wonderful challenge."

The first program implemented, Felton recalls, was the weekly bulletin. Continuing legal education programming followed. The Lawyers Referral Service, which was administered by the Legal Aid Society, was brought back in-house. The Young Lawyers Division, which had been instituted in 1969, was joined in 1977 by the Women and the Law Division.

But Felton believes the best of the early programming was the Ask A Lawyer service. The association's first serious foray into public relations and image-building, Ask A Lawyer was telecast live on the local PBS station, WFYI Channel 20. Felton approached Indiana Bell Telephone for a grant to cover the cost of telephones and the program went on the air in the mid-1970s. Lawyers staffed the phones as viewers with real legal problems called in seeking real legal advice. The on-air program was so successful that the association

134   LAW IN AMERICA'S CROSSROADS

tacted while in the Netherlands by another Indianapolis art dealer, Robert Fitzgerald, about the availability of "four early Christian mosaics." She met in Amsterdam soon after with a Dutch art dealer, Michel van Rijn, and a California attorney, Ronald Faulk. She said van Rijn claimed to be an expert on Christian icons and a descendant of Rembrandt and Rubins. He also admitted to a French conviction for art forgery.

At that meeting, Goldberg was shown the mosaics and told the asking price was $3 million. As negotiations escalated and a firm price of just over $1 million was finally established, Goldberg brought Indianapolis banker Otto N. Frenzel III into the deal to provide financing for the purchase. The sale was consummated in the Geneva, Switzerland, airport after, Goldberg said, she spent two days investigating the legitimacy of the mosaics' ownership.

When she returned to Indiana, she began merchandising the artwork (with an asking price of $20 million) and it came to the attention of Dr. Marion True at California's Getty Museum. It took little effort for True to discover that the mosaics were in fact plundered treasure from the Cypriot church and for Greek-Orthodox officials to request their return from Goldberg. When she refused, the Republic of Cyprus and the Church of Cyprus sued in the United States District Court for the Southern District of Indiana, with Judge James E. Noland presiding. A petition signed by some 2,000 academics and cultural figures supported the Cypriot position.

The trial began on May 30, 1989, and lasted six days under the microscope of widespread international attention. Noland clearly questioned the credibility of Goldberg's claim to have purchased the mosaics from a Turkish art dealer after thoroughly investigating their provenance. One by one, he also dismissed her arguments on issues of statute of limitations, replevin and the legitimacy of Turkish Republic of Cyprus government edicts claiming such works were "abandoned movable property."

Noland ordered the mosaics returned to their rightful owners in Cyprus (717 F.Supp. 1374 (S.D.Ind., 1989) and, in 1990, the Seventh Circuit Court of Appeals affirmed his decision in rulings hailed throughout the international art community.

"Only the lowest of scoundrels attempt to reap personal gain from this collective loss (of antiquities)," the Seventh Circuit decision said. "Those who plundered the churches and monuments of war-torn Cyprus, hoarded their relics away, and are now smuggling and selling them for large sums, are just such blackguards." (917 F.2d 278 (7th Cir., 1990))

---

[1] *The Siege of Corinth*, George Gordon (Lord Byron), as quoted in *Autocephalous Greek-Orthodox Church of Cyprus v. Goldberg*, 917 F.2d 278 (7th Cir., 1990)

---

took it on the road—to shopping malls and the City Market. Young attorneys were recruited to sit in booths listening to and advising people who took advantage of the opportunity to consult an attorney. Not only was it a terrific opportunity for the individuals who obtained legal help, it provided "wonderful experience in interviewing" for the young lawyers, Felton says.

Two other programs begun during the era draw special praise from Felton. Children's Haven provides a special room at the City-County Building for children involved in domestic violence cases. And the Court Appointed Special Advocates for Children (CASA) program made a dramatic and lasting impact throughout Indiana.

The Indianapolis Bar Association was approached by the National Legal Resource Center for the Protection of Children in 1981 asking it to partner with the American Bar Association in developing a model program in Indiana, one of only 11 states at that time that had no provision in law mandating guardians ad litem (GAL) or court appointed special advocates. With a grant from Lilly Endowment providing funding for the first five years, the association hired a director in November 1981. In that year, there were 260 new child abuse and neglect cases filed in Marion County, but only two guardians ad litem were appointed, and both were in high profile cases. By 1989, Indiana boasted the largest organized CASA program in the nation, with 2500 volunteers, plus attorneys and staff operating throughout the state. "In human services terms," says Rebecca M. Pryor, former director of the program, "it was the most important thing the Indianapolis Bar Association has done."

By the time the association's participation ended, children were made parties to their own cases in Indiana; courts were given the right and ability to appoints GALs or CASAs; and 65 percent of cases involving juveniles mandated that appointment, including cases where the child was deemed a danger to himself or others, cases involving sexual abuse, mental illness, or an obvious conflict between parent and child. That list was later expanded to include cases of delinquency, family violence, child custody and visitation issues, guardianships and adoptions.

REFORMING THE BAIL BOND SYSTEM

The first four judges of the Municipal Court in Marion County made it a point to limit the practice of bondsmen who "loiter in the corridors of the Police Station or the Turnkey's office at unusual hours of the day or night for the purpose of soliciting business, or who divide fees with attorneys...." It was an admirable recognition of the problems faced by families of defendants, but not altogether successful.

By 1970, Presiding Judge William T. Sharp recognized the need to reform the system. Working with Indianapolis lawyers, the Indiana University School of Law in Indianapolis and the Indiana Criminal Justice Planning Agency, Sharp engineered the Indianapolis Bail Bond Project. Begun as a trial project with funding from a federal grant, the program utilized the staff and administrative facilities of the law school, with senior law students acting as bail commissioners who interviewed misdemeanor defendants and made bail recommendations to the courts. With many defendants released on their own recognizance following the students' evaluations, jail populations were reduced and defendants saved significant sums. The project also involved monitoring of defendants on release, investigating missed court dates, and diversion programs channeling some defendants into rehabilitation programs instead of incarceration.

In 1976, the courts adopted a 10 percent cash bond system and soon boasted a 97 percent court appearance rate. In 1988, the program was transferred to the Marion County Justice Agency and expanded to include professional staffing for a 24-hour Pre-Trial Service Diversion. A jail ombudsman, lock-up services, diversion program and fail-to-appear office are under its umbrella.

INSIDE THE COURTROOMS

As Indianapolis grew in size and sophistication, its courtrooms would host new, sometimes complex, sometimes tragic and sometimes grizzly dramas. Four were of particular interest in the city at a crossroads. The first, played out on live television on February 8, 1977, would eventually add another possible verdict in Indiana criminal cases. On that cold morning, an angry Anthony G. "Tony" Kiritsis, facing a looming $130,000 mortgage payment on a 17-acre property he had hoped to develop as a shopping center, decided Merid-

Rosie Felton began her career with the Indianapolis Bar Association in 1971. (Courtesy Indianapolis Bar Association)

ian Mortgage Company had sabotaged the project and was responsible for its failure. He walked into the office of Meridian Mortgage executive Richard O. Hall and took him hostage. A sawed-off 12-guage shotgun was wired to Hall's neck and the two men left the building, parading through downtown Indianapolis streets with an entourage of police officers, reporters, and television cameras. Hall was forced behind the wheel of an Indianapolis Police Department cruiser and ordered to drive to Kiritsis' westside apartment, where the kidnapper told police he had wired the flat with explosives and fashioned a "deadman's switch" on the shotgun still trained on Hall.

For 63 hours, the stand-off continued, with Kiritsis demanding an apology and $5 million dollars in compensation for his failed business deal, plus the promise of no state, federal or civil prosecution. When officials agreed to his demands, Kiritsis and Hall, the gun still fixed to the executive's neck, stood before news media for an agonizing 23 minutes, while Kiritsis delivered a disjointed, obsenity-laced speech carried live on local television. As soon as Hall was released, Kiritsis was taken into custody and charged with kidnapping, armed robbery and armed extortion. He pleaded not guilty by reason of insanity, and the jury returned that verdict on October 21, 1977.

Once again, though, Kiritsis was ordered into custody and, two weeks later, was declared incompetent and committed to the State Department of Mental Health. When he refused to submit to the state's psychiatric examination, he was found in contempt of court. For four years, he was transferred from one state hospital to another and, in 1981 he was sent to the infirmary of the Indiana State Reformatory on yet another contempt citation for his continuing refusal to submit.

In January 1985, the Indiana Supreme Court agreed with Kiritsis that he could not be forced to undergo an examination, so he was released from the Reformatory and returned to a state hospital. He remained there for two more years before agreeing to be examined by a private psychiatrist. Kiritsis was released in December 1987 and, in 1990, filed 101 ultimately unsuccessful lawsuits in Marion Superior Court. Defendants included everyone who had been involved in the case—and many who had not. In the meantime, Indiana law had added the option of a "guilty but mentally ill" criminal plea, largely in response to the verdict returned in the Kiritsis case in 1977.

Although tried and convicted in Morgan County, Steven T. Judy was an Indianapolis native and his horrific crime attracted enormous attention in the capital city. Judy's background included significant child abuse and neglect, and he got an early start in the juvenile justice system. At least four violent sexual assaults were attributed to him, the first when he was just 13 years old. In 1979 he was free on $75,000 bond for the 1977 robbery of a supermarket. That's when he met Terry Lee Chasteen and her three children. His brutal rape and murder of Chasteen was made even more appalling by the drowning of her three children.

Judy was labeled a sociopath and confessed to the murders; but he pleaded not guilty by reason of insanity. When the jury returned its guilty verdict, Judy asked for the death penalty because, he said, he believed in reincarnation.

In 1981, he got his wish. Steven Judy became the first person executed in Indiana in 20 years, and died in the electric chair at the Indiana State Prison.

Just a year later, a civil case out of Bloomington focused the city's attention on a different kind of life and death issue. Baby Doe was the third child of a Bloomington couple and was born following a pregnancy labeled "uneventful." The tragically disabled child was born blue from lack of oxygen, had a closed and undeveloped esophagus, a constricted artery, an enlarged heart, and exhibited signs of Down Syndrome. Doctors offered the Does limited options for their baby. The parents could agree to transfer the child to another hospital for surgery to open the esophagus, and expect half-a-dozen or more surgeries in the next few years to repair the baby's heart and other damaged organs. Without the operations, the child would die. The parents, with the agreement of their primary physician, elected to do nothing and allow the baby to die.

When word of the situation filtered outside the hospital, however, the Monroe County prosecutor intervened. Reportedly, the hearing was held in a utility closet at the hospital in recognition of the urgency of the case, the lack of an available room at the hospital, and the privacy rights of the family. The judge ruled in favor of the family, recognizing that there were differing medical opinions and granting the baby's parents the right to decide between them. The prosecutor raced to Indianapolis in an attempt to overturn the decision, but the Indiana Supreme Court, too, refused to require the surgeries. Six days after birth, Baby Doe died without medical intervention.

It was not personal tragedy that drove the fourth case, but the converging agendas of two very diverse groups: a band of fundamentalist, evangelical Christian ministers and the radical feminists who agreed with them that pornography had to be banned from Indianapolis. Then-Mayor William H. Hudnut III supported the City-County Council's effort to make that happen and, in 1984, an ordinance passed prohibiting "all discriminatory practices of sexual subordination or inequality through pornography." The purpose of the ordinance was to define pornography as discrimination against women and subject to regulation by the Indianapolis Human Relations Commission. A lawsuit was filed by a large group of plaintiffs including the American Booksellers Association, the Association for American Publishers, the Council for Periodical Distributors, and the Freedom to Read Foundation. The Indiana Civil Liberties Union, Indianapolis Urban League and other civil rights organizations supported the plaintiffs.

Judge Sarah Evans Barker declared the ordinance unconstitutional on November 19, 1984, reminding the city that the First Amendment to the United States Constitution protects the right to free speech, even when the speech is evil. She also found the ordinance to be unconstitutionally vague, and declined to define the production, dissemination and use of sexually explicit works as conduct rather than speech, as the defendants had asked.

On August 27, 1985, the Seventh Circuit Court of Appeals affirmed Barker's decision and, on February 24, 1986, the U.S. Supreme Court unanimously agreed, without opinion.

CHAPTER EIGHT
(1990s AND BEYOND)

A CITY POISED FOR GREATNESS

AT THE END OF THE SECOND MILLENNIUM, INDIANAPOLIS WAS A city justly proud of how far it had come—and with how few stumbles—since 1819 when the first permanent white settlers arrived to carve a future from the dense forest.

Created as a planned city and named as an amalgam of the Greek word "polis," meaning city, and the state name "Indiana" to "indicate to all the world the locality of the town," the Hoosier capital city had outgrown and outlasted the derogatory twists on that appellation. No more "India-no-place." No more "Nap-town." Indianapolis was a national city—an *international* city—with a glowing reputation earned by its innovative leadership, strong economy, dedicated volunteer base, and labor force endowed with a powerful work ethic and enviable clarity in its values.

The final decade of the 20th century had seen phenomenal expansion not just within the city-county limits, but throughout the metropolitan area including the so-called "donut" counties that surround the Circle City. Indianapolis may not have had the navigable river its founders mistakenly identified; but by the turn of the century it had a maze of interstate highways and a central location that made it not just a regional powerhouse for manufacturing and distribution, but a national one as well. Air cargo, in particular, found Indianapolis an attractive home. First United Airlines came to the city, investing $800 million to build its second U.S. maintenance facility in Indianapolis rather than expand-

Victory Field, home of the Triple-A champion Indianapolis Indians, has been called "the best minor league ballpark in America."
(Courtesy Indianapolis Indians)

138 LAW IN AMERICA'S CROSSROADS

ing its existing operations in San Francisco. By the end of the decade, Federal Express, too, had made a major commitment to Indianapolis; the city was tapped for a 300,000 square foot expansion of a package-handling facility that was already FedEx's second largest in the nation.

While elsewhere in the nation politicians would sniff at manufacturing as part of a "rust belt" economy unsuited for a high-tech world, Indianapolis recognized the worth of an industrial base that had kept its people employed and its standard of living growing for generations. The city courted and catered to its manufacturers and was rewarded with more than $2 billion in industrial investment in the 1990s. Automotive manufacturers DaimlerChrysler, Ford, General Motors, Navistar and Rolls Royce-Allison each completed major construction valued at more than $100 million during the period. The expansions kept Indianapolis workers working, with one of the lowest unemployment rates in the nation—four percent statewide, and as low as two percent or less in suburban Hamilton, Boone, Johnson and Shelby counties.

Homegrown industries, too, liked what they found in Indianapolis and committed ever more dollars to expansion in the city. Eli Lilly and Company promised to spend more than $1 billion enlarging and improving two of its near-downtown plants, and Anthem Inc. built new headquarters nearby.

Bank One, Indianapolis, opened the decade of the '90s by changing the skyline of the city with its 51-story downtown office tower, while other local banks changed owners and names throughout the decade. Cleveland's National City Corporation acquired Merchants National Bank and NBD Bancorp of Detroit bought INB Bank in 1992. Other purchases and mergers throughout the decade would leave just one locally owned bank by the turn of the century.

LEFT: *The Maennerchor Building located on the corner of Illinois and Michigan Streets, served as the home of the law school from 1945 to 1970.*
BELOW: *The IU School of Law-Indianapolis was housed in this bulding at 735 West New York Street from 1970 until 2001.* OPPOSITE PAGE: *Lawrence W. Inlow Hall, located at 530 West New York Street is the new home of the IU School of Law-Indianapolis.*

What might have been considered more bad news for downtown retailing—the closing of the L.S. Ayres and Company landmark department store at Meridian and Washington streets—instead cleared the way for the long-anticipated Circle Centre Mall. Nordstrom and Parisian anchored a gallery of national shops, dining and entertainment options when the mall finally opened in 1995, bringing new life and opportunity to the city's center. Indeed, entertainment flourished in the revitalized downtown district. The Capitol Improvement Board struck a 10-year, $10 million deal to rename the Hoosier Dome the RCA Dome in 1994. Two years later, the minor-league Indianapolis Indians proudly opened their season in a beautiful new Victory Field at the western edge of downtown. The opening of Conseco Fieldhouse in 1999 as home of the Indiana Pacers capped a decade of sports-related construction that included luring the NCAA to relocate its headquarters to the "Amateur Sports Capital of the World."

The city took two more giant steps forward and, some say, one backward as a sports mecca, courtesy of Indianapolis Motor Speedway owner Tony George. The grandson of Tony Hulman, who is credited with building the prestige of the Indianapolis 500 Mile race as a Memorial Day classic, opened the track to a second blockbuster event with the inaugural Brickyard 400 NASCAR race that pumped an estimated $31.5 million into the local economy in 1994. The backward step, in the view of many local racing fans, came with the CART/IRL breach that substantially reduced inter-

A History of the Indianapolis Legal Profession   **141**

est and income from the May festival. In 2000, though, Hulman added a third payday to the track, with a Formula One race, bringing more racing fans—and millions more in fan spending—to Indianapolis.

The long-stalled White River State Park began to return on its promise during the 1990s, with the opening of the Eiteljorg Museum of American Indian and Western Art at its entrance. A new Imax Theatre soon followed, while White River Gardens and the start of construction on an $84 million Indiana State Museum rounded out the decade.

A LAWYER TAKES THE REINS

Much of the credit for what went right—and the blame for what went wrong—in the 1990s was heaped on the first lawyer to lead the city as mayor since Alex M. Clark stepped down in 1956. Like Clark, Stephen Goldsmith was an Indianapolis native and a former Marion County prosecutor. Both were young men when they took office (Clark was 36, Goldsmith 46); both stumbled in later political efforts; and both Republicans handed the office keys to a Democrat as they left. In Goldsmith's case, his successor Bart Peterson would return Democrat control to the mayor's office in 2000 after a 32-year absence.

Goldsmith was elected to the office in 1992 focused on reorganizing the delivery of government services, especially through privatization. He talked fiscal responsibility and balked at adopting the expansive practices of his predecessor, popular three-time Republican mayor William H. Hudnut III. Plums like Circle Centre Mall and the United Air Lines Maintenance Center that had been brokered by Hudnut were concerns to Goldsmith, who believed the city was overextended in its development deals and that taxpayers were supporting too much private expansion. But he stepped to the plate quickly when faced with the potential loss of jobs with the closing of the Department of Defense finance center and again when professional baseball threatened to pull the city's baseball franchise if it was forced to continue playing at the old 16th Street stadium.

The deal Goldsmith put together to save 2000 jobs at the aging Naval Avionics Center in 1996 was more to his taste, however. An innovative public/private partnership between the city and Hughes Technical Services, the pact was the first full privatization of a military facility in the nation. It was a fitting next phase for the property that had built the Norden Bombsight credited with ensuring Allied air prowess in World War II.

Stephen Goldsmith, shown here in 1977, served as Marion County prosecutor and was elected mayor in 1992. (Courtesy Indianapolis Bar Association)

By then, Goldsmith's national star was rising as word of his successes in contracting with private companies to deliver government services in Indianapolis spread. But his popularity at home was strained and he embarrassingly failed to carry the city in his losing 1996 bid for the Indiana governor's office. He declined to run for a third term, but was making headlines at the end of the century by advising Republican presidential candidate George W. Bush. The former mayor was not to win the cabinet-level position he had sought in the Bush administration and, like Hudnut before him, began a self-imposed exile from the city where he made his name.

LEGAL SERVICES ORGANIZATION CHANGES, TOO

Embattled for much of its life, Legal Services Organization would enter the new millennium with an altered structure, an expanded purpose and a new name. Founded within the Office of Economic Opportunity as part of President Lyndon B. Johnson's Great Society in 1966, the Office of Legal Services was intended to enhance delivery of legal services to the poor through existing local organizations. But in conservative Indianapolis, the federal dollars were not worth the federal obligations that came with them, and the Legal Aid Society formed in 1941 with the assistance of the Indianapolis Bar Association declined to participate. So Legal Services Organization of Indianapolis (LSO) was created and opened six neighborhood branches in storefront offices.

The organization was controversial from the beginning. Two arguments bolstered criticism: first, that there was no need for poverty law practice and, second, that attorneys in the city already provided those services either pro bono or through Legal Aid. LSO's Executive Director Norman Metzger recalls those early years as a fight to gain "a toehold" in the city. His job, he says, was to hire the best lawyers he could find who would be zealous in the pursuit of the rights of the poor. And, in an era when women were just starting to find a place in Indianapolis law firms, more than half of Metzger's LSO law staff was female.

The concept was no more popular in Washington than it was in Indianapolis. In his last official act before stepping on the helicopter to leave the capital, President Richard M. Nixon signed an act reorganizing Legal Services into a quasi-public corporation funded by Legal Services Corporation. With the static funding that followed, LSO in Indianapolis closed its neighborhood offices and consolidated into a single office. Ultimately, Metzger said, moving out of the neighborhoods probably benefited clients. It was frequently safer to board a bus and ride downtown to see a lawyer than to walk through the drug dealers and prostitutes who peopled the neighborhood streets where the offices had been located.

In the late 1970s, things again looked up for LSO as President Jimmy Carter acted on his plan to expand legal services to every county in the United States. In Indianapolis, LSO expanded from one office with 35 staff to 11 offices representing 59 Indiana counties with 185 staff serving not only Indianapolis clients, but the rural poor across the state. The expansion was brief. President Ronald Reagan was elected and made good on his promise to gut the California Rural Legal Aid systems that had represented migrant farm workers and so angered the California farmers and ranchers who supported the new president. Funding cuts closed six of the 11 LSO offices in Indiana and 40 staff were terminated.

The 1990s saw even more restrictions on LSO and its mission. In 1996 Congress took away the right of LSOs across the nation to file class actions, represent prisoners, assist clients in lobbying efforts, or represent anyone other than a U.S. citizen or documented alien. "The times and priorities have changed," Metzger says. "The task is how to endure, to be effective, to provide services." The answer, he adds, was

FRED SANDERS AND THE IPD

FRED SANDERS TAUGHT SCHOOL AT ST. LUKE SCHOOL ON THE Indianapolis northside. But he was at home in his Forest Manor neighborhood on August 14, 1988, when IPD Officer Matt John Faber responded to a complaint that Sanders' dog was running loose. The confrontation between the officer and the teacher escalated; Faber called for back-up and Sanders retreated inside his home. When Faber's help arrived, the officers forced their way into Sanders' home. Sanders fired at the police, striking Faber in the back. The officers returned fire, hitting Sanders three times before subduing and beating him. Faber died nine days later and Sanders was charged with murder.

On March 3, 1989, Sanders was sentenced to seven years in prison on a plea agreement that reduced the charge to involuntary manslaughter. Two police officers were indicted in the post-arrest beating of Sanders; one was convicted; and several officers were disciplined by the department.

Sanders filed a lawsuit against the city and 20 police officers, charging they had violated his civil rights. He withdrew his guilty plea and was released from prison in May 1991. In July 1992, the Indiana Supreme Court reversed the Marion Superior Court judge who ordered Sanders' release and Sanders appeal to the U.S. Supreme Court was unsuccessful. He was returned to prison in mid-1993.

In the meantime, though, a federal jury on November 11, 1992 awarded Sanders $1.5 million in damages on his civil rights claim, an amount reduced by District Court Judge Sarah Evans Barker to $78,000.

A TALE OF TWO MIKES

It was with great pride that then Marion County Republican Chairman L. Keith Bulen talked about why Indianapolis was spared the race riots that burned parts of so many U.S. cities during the 1960s. He, Mayor Richard G. Lugar and other city leaders—both white and African-American—made "a concentrated effort to keep it cool," he told an interview in the Senior Lawyer's Project.

But managing to keep it cool in the '60s didn't mean that relations between the races in Indianapolis were open and trusting. It was, at best, an uneasy peace and the political and courtroom battles over Uni-Gov and school desegregation were evidence of the often unbridgeable differences. Other cases as well demonstrated how differently the races viewed the city and their places in it. Of them, two were significant: those of Michael Taylor and Mike Tyson. The only thing the two men shared was race, but that was enough to make each of them a cause celebre in Indianapolis

Michael Taylor Jr. was 16 years old when he was arrested on September 24, 1987 for attempted auto theft. At 5:04 p.m., he was sitting in the back seat of an Indianapolis Police Department car in front of the Juvenile Detention Center when a gunshot exploded. Taylor died at 1:40 p.m. the following day. From the beginning, police insisted that, with his hands cuffed behind his back, the teen-ager had nonetheless managed to pull a hidden gun from his high-topped athletic shoes and shoot himself. That was an act of legerdemain Taylor's family and the African-American community were not prepared to believe. Police Chief Paul A. Annee confirmed on October 7 that a police investigation determined the bullet that killed Taylor was, indeed, self-inflicted; the only blame attached to the two officers who had arrested and transported the youth was that they had been negligent in their search for weapons on him.

African-American ministers demanded that the Marion County Coroner and U.S. Justice Department re-investigate Taylor's death, and hired their own private investigator to look into the matter, as well. None of the investigations disproved IPD's initial findings, but members of the black community continued to distrust both the police and the verdict.

Taylor's family filed a lawsuit against the city and the detectives and, on March 21, 1996, a Hancock County jury deliberated 12 hours before returning a $4.3 million verdict in favor of the Taylors. One of the jurors bluntly endorsed the family's fears. "He (Taylor) died as a result of being in the back of a police car," she said, "and it was not of his own hand." (Indianapolis *Star*, March 22, 1996) The verdict was reduced to $2.6 million and, on October 29, 1999, the Indiana Supreme Court refused to hear the city's appeal.

Mike Tyson was a celebrity, former world heavyweight boxing champion, in town to help celebrate Black Expo in July 1991. His stay was brief and notorious, a round of clubbing, hand shaking and, according to later reports, making crude passes at most of the women he met in the slightly more than 48 hours he spent in the city. One of those women, an 18-year-old Miss Black America pageant contestant, would cry rape. And her credentials—varsity cheerleader, softball player, National Honors Society member, recipient of an Outstanding High School Student Award from her school—would lend credibility to that claim.

The two met when Tyson attended a pageant rehearsal. He invited the young woman out that evening and she

---

to cannibalize the organization, to shrink offices and staff. By 1999, LSO still had five offices, but only 80 staff.

The job was accomplished, Metzger says, through a variety of creative processes. First, staffing was reduced to a core group of people who made a commitment to LSO and were dedicated to the bottom line mission. LSO then began effectively contracting at reduced rates with private attorneys, and utilizing the services of volunteer and pro bono attorneys from outside the organization. Law students were employed in clinical settings which, Metzger says, has the additional benefit of not only helping clients but introducing students to the concept of poverty law practice. A strong community legal education program also was initiated, with staff attorneys and paralegals offering programs in senior

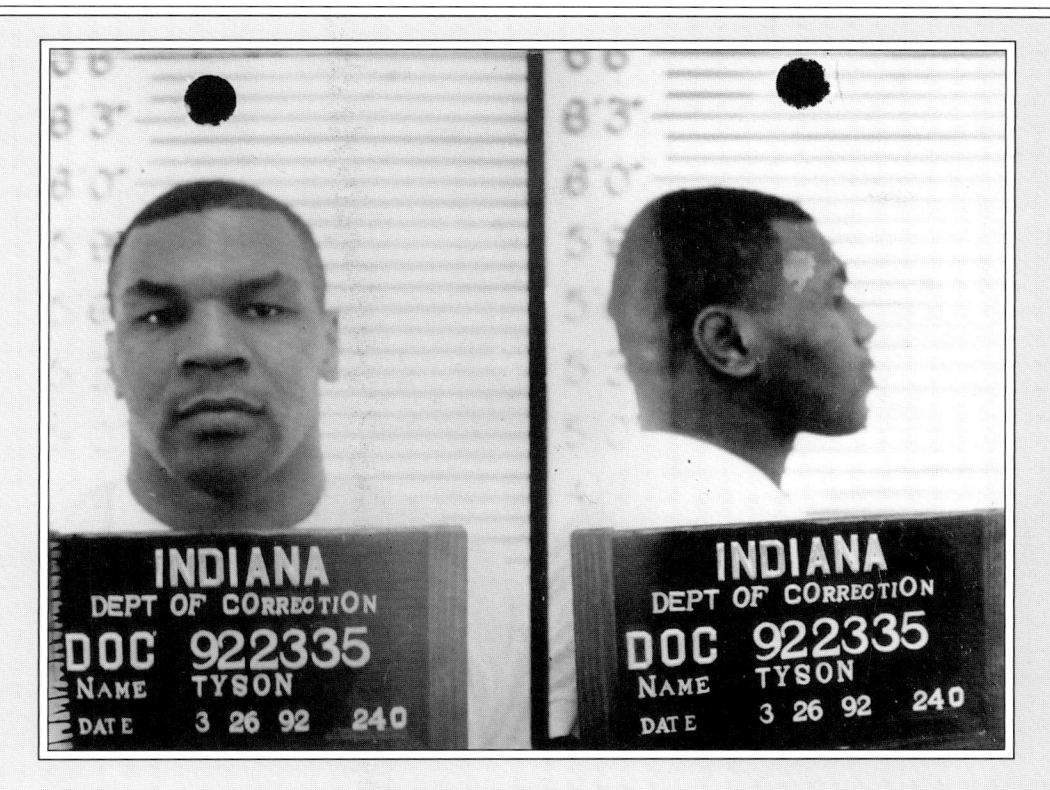

Mike Tyson's prison mug shot, taken when he entered the Indiana Department of Correction system on March 26, 1992.

ward on January 27, 1992 with Indianapolis attorney and former deputy prosecutor J. Gregory Garrison serving as special prosecutor and local defense attorney James H. Voyles Jr. assisting Tyson's team. Jurors were sequestered at the Indianapolis Athletic Club and, just a week into the trial, fire broke out at the club. Jurors were fortunate to escape uninjured; two firefighters and another hotel guest died. Initial concerns that the fire and the trial were related proved false; the fire was blamed on faulty wiring in a refrigerator. Still, one juror was excused when he said he could no longer concentrate on the trial.

agreed. She also agreed to visit his suite at the Canterbury Hotel, but the stories of what happened there were dramatically different. Although Tyson voluntarily testified, a Marion County grand jury believed Desiree Washington's version and Tyson was indicted.

Although Desiree, like Tyson, was African-American, much of the black community in Indianapolis and around the nation attacked the indictment as racist. Tyson's legal team, led by Vincent L. Fuller, the Washington D.C. attorney who had successfully defended John W. Hinckley Jr. for the attempted assassination of President Ronald Reagan, fed the flames. They fought to exclude the entire Indianapolis jury pool, arguing that the selection system used in the city was racially biased. The motion failed and the trial went for-

The jury deliberated 10 hours before returning a guilty verdict on February 10, 1992. Tyson was sentenced to six years in prison and four years on probation. He was denied bail and entered the Indiana prison system on March 26.

Tyson hired Harvard law professor Alan M. Dershowitz to handle the appeal to the Indiana Court of Appeals, which affirmed the conviction on September 22, 1993. The Chief Justice of the Indiana Supreme Court recused himself when he discovered his wife and Dershowitz had discussed the appeal at a Yale Law School alumni reunion. Without his vote, the court split 2-2 on Tyson's appeal and the Court of Appeals denial was upheld.

Tyson was released from prison on March 25, 1995 after serving three years of his sentence. While in prison, he converted to the Muslim faith and was chauffeured directly from the prison to a mosque for prayer before leaving Indiana.

---

centers and community centers to teach clients how to help themselves use and navigate the system and prevent legal problems.

As 2001 began, Legal Services Organization of Indianapolis made yet another change in its organization, its name and the way it would provide services. Indiana Legal Services, Inc. is now the one organization authorized by the national Legal Services Corporation to provide poverty law services in Indiana, taking over the responsibilities formerly under the wings of four separate LSO organizations in Indianapolis, Fort Wayne, South Bend and Gary. As a result, the Indianapolis office is now empowered to offer specialized services throughout the state, including prisoner rights, children's rights, economic development law and elder law. Among the projects managed from the office are programs for migrant farm workers, the homeless, and victims of domestic violence. There is a hot-line service for seniors and a state-funded ombudsman program. For Metzger, that translates as a revitalized program able and prepared to provide highly specialized legal services for some of the neediest of Indiana's citizens.

PUBLIC DEFENDER SYSTEM EVOLVES

The path to develop a system of legal representation for the neediest criminal defendants was no less serpentine. In fact, for many years the decision of whether or not a defendant should be provided an attorney at public expense was left entirely to the discretion of the judge. As the United States Supreme Court began to mandate the right of defendants to counsel, Marion County courts pieced together their own patchwork system of public defenders—some with full-time staff, some independent contractors, with varying levels of support staff and compensation.

The most sophisticated and organized systems developed in the Municipal and Juvenile courts. There full-time public defenders worked with a full complement of staff, including investigators and paralegals. Funding was through the court system and defendant eligibility was determined by the individual judge, based on a prescribed formula. At the opposite extreme, criminal court judges appointed private attorneys as part-time public defenders when they determined a defendant was entitled to the representation, but provided virtually no staff or other support. Public defenders were required to petition the court for resources at each step.

JUDICIAL CASELOADS MOUNT

When Richard M. Given was in law school in the late 1940s, he was appointed as one of the first law clerks for the Indiana Supreme Court where he would one day serve as chief justice. He served five justices. Prior to that time, the court had turned to its assistant librarians for research help.

When William E. Steckler became judge of the U.S. District Court for the Southern District of Indiana, he was the only person holding that title.

In the early 1960s, Indianapolis courts still took summer term vacations, with only one courtroom remaining open during July and August. Indianapolis Bar Association members, concerned about the increasing backlog of cases pending before the courts, offered to help by serving as volunteer pro-tem judges.

When Patrick D. Sullivan left the Municipal Court bench for the Indiana Court of Appeals, his statehouse office staff included one secretary and one clerk—the same allocation for each of the eight judges on the appeals bench.

Today each justice on the Indiana Supreme Court is assisted by at least two clerks, and some have three. The court also employs librarians, assistants and secretaries to the justices, and a court administrator with a full complement of staff.

The U.S. District Court for the Southern District of Indiana has five judges.

The Indiana Court of Appeals has 15 judges, each with one secretary and three clerks; five senior judges; and an administrator and a commissioner.

And the 35 Marion County courts are open year around.

Without exception, judges interviewed for this book noted increased caseloads as the most striking difference in the practice of law over the past half century. Given recalls that, when he was elected to the Supreme Court in 1968, the caseload was "reasonable." But today, he said, there is a "tremendous backlog" and no obvious way to reduce the strain. "Every judge has to read every case," he explained. "The only efficient way to deal with it is to send more cases to the Court of Appeals." At that level, he said, adding judges to deal with the volume can have an effect.

But the additional faces at the Indiana Court of Appeals hasn't stemmed the tide of backlogged cases there, Sullivan said. "We've had a twofold increase in judges (since 1969), and a tenfold increase in cases," he said. Although the types of cases are not dramatically different, they are more complicated, and that, too, slows the process. To deal with the

146   Law in America's Crossroads

By the early 1970s, critics including the Indianapolis Bar Association found fault with the all of the various systems, most significantly with the level of control exercised by the judges before whom the public defenders practiced. Three Bar Association studies—in 1976, 1979 and 1985—recommended substantial changes. None were forthcoming and, by the time the IBA began its fourth study in 1990, the Marion County public defender system was disparaged as among the worst in the nation. But it was not until the Indiana Civil Liberties Union filed suit in 1992 that the City-County Council took action to reform the public defender system. By mid-1993, the Marion County Public Defender Agency had been created, based in part on recommendations found in the 1985 Bar Association study.

The Agency is under the direction of a nine-member board and a chief public defender and provides representation for defendants in all of the Marion County court systems, including appeals. While not yet an ideal situation, the new agency is a step forward, at least creating public defenders independent from the judges.

LAWYERS FACE PRO BONO RESPONSIBILITIES

Not every lawyer can or should make the decision to dedicate his or her career to the representation of indigent clients, criminal or civil. But Indianapolis lawyers have a long and honorable tradition of sharing their expertise with those who cannot afford to pay for the service. The importance of doing so was even included in the statement of purposes in the Indianapolis Bar Association's initial Articles of Incorporation. "To apply knowledge and experience in the field of

---

substantial increase in cases involving children (particularly cases of children removed from their home or cases involving alleged child molestation), the court has established a strict priority: any case involving children goes to the top of the assigned judge's caseload stack.

Still, there's no way to maintain the highest level of quality judges seek and the citizenry deserves when the caseload becomes so overwhelming. "It's a numbers game," Sullivan pointed out. "When you crank out more decisions, it dilutes careful deliberation."

He recalled the luxury of a leisurely caseload when he became an appeals court judge in 1969. He arrived at an office that held 10 cases in inventory and, over the first year, was assigned an additional 14 cases. In contrast, he began 1999 with 69 cases pending and was assigned an additional 107; at the end of the year, all but 19 had been disposed of. Such a schedule leaves no time for the contemplative hours of research and reflection that leads to the scholarly opinions both judges and advocates favor. Sullivan recalled one such opinion in particular—a 1971 case in which he was free to spend three full days researching and crafting a single paragraph and its attendant footnotes. The case (*Cox v. Winklepleck*, 271 N.E.2d 737 at 740) involved the appeal of a $500 award in a personal injury matter. But the small stakes didn't prevent Sullivan from giving it due consideration and contributing a particularly esoteric aside:

"We now express the hope that the highest court of this state will reconsider the posture of the law in this regard and that in the future evidence of prior convictions for impeachment purposes will be limited to those crimes which clearly bear upon the credibility of the witness or at least to crimes clearly involving moral turpitude. After all, angels[1], bishops[2], kings[3], and even judges[4] upon rare occasions, are subject to human frailties and commensurate with such characteristics have been and might be convicted of transgressions against established law. One's credibility might well be destroyed were he to quarrel on Sunday, IC 1971, 35-1-86-1, being Ind.Ann.Stat. § 10-4301 (Burns' 1956), ride a horse within the city, IC 1971, 35-1-119-2, being Ind.Ann.Stat. § 10-2702 (Burns' 1956), or gather cranberries on public lands, IC 1971 35-27-3-1, being Ind.ann.Stat. § 10-4508 (Burns' 1956)."

---

[1] "How art thou fallen from heaven, O Lucifer, son of the morning"! Isaiah 14:12.

[2] "Give me chastity and continence, but not just now." Confessions of St. Augustine. Book 8, Chapter 7.

[3] "If Henry III had been capable of being sued, he would have passed his life as a defendant. In the opinion of many of his subjects, he was forever breaking the law." 1 Pollock and Maitland (1895) History of English Law, page 501.

[4] In 1621, philosopher, scientist and Lord Chancellor Francis Bacon, the highest judicial officer of England, was impeached for accepting bribes from litigants—sometimes from both parties to the controversy. His only defense was that he never gave the briber value in return unless he deserved it upon the merits. Impeachment of Federal Judges: An Historical Overview. Thompson and Pollitt. 49 N.C.L.Rev. 87 (1970).

law to the promotion of the public good," the founders wrote.

But it was not until October 22, 1997 that the Indiana Supreme Court put into place a framework to encourage and enable pro bono efforts by attorneys throughout Indiana. The purpose of Rule 6.5 of the Rules of Professional Conduct was clearly enunciated as:

"to promote equal access to justice for all Indiana residents, regardless of economic status, by creating and promoting opportunities for attorneys to provide pro bono civil legal services to persons of limited means."

Court of Appeals Judge L. Mark Bailey was appointed chairman of the 21-member Indiana Pro Bono Commission, and recently identified four primary goals: "(T)o improve the (local) district plans and assist the districts in accomplishing their goals, to develop a curriculum of training seminars with a certificate of 'graduation,' to continue to enlighten the bar about the need for pro bono service through marketing and publicity, and to develop the Web site and technology to further the goals of the rule and develop the culture of pro bono." ("An invitation to become part of the solution," the *Indiana Lawyer*, April 11, 2001) He stressed the necessity of a "culture change" to bring more attorneys into the pro bono system.

Indiana Legal Services Executive Director Norman Metzger hailed the new emphasis. "Some people worry about duplication of service," he said. "It's an interesting concern to me. There are plenty of clients out there and, no matter how hard we work, we are never going to have enough services to meet the basic legal needs of all the poor people out there. But the cooperation that's taking place is all coming together and is vastly superior to what we had five years ago." ("Legal Services expands into new roles," *Indiana Lawyer*, April 11, 2001)

PRACTICING LAW INTO THE 21ST CENTURY

Harry T. Ice foretold the future as early as the mid-1930s. In *History of a Hoosier Law Firm*, his book about the firm now known as Ice Miller, he wrote:

"One day, at the weekly roundtable luncheon of Harvard Law School graduates at the Athenaeum, Pierre Goodrich ignited an argument by saying the New Deal was destroying the country in general and lawyers in particular. I took the position that the New Deal was creating business for lawyers and they had to follow their brethren in the medical profession and specialize. I argued that lawyers could neither serve their clients well nor prosper if they did not do so. The law was now too vast and so full of pitfalls that the day of the generalist was over. I contended that specialists would ultimately take over the practice. ...

"Kurt Pantzer's response, designed perhaps to keep the discussion going, was that his firm specialized in clients. I replied that clients ultimately would recognize the need for and go to experts in the various fields."

For the Ice Miller (then Matson Ross McCord & Clifford) firm, the expertise was in the municipal bond business. But it, like many of the large and growing larger firms of Indianapolis, began shortly after World War II building other areas of focused competence within the firm. In those years, new associates were assigned an initial "rotation," working with different partners to develop their skills and knowledge in several areas of practice. By 1960, that had changed, Ice recalled. Newly hired associates were now assigned to a specific practice section within the firm, and expected to remain in that "specialty" throughout their careers. Those sections were competing with new and established small firms known as "boutiques," where attorneys largely limited their practice to one or at most a small number of closely related specialties and subspecialties.

That firms of all sizes were in fact competing for business was a rarely acknowledged reality in Indianapolis—at least until 1983. That's when a young attorney named Stanley Kahn moved to Indianapolis and opened his personal injury practice. Kahn took to the television airwaves with low-budget advertisements urging individuals who had been injured in an accident to call him. Established Indianapolis law firms and lawyers may have sniffed their disdain for Kahn and his business development style, but the ads were well within the guidelines of the U.S. Supreme Court's 1977 ruling that permitted lawyer advertising so long as it was not deceptive. Equally important for the future of legal advertising in the city, they quickly turned the unknown sole practitioner into the leader of a large and successful firm.

Other new and small firms followed Kahn's lead and upped the ante, with ads that shouted from the yellow pages, newspapers and magazines, television and radio. One, Frank & Kraft, placed an advertisement in local newspapers offering a free seminar about living trusts. To their surprise, 256 people responded to that single advertisement, launching a marketing program based on seminars and retail-oriented customer service. Keeping their forward-thinking approach to marketing, the firm today conducts 48 seminars each year, teaches continuing professional education classes for certified public accountants and insurance agents, and operates an interactive Web site for clients and potential clients.

Gradually, the established firms bought into the marketing concept, too, albeit with what they still insist is more dignity and targeted marketing. By the beginning of the 21st century, most of the city's largest firms and many of its smaller ones were actively engaged using sophisticated advertising and marketing programs to seek new business. Some hired full-time marketing or business development managers. Others used outside consultants to design and coordinate materials from letterhead and business cards to consumer advertisements, marketing slogans, newsletters and internet web sites. But all are aimed at building an image for the firm. And that, says Kahn, proves he was right back in 1983, and they were wrong.

"Have they raised advertising to a level of decency or integrity?" he asked an *Indianapolis Star* reporter. "I don't think so. Just because they are (a large firm) doesn't mean their ad is more dignified or less dignified, more tasteful or less tasteful than anybody else's. ... The very same people who were so critical of me are doing it themselves. It sort of validates what you do." ("Law firms cautiously embrace advertising," *Indianapolis Star*, August 20, 2000)

NEW DIRECTIONS IN LAW

Forty lawyers met in the Indianapolis law offices of Dye & Harris on November 30, 1878 to form the Indianapolis Bar Association. Today the membership of the organization numbers more than 3,200. The association has matured along with the city whose name it bears, growing more sophisticated in anticipation of and response to the needs and desires of its members. Initially a fraternity of white males, it has become a diverse group, boasting both men and women representing varied ethnicities.

Most of those original 40 members were sole practitioners or shared a practice with, at most, one or two other lawyers. Although many independent lawyers and small firms operate within the city today, there also are mega-firms spilling across several floors of high-rise office towers and filling up satellite offices in the city's suburban office parks. More than a few have partners and associates stationed in other cities—north and south in Indiana, in Washington, D.C. and in other national centers of commerce and government.

The original 40 members lived and practiced law in Indianapolis. Through the years, firms in nearby cities joined the Indianapolis Bar Association in recognition of the importance of maintaining a presence in the capital city. In the last few decades, large firms from other cities and states forged alliances with Indianapolis firms, seeking representation as co-counsel from the local bar. But it was not until the 1990s that firms from distant cities boldly opened their own local offices, typically with lawyers lured away from Indianapolis firms.

Such temerity would not have existed in an earlier era. Loyalty was paramount between lawyers and their firms until recently, says Harold R. Woodard. "We had an understanding between firms," he says. "It was an unwritten understanding not to raid; there was no lateral hiring. Now, if a lawyer feels he or she can get a better deal from another firm, there is no loyalty. They go." When in 1946 he joined the firm that now bears his name, Woodard says, he knew it was likely he would spend his entire career there. And he has done so. But younger lawyers feel no such obligation, ricocheting from one firm to another, taking their training, their expertise, and sometimes large client bases with them.

Most of the original 40 members of the Indianapolis Bar Association who were in practice with other attorneys were in partnerships, and though the details of those partnerships were confidential between the partners, they undoubtedly shared many qualities. It is likely the law partnership of Matson Ross McCord & Clifford was configured similar to others in the early 1930s. It was known as "the Matson firm," and Frederick E. Matson was not only the founder and senior partner, but the governing partner, as well. Harry T. Ice said Matson set compensation for all employees and partnership percentages. At the beginning of each year, he handed each partner a new partnership agreement. "It was signed and returned without questions being asked," Ice wrote. "The process was never challenged, undoubtedly because of his position, but also because he was an unselfish and generous man."

As law firms grew and formed and re-formed in the city, there probably were few if any others that gave such unquestioned control to a single partner. Still, the partnership was the dominant form of organization for lawyer groupings during most the 20th century. Today, the complexity of the practice has spawned a variety of organizational styles—and not just for partnerships. Indianapolis law firms are structured as limited liability partnerships, professional corporations, and professional associations, and other types of practices surely will develop in the future.

The original 40 members of the Indianapolis Bar Association were primarily general practitioners. They practiced the law their clients required: business law, wills, real estate, a smattering of criminal law now and then. Few modern law-

RAISING THE BAR... FOR INDIANAPOLIS

THE INDIANAPOLIS BAR FOUNDATION, ESTABLISHED IN 1968, EXISTS to advance the administration of justice and an understanding of the law. The philanthropic arm of the Indianapolis Bar Association, the foundation holds total endowment of $1,000,000 in six designated funds: the Hon. Paul H. Buchanan Jr. Ask a Lawyer Endowment, Pro Bono Initiatives, the Neil E. Shook Scholarship Endowment Fund, Foundation Program Grants, the General Endowment Fund, and the Unrestricted Gifts Fund.

With the generous support of directors, fellows and donors, the Bar Foundation provides a variety of on-going programs. Since 1995, it has awarded more than $250,000 in community grants and scholarships to Indiana University School of Law students in Indianapolis and Bloomington.

Equally important are the many innovative programs that exist only because of Bar Foundation support. Among them are the annual Ask a Lawyer event that involves hundreds of Indianapolis lawyers providing pro bono advice at community centers throughout the city, and the IBA Legal Line, a bi-weekly pro bono telephone bank. The Homeless Project giving pro bono counsel to the homeless, and the Juvenile Project offering counsel to families within the juvenile justice system are other Bar Foundation supported programs.

Marion County's "Settlement Week," an intensive program aimed at resolving pending cases through mediation is funded by the Bar Foundation, as is the IBA's Gold E. Locks program designed to educate children about the legal process through the trial of Goldilocks.

Program and financial assistance is also made available through the Bar Foundation to the Legal Aid Society and Indiana Legal Services Corporation.

The Bar Foundation is especially proud of its instrumental role in developing and funding A Child's Haven, the children's waiting room at the City-County Building where children are made to feel safe and secure while waiting to testify or for parents or guardians to complete court business.

---

yers range so widely. Most have settled, as Harry Ice predicted, into areas of specialty or concentration.

Labor and employment law, family law, business and tax law, estate planning and administration law, patent and trademark law, and litigation concentrations were some of the earliest specialties embraced by Indianapolis lawyers, but ballooning federal and state laws and regulations soon added others: environmental law, health care law, sports and entertainment law, and elder law all reflected the changing society in which Indianapolis lawyers practiced.

Patricia Orloff Grow of Lamberti & Grow perhaps exemplifies the new face of law in Indianapolis. She practices discrimination and constitutional issues within a female firm, and she expects to see new subspecialties within that practice reflecting the changes in society. As the population ages, she believes there will be increasing emphasis on age discrimination in the workforce, and on discrimination under the Americans with Disabilities Act. She also believes attorneys will continue to explore alternative remedies through the Indiana state constitution. And, with the explosion of technology changing the ways and the places Hoosiers work, she anticipates much more concentration of legal challenges and protections in those ways. Most important, Grow believes, is that the bench and the bar of the future reflect the diversity of the workplace.

A PROFESSION POISED FOR GREATNESS OR...

"I have observed that lawyers do more than their share of the civic and charitable work," said Indiana University Chancellor Herman B Wells. So it certainly has been with the lawyers of Indianapolis. From the beginning, their numbers have included men and women of greatness, dedicated to justice.

Such a man was Judge Isaac Blackford who wrote what was probably the first decision in the nation acknowledging the civil rights of Native Americans in 1825.

So, too, were Ovid Butler who helped fund the antislavery newspaper, the *Free Soil Democrat*, a newspaper for "Free

Soil, Free States and Free Men," and its editor, lawyer Lewis "Lew" Wallace, both supporters of the Free Territory party which opposed expansion of slavery into western territories and supported free-soil settlers in Kansas.

Perhaps the first woman to be counted among that group was Bessie Eaglesfield who was graduated from the University of Michigan School of Law and successfully petitioned for admission to the Vigo County bar in 1875, later practicing in Indianapolis, Terre Haute and Grand Rapids, Mich. She cracked the door Antoinette Dakin Leach opened fully in 1893, when she successfully petitioned the Indiana Supreme Court for the right of women to practice law in the state.

Indianapolis attorney George W. Stubbs, whose concern for children being tried as adults led him to draft legislation for the 1903 General Assembly creating the first juvenile court in Indianapolis, was another.

And Lewis A. Coleman, who probably exemplified the Indianapolis Bar Association, memorialized upon his death in 1940 as a man with "a clean mind" who was "always friendly, always kindly, and always a gentleman."

The profession poised at the beginning of the 21st century has decisions to make: will it continue in the tradition of those generous lawyers or forge a new, more ruthless culture mirroring the distasteful lawyer jokes popularized in the 1990s. "Grasping, over zealous, unethical, flamboyant self-seekers," retired Court of Appeals Judge Paul H. Buchanan Jr. described them. He lamented that "by the very nature of the legal process, lawyers are intimately involved as partisans in controversies which are often bitter." Yet, he believes, "the vast majority of lawyers are hard working, loyal to their clients, and serve the basic needs of a civilized society. They make our system of justice and freedom work."

He, like many of the attorneys whose names dominated the profession in Indianapolis during the last half of the 20th century, expressed concern about a new trend toward incivility and even deceitful behavior among some contemporary attorneys. When he started practicing in 1961, said John Moss Jr., "your word was your bond." Any lawyer could rely on what another lawyer said. The reluctance to take a fellow lawyer at his word today may be less a matter of untrustworthiness among practitioners, he believes, than the fact that lawyers today are not speaking as clearly or listening as well. Combativeness and posturing were always around, Moss said, recalling an incident several years ago when one attorney's parting words to an adversary as he left the courtroom were "the next time you speak to me, speak with your fists!"

Former Indianapolis Bar Association president John Houghton believes the change in attitude evidenced by some modern lawyers is no more than a reflection of contemporary society. It is akin, he says, to road rage among the general population, and may be brought about simply because the competition among lawyers has become so vicious.

Former Marion Circuit Court Judge and U.S. District Court Magistrate J. Patrick Endsley places some of the blame for any increased incivility among lawyers on law school curricula which may leave young lawyers less well prepared than previous generations. "We studied evidence, procedure, constitutional law," he said, pointing out that many more elective courses now take up students' time.

Retired attorney Alan T. Nolan questions whether the difference in attitude might be attributable to the "bottom line business" approach to law. Nolan's father was an attorney, he said, when "the practice of law was a learned profession—there were doctors, lawyers, ministers and teachers." None was considered a lucrative career so much as a public service occupation, with social obligations to represent some people and organizations without charge. To some degree, that changed when the pressure of billable hours intensified as clients sought to minimize legal costs. "The minute you start taking a unit of time and putting a price tag on it," he said, "it becomes very unprofessional, like a surgeon charging for the time it takes to remove tonsils."

Court of Appeals Judge Patrick D. Sullivan blames some of the problem on societal changes. "Our system is admittedly overburdened with disputes more imagined than real, often created by those who seek causes to champion," he said. "It is admittedly overburdened by a natural, necessary increase in litigation brought about by population shifts, unemployment, economic failure. … Keep in mind that the paramount factor which should be in all our procedures is to facilitate the resolution of the dispute."

That thought is echoed by former U.S. Attorney Virginia Dill McCarty, who believes that too many lawyers may have lost sight of the primary purpose of a lawyer. "It is not to win," she said, "but to stand between two emotionally involved clients and help them solve their problems."

"Beyond peacemaking, beyond public service," Buchanan said, "it should be remembered that lawyers are the lubricant that makes the wheels of justice turn—a vital factor in domestic tranquility. Civilization cannot exist without a system of justice, civil and criminal."

LAW IN AMERICA'S
CROSSROADS

LAW FIRM HISTORIES

THIS HISTORIC ACCOUNT OF INDIANAPOLIS' LEGAL PROFESSION would not be complete without including descriptive profiles about the men and women who make up this notable profession. Working within a firm or as a solo practitioner, attorneys stretching from Johnson County up to Hamilton County have influenced the growth and development of not only the legal profession, but also the city of Indianapolis and its surrounding communities. Although many of the following profiles describe the areas in which these firms and lawyers practice, these firm histories are not to be taken in any way as a representation of the quality of the firm's service.

Through these profiles one gets a glimpse of how the city has been shaped by the legal profession and the men and women who form it. The dedication of so many has left an impression on the community not only through their legal work, but through their commitment to their families, their churches, professional organizations, and a variety of charitable organizations. The traits of dedication, good character, and commitment to public service will continue impacting the growth of their communities for many years as they are passed through the generations.

This Bench and Bar composite photograph portrays Indianapolis lawyers in 1897. Pictured in the center is former U.S. president Benjamin Harrison.

152   LAW IN AMERICA'S CROSSROADS

A History of the Indianapolis Legal Profession

THE INDIANAPOLIS BAR ASSOCIATION

From 40 members to more than 3,700, from an amiable fraternity to a professional organization of gender, racial and ethnic diversity, the Indianapolis Bar Association has always reflected the growth in size and sophistication of its namesake city. But more than a mirror of its urban environment, the Indianapolis Bar Association has throughout its history been a catalyst, a driving force in the development of the city.

The Indianapolis Bar Association first met on November 30, 1878 when 40 local attorneys came together in the offices of Dye & Harris to establish a professional organization. Among its first members were Benjamin Harrison, who would serve as the nation's 23rd president, and Charles W. Fairbanks, who would be elected vice president under Theodore Roosevelt. The noble purposes set forth for this new league have been its guiding principles for 123 years, steering the Indianapolis Bar Association through the 20th century and into the new millennium. They remain as part of the Association's Articles of Incorporation in 2001:

To develop and maintain the integrity and impartiality of the administration of justice; To promote reforms in the law and modernization of the judicial system; To cultivate jurisprudence ...

From its earliest inception, the Indianapolis Bar Association has been vigilant in seeking justice for all citizens and in its oversight of the judicial system in Indianapolis and Marion County and at the appellate levels. Before the end of the 19th century, committees had been formed to investigate local court practices, and the association would take an active role in judicial reform throughout its history.

The Bar Association was instrumental in designing the Marion County Municipal Court system that replaced the City Court and Center Township Justice of the Peace courts in 1925.

Julie Armstrong, Executive Director of the Indianapolis Bar Association, right, and Kari Hartman, Assistant Executive Director.

When the integrity of that system came under fire again in the 1960s, the Bar Association led the charge to restore public confidence in the judiciary; at its urging, the practice of gubernatorial appointments was replaced in 1971 with a mini-Missouri Plan merit system for the selection and retention of Marion County Municipal Court judges.

The Bar Association also worked tirelessly to extend access to justice to all citizens. As early as 1917, its War Committee established procedures to ensure that matters in the offices of Indianapolis lawyers serving in the military were smoothly transferred to other attorneys. In 1941 it launched the Legal Aid Society to make legal services more widely available and, in March 1954, established the Lawyers' Referral Service. The Ask A Lawyer program was initiated in the early 1970s to take legal services even more directly to the public, with Bar Association members donating countless hours answering questions and advising citizens in shopping malls, on radio and on television. All three services continue today with financial backing from the Indianapolis Bar Foundation.

The 1993 creation of the Marion County Public Defender Agency was based in part on recommendations from three Bar Association studies urging reform of the much disparaged previous system administered by the various courts.

The Indianapolis Bar Foundation was established as the philanthropic arm of the Indianapolis Bar Association in 1968 to advance the administration of justice and an understanding of the law. With a current endowment of nearly $1 million, it supports several on-going programs, including the IBA Legal Line, a bi-weekly pro bono telephone bank; the Homeless Project, giving pro bono counsel to the homeless; and the Juvenile Court Project, offering counsel to families in the juvenile justice system. The Foundation was instrumental in the development and funding of A Child's Haven, the children's waiting room at the City-County Building.

50 year practitioners of the Indianapolis Bar Association, 2000: front row, left to right, Ms. Virginia Dill McCarty, Mr. William H. Wolf, Mr. Richard P. Stein, Mr. Thomas L. Davis, Mr. William B. Patrick; middle row, left to right, Mr. Joseph H. Greenberg, Mr. Stanley Talesnick, the Hon. Richard M. Salb, Mr. John C. Christ, Mr. Charles W. Hunter; back row, left to right, Mr. Andrew Steffen, Mr. William E. Roberts, Mr. Thomas L. Davis.

TO ENCOURAGE AND PROVIDE for continued education of the practicing lawyer and cultivation of professional excellence and maintenance of high ethical standards; to uphold the honor of the profession of law ...

Providing a complete law library for the use of its members was one of the most pressing early goals of the Indianapolis Bar Association. The organization has continued to look to the development of professional excellence among its members ever since. In 1925, members voted unanimously to raise the standards for admission to the practice of law from the broad permission granted in the 1851 State Constitution that opened the door to any voter "of good moral character." Similar attempts had been turned back in 1906 and 1910, but a 1931 constitutional amendment granted new powers to regulate admissions to practice to the Supreme Court and a bar examination was established in 1933.

In 1949 the Indianapolis Bar Association began an ambitious program of seminars conducted in conjunction with association meetings to continue the educational process for practicing lawyers. A placement committee was established in 1954 to assist young lawyers seeking to begin practicing in Indianapolis.

Club rooms were opened in 1956, providing library facilities, conference rooms for depositions and dictation and a

A History of the Indianapolis Legal Profession 155

Rosie Felton, left, and the Hon. Sarah Evans Barker on the occasion of Rosie's retirement in September, 1995.

dining room for client entertainment and attorney fellowship. They remained available to Bar Association members until the building in which they were housed was demolished in the late 1960s.

In the 1970s, with the appointment of Rosie Felton as the Indianapolis Bar Association's first executive director, services began to multiply. Continuing legal education, the Young Lawyers Division, the Women and the Law Division, and the Bench/Bar Conference were created. Committees were formalized to oversee client grievances against attorneys, judicial evaluations, professional responsibility and to encourage pro bono work by members. Currently, additional task forces on continuing legal education, placement services and small firm crisis management support the professional development of members.

TO CARRY OUT THE FOREGOING PURPOSES in concert and cooperation with other agencies or organizations when deemed appropriate to do so …

In 1945 the Indianapolis Bar Association partnered with the law school deans to provide a refresher course for attorneys returning from World War II, helping update them on changes in the law during their absence. Other partnerships—both formal and informal—have been formed over the years to offer the services of the Indianapolis Bar Association and its members for the benefit of the community.

One such partnership stands as an extraordinary example of the Bar Association's efforts. Its partnership in 1981 with the National Legal Resource Center for the Protection of Children, the American Bar Association, and Lilly Endowment resulted in the development by 1989 of the nation's largest organized Court Appointed Special Advocate (CASA) program.

The work of individual Bar Association members in concert with other citizen groups has been among the most far-reaching of those partnerships. Indianapolis lawyers can take justifiable pride in their front-line participation in such monumental efforts as the Indianapolis Public School desegregation cases and the development of Uni-Gov.

The Indianapolis Bar Association has been at the forefront of change and growth in the city for 123 years. Today it boasts more than 3,700 members and is administered by a 26-member Board of Managers. There are 17 Sections, three Divisions, 11 Committees and six Task Forces.

In 1995 Julie Armstrong, who had joined the Indianapolis Bar Association staff as public affairs director in 1991, took the helm from a retiring Rosie Felton. As executive director, she presides over a full-time staff of nine functioning with upgraded technology in new quarters that house the association's first on-site education center. Under Armstrong's direction, the organization has focused significant effort on increasing the pro bono work of its members. An extensive Task Force on Pro Bono Civil Matters resulted in the creation of a Standing Committee on Pro Bono.

The Indianapolis Bar Association's rich history of professionalism, civic awareness and tireless contribution to the quality of life in Indianapolis have earned it a deserved place at any table where important decisions on the city's future are discussed. It speaks with a respected voice on policy issues not only within the legal and judicial communities, but at the General Assembly and in partnership with other public and private entities.

The Indianapolis Bar Association will respond to the challenges of the new century with the same spirit of innovation, cooperation, determination and professional excellence that have brought it to its current position of respect within the community.

BAKER & DANIELS

Since 1863, the law firm of Baker & Daniels has been helping clients do business throughout Indiana, across the country, and around the world. The firm's clients are served by more than 325 professionals located in seven offices. Despite the firm's long involvement with Indiana's growth, its reach extends far beyond state boundaries. Clients affected by federal legislation and regulations have access to the expertise of attorneys in the firm's Washington, D.C. office and the D.C. federal affairs consulting subsidiary, Sagamore Associates, and its public affairs consulting organization, Capitol Direct. On the international front, Baker & Daniels is one of only 26 U.S. law firms licensed to practice in China, where the firm counsels international businesses and facilitates partnerships and joint ventures. Finally, as the exclusive Indiana member of Lex Mundi, the world's leading association of independent law firms, Baker & Daniels attorneys have access to legal professionals throughout the United States and the entire world.

Baker & Daniels' guiding principle is to provide practical business and legal advice and build strong, human relationships. "One of our strengths is that we are constantly thinking of how we can improve the client's business in ways that just wouldn't be possible if we were merely responding to isolated issues," said Managing Partner Brian Burke. In addition, the firm's systems and structures are designed to encourage teamwork and enhance client service, and Baker & Daniels takes great pride in conducting client satisfaction interviews throughout the year. This focus on client service is a strategy that has served the firm well, evidenced by the fact that companies such as Eli Lilly and the Indianapolis Water Company have been loyal clients for much of the firm's 137-year existence.

The new economy is challenging Baker & Daniels to transform itself to meet and exceed the expectations of performing services better, cheaper and faster across a broader spectrum of disciplines. "There is less distinction between what we've traditionally done and what other professionals are doing, so we know that we must be nimble in identifying multidisciplinary solutions and adding expertise," Burke said. By embracing technology, Baker & Daniels also has improved the efficiency of its own operations and positioned itself to understand clients who use or make technology.

In addition to client service, the firm prides itself on its civic contributions. Starting with its founder, Baker & Daniels attorneys have been well-known for their involvement in bi-partisan politics and government. Thomas A. Hendricks, one of the founders of the firm, was vice president of the United States in 1885. The firm's lawyers have represented Indiana in the Congress and the Indiana General Assembly, and others have served as governor of Indiana, and mayor of Indianapolis.

As a value-centered organization, Burke said the firm has an obligation to be involved in its home communities, not just by supporting the causes of other organizations, but also through its own initiatives. In the late 1990s, Baker & Daniels embarked on an ambitious initiative to help build neighborhood parks and green space. As of the summer of 2000, four parks or green space projects have been completed, and the firm has committed to continue to provide volunteers, financial support, private sector sponsorship coordination, and pro bono legal work to serve the community in the future.

As it braces for the challenges of a more global economy and greater competition for talent, Baker & Daniels' competitive strategy includes building the same kind of loyalty among legal professionals and support staff as it does with clients. In a profession known for its rigorous workload, the firm encourages employees to strike a balance between work and life. "If all we do is pursue our profession, we don't have much to offer our clients, our communities or our families," he said. The firm continually evaluates how it can shape the organization to encourage legal professionals and staff to come and stay.

A History of the Indianapolis Legal Profession

BINGHAM SUMMERS

MAKING PEOPLE FEEL AT EASE HAS DONE A LOT FOR INDIANA'S FIFTH-largest law firm. It has positioned the firm for significant growth in size within the next few years. It has attracted an expansive list of top state and regional companies as clients. And it has cultivated a loyal base of staff and attorneys who are responsible for the Bingham Summers Welsh and Spilman culture.

"Our people are very down to earth," said Nikki Schofield, a 26-year veteran who serves as the firm librarian. For most of her career, Schofield has enjoyed a ringside seat near what was once the center of activity in any law firm. "They aren't in the library as much any more, but this was the place to meet and strategize about important cases, before technology and conference rooms came along," she said. With her office just steps away from attorneys at work, she came to know what continues to make the firm unique: the ability of its people to balance personal, professional and financial goals.

As the firm librarian, Schofield is the keeper of the firm history, chronicled by decades of photographs and historical documents. Among them is a typewritten manuscript by founder James E. Bingham, which he authored at the age of 95. In it, Bingham describes his first work experience as a "printer's devil" for the Veedersburg News at the age of 12. There he was responsible for opening the offices every morning at 6 a.m., building the fires in the winter, carrying water and performing various duties which he called "slavery."

By the time he started college in 1907, Bingham had learned the printing trade, having worked his way up from printer, typesetter, press operator, and proof reader to reporter. His classes at Wabash College were scheduled in the mornings, allowing him to work for the Crawfordsville Journal during afternoons. After graduating from Wabash College in 1911, Bingham followed the custom of that era by studying law under an attorney, in this case, his uncle. He later served as an associate in the law firm of Henderson & Marshall until he founded his own firm in 1914. Bingham's father—a teacher, farmer and practicing attorney—joined the practice four years later and remained there until his death in 1947.

According to Bingham's manuscript, the early years of the practice were lean but they survived, aided by an excess of office space in Indianapolis. "Tenants could move from one building to another, rent-free for a few months, plus moving expenses," he wrote. "This was quite helpful for the first few years of scarce clients and scant fees, although it had no benefit to some building owners."

As the father-son law firm became more established, they recruited other attorneys to their practice. If one of their early recruits had found practicing law as interesting as writing music, the world might never have danced to the tunes of "Stardust" and countless other hits he composed. Bloomington native Howard "Hoagy" Carmichael, composer of "Ole Buttermilk Sky," "Georgia on My Mind," and "Lazy River," joined the firm in 1925 after receiving his law degree at Indiana University. Whether he resigned or was asked to leave is a matter of speculation, but two years later the piano-playing lawyer left the firm and followed a path that led to fame.

Later the firm added notable partners such as Claude M. Spilman, Jr. in 1945, Paul R. Summers in 1949 and Matthew Empson Welsh in 1965. Spilman was a young lawyer who received The Silver Star for his service in World War II before joining the firm. Paul Summers was a veteran of World War I, well-known for his community deeds and service to his alma mater, Indiana University. Prior to joining the firm, Mathew Welsh served as governor of Indiana from 1961 to 1965.

Today, Bingham Summers attorneys continue their forefathers' legacy of political involvement and community service.

One of their proudest community service achievements in recent history is a relationship with Howe Middle School which began in 1994 through Indianapolis Chamber of Commerce's Partners in Education program. Every week members of the firm visit the school to participate in reading and mentoring programs. Bingham Summers also hosts other special programs for students, including job fairs and tours of its offices, the state capitol building, and area courts. "When I hear a student say, 'I think I might want to be a lawyer someday,' it makes me realize how much we can do to raise the level of expectation they have for themselves," one employee said.

Bingham Summers' people-first attitude attracts a certain kind of lawyer—one who is just as interested in attending a daughter's soccer match or mentoring an at-risk child, as securing a new client or winning a big case. Their monthly breakfast meetings for partners are part-business, part-social events, where consensus is built for issues like the firm's ambitious growth initiatives which will significantly increase its 72-attorney count within the next few years. The execution of this plan will be based on the management and development of Bingham Summers' 18 practice groups, with emphasis on those that have the most strategic importance to clients or prospective clients.

In a business that's built on the individual reputations of its attorneys, part of Bingham Summers' growth strategy includes recruiting talented people who feel they have a stake in the firm. "The partners of this firm are the owners of this enterprise and their voice is important," said Michael D. Arnold, Chief Operating Officer. Bingham Summers' open-door policy and democratic management structure reflect the value it places on communication among all employees.

A commitment to practicing law with a personal touch has placed one stipulation on Bingham Summers' plans for bolstering its state and regional practice: growth must not come at the expense of client satisfaction. "We don't want to become big just for the sake of size," Arnold said. "Our goals are really about adding breadth and depth for our clients and recognizing that there is a layer of business out there that can benefit from the personal attention we give," he said.

A History of the Indianapolis Legal Profession 159

BARNES & THORNBURG

BARNES & THORNBURG IS THE PRODUCT OF A 1982 MERGER BETWEEN two well-established Indiana law firms, one in Indianapolis, the other in South Bend. The marriage of Indianapolis-based Barnes, Hickam, Pantzer & Boyd and South Bend-based Thornburg, McGill, Deahl, Harman, Carey & Murray formed one of the largest firms in the Midwest and led to its current national stature. Since that time, there have been mergers with other specialized firms whose focuses have ranged from intellectual property to labor and banking.

Barnes & Thornburg has offices in Indianapolis, Fort Wayne, South Bend, Elkhart, Chicago, and Washington, D.C., but clients are drawn more by what the firm offers than by where it's located. With more than 300 attorneys, the firm counsels clients in many areas including business, creditors' rights, environmental law, estate planning and administration, governmental services and finance, healthcare, intellectual property, international, labor and employment, litigation, public utilities, real estate, securities, taxation, and transportation. Its clients range from individuals and small businesses to multinational corporations. "When we opened an office in Chicago about five years ago and competed there successfully, it became evident that this was no longer an Indiana law firm," said Don Knebel, partner. "If you look at our client list now, you'll find a number of clients with Silicon Valley addresses; geographic boundaries have virtually disappeared."

The firm's willingness to think beyond state boundaries and its early participation in e-commerce has prepared Barnes & Thornburg for the Internet's expanding role in business. Its Business and Technology practice group was formed specifically to help clients develop their virtual worlds. With a base of technologically-savvy clients scattered across the globe, Barnes & Thornburg must continually leverage technology to be responsive. Video conferencing, for example, has become an integral part of how the firm practices law. "If we have a client that has a specific issue and our best experts on that issue are in different offices, video conferencing allows us to bring those people together without leaving their offices," Knebel said. "The client still meets the people who are doing its work, without feeling like it's being shipped off to some unknown outpost."

This modern firm retains evidence of its heritage. Barnes & Thornburg's conference rooms chronicle the firm's corporate citizenship in the communities it occupies. The walls are lined with memorabilia from the cultural and human service organizations the firm has supported over the years. "We place a lot of importance on community life and look for projects which will involve our lawyers and staff," said Wayne Kreuscher, a partner in the Indianapolis office. He joined the firm in 1974, in part because of the individual commitment to community service among the firm's attorneys. "The causes we've supported make our cities better places to live and they also attract diverse, dynamic people who can enrich our communities," Kreuscher said.

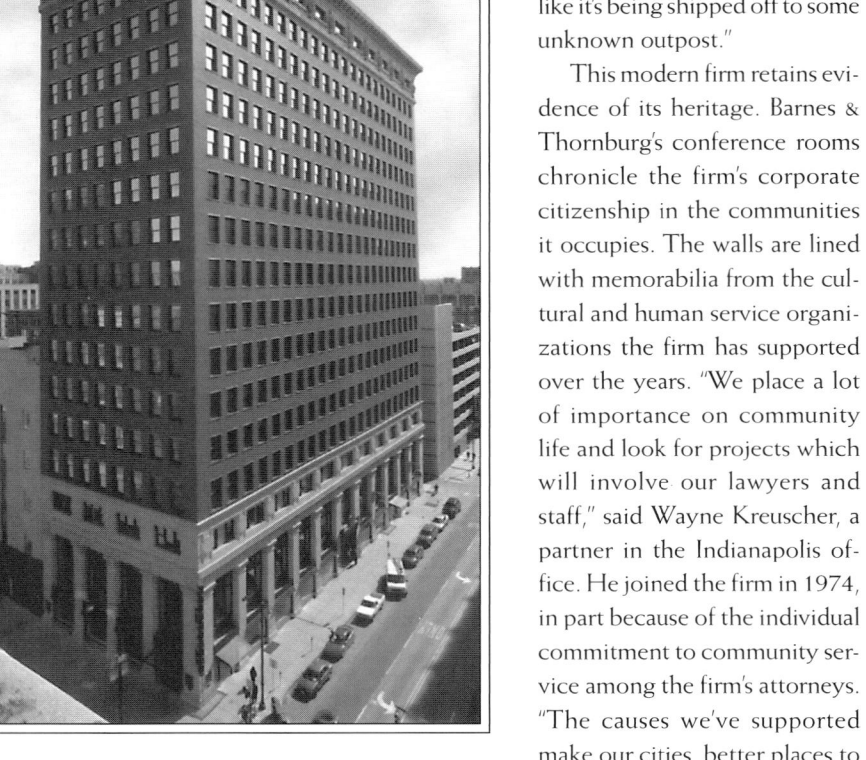

Having been ranked as one of America's greatest places to practice law, Barnes & Thornburg also concentrates on being a model employer. The firm helps develop its associates by giving them substantial responsibilities and the ability to determine their own destiny. "In my first year, I tried a jury trial and argued an appeal in the Seventh Circuit," one attorney said. "You won't find that very often at law firms the size of Barnes & Thornburg."

As it looks to future growth, the firm remains committed to its foundation: Tradition. History. Excellence.

BOSE McKINNEY & EVANS LLP

BOSE MCKINNEY & EVANS LLP OFFERS THE STRENGTH OF 21 PRACTICE groups and a corporate culture that values congeniality, cooperation and open communication.

Lewis Bose founded the firm, originally named Cook Bose & Buchanan, in the 1950s. Bill Evans joined the firm in 1957 and Robert McKinney in 1963. In 1971, the firm became known as Bose McKinney & Evans. Today, with more than 90 associates and partners, Bose McKinney & Evans has grown to what partner Joe Russell likes to describe as a "large small firm."

"Bose McKinney & Evans dispels the myth that as a law firm grows, its atmosphere becomes formal and cold. There's no hierarchy here, no internal competition, but rather a feeling of cooperation and mutual assistance. To more effectively serve our clients, we often form work teams with attorneys from different practice groups," Russell said.

The firm has played an active role in key developments in the city of Indianapolis and the state of Indiana. Beginning in the 1950s, Lewis Bose and Bill Evans were instrumental in drafting most of the major legislation relating to school issues, including school consolidation, school finance and student due process. Education law remains a strong practice group to this day, with Bose McKinney & Evans representing two-thirds of the school corporations in Indiana. Members of the firm also helped draft the plan that created Unigov, which consolidated Indianapolis and Marion County in the 1970s, and assisted the then-Baltimore Colts in moving to Indianapolis in the early 1980s.

One of the keys to the growth of Bose McKinney & Evans is its commitment to serving the changing needs of clients. This is especially true in the area of technology.

"As Indiana works to attract high-tech business, the businesses need to know that they can get the high-tech support they need. That includes legal service. The core needs of a high-tech firm related to compensation strategy or growth strategy may be different from the needs of a more traditional client.

"High-tech businesses have options for legal services in the Midwest, not just on the East Coast or the Silicon Valley. We can provide them with high quality, cutting-edge legal service in their own backyard," said Robert Kassing, managing partner.

Firms that are not necessarily categorized as "high-tech" also find that technology is changing the way they do business.

"Financial institutions, for example, have many high-tech issues to consider, including issues related to the Internet and e-commerce. We explain the pros and cons of the situations our clients face so that they can make informed decisions," Kassing said.

The three name partners of Bose McKinney & Evans LLP in Indianapolis, Indiana, left to right, William Evans, Lewis Bose, and Robert McKinney.

Some key practice groups at the firm include business services (including equity formation, business finance, and M&A transactions), employment law, taxation, financial institutions, intellectual property, real estate and litigation. Bose McKinney & Evans also has one of the largest utility law practices in the state. The firm's client list includes Duke-Weeks Realty Corporation, Emmis Communications Corporation, First Indiana Bank, MCI Worldcom, USX and WebAssured.com.

Bose McKinney & Evans maintains an active presence in city, state and national bar associations. The firm encourages employees to perform volunteer work and serve on the boards of directors for not-for-profit organizations, churches and schools. In addition, a scholarship in the name of founder Bill Evans is awarded each year to an Indiana special education student who is planning to attend a university, college or trade school in the state.

"This is such a satisfying and supportive place to work that we retain our attorneys extremely well. We are also able to devote more time and energy to serving our clients and finding new and better ways to carry forward our business," Russell said.

CAMPBELL KYLE PROFFITT

Campbell Kyle Proffitt has provided legal services to clients in central Indiana since 1915. Founded by Cassius M. Gentry and Frank S. Campbell, the firm has changed names throughout the decades but its approach to the practice of law has remained constant. For more than 75 yeas the firm has been blending traditional attitudes and contemporary methods with the objective of providing high quality legal services to every client.

A general practice firm from the beginning, Campbell Kyle Proffitt has many areas of specialty through its individual lawyers. The firm serves individuals, partnerships, corporations and various municipal and other public entities.

Colorful clients and cases have passed through the firm. In 1940 the firm was hired by former Klu Klux Klan grand dragon D.C. Stephenson, who was serving a life sentence in the Indiana State Prison in Michigan City. Having exhausted all available appeals, Stephenson hired the firm to prepare and present a petition for a new trial based on newly discovered evidence. In the end, the firm's attorneys spent most of a year building a case only to be relieved the morning they were to present the case. Stephenson claimed that he had made an arrangement with the governor for a pardon.

Campbell Kyle Proffitt's impact on the community can be seen in businesses ranging from the development of Riverview Hospital to the explosive growth of the Carmel-Clay and Hamilton Southeastern school districts. Frank S. Campbell, serving as Hamilton County attorney, worked in conjunction with his son and other community leaders to formulate a plan to move the Hamilton County Hospital, which was renamed Riverview Hospital. In the 1970s the firm represented the Carmel-Clay and Hamilton Southeastern School Districts to counter court-ordered busing of students across county lines to achieve desegregation.

In addition to serving its clients, another constant with the firm is its commitment to serving the community. Lawyers with the firm can be found supporting growth and betterment of the community across Hamilton County. Campbell Kyle Proffitt has produced five judges to the bench in Hamilton County—more than any other firm. The firm also encourages involvement with the Bar Association. All members of the firm are members of both the Hamilton County and Indiana State Bar Association. Campbell Kyle Proffitt has furnished two presidents of the Indiana Bar Association in 14 years, Frank W. Campbell and John Proffitt. Many other lawyers in the firm chair various segments of the Bar Association and have served on the Board of Governors. Frank W. Campbell and John Proffitt are the only lawyers in the county to be admitted as American College of Trial Lawyers Fellows. John Proffitt and Debbie Farmer are the only lawyers in the county to be recognized as American Academy of Matrimonial Lawyers Fellows.

Due to the continued growth in Hamilton County, Campbell Kyle Proffitt believes expansion of its firm must continue to happen. As in the past, expansion of the firm is done with great care and always with the purpose in mind of improving client services rather than merely serving more clients.

CONOUR DOEHRMAN

While there are dozens of well-respected firms handling personal injury cases, very few can carve out a niche in the area.

Conour Doehrman was founded in 1988 by William Conour and Thomas Doehrman to offer dependable and affordable legal representation to the injured. But as their reputation for winning arguments and favorable settlements for their clients grew, Conour Doehrman decided to focus its practice on serious injury cases.

Today, nearly all of their cases are referred to them by other attorneys, and deal almost exclusively with brain injury and serious bodily injury suffered on construction sites.

"When Bill and I got together, we were both handling general personal injury cases," Doehrman recalled. "The people who are hurt the worst usually need the most help, so there is something rewarding about winning those types of cases.

The most gratifying thing for me is getting these people the kind of treatment they need to sustain them for the rest of their life."

The firm is not only committed to representing its clients but to help directing the law, when possible. As a result, dozens of the firm's cases have risen through the appellate ranks.

"When we see issues that we think will advance the law toward compensation of the injured, we've taken those cases," Conour explained.

An illustration of this practice comes from what Conour called one of the firm's most rewarding actions, which made a significant impact on the law.

Conour represented a client injured by a drunk driver and won compensatory and punitive damages against the tavern that supplied the alcohol to the drunk driver. The Indiana Court of Appeals reversed the decision claiming the law does not allow the action since it was made under a common law claim as a "dramshop action."

The Indiana Supreme Court disagreed with the appellate court and upheld the lower court ruling. The punitive damage from the case, *Picadilli vs. Colvin*, was the largest ever affirmed in Indiana at the time.

Conour and Doehrman agree their practice will continue to evolve and challenge them, but do not see the need to add more lawyers or support staff.

"We benefit greatly from staying in a practice area," Conour said. "When a case involving a serious construction site injury lands on the desk of a lawyer doing general injury cases they usually cannot afford the time to learn the complex case law, government regulations and the intricacies that surround it."

In order to maintain their reputation in the bar, firm lawyers routinely teach and attend Continuing Legal Education courses. Conour is actually an OSHA-authorized safety instructor, a designation he earned in order to better understand the legal realm in which he operates.

He is a member of the city, Indiana State, and American Bar Associations. He has been a member of the Indiana Trial Lawyers Association Board of Directors since 1993. Certified as a civil trial attorney by the American Board of Trial Advocates, Conour served on the organization's National Board of Directors and was president of the Indiana Chapter. He is President of the Sagamore American Inn of Court and is currently nominated to serve on the National Inns of Court Board of Directors. Conour is a member of the Indianapolis Law Club and a Distinguished Fellow with the Indianapolis Bar Foundation and the Roscoe Pound Foundation.

Much of Doehrman's charitable work reflects his professional interests. He has served on the board of the Brain Injury Association of Indiana for 16 years and will serve as its chairman in 2001 and 2002. He also serves on the executive committee of the Traumatic Brain Injury Litigation Group of the American Trial Lawyers Association.

He is certified as a Civil Trial Specialist by the National Board of Trial Advocacy and has been a member of the Indiana Trial Lawyers Association Board of Directors since 1989 and is a member of the Indianapolis, Indiana State and American Bar Associations. He also is a member of the Association of Trial Lawyers of America, the Indianapolis Law Club and is a Distinguished Fellow of the Indianapolis Bar Foundation.

COOTS, HENKE & WHEELER

FOUNDED IN 1978 BY E. DAVIS COOTS AND STEVEN H. HENKE, Coots, Henke & Wheeler is an established law firm serving the Indianapolis, Carmel and Hamilton County areas. James K. Wheeler joined the firm two years later to help serve the growing Carmel community. Together these founding partners made a commitment to maintain a firm that was small enough to develop personal relationships with its clients, yet comprehensive enough to handle complex litigation matters. Through the years the firm has served a range of clients, from major established corporations planning for long-term growth, to individuals hoping to purchase a new home. Every client is served with the same commitment—achieving successful outcomes while developing a strong attorney-client relationship.

Today, Coots, Henke & Wheeler has grown to twelve lawyers. The firm offers a full range of legal services for both businesses and individuals including corporate commercial and business law, civil and criminal litigation, real estate, estate planning and family law. Coots, Henke & Wheeler is dedicated to developing innovative ways to provide cost-effective, quality solutions to legal issues and conflicts for both individuals and businesses. The firm has a proven record of powerful litigators who are capable of handling complex litigation matters. Several members, including two of the founders, have expanded the firm's practice by providing legal services as Certified Mediators. The firm also has an experienced Registered Nurse on staff, which serves as a valuable asset in evaluating medical issues in civil litigation.

Coots, Henke & Wheeler encourages members of the firm to become active in the Bar Associations serving their areas of practice. All lawyers are active within the community and participate in professional events. Every member of the firm is a member of the Indianapolis, Hamilton County, Indiana State, and American Bar Associations. Several are involved with a variety of other associations both within the legal field and within the community. Members of the firm have served on the Board of Directors of the Indianapolis Bar Association as well as the Board of Managers, served on the American Board of Trial Advocates, the Defense Trial Counsel of Indiana, and the Defense Research Institute. Firm members can be seen serving their community through the local Chamber of Commerce, the Planning Commission, and many nonprofit organizations.

While Coots, Henke & Wheeler has witnessed significant changes in how the legal profession delivers its services, the firm anticipates and is posed to meet the increasing need for legal service, in the Indianapolis, Carmel and Hamilton County areas as the community continues to develop and prosper. The firm remains committed to continuously updating its areas of practice to reflect the contemporary needs of its clients. Coots, Henke & Wheeler is committed to developing and strengthening its client-attorney relationships. The firm prides itself on being a true advocate for its clients. Acting as both a business partner and consultant for those they serve has been a primary focus for Coots, Henke & Wheeler, and is one that will continue well into the future.

DALE & EKE

Founded by William J. Dale, Jr., and Joseph W. Eke in September, 1978, the firm has grown to include seven lawyers in 2001. The firm began with an idea of developing a smaller-sized firm providing one-on-one service to its clients. The firm has remained true to its mission throughout its more than 20-year practice.

Dale & Eke provides a broad spectrum of legal services that include corporate, tax, estate planning, bankruptcy, probate, real estate and civil and business litigation, with emphasis on providing legal services to small and medium-size closely held businesses and professional corporations. It is one of the few smaller firms in the city that has managed to hold its size and focus throughout the years. Dale & Eke is proud to have a long-standing client list. A majority of the firm's new clients are referred from existing clients and other professionals.

The businesses represented by Dale & Eke have shaped the business world within Indianapolis. The firm has played a major role in several business mergers and consolidations that, in turn, have helped shape the community. Such mergers and consolidations have included large health care organizations as well as a major Indianapolis company involved in the satellite equipment and programming business.

Dale & Eke is proud of the work it provides to its clients and the impact it makes on the city of Indianapolis. The firm plans to continue its practice of remaining true to its size and focus in the years to come. It is proud of the lawyers in its firm today. Principal members of the firm include:

William J. Dale, Jr., is both an attorney and certified public accountant. He is a member of the American, Indiana, and Indianapolis Bar Associations, as well as a Fellow of the American College of Trust and Estate Counsel and of the American College of Tax Counsel. He is also a distinguished fellow of the Indianapolis Bar Association. He is an adjunct professor of law at the Indiana University School of Law in Indianapolis. Mr. Dale is the Indiana practice consultant for Matthew Bender's Midwest Transaction Guide, a member of the Board of Reviewers and a contributing author to Matthew Bender's Indiana Estate Planning and Probate Practice.

Joseph W. Eke is both an attorney and certified public accountant. He is a member of the American, Indiana and Indianapolis Bar Associations and works extensively in the areas of corporations, taxation, health care law, employee benefits including retirement plans, estate planning, corporate compliance and health care fraud and abuse.

Deborah J. Caruso focuses her legal work in the areas of bankruptcy, creditors' rights, and commercial and business litigation. She has been with Dale & Eke since 1980 and is a member of the American, Indiana, and Indianapolis Bar Associations, as well as the Association of Trial Lawyers and the National Association of Bankruptcy Trustees. She is also a distinguished fellow with the Indianapolis Bar Association. Ms. Caruso was appointed to the panel of Chapter 7 Trustees in 1997. She was General Chair of the Indiana State Bar Association's Annual Meeting for 2000 and is the President of the Bankruptcy and Creditors Rights Section. Ms. Caruso is a contributing author to Matthew Bender's Civil Trial Guide.

BRATTAIN & MINNIX

BRUCE D. BRATTAIN, A FOUNDING partner of four-member firm Brattain & Minnix, is no stranger to conflict. In fact he was prepared to do battle in the courtroom in an arena far less forgiving than a court of law: the military.

Brattain entered law school a decorated veteran; he earned a Distinguished Flying Cross; Army Commendation Medal and the Vietnamese Cross of Gallantry. Perhaps that's why opposing counsel from outfits 50 times larger do not intimidate the firm.

"We take pride in the fact that while we can't match a big firm in volume of cases, we can match a big firm in any case," Brattain said. "We are a small firm intentionally and our focus is all litigation."

Technological advances over the last seven years have helped Brattain and co-founder Larry C. Minnix serve clients better because so much information is at their fingertips.

"All of our briefs are on a database so I can find what we've done on prior cases even though I can't recall the case or the client."

The lawyers at Brattain & Minnix maintain a unique caseload, where at any one time they may handle a civil or criminal case for a plaintiff or a defendant instead of sticking to one side or the other.

"A trial is a trial and although the burden of proof between civil and criminal cases is different, there are a lot of similarities," Brattain said. "The way you interrogate eyewitnesses is the same; the way you analyze the issues is the same and the way you present the evidence is the same."

While Brattain does not want to increase the size of the firm or expand its practice area, he does eagerly anticipate new technology that will help level the playing field even more between larger firms and small firms. But ultimately, he explains, a successful argument comes down to ancient lawyering abilities.

"They can give you a fancier bike to ride, but you still have to know how to pedal," Brattain said. "Jurors won't decide in your favor just because you have a more slick presentation, ultimately you must convince them to agree with you rather than the other guy."

CLINE FARRELL CHRISTIE LEE & CARESS

CLINE FARRELL CHRISTIE LEE & CARESS IS STOCKED WITH VETERANS of the Indianapolis plaintiff's bar. Each of the partners has served with many other personal injury attorneys in town and has handled many challenging cases. But this firm is different.

"When we prepare a case, we probably spend as much time at the medical library as we do the law library," Kevin Farrell said.

Partners Lee Christie, Lance Cline, Kathy Lee and Tim Caress round out an eight-year-old firm that has become an innovative specialist in representing people injured from auto accidents, medical malpractice and defective products.

Because determining the true financial impact of an injury requires familiarity with medical issues as well as the law, the firm's lawyers spend more time than many of their peers preparing for trial.

In order to accomplish this task, the firm has added medical expertise that rivals the much larger firms. Partner Kathy Lee is not only a seasoned trial lawyer, but also a registered nurse who worked extensively in area hospitals prior to law school. Additional expertise is provided by a full-time registered nurse paralegal who spends much of her time reviewing medical charts, consulting with physicians, and reviewing medical literature to assist the attorneys in properly understanding and presenting complicated medical issues in both injury and medical malpractice cases.

Lee Christie is well known to area attorneys and insurance companies. His assistance has been sought in over 2,000 personal injury mediations.

Lance Cline is widely regarded as one of the most effective plaintiffs attorneys having successfully concluded over 200 medical malpractice claims as well as hundreds of personal injury claims. He has been listed in *The Best Lawyers in America* since 1995.

The firm requires continuing professional development of all partners including its two associates, and all partners are frequent speakers at and attendees of continuing legal education seminars. Farell has served as an instructor at the Indiana Trial Academy since 1997 and, along with Cline, was selected as one of Indianapolis' best trial attorneys by area peers.

Caress, the newest partner, has been a contributing author to *The Indiana Lawyer*, and has brought in considerable knowledge of products liability law to a firm that handles cases in state and federal courts in Indiana, as well as other states.

The firm has handled cases that received widespread publicity as well as refining and creating new areas of Indiana law.

DOYLE, WRIGHT & DEAN-WEBSTER, LLP

Rick D. Doyle, Robert W. Wright and Deanna A. Dean-Webster joined forces January 1, 2000 to form Doyle, Wright & Dean-Webster, LLP in Greenwood, Indiana. The creation of that firm reunited three friends. Doyle and Wright are law school friends who clerked together at Locke Reynolds, LLP. Doyle subsequently worked as an associate at Bingham Summers Welsh & Spilman, LLP with Dean-Webster, who left that firm to join Locke Reynolds in 1994. Doyle started his own practice in Greenwood in 1994, and was joined by Wright in 1999 and by Dean-Webster in 2000.

Doyle, Wright & Dean-Webster, LLP focuses its practice on litigation, including insurance defense, direct corporate defense and representation of individuals in both state and federal court. The firm also represents clients in utility matters before the Indiana Utility Regulatory Commission. The three attorneys complement each other with their individual experiences: Doyle in handling criminal matters, having served as a special prosecutor and a public defender; Wright in handling insurance coverage and appellate matters; and Dean-Webster in defense litigation and handling family law matters.

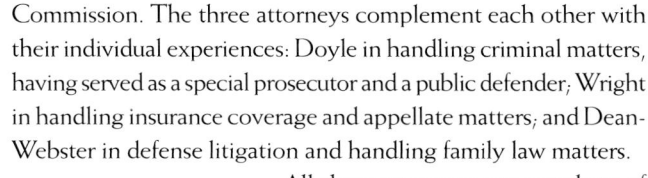

All three attorneys are members of the Johnson County, Indianapolis and Indiana State Bar Associations. Doyle also serves on the Energy Sub-Committee of the Utility Law Section of the Indiana State Bar Association. Wright is active in the Defense Trial Counsel of Indiana, where he has served as chair of the Insurance Coverage Section and is a member of the Defense Research Institute. Dean-Webster has lectured on various issues of law, including trial tactics, depositions, expert witnesses and case law updates.

FINDLING GARAU GERMANO & PENNINGTON, P.C.

Since its inception in 1997, Findling Garau Germano & Pennington, P.C. has rapidly established itself as one of the leading plaintiff's litigation practices in Indianapolis. Attorneys from the firm have earned inclusion in the Bar Register of Preeminent Lawyers and Best Lawyers Consumer Guide.

The firm was formed in 1997 when Mary Findling, Jerry Garau, Barbara Germano, Deborah Pennington, and Jennifer Stephens Love decided to form their own firm after having worked together for a number of years. Marshall Hanley joined the original members of the firm in 1999.

The firm represents individuals injured by medical negligence, automobile accidents, or unfair business practices. The firm's practice is devoted exclusively to litigation on behalf of plaintiffs.

The firm is best known for its work in the medical malpractice field and has pursued cases that changed the landscape of Indiana medical malpractice law. In *Martin v. Richey*, Mary Findling challenged the Indiana Medical Malpractice Act's occurrence-based statute of limitations.

In that case, the firm's client discovered that her physician had negligently failed to diagnose her breast cancer three years earlier. Because the malpractice had occurred more than two years before the client's discovery of the malpractice, the claim was barred under the terms of the malpractice statute. Findling argued that such a result violated the terms of Indiana's Constitution, and in 1999, the Indiana Supreme Court agreed. For her efforts in this case, Ms. Findling was named Trial Lawyer of the Year by the Indiana Trial Lawyers Association.

The firm also successfully litigated the first Indiana appellate case upholding the availability of punitive damages under Indiana's Medical Malpractice Act. Attorneys from the firm have devoted their time and talents to author numerous amicus curiae briefs filed on behalf of the Indiana Trial Lawyers Association.

The firm prides itself on providing effective advocacy for individuals in need. "Most of our clients have been placed in difficult circumstances and are facing an uphill struggle," said Deborah Pennington. "We try to level the playing field."

DANN PECAR NEWMAN & KLEIMAN, PC

As one of the oldest full-service law firms in Indianapolis, Dann Pecar Newman & Kleiman's roots trace back to 1911 when Jackiel Joseph began practice. As his practice grew, others joined his ranks, including Theodore Dann, who became his partner. It is Dann the firm credits with establishing many of its philosophies and practices still being modeled today. He established a solid foundation for the firm that each generation has strived to maintain as they serve clients from a local, national & international client base.

Dann joined the firm in 1931, with degrees from Harvard University and Indiana University. He believed that bigger wasn't necessarily better and that just because a firm is smaller didn't mean it couldn't offer the same—or more—than its larger-sized competitors. That grounded belief has guided the firm throughout the years. The size of the firm allows them to develop long-term relationships with clients, offering specialized services and counsel in large, and often complex, transactions.

Philip Pecar and Norman Newman began practicing at the firm in 1956 and 1960, respectively, and established themselves as experts in the shopping center industry. Today, Dann Pecar Newman & Kleiman has a well-deserved reputation as a premier real estate firm in the country. It houses one of the largest real estate practices in Indiana and has been involved in a number of firsts, including the development of the Mall of America, the largest and most-unique shopping center in the United States. Dann Pecar has been involved in a number of real estate projects including shopping centers, industrial parks, office buildings, apartment projects and residential subdivisions. The firm provides counsel in all phases of a real estate project: land acquisitions, zoning, environmental compliance, financing and construction.

Posed in front of a portrait of Theodore Dann are, left to right, Mark R. Waterfill, Jon B. Abels, Melvin R. Daniel, David H. Kleiman, Michael J. Gabovitch, Norman R. Newman, James H. Schwarz, and Jeffrey A. Abrams.

David Kleiman became a shareholder of the firm after a merger in 1974 and brought tremendous skill and experience in bankruptcy and reorganization to the firm. He is respected as one of the top bankruptcy attorneys in the country, having worked on many national cases. The firm has represented lenders, debtors and other parties in many of the larger reorganization cases in Indiana during the past 30 years.

Now, more than 90 years since its founding, the firm consists of nearly 30 attorneys and nine major practice areas:
- Real Estate, Construction and Environmental Law
- Corporate, Partnership and Venture Law
- Commercial, Reorganization and Bankruptcy
- Governmental Law and Finance
- Trial Practice and Litigation
- Employment Law
- Technology
- Estate Planning, Probate and Taxation

Dann Pecar's lawyers pride themselves on being responsive to clients and delivering service better than their competitors. They understand that time is of the essence, particularly in real estate and bankruptcy transactions. Their efficiency, responsiveness and high-level of service is evident with the long-standing clients they have maintained. In addition, their reputation as "attorneys that deliver" has involved them in several major city projects, including Circle Centre, the revitalization of downtown, White River State Park, the downtown canal development, the bonds for Victory Field and the Convention Center, and privatization of the Indianapolis International Airport and municipal golf courses.

As Dann Pecar Newman & Kleiman looks to the future, one thing is certain: They will continue to work to satisfy the needs of their clients, believing that, "You take care of business and business will take care of you."

FEIWELL & HANNOY, P.C.

Having spent 22 years with another Indianapolis law firm, Murray J. Feiwell opened his own law office, Feiwell & Associates, in April of 1986. Born in South Bend, he began practicing law in Indianapolis in 1963 after he graduated from the University of Michigan and its Law School. In 1988, Union City native Douglas J. Hannoy, a graduate of Indiana University and its Law School and a lecturer and author of *Indiana Foreclosure and Repossession*, joined him. This union led to the partnership of Feiwell & Hannoy, P.C.

The firm has concentrated on being a boutique or niche firm. They focus on the following areas:

- Real estate and foreclosure
- Bankruptcy
- Creditors' rights
- General civil practices
- General business
- Commercial law

Feiwell & Hannoy has extensive experience in the real estate field and, in particular, the handling of residential and commercial mortgage foreclosures in Indiana. The U.S. Department of Housing and Urban Development approve them to act as foreclosure commissioner in Indiana.

Feiwell & Hannoy credits its growth to the sophisticated use of information technology systems as well as to the quality of work, quick service, at minimal expense as possible, and the hands-on treatment they provide for their clients. Each employee has his/her own email account and is able to communicate to clients instantly. With the tailor-made case management program, Feiwell & Hannoy can provide each client with detailed status of its files. The Firm also uses state of the art technology to access and update clients within their own websites. By using these types of communication, each client is kept well-informed.

Entering the 21st century, Feiwell & Hannoy will continue to serve each client's need in the most efficient, expedient way possible. The Firm looks forward to the new challenges that demonstrate their exceptional service and system capabilities.

Several of the attorneys in the Firm are presenters of seminars and have written many articles for various publications. They are actively involved in committees of the Indianapolis Bar Association. Douglas Hannoy is a frequent presenter on foreclosures and bankruptcies in the State of Indiana and is a member of the Attorney Grievance Committee. Both he and Murray Feiwell are members of the Commercial Law League and American Bankruptcy Institute. Michael Feiwell has written articles on the Fair Debt Consumer Practices Act (FDCPA). David Jurkiewicz has led seminars on bankruptcy actions and Susan Woolley has conducted a seminar on the Veterans Administration and foreclosure. All of the attorneys in the Firm are members of the Indiana and Indianapolis Bar Associations.

Internally, the firm works hard to provide a working environment that is conducive to keeping employees for a long time. Such things as saying hello and taking a personal interest in employees' families have developed an atmosphere at Feiwell & Hannoy that is family-like itself. "There's more to it than paying an employee," says Feiwell.

In the early days, Feiwell & Hannoy had a minimum staff of 4 or 5 employees. Today with its ever-expanding staff approaching 100, the practice is national in scope, serving local and national companies with business interests in Indiana.

"When I look at how our firm has expanded over the last fifteen years, I am extremely proud of the services and dedication to excellence that our firm has shown," said Feiwell.

FOLEY & POOL, LLP

When Donald F. Foley and Douglas W. Pool joined forces to form Foley & Pool in 1991, they were combining over 40 years of business law expertise. The firm's core clients have remained clients of the firm for decades.

Foley & Pool takes pride in providing expert legal advice for its clients at a reasonable cost. The firm's business expertise and flexibility continues to attract new business and start up clients.

"We try to enable our clients to accomplish their goals legally," Foley said. "We've represented some of the same clients for over 20 years and I believe that tells an important story."

Any lawyer or business professional will tell you that it is difficult to maintain a long-term professional relationship with clients, yet Foley & Pool have been able maintain those relationships, because a very personal interest is taken in each clients' problems.

Clients demand what the firm provides: responsive, effective and reasonably priced legal services. In addition, Foley & Pool makes it a priority to deliver on the client's schedule.

"We guide our business clients through the maze of governmental regulations that are such a burden in today's business environment," Foley said. "When you represent Indiana businesses and business owners, you may be helping them start up a business, limit liability or even take care of their estate planning at the same time; it all fits together."

While the firm handles a wide range of business matters for a diverse group of clients, many of its clients fall into the areas of construction (both general and subcontractor groups) solid waste collection, recycling and landfilling, environmental and warehousing.

The firm also provides legislative lobbying service for many of its clients. In 1999, the firm worked on legislation that extended the time for mechanic's liens to be filed for subcontractors, gave subcontractors more payment protection and provided other benefits to them. The legislation also abolished no lien contracts for commercial and industrial projects, which has been very beneficial to many in the construction industry.

"Frequently we represent contractors when their projects become problematic with disputes, but we also work with them to impact changes in the law and the future of their industry," Pool said.

The firm has also helped the public warehousing industry with legislative issues over the years. In 1999 the firm provided assistance in pushing for changes in inventory tax legislation and improving regulations for the industry.

"There are some firms where there are multiple departments and a multitude of lawyers handling the same matters Don and I handle," Pool said. "We stay current in many areas so that when we're advising clients we can guide them as to how a specific issues may relate to many different areas within their business."

Foley & Pool plan to increase the number of lawyers within the firm over the next few years as they anticipate new clients will be added to their already impressive client base.

Don Foley (seated) and Douglas Pool joined forces to form Foley & Pool in 1991.

FRANK & KRAFT, P.C.

When they opened their doors in 1990, Frank & Kraft decided to take a different approach to the practice of law, particularly within the area of estate planning. Their approach was personal and completely geared toward the client. "We are dealing with more than business—we're dealing with people," says Marvin J. Frank, senior principal. "We ask instead of tell. We want to know their goals—what they want to achieve."

That approach has helped Frank & Kraft become a leading estate planning firm in Indiana. For more than a decade, they have helped families plan, protect and preserve their wealth. In addition to estate planning, the firm provides services in the areas of probate, tax, corporate and business law.

Frank & Kraft offers services that are efficient, helpful and attentive to every detail. Above all, they pride themselves in taking the mystery out of the law. "We discuss opportunities and methods of accomplishing them in a straightforward manner. We make sure clients know exactly what to expect at every step of the process," says Paul A. Kraft, administrative principal. "A lot of the time, particularly with estate planning, people know they should do something, yet they are unsure of their options. We make it clear and understandable."

In one of their many efforts to reach out and educate people, Frank & Kraft formed the Indiana Network of Estate Planning Professionals in 1993. The organization is comprised of accountants, insurance and financial planning professionals. They offer articles, continuing education classes, roundtable discussions and a web site featuring specialized cases and information.

Marv Frank graduated from Indiana University with a bachelor's degree in Accounting in 1962, and while working as a CPA, he attained his Juris Doctor degree in 1966 from Indiana University. Paul Kraft graduated from Indiana University with a bachelor's degree in Accounting in 1983, and he completed his Juris Doctor at Indiana University in 1986.

Today, Frank & Kraft spend a great deal of time presenting public and private seminars on a wide variety of tax and estate planning topics. They also have authored various articles on estate planning and are contributing authors of *LEGACY: Plan, Protect, and Preserve Your Estate—Practical Answers from America's Foremost Estate Planning Attorneys*. They are charter members of the American Academy of Estate Planning Attorneys and founding members of the National Network of Estate Planning Attorneys.

Like the founding partners, most of the firm's attorneys have significant experience in business matters to complement their backgrounds. This experience allows them to consistently meet the ever-changing needs of clients, whether through a simple document or a complex merger.

Referrals from clients have propelled continued growth in the past decade. Frank & Kraft predicts that client demand will dictate future growth.

HACKMAN HULETT & CRACRAFT, LLP

IT MUST HAVE TAKEN GUTS TO OPEN A LAW FIRM IN 1929, THE YEAR the U.S. stock market crashed, triggering a worldwide economic depression. Despite adverse conditions, an eminent Indianapolis public utility attorney, William Thompson, and his partners Albert Rabb and Thomas Stevenson forged ahead to start their own practice, known today as Hackman Hulett & Cracraft, LLP.

Though they now practice law in history's most prosperous era, the firm's 13 attorneys greet the complexity of the future with the same sense of solidarity that helped their founders weather the past. Even through times of radical change, Hackman Hulett & Cracraft is sticking with what it does best.

"Our signature is quality and personal attention," said Bob Hulett, who joined the firm in 1969, the day after he received his law degree from Indiana University. "Our clients count on those characteristics, so we're convinced that remaining a comfortable size is still very important to our clients and viable for us."

The firm serves a broad range of clients, including local and regional utilities, real estate companies and other corporate and individual clients that have been with the firm for decades. Hackman Hulett & Cracraft's practice is focused mainly on business organizations and transactions; administrative and legislative relations; litigation; and all phases of utility practice. They also represent individuals in such matters as estate planning and administration, charitable giving and guardianships.

As a business-oriented practice, the firm's attorneys are bright, flexible people, all of whom graduated near the top of their class. "We can't be all things to all people, but to succeed in a small practice, we all have to be generalists to some extent," Hulett said. "I think that makes practicing law more interesting and I think it makes us better attorneys."

Because the firm's clients are not served exclusively by an individual attorney, Hackman Hulett & Cracraft places a high value on interpersonal skills that help the attorneys work together in a meaningful way on behalf of clients. Like most of the firm's decisions, adding a new person to the mix is a careful choice, based on the person's ability to become an immediate contributor to the firm and its clients. Generally, recruits are interviewed by every attorney in the firm and hired only by consensus.

Having a clear sense of purpose has allowed Hackman Hulett & Cracraft to bypass an activity that's become a hallmark of most modern organizations: elaborate strategy sessions to develop future business plans. Their interest in delivering quality products at a reasonable cost has easily classified such meetings as a process that adds little value to their clients. "We do our work well and respond quickly," said Vicki Anderson, a 15-year veteran of the firm. "We have clients who love walking down our halls and saying hello to each of us. They enjoy knowing they are important to us. We are able to maintain an atmosphere of quality and stability in a changing environment, and our clients are drawn to that."

HARRISON AND MOBERLY

AFTER 50 YEARS AS A VENERABLE INDIANAPOLIS LAW FIRM, Harrison & Moberly is back where it started: serving the legal needs of medium-sized businesses.

But as any of the firm's 24 lawyers will tell you, the firm has evolved into a nimble, specialized outfit. It is focused on aggressively expanding its practice areas, which means its lawyer ranks will grow as well.

James Harrison, a founding partner, has been at the helm of much of this journey and although he is no longer steering the ship himself, managing partners rely heavily on his wisdom.

"We always served business needs in some way but never as thoroughly as we do today," Harrison recalled.

Warren Moberly, who founded the firm with Harrison, helped create the Marion County Health and Hospital Corporation and then served as its legal counsel for 17 years while at the firm. The trucking industry, a very dominant business force in Indiana in the 50s and 60s, attracted much of the firm's attention up until the mid-1980s. The firm also developed a well-respected insurance defense practice over time.

"At one point we were so heavily in insurance defense, it didn't seem as if we did much of anything else," Harrison said.

But as federal and state government regulations on businesses expanded over the last 20 years, so too did Harrison & Moberly's practice areas. Instead of a single lawyer performing a wide range of tasks for a client, a team of lawyers is now required to handle the more complex and specific legal challenges businesses face today.

"A perfect example of how this firm has developed is to look at our environmental practice," said Patricia McCrory who, when named a managing partner in the mid-1990s, became the first woman elevated to such a post in a Hoosier firm. "We used to have one person who did nothing but environmental work and that person hired an associate. Then they hired another lawyer for that team who also had an insurance defense background. We kept hiring to meet the needs of our client list."

Operating in an ever-changing business climate means the firm must have a rock-solid vision of where it's going. Harrison & Moberly has identified the practice areas it wants to develop and created a strategy in order to become a major player in that area, according to Tim Hulett, the firm's managing partner from 1997 to 2000.

Founding partner James Harrison

"Just in 1999 and 2000, we have hired lawyers with construction, complex litigation, and commercial real estate practices," Hulett said. The firm recently added an office north of Indianapolis in Hamilton County to enhance its real-estate practice. "We have picked the areas we want to grow in and gone out to find the best talent to grow it. It is as simple as that."

But the firm's management team also realizes that for it to remain focused, personal dynamics can be a positive, or negative factor.

"Even though we want to grow, we also bring in people we like," Hulett added. "We do not want to create a cut-throat atmosphere that is sometimes associated with the culture in a big firm.

"Our firm is a fun, friendly and a challenging place to practice."

A History of the Indianapolis Legal Profession

HENDERSON DAILY

HENDERSON, DAILY, WITHROW & DEVOE IS A MID-SIZED LAW PARTnership founded almost four decades ago. Their first office was a large house at 38th Street and Washington Boulevard. When the Indiana National Bank Tower opened in 1970, as the then tallest building downtown, the firm became one of the original tenants and still maintains its offices at this site, although the building is now known as One Indiana Square. The firm is proud of the fact that Elisabeth M. Daily, a named partner, was one of the first women lawyers to become an acknowledged expert in corporate and securities matters, at a time when many business clients were reluctant to accept women lawyers. The firm's size and mix of legal specialties promote personalized service, while offering the support and expertise found in much larger practices. Henderson Daily has focused on corporate and securities law from its formation and is known for counseling entrepreneurs from the start up phase through initial public offerings. Over the years the firm has added additional areas of concentration, including estate planning, real estate, family law, health care law, employment law, insurance defense and a large litigation and appellate practice.

The firm represents a number of financial institutions and organizations, which have provided opportunities to engage in complex real estate and financial transactions on both a regional and national basis. Its representation of high tech and venture capital companies has kept it abreast of developing law and national and international joint venture transactions involving trademark and intellectual property matters. Henderson Daily serves a broad base of corporate clients, including banking and insurance companies, professional organizations, charitable societies, construction and engineering firms, and manufacturing and energy companies. In addition the firm is privileged to represent individual clients, including physicians and other professionals, corporate executives, and other high net worth individuals and families. Clients are represented before the Securities and Exchange Commission, the Department of Justice, the National Association of Securities Dealers, Inc., the Indiana Department of Insurance and other local, state and federal regulatory agencies. Trial lawyers litigate in state and federal courts throughout the country, but concentrate the practice in Indiana, where major construction, commercial, tax, securities and product liability cases are undertaken.

Henderson Daily encourages its attorneys to become involved with the American, Indiana State and Indianapolis Bar Associations and to assume leadership roles through a variety of civic groups and organizations. The firm is committed to excellence in providing client services and in serving the community.

HOVDE LAW FIRM

Hovde Law Firm was founded in 1996. Formely known as Townsend Hovde & Montross, the Hovde firm can trace its beginning back to 1969 when F. Boyd Hovde joined Earl C. Townsend and John F. Townsend Jr. in the plaintiffs practice after serving 10 years as a defense lawyer with Ice Miller Donadio & Ryan. Frederick R. Hovde joined the firm in 1980.

Hovde Law Firm has limited its practice to representing injured plaintiffs. . Its members have devoted their careers to trial work and have been actively involved in trail lawyer organizations dedicated to preserving client rights and the jury system.

A year before the U.S. Supreme Court's landmark *Roe Vs. Wade* decision that legalized abortion, F. Boyd Hovde handled one of his most memorable cases, *Britt vs. Sears*. The case allowed the wrongful death action by the parents of a viable fetus.

In *Poehlman vs. Fefferman*, Hovde convinced the Indiana Supreme Court that a medical malpractice plaintiff who had succeeded in winning a judgment against a health care provider in excess of its insurance limit was entitled to recover interest on the judgment to the day it was paid, even though the total payment exceeded the state's provider liability cap.

While courtroom methods and strategies have changed little over Boyd's career, the practice environment has changed dramatically.

"Legislatively, whether it be local or national, there is a constant assault on the rights of people to file suit," Boyd Hovde said. "By forcing limitations on penalties and eliminating causes of actions by granting immunities and restricting tort remedies, big business and insurance are constantly trying to legislate away the rights of people who are injured."

Boyd and Rick both have had a major impact on in the legislative enactment and changes in Indiana's statutes regarding medical malpractice.

Boyd Hovde represented the Indiana Trial Lawyers Association's interest in the legislature when Indiana's Medical Malpractice act was passed in 1975. Rick has served as the association's legislative co-chairman for nine years and will serve as ITLA president in 2002. Rick chaired the committee whose work lead to the 1999 changes in the medical malpractice statute that, among other things, raised the liability cap to $1,250,000. Rick has also played a key role in revamping ITLA's legislative programs and strategies while creating an extremely effective in-house legislative lobbying team.

The firm has handled a number of large and complicated cases and won significant jury verdicts in medical malpractice, construction site, railroad crossing, automobile and truck accidents as well as product liability claims. Firm lawyers have also been involved in class action cases and are currently representing dozens of Indiana litigants in actions against the drug industry for the diet medication "fen-phen." In the late 1990s, health officials linked the drug to heart valve disease and pulmonary hypertension.

The firm is dedicated to perpetuating its history of quality legal representation. Robert T. Dassow and Nicholas C. Deets are recent members of the firm. Rob brought with him trail experience in personal injury and commercial litigation with both plaintiff and defense experience. Nick developed extensive trial experience in personal injury and criminal defense in Lafayette, Ind, where he was a member of his father's law firm.

ICE MILLER

For a law firm that emerged at the start of one century and is still thriving at the turn of another, Ice Miller has a remarkably modest self-image. "Even though we've been around since 1910, I doubt we fully understand the role we have played in our community," said Philip Genetos, a managing partner who joined the firm in 1977. This effacing attitude has much to do with Ice Miller's enduring philosophy about the practice of law: that lawyers and law firms exist to add value for their clients.

The major architect of what Ice Miller is today was Harry Ice, an attorney who joined the firm in 1929, fresh from Harvard Law School. He devoted the next 50 years of his life to growing what is now Indianapolis' largest law firm. Under Harry Ice's leadership, Ice Miller acquired a national reputation, partially due to his predictions about the future of the legal profession.

"Mr. Ice believed the practice of law was headed toward specialization," said Genetos. In an era when most firms were trying to be all things to all people, he believed that clients would be drawn to attorneys who devoted themselves to a particular aspect of law. He gradually organized the firm into core disciplines, a system that still exists not only at Ice Miller, but also throughout the legal profession. "That was the beginning of our growth," Genetos said. "It allowed a lot of things to happen, including the accumulation of higher levels of expertise, and more focus on client needs in specific industries and disciplines."

Having known all but two of the firm's partners, no one was better qualified than Harry Ice to write the firm's history, which he published in 1980, just two years before his death. In his book, *History of a Hoosier Law Firm*, Ice describes how the firm began, recalling a conversation with the firm's founder during an overnight train ride to Washington, D.C. in 1938.

Originally known as Henley, Matson & Gates, the firm was founded by Frederick E. Matson, a leading Indiana attorney who served in the early 1900s as a state senator for Marion County and as corporate counsel for the city of Indianapolis. At the age of 40, Matson was highly regarded by local Republican leaders who wanted him to run as prosecutor. They were confident he could rise high in public office. Matson was friendly with Indiana politicians who were prominent in national politics, so there was nothing far-fetched about their suggestion.

Despite their encouragement, Matson bypassed a political future and chose to start his own firm, with William Henley and Ed Gates as partners. Both partners left during the firm's first decade. Matson remained a dominant figure there until his death in 1941. By that time, the firm's name had changed five times, reflecting new partnerships and growth.

Four name changes have followed. The most recent came in 2000, when the firm shortened its name from Ice Miller Donadio & Ryan, the name it had used since 1963, to Ice Miller. The change reflects the evolving role of law firms in an increasingly competitive environment. "The new economy is pushing professional service organizations like ours to provide a broader scope of guidance," said Genetos. "We're excited about the things this may hold for us."

With a vast client base of small and medium-size businesses and regional, national and international clients, Ice Miller continues to position itself for expansion, both geographically and by practice. "The firm has invested in technology and encouraged our practice groups to identify new markets we can serve," Genetos said. By managing its cost structure and delivering legal and business advice that consistently adds value for clients, he believes Ice Miller can compete with any firm in the country.

Ice Miller's role in building the area's infrastructure and its influence on the state's legislative framework for gaming and public employee benefits are among the firm's Indiana legacies. It has successfully exported its expertise in these areas to other states. In a new economy that has fewer geographic boundaries, the firm expects to repeat that success in other areas such as intellectual property.

Serving Central Indiana's vibrant and diverse economy has contributed to Ice Miller's steady growth. With additional offices in Chicago, Washington, D.C., Kansas City, and South Bend, it has more than 240 lawyers and non-lawyer practice group specialists, 40 paraprofessionals and 250 staff members. Ice Miller's practice areas are divided into five sections: Business, Labor and Employment, Litigation, Public Finance, and Real Estate, which still reflect Harry Ice's influence.

This broad array of services, offered by people who are committed to teamwork, creates one of Ice Miller's distinguishing features: the ability to move client matters seamlessly from one part of its organization to another. "If we're working through a business issue and it somehow becomes an estate-planning issue, we think it should be an easy, painless transition for our clients," Genetos said. The firm rewards teamwork, training, mentoring and cross-marketing, believing that Ice Miller should be far more to its clients than a collection of individual attorneys who operate under a single brand.

Ice Miller's longevity and unity has been fortified by its penchant for attracting and keeping the brightest lawyers in an environment where people love their work and take satisfac-

Young partners at Ice Miller bring a fresh perspective as legal and business advisors.

tion in helping others. "This is a people business and we invest in people," one partner said. "That has served us well."

Given the firm's large number of clients from a vast range of businesses, organizations and government entities, there is no prototype for a typical Ice Miller client. This diversity has prevented Ice Miller from becoming dependent on a single client or industry. "Assuming there is a fair economic exchange, we'll do whatever it takes to serve our clients efficiently and effectively even if we have to learn a new business at our own expense," Genetos said. That approach has developed some substantial relationships. It has also positioned the firm to respond to the rapidly changing needs of its clients in an unpredictable world.

A History of the Indianapolis Legal Profession 177

KIGHTLINGER & GRAY, LLP

ERLE A. KIGHTLINGER AND MARK W. Gray began practicing law together in Indianapolis upon returning from World War II in 1946. They rejoined the Indianapolis legal community with the firm of Armstrong & Gause, a firm established locally in 1939, which eventually would become Kightlinger & Gray, LLP.

Kightlinger & Gray, LLP has been part of many key developments in the city of Indianapolis throughout its history. Notably, during the 1960s development of the unified government of Marion County and the City of Indianapolis—commonly referred to as "Unigov"—the firm presented arguments all the way to the Indiana Supreme Court to assure that all elements of the plan were constitutional. In addition, the firm has pioneered new rules and methods within the judicial system and is considered one of Indiana's most innovative and experienced litigation firms.

Litigation expertise largely contributed to the firm's early reputation, as Erle A. Kightlinger and Mark W. Gray established national reputations as insurance litigators. "The best form of advertising is doing good work," was Kightlinger's philosophy. Today, the firm is a full service, general practice legal and business advisory firm. The focus has expanded beyond insurance to include complex, class action, commercial and product liability litigation, business transactions and consulting, real estate and land use, estate planning, administration and probate, creditor's rights, professional liability, and employment law, including workers compensation and civil rights. Kightlinger & Gray, LLP is still regarded as one of the Nation's leading specialists in the field of insurance litigation, representing America's largest insurance companies.

Involvement in the community and in professional associations has always been a cornerstone of the firm's business philosophy. While Kightlinger was active in the Republican Party, Gray was equally active in the Democratic Party. Both Kightlinger and Gray served terms as president of the Indianapolis School Board. Gray has been active with the Indiana Convention & Visitors Association since 1947, having most recently served as board treasurer. Kightlinger served as president of the Indianapolis Bar Association and was a state bar examiner. Partners in the firm actively participate in civic, legal, professional and other trade organizations. The firm also recognizes the contribution that teachers make to our community by sponsoring the annual "Kightlinger & Gray Outstanding Arts Educator Awards" presented during the annual ceremonies for the Prelude Awards.

While the firm has grown in size to 50 lawyers, 100 staff, and three offices in Indiana including Indianapolis, New Albany, and Evansville, the newest generation of lawyers is continually being brought into the firm. Kightlinger & Gray, LLP is proud to play an active role in this process, and with lawyers in the firm ranging in age from 80 to those fresh out of law school, the firm encompasses a wide range of perspectives and experiences. "Law firms can't stay static," Gray said. "The world is changing and so must we."

Erle A. Kightlinger (top) and Mark W. Gray (above).

KNOWLES & ASSOCIATES, LLC

Knowles & Associates, LLC offers a team approach to high quality yet cost-effective legal services designed to save money through estate and business planning, and to protect the rights of individuals, families, and businesses.

The firm originally began in 1934 under the name of Binkley & Baker with a legal focus on estate planning and litigation. Through the generations the name of the firm has changed; however, its focus has remained constant with estate planning, probate and trust administration, and litigation, both civil and criminal, as its primary emphasis.

Today there are three principle lawyers in the firm: William W. Knowles, Millicent E. Hatch, and Nicholas T. Buschmann. The firm is committed to serving clients across the state and to involvement with the city of Indianapolis and city of Carmel.

One of the things that sets Knowles & Associates apart from many other firms in the city is its team approach. Instead of one lawyer working with each case, all lawyers and appropriate staff take an interest and participate in the development of a case as needed, which results in time being billed at lower rates.

The firm believes in and practices a Christian approach to each client matter. The firm does not plan to grow in size by great measure, as it believes that by limiting its areas of practice together with the implementation of modern technology it has the ability to compete with all other firms in the services it provides.

The firm's services include: Comprehensive estate planning; counseling trustees with respect to the administration of trusts; counseling personal representatives with respect to the administration of probate estates; establishing guardianships of the person, or the estate, or both; and coordination of business succession planning with the client's underlying estate planning objectives.

In addition to the complex area of estate planning, the firm engages in general civil and criminal litigation (appeals as well as trials) with an emphasis on breach of fiduciary duty issues, will and or trust construction issues, inheritance tax controversies, estate tax controversies, litigated claims, will contests, objections to accountings, and elder law issues.

Mr. Knowles' community activities include being a former Young Republican Chairman of Hamilton County and being a life member of Sertoma International (since 1966). He has served as a Director of the Carmel Symphony Orchestra, Indianapolis Interfaith Hospitality Network, Inc. (which he serves as legal counsel), and is a sustaining member of the Indiana Trial Lawyer's Association.

Mr. Buschmann is a former member of the Board of Directors for IndyReads, a not-for-profit organization that works with the Marion County Public Library to promote adult literacy, and is a former member of the Board of Directors of the Indiana State Chapter of the National Multiple Sclerosis Society. He has served the public professionally as Deputy Attorney General for the State of Indiana.

Ms. Hatch is president-elect of the Washington Township Neighborhood Trustees Association. She is actively involved in the Church at the Crossing, assisting in the International Neighbors ministry and serving in leadership in the area of children's ministries.

A History of the Indianapolis Legal Profession

KRIEG DEVAULT ALEXANDER & CAPEHART, LLP

FOUNDED IN THE MID-1870S, KRIEG DEVAULT ALEXANDER & Capehart, LLP originally began as a two-lawyer practice headed by Indianapolis attorney and civic leader Aquilla Q. Jones. Its rich history of involvement in community affairs, coupled with its experience during tumultuous times in America's history, are the foundation for the firm's philosophy and business practices today.

Jones began the practice with William W. Hammond, who previously served as first headmaster of Culver Military Academy. In 1921, they added C. Severin Buschman and Alan W. Boyd and the firm became known as Jones Hammond Buschman & Boyd.

In the years to follow, Boyd left the practice and Leo M. Gardner joined their ranks. In 1932, the firm became known as Jones Hammond Buschman & Gardner. Around that time, two associates, William H. Krieg and Paul J. DeVault joined the law practice, having just graduated from Harvard Law School and Indiana University School of Law, respectively. These young lawyers were eager for work, and much was available as this was a time when the county struggled from the effects of the Great Depression. During these years, Congress enacted legislation reforming financial institutions which brought important work to the firm.

By 1939, Gardner had left, and the firm changed to Hammond Buschman Krieg & DeVault. World War II created a severe challenge to the survival of the firm as it called into service three of its four partners. Krieg was the first partner to depart for military service, serving from 1940-1945. He returned from war as a Lieutenant Colonel having received The Legion of Merit. Buschman had been a Lieutenant Colonel in the U.S. Army Reserve during World War I and was sent overseas shortly after the bombing of Pearl Harbor in 1941. He returned to the firm in 1945. DeVault was commissioned in 1943 as a Lieutenant (jg) in the U.S. Naval Reserve. Ultimately he participated in the Normandy Invasion at Omaha Beach. He was released from duty in 1945 with a rank of Lieutenant and a Letter of Commendation for his service in Normandy.

Much of the firm's success during World War II years can be attributed to John A. Alexander, a graduate of the law school of Northwestern University and an associate of the firm when the exodus of partners for military service began. Alexander carried on representation of long-time corporate and banking clients, including the Indiana Bankers Association, and performed substantial work for the Federal Home Loan Bank of Indianapolis and the Indiana National Bank. In addition, the Honorable

ABOVE: *The firm's reception area in the early 1960s.* OPPOSITE PAGE: *The firm's reception area in 2001.*

Curtis W. Roll, a member of the Supreme Court of Indiana, joined the firm upon leaving the bench in 1943. It was at that point that the firm name was changed to Hammond Buschman Roll & Alexander.

Upon returning from military service, Buschman and DeVault rejoined the firm as partners, and the firm became known as Buschman & Roll. Krieg accepted a position as President and General Counsel for Packard Manufacturing Corporation, an Indianapolis company owned by Senator Homer E. Capehart. In 1947, Roll returned to his hometown of Kokomo, and Hammond decided to retire. Upon their departures, Krieg rejoined the partnership, and the firm name became Buschman Krieg DeVault & Alexander.

Additional lawyers were added after the war, including H. Earl Capehart Jr., a graduate of Harvard Law School. In 1961, the firm changed its name to Krieg DeVault Alexander & Capehart.

The full-service capabilities of the firm today can be traced back to the four name partners. Each one brought different strengths to the law firm, allowing the firm to develop expertise and a client base in several areas.

Krieg specialized in federal and state taxation and corporation law, and possessed an excellent sense of business strategy which attracted many corporate clients. He served on numerous corporate boards and was a member of the Purdue University Board of Trustees for four, three-year terms.

DeVault pursued a general civic practice and was engaged in an extensive variety of litigation in both federal and state courts. He became proficient in antitrust law and successfully tried a substantial number of cases filed under the Sherman and Clayton Antitrust Acts. He engaged in numerous civic and charitable endeavors and served on several State commissions. He was the recipient of Sagamore of the Wabash awards from both Governor George N. Craig and Governor Otis R. Bowen.

Alexander was the dean of Indiana banking law. He was knowledgeable in all phases of financial institutions law and was often consulted concerning amendments to the Indiana Financial Institutions Act. He formed the first major bank holding company in Indiana. Alexander was also well known in business and corporate law.

Capehart was engaged in general civil practice, with emphasis on real estate, probate and municipal law. He represented the interest of the firm in numerous government and community affairs.

Today, Krieg DeVault has evolved into a prominent business and corporate law firm with a fully diversified civil practice. The firm represents a wide variety of local, regional and national clients in matters throughout the Midwest and the nation. Practice areas include:

- Corporate and securities
- Creditors' rights and bankruptcy
- Employee benefits/executive compensation
- Employment law
- Environmental law
- Financial institutions
- Governmental and legislative services
- Health care
- Insurance
- Intellectual property
- Litigation
- Municipal law
- Real estate
- Taxation
- Technology and e-commerce

As the seventh largest law firm in Indianapolis, Krieg DeVault prides itself on its ability to provide excellent, timely legal service.

As a member of the Commercial Law Affiliates, an international organization of mid-sized commercial-based firms, Krieg DeVault offers a national and international network of law firms to assure its business clients access to cost effective, quality legal representation by like-minded firms wherever they have legal needs.

Although known throughout the years as a business and banking law firm, Krieg DeVault is a full service law firm, working with healthcare professionals and institutions, entrepreneurs, people with complex estate planning needs, organizations with interests in specific items of legislation, and executives who are negotiating their compensation packages. In addition, the firm has created a financial consulting subsidiary, Krieg DeVault Financial Consulting, that develops creative sources of financing for its corporate clients.

Krieg DeVault holds much of its past: excellent legal services with creative solutions while being a good community citizen through its support of civic and charitable endeavors.

A History of the Indianapolis Legal Profession   181

CHARLES HANKEY LAW OFFICE

For more than 25 years Charles D. Hankey and associates have been serving people's legal needs within a community that is easily overlooked. The firm focuses its efforts on serving injured people or people with disabilities, including work-related injuries or other accidents. The firm has the largest disability practice in the state of Indiana. Mr. Hankey has found that being located in the state capital has served the firm and his clients well through the years by having access to state and federal offices.

In the year 2000 the firm size totaled 12 people, three lawyers accompanied by nine staff members. The ratio of staff to lawyer is inline with the national average for firms with a focus on serving injured and disabled individuals.

Although the firm may run into frustrations in its field, Mr. Hankey focused the firm in this way throughout the years for the many rewards it brings in helping his clients. Mr. Hankey is highly involved with the national organization the American Trial Lawyers Association and the National Organization of Social Security Claimants Representatives (NOSSCR). He has been a member of NOSSCR for more than 20 years.

As for the future, Charles D. Hankey law office will continue working to make sure ordinary people get the representation they deserve by people who care about representing them. He feels his firm plays a vital role in the city of Indianapolis and plans for it to continue fulfilling that role.

HOLLINGSWORTH & ASSOCIATES

J. David Hollingsworth has spent his 27-year legal career serving the general legal needs of families and small businesses in Central Indiana. Whether it's domestic disputes, simple truancy matters or EEOC complaints, Hollingsworth serves his clients with a warm, personable manner.

The first thing you notice about Hollingsworth upon introduction is that he's a good storyteller, and that has paid dividends both in the courtroom and with his clients throughout his career.

He recalled being thrust into the lead counsel role for an emergency hearing only hours before it was scheduled to begin.

"I was assigned to assist on the case the day before the hearing, but that morning my co-counsel dies," Hollingsworth explained. "I rush up there trying in vain to prepare for this case, a continuance was not an option; I just didn't know what I was going to do. Not a minute after we got into the courtroom we were evacuated because a bomb threat had just been received.

The matter was rescheduled and I was never more happy to receive bad news than I was on that day."

Hollingsworth has served with many lawyers over the years including Gary Miller, who serves as a judge in the Marion County Superior Court's Criminal Division. Lindley Pearson joined Hollingsworth in practice after his failed state gubernatorial bid in 1996. Pearson was later elected to the Clinton Circuit Court bench.

Hollingsworth's work with families in positive and negative situations has taught him the value of giving back to the community. The firm supports the 32nd degree Masonic Learning Center for children, which provides members an opportunity to perform one-on-one tutoring for children with dyslexia. The firm has also supported Daymar, an agency for people with mental handicaps, as well as Goodwill Industries.

Despite his long legal career and community involvement, Hollingsworth's mark on the Indianapolis legal landscape may be more for what he didn't do than for what he did.

"We don't give anyone a bill for a simple will; we just ask the client to pay us what they think its worth," Hollingsworth said. "A probate judge recommended that to me once and he was right when he said it would do two things: you'll ingratiate yourselves to your clients and two you'll get two or three referrals."

KIEFER & McGOFF

J. RICHARD KIEFER AND KEVIN P. MCGOFF BEGAN PRACTICING LAW together in 1986. They established their partnership in 1992, and in nine years the firm has grown to nine lawyers. Defending the accused in state and federal criminal cases, at the trial and appellate levels, is the largest segment of the firm's practice. The firm defends major felony and white-collar crimes, as well as less serious charges, practices family law and complex civil litigation. Kiefer also defends nursing home corporations and other health care professionals in criminal and administrative proceedings. A significant part of McGoff's practice is representing lawyers and judges charged with ethical violations by the disciplinary agencies of the Indiana Supreme Court.

Both partners are named in *The Best Lawyers in America* and train lawyers throughout the state on topics of criminal defense.

McGoff addresses hundreds of lawyers each year on the subject of legal ethics and Kiefer is a frequent lecturer on criminal health care issues.

Kiefer is past chairman of the Criminal Justice Section of the Indiana and Indianapolis Bar Associations. He was President of the Indiana Association of Criminal Defense Lawyers' Board of Directors from 1992 to 2000, and a member of the National Health Care Association and Association of Trial Lawyers of America.

McGoff is past chairman of the Indiana Public Defender Council Board of Directors. He served on the Supreme Court Committee that wrote the Indiana Rules of Evidence. He also serves on the Indiana State Bar Association's Legal Ethics Committee, and the Ethics Advisory Committee for the National Association of Criminal Defense Lawyers.

KORTEPETER McPHERSON HUX FREIHOFER & MINTON

KORTEPETER MCPHERSON HUX FREIHOFER & MINTON'S TIES IN THE Indianapolis legal community date back to the late 1890s when Carson & Thompson, a prominent Indianapolis law firm, opened its doors. Early in the next century, Herman Kothe and Grier Shotwell joined the practice, and the firm changed its name to Kothe & Shotwell. Kothe's son, Shubrick, joined the firm in 1947.

After Paul Kortepeter joined the practice, the firm changed its name again—to Kothe Shotwell & Kortepeter. In 1970, a merger added brothers Robert and John Claycombe and Harry Hendrickson. Shortly after, Heather McPherson joined the firm, and in the early 1980s, the firm became known as Kothe Claycombe Kortepeter & McPherson.

Another merger in 1998 added William Freihofer and Phillip Minton, both of whom have practiced more than 40 years, and Sarah Frank and Alan Hux, who have each practiced for more than 20 years. The firm added Kristina Keener Yeager in 1999.

Throughout the years, the firm has changed its name and personnel, but it has not strayed from its mission. The firm provides quality legal services in a timely, efficient manner and at a fair and reasonable cost. The firm offers continuity of service and, with the aid of its entire staff, a personalized, client-focused approach to handling its clients' legal issues.

The primary practice areas for Kortepeter McPherson Hux Freihofer & Minton are:
- Probate, estate planning and trusts
- Real estate
- Non-profits (health care)
- Utility regulation
- Business organizations
- Income, estate and gift taxation
- Civil litigation
- Family law

A History of the Indianapolis Legal Profession

LAMBERTI & GROW

WHILE AN EQUAL NUMBER OF MEN AND WOMEN ARE ENROLLED IN Indiana's law schools today, very few women run their own firm. Ida Coleman Lamberti and Patricia Orloff Grow are exceptions. But what also makes Lamberti & Grow unique is their firm's concentration on discrimination and constitutional issues in employment and educational settings.

Lamberti began practicing law in 1992 after an internship for a federal judge. She had a prior career as an English teacher at the university level and as a field editor for several educational publishing companies. Grow began practicing law in 1987. She served as Legal Director of the Chicago Bar Association's Legal Clinic for the Disabled, and subsequently served as Attorney-Advisor to the U.S. Commission on Civil Rights, and legal consultant to the Equal Employment Advisory Council and National Foundation for the Study of Employment Policy in Washington, D.C.

With a common interest in discrimination cases, and having successfully teamed efforts on federal cases, Lamberti & Grow formalized their association in 1997 and hung out their own shingle down the street from the federal court house.

"There is a real need for legal representation in this area. Many people are denied access to the legal system, and without effective representation there cannot be meaningful enforcement of our discrimination and civil rights laws," Grow said. "On a professional level we deal with novel and complex legal issues, and our practice addresses the demands, challenges, and opportunities inherent in a changing workforce and legal landscape."

Through advocacy efforts, training and policy drafting and analysis, these attorneys have also assisted organizations and entities in better understanding and complying with the law. Lamberti and Grow's combined experience in the public and private sectors allows them to provide a unique insight and understanding of the legal, as well as practical, considerations relevant to employment law and proper development and application of policies and procedures.

"We represent the individual and advocate on their behalf, but we also look at the management end by providing training and solutions to employers, educational institutions, and governmental entities." Lamberti said. "By learning about their legal responsibilities and how to properly enforce their policies, employers can reduce their exposure to litigation and liability. It also helps employers to be more aware of their legal obligations to their employees."

Both Lamberti and Grow are active in a variety of civic and philanthropic organizations. Grow was appointed by Governor O'Bannon to the Indiana Commission on Rehabilitation Services and by Governor Bayh to the Meridian Street Preservation Commission. Lamberti donates her time to help the

Patricia Orloff Grow, left, and Ida Lamberti of Lamberti & Grow.

poor access vital legal services by serving as a pro bono mediator in family law and other civil disputes.

Lamberti and Grow are affiliated with the American Bar Association, Federal Bar Association, National Employment Lawyers Association, Indiana State Bar Association, and Indianapolis Bar Association. Lamberti is admitted to practice in Indiana, the Seventh Circuit Court of Appeals, and the federal bar for the Northern and Southern Districts of Indiana. Grow is admitted to practice in Indiana and Illinois, and the U.S. Supreme Court, Seventh Circuit Court of Appeals, federal bar for the Northern and Southern Districts of Indiana and Northern District of Illinois.

Whether through litigation, advocacy or training, Lamberti & Grow has dedicated its service to enforcing and improving equal employment opportunities and civil rights.

LEWIS & WAGNER

Since its inception, Lewis and Wagner lawyers not only helped shape Indiana law, but the Indiana political landscape as well.

Ed Lewis, a Democrat who founded the firm in 1950, was heavily involved in the often thankless but crucial job as a consultant and fundraiser for political campaigns. Lewis was passionate about the abilities and political promise of Evan Bayh and played an instrumental role in his rise to governor. "Ed Lewis came from humble beginnings but made a tremendous contribution to Indiana, and Indianapolis." said Bayh, who now represents the state in the U.S. Senate. "He was a friend and advisor, and he played an important role in the success of our administration."

Many of Indiana's brightest lawyers who were influenced by Lewis while at the firm have gone onto serve the public as judges on the state, federal and appellate bench, as well as for the U.S. Justice Department as U.S. Attorneys.

A lawyer who shared Lewis' passion for the law and promoting good government joined the firm in 1971. Robert Wagner would go on to chair Vance Hartke's Senate campaign and assisted in his presidential bid. In the early, 1980s, shortly after his work for Hartke, Wagner was asked by Democrats to run against Sen. Richard Lugar, but decided instead to concentrate on the firm.

"I had to decide whether to build a law firm or run for office, and I chose to build a law firm," Wagner said.

At that time, the firm was in transition as it rapidly expanded its labor law and insurance defense practice to complement the commercial and business litigation practice Lewis founded. Wagner, however, maintained his political influence as he later managed Larry Conrad's campaign for Indiana Secretary of State and Governor.

Despite Mr. Lewis and Mr. Wagner's devotion to politics, they were never motivated by a desire to seek business from the people they supported or worked with in politics. And even though the firm has evolved dramatically over the last 15 years, this policy to separate the practice from the political figures they advise has gone unchanged.

Since the firm's 22 lawyers are split evenly into Democrat and Republican political camps, the management team doesn't hire lawyers who prefer one political persuasion to another — as long as they are not a-political. The firm's lawyers understand that out of the firm's political involvement has grown a spirit of support for civic and bar association activities.

While politics and civic duty is a common thread that runs through the firm, Lewis & Wagner lawyers also plan to do in the future what they've always done in the past: try cases.

"We may have as many litigators in this firm as some of the big firms have; that's because the big firms are doing everything," Wagner said. "Someone asked me if we had carved a niche out for ourselves and I told them yes, we try lawsuits."

Arguing a case before a judge and jury is what lawyers have been doing for hundreds of years and Lewis & Wagner is committed to continuing the tradition. But there are plenty of opportunities for practice advancement while honing ancient lawyer skills.

According to the management committee, the firm will expand its commercial and insurance coverage litigation as well as their already active defense work. The firm plans to branch out into employment litigation and environmental litigation as well as develop an estate and business formation practice.

To support this growth, the management committee expects to add lawyers as needed, but did not commit to a particular size.

While firm lawyers are active in charitable and bar association activities, the firm as a whole devotes much time to assisting nearby Indiana University School of Law – Indianapolis. They have been called upon to serve as adjunct professors, mentors, alumni board leaders, employers and financial donors. Each year, attorneys in the firm also serve as presenters in an average of 25 continuing legal education seminars at the law school and elsewhere.

Robert Wagner has served the last few years as chair of the White River State Park Commission when the grounds of the park were completely overhauled and beautified. The NCAA relocated to the park and an IMAX theatre was built there. Wagner worked with Indianapolis Power and Light in 1999 to bring the U.S. Medal of Honor recipients to Indianapolis to open a memorial dedicated to them on park grounds.

His most cherished and ambitious project has been his devotion to the tree beautification project on the near-west side along Dr. Martin Luther King Street. Hundreds of trees and landscaping changes will transform the area into a location worthy of the name of the street it will beautify.

When asked about his favorite aspect of the modern Lewis & Wagner, co-founder Wagner remarked "We are proud to be a place where people look forward to coming to work every day, and our clients and friends in the bar enjoy coming to visit. We hope that we are viewed in the community as problem solvers who try to uphold all of the very best characteristics of the legal profession."

A History of the Indianapolis Legal Profession

LOCKE REYNOLDS LLP

THE HISTORY OF LOCKE REYNOLDS DATES TO 1917 WHEN THEODORE L. Locke, Sr., a University of Michigan law graduate, came to Indianapolis and associated with an established solo practitioner, Charles Dryer. Locke quickly grew from a young lawyer to a very seasoned trial attorney. For many years up to his retirement, Mr. Locke managed the firm with a strong and steady hand. Ted Locke was widely known as a careful and diligent lawyer who zealously represented his clients. We remain grateful for the excellent example that he set so many years ago.

While the firm's main office was located in the Consolidated Building in downtown Indianapolis, a satellite office was soon established in Chicago. The firm's practice expanded rapidly in the 1920s, particularly its insurance work. Locke felt strongly that the firm's past, present and future could be found in its insurance defense practice. In 1955, the firm became known as "Locke Reynolds Boyd & Weisell." By the 1960s, things began to change in the way the insurance industry managed its claims. As a result, by the late 1960's, the firm began to diversify and expand its legal practice beyond insurance defense.

Hugh Reynolds, Jr., became managing partner in the early 1970s, and vigorously guided Locke Reynolds in its new direction. The 1980s involved a period of very significant growth and tremendous diversification for the firm. After nearly twenty years of practicing law in the Indiana National Bank Tower, the firm outgrew its space and, in 1989, relocated to the Capital Center at the northeast corner of Illinois and Ohio Streets. Today, the Capital Center remains the headquarters location for Locke Reynolds. In 1999, in an effort to expand our geographic service for clients, as well as our capabilities, Locke Reynolds merged with the highly regarded Hammond, Indiana, law firm of Galvin, Galvin & Leeney.

Over the last several years, we have successfully expanded our practice into virtually all areas of law, including Appellate, Banking and Creditors' Rights, Business Litigation, Construction, Corporate, Environmental and Toxic Exposure, Estate Planning, Family Law, Governmental Services, Healthcare, Intellectual Property, Labor and Employment, Medical Malpractice, Products Liability, Real Estate, Tax, White Collar Criminal Defense, and Worker's Compensation. While the firm maintains an impressive breadth of services, our primary concentration is on the needs of business. This concentration permits us to strategically develop the legal services that our clients need, by attracting attorneys who are leaders in their respective areas of law.

Throughout Locke Reynolds' history, the firm has offered and supported many involvements and contributions to the professional community and the Indianapolis Bar Association. For example, over the years, seven partners have served as IBA President, including two of the firm's senior partners, Theodore L. Locke, Sr. (1947) and Emerson Boyd (1977). As another example of community involvement, William B. Weisell, served for a number of years as President of the Indianapolis Symphony Orchestra. In addition, firm members have been very active politically. Paul S. Mannweiler served as Speaker of the Indiana House of Representatives and William H. Vobach served in the Indiana Senate. In 2000, Judge Steven R. Eichholtz retired from the Marion Superior Court and joined Locke Reynolds. The firm is deeply committed to the success of Indianapolis and encourages and supports many charitable and benevolent causes in our community.

Even though we look very different today than we did during our humble beginnings, Locke Reynolds starts the new millenium in the same way we completed the last one: committed to the success of our clients. Locke Reynolds' clients are experienced. Locke Reynolds' clients are cost-conscious. Locke Reynolds' clients are creative. Our clients are the reason for our existence, and we remain committed to their success.

Julia Blackwell Gelinas, Chair, Management Committee.

LOWE GRAY STEELE & DARKO, LLP

A FATHER AND SON TIE THE PAST AND PRESENT TOGETHER FOR Lowe Gray Steele & Darko, LLP. The firm's roots trace back to 1911, when Whitcomb Dowden & Stout was established. Louis R. Lowe joined the firm in the early 1950s, eventually becoming a partner and its sole practitioner.

Lowe's son, L. Robert Lowe, Jr., proudly followed his father's footsteps. After graduating from law school, he became a member of the firm. "I joined Dad in 1967. We got to work together for a year, even trying cases together. He died the following year," remembers Bob Lowe. "I have great memories of the enjoyable time we spent together."

After his father's death, the younger Lowe was on his own. In 1970, he added to the practice two friends: Maxwell Gray and Sydney L Steele. Together, the three became founding partners of Lowe Gray & Steele. Today the firm's founding partners remember their earlier, lean years and the teamwork and loyalty to each other that has been a constant in the ever-changing legal profession.

They remember with fondness how they used a little red wagon to move furniture to their new offices. As they grew and occupied a second floor, they had to connect one of the founding partner's phones by running the cord outside through a window, down a floor and through the window of his office.

Memories from the early years also focus on how the partners built the practice areas of the firm. When father and son were together, the firm primarily focused on general litigation and insurance defense. The firm gradually added new areas of service as its members became specialists. With the addition of Richard J. Darko in the 1980s, the firm continued to expand its expertise and its name: Lowe Gray Steele & Darko.

Today, the firm concentrates its practice in the following areas:
- Construction claims and litigation
- Estate planning, succession planning, estate and trust administration, and elder law
- Family law and domestic relations
- Entertainment, advertising and intellectual property
- Health care law and medical malpractice defense
- Labor relations and employment law
- General litigation and dispute resolution
- Corporations, business organizations and securities

Lowe Gray Steele & Darko, LLP has been instrumental in shaping the growth of the city by being a part of the creation of major Indiana business laws. Attorneys in the firm have participated in the drafting of the Indiana Business Corporation Law, the Indiana Nonprofit Corporation Law of 1991, the Indiana Revised Uniform Limited Partnership Act, the Indiana Limited Liability Company Act, and the Indiana Limited Liability Partnership Act. They also helped shape laws for families in the community by assisting in authoring the Rules of Procedures of the Marion County Superior Courts pertaining to family law matters.

LGS&D attorneys have contributed to Indianapolis' development by taking law off the bookshelf and putting it into the client's hands. The firm's enthusiasm, responsiveness and proactive nature have allowed it to foster unique relationships with clients. Future growth will continue to be dictated by client needs and market trends. Intellectual property will play a significant role in the practice as high technology continues to explode on the market. The firm also will strive to provide more one-stop shopping with the addition of multi-disciplinary practices.

Partners of Lowe Gray Steele & Darko, left to right, Richard J. Darko, Sydney Steele, Maxwell Gray and L. Robert Lowe, Jr.

A History of the Indianapolis Legal Profession   187

LADENDORF & LADENDORF

After seventeen years of practicing law, Mark C. Ladendorf opened his own office in 1997 continuing his specialty as a trial lawyer exclusively devoted to personal injury, medical malpractice, wrongful death, and product liability. In June 2000 he expanded his office to include his brother, Daniel A. Ladendorf, as a partner. The firm has seven additional staff members including a nurse-attorney, Gloria Gradeless, who spent 25 years as a practicing nurse.

Born and raised in Lake County, Mark and Dan appreciate the value of hard work to attain a goal. Their commitment to justice on behalf of the citizens of Indiana is reflected in numerous accomplishments at the trial and appellate levels.

Mark Ladendorf has represented clients throughout the state as well as nationwide. He is an active member of the Indiana Trial Lawyers Association and has served on its Board of Directors since 1990. He is a member of the American, Indiana, and Indianapolis Bar Associations, and a sustaining member of the Association of Trial Lawyers of America.

Before going into private practice, Dan Ladendorf served as legal counsel to the Marion County Grand Jury and as Deputy Prosecuting Attorney during the terms of Steve Goldsmith, Jeff Modisett, and Scott Newman. He is a member of the Indianapolis Bar Association and the Indiana Trial Lawyer's Association.

Ladendorf & Ladendorf believes in dedication to their clients to help them successfully resolve their legal struggles. Their unique and diverse experiences provide their clients with a blend of service, commitment and integrity.

LEE BURNS & COSSELL, LLP

Established in 1985 as Lee & Clark, the firm changed to Lee Burns & Cossell in 1998. The current partners include Nathaniel Lee, Robert A. Burns, and Marcia J. Cossell. Established as a general civil practice firm, it is comprised of skilled and experienced attorneys, paraprofessionals, and support staff dedicated to providing its clients with high quality, efficient, effective, and economical legal services.

Located in downtown Indianapolis, the firm's litigation practice focuses on personal injury action, which may include automobile accidents, medical mal practice, product liability, and breach of warranty. In addition, the firm provides general litigation services, in both the claimant and defense areas, to its business and insurance clients.

The firm's senior partner, Nathaniel Lee, chaired the Marion County Bar Association Board of Directors for 10 of its past 13 years and serves as counsel to the Ronald McDonald House. He has handled hundreds of litigation matters and lectured on litigation issues across the country. Since 1996 Mr. Lee has co-hosted a weekly radio program, "Legally Speaking," which offers discussions on different legal topics. He is also involved in a multitude of community projects.

Mr. Burns was an Associate Editor of the Indiana Law Review in 1978 and has done extensive trial and appellate work, with a favorable Indiana Supreme Court decision, which has significantly affected both domestic and personal injury law. Ms. Cossell has developed a social security practice brochure and presents at seminars on this topic. She also serves as Judge Pro-Tem in the Marion County Superior Courts.

DIANE L. LIPTACK, P.C.

DIANE LIPTACK CAME TO INDIANAPOLIS AFTER LAW SCHOOL TO WORK with Arthur Anderson. After one year she decided to join the law firm of Bamberger & Feibleman to engage in legal work. Knowing she wanted to pursue estate-planning work, Ms. Liptack left the firm in 1981 and joined Ray Hilgedag in his practice, which was a great match for both Mr. Hilgedag and Ms. Liptack.

Mr. Hilgedag's firm was splitting up and he wanted someone to join him to keep his practice alive once he retired. When Ms. Liptack began working with Hilgedag, the firm was sharing space in Circle Tower downtown on Monument Circle. They remained there until Hilgedag's sudden death from a heart attack in 1986. In 1987 Liptack moved to her current location on New York Street.

During the five years Liptack practiced with Hilgedag, she learned a great deal about the profession. "Hilgedag was a great mentor and helped me get a foot in the door in the probate court," Liptack stated. "I began working with Ray at a time when he wanted to cut back so I got to handle more clients and office matters than one usually would at that stage," she continued.

The firm was called Hilgedag & Liptack until the year 2001 when she decided to use Diane L. Liptack, P.C. The constant focus of her work has been estate planning and administration. Since she is a certified public accountant, she also does some business consultation and incorporation work and is counsel to the firm McCrosson & Nerz.

MADDOX KOELLER HARGETT & CARUSO

MADDOX KOELLER HARGETT & CARUSO HAS the unique experience to represent investors who have been victims of stockbroker fraud or have been defrauded by brokers, brokerage firms, or insurance companies. The firm includes a former State Securities Commissioner in Mark E. Maddox, a former broker in Thomas A. Hargett and a former general counsel to a national brokerage company in Steven B. Caruso. By providing its clients with insightful, knowledgeable and ethical advocacy, the firm is able to represent victims of broker or brokerage company fraud in both arbitration and litigation.

In 1991 Mark E. Maddox left the Indiana Securities Division and opened his own practice concentrating on representing investors in securities arbitration and litigation proceedings. He is the past president of the Public Investors Arbitration Bar Association, having served from 1998–2000.

Robert Koeller is the senior founder of the firm and has an extensive background in publicly and privately held businesses. He has been involved in various state and federal securities registrations, including initial public offerings, registrations and Blue Sky filings.

Thomas Hargett joined the firm in 1994 bringing with him significant securities industry experience. Combined with Maddox, the firm is highly qualified to represent investors in NASD and NYSE arbitration and general securities arbitration.

In 1997, Steven B. Caruso joined the firm as the resident partner in New York City. Caruso brought with him significant securities arbitration experience as general counsel to a national brokerage firm.

Today, Maddox Koeller Harget & Caruso has one of the largest practices that concentrates in the area of securities investors in the United States.

A History of the Indianapolis Legal Profession

McNAMAR, FEARNOW & McSHARAR, P.C.

Three years after graduation from law school, David S. McNamar took a routine case that would have a major impact on the next 30 years of his legal career. He successfully represented a nursing home in some administrative matters where he squared off against the various state and federal health agencies that were beginning to usher in a line of regulations that inundated his client.

He was successful in the matter and soon, nursing homes from all over the state chose Steers Sullivan McNamar and Rogers as their firm.

In 1993, the Steers firm broke up and McNamar formed McNamar, Fearnow & McSharar, P.C. with Randall R. Fearnow, who served as general counsel of the Indiana Health Care Association and Janet A. McSharar who served as trial counsel for the Indiana State Department of health. That added up to more than fifty years combined experience in the representation of health care providers.

The firm today handles litigation, transactional and general corporate matters on behalf of a wide array of health care and related clients and offers special expertise in the areas of long term health care, home health, medical transportation, and Medicare and Medicaid reimbursement. The firm also has considerable experience in defending health care providers charged with Medicare and Medicaid fraud and abuse violations, and in the development of health care organization fraud and abuse compliance programs.

Several state and federal agencies oversee what is a now a heavily regulated nursing home industry. The McNamar firm has positioned itself to offer effective legal counsel to help nursing homes in the state navigate the complex legal environment.

"The key to effective representation in this area is knowing which federal or state agency has jurisdiction in a case and then determining a course of action," McNamar said. "With so many regulations, it can be a very murky area so that's why our clients prefer us, we have many years of experience dealing with these matters."

While the firm does handle some business litigation, it is clear that because regulations on nursing homes will only continue to expand, the McNamar firm will continue to expand its niche in its representation of nursing homes.

"Nursing homes are beginning to see big tort claims filed against them where families of residents are suing them for wrongful death," McNamar said. "They, for instance, claim that the nutrition was not adequate enough and lead to an earlier death, where our position is that they lived a longer, better quality of life because of the care they received."

McNamar predicted that regulations governing assisted living will soon appear and that the firm will represent many of those organizations much as they do nursing homes.

"Assisted living facilities are there to provide a place for seniors to live but they do not provide nursing care. Residents can come and go as they please and receive meals and have emergency care available if needed." McNamar said. "The state does not require licensure in this area and therefore its not yet very regulated. But that will change."

One of the firm's most significant actions is coming to a close after 11 years of work. The Tioga Pines class action suit was filed by nursing homes against the state for instituting unfair Medicaid rate settings. The action has involved five appeals to the Indiana State Court of Appeals and the Indiana Supreme Court as well as additional matters filed in the Seventh Circuit U.S. Court of Appeals and the U.S. Supreme Court.

The nursing homes recently settled with the state and are, for the most part, receiving the relief they sought in court, McNamar said.

In addition to maintain on of the busiest nursing home practices in the state, the seven members find time to serve on Indianapolis and Indiana State Bar Association Committees as well as Nursing Home and Nursing home association boards. The firm also supports the Ronald McDonald House and local symphonies and theaters.

GLORIA K. MITCHELL

GLORIA MITCHELL RECALLS EARLY FAMILY LAW CASES AS SHAPING HER family law practice. It was readily apparent to Mitchell that too often, divorcing parties were more invested in inflicting emotional wounds than in resolving their differences. It was often that attorneys became embroiled in the conflict due to the need to zealously represent clients who needed various levels of assurance to keep them happy.

With the potential for disaster looming, "everywhere you looked" when the cases involved children, Mitchell began working harder to alleviate conflict when possible, as soon as possible, and to redirect families to resources outside the courtroom to settle their disputes.

After much trial and error, Mitchell was finally able to create some effective composite strategies which advance a client's position but also reduce high conflict to allow the parties to avoid the fatal blows to future communications which are so necessary to effectively co-parent children.

While Mitchell now practices exclusively in the area of family law litigation and as a certified family law mediator, this was not her original plan. While enrolled at Indiana University School of Law-Indianapolis, and upon her graduation from there in 1988, she hoped to continue to write briefs as an appellate attorney, practice criminal defense and work as a personal injury litigator. Mitchell did so by joining Landwerlen and Rothopf in 1988 and by later affiliating with Pardiek Gill & Vargo, while maintaining a general practice. With the support of her valued mentors at both firms, Mitchell accepted the position of Master Commissioner of the Marion Superior Court in 1992, where she heard primarily family laws cases. Over the next five years Mitchell lost her comfort level in the general practice.

"It was unmanageable for me to keep track of the constant changes in family law, criminal law appellate law and personal injury litigation to my satisfaction," Mitchell recalled. "I picked the area in which I had the highest referral rate and the highest level of personal satisfaction on the conclusion of the case; and that was family law."

Mitchell now practices with fellow family law attorneys R. Gayle Mack and Robin Neihaus. She continues to focus on the provision of various family law services to area clients in Marion and surrounding counties. Mitchell hopes that the idea of a unified family court will become a reality in the near future which would provide global benefits to clients and their families in their time of need. Mitchell, also a former hearing judge for the Indiana Alcoholic and Beverage Commission is a member of the Indianapolis Bar Association and has been seated on the Family Law Executive committee since 1994. She has been a Distinguished Fellow of the Indianapolis Bar Foundation since 1995, a member of the National Association of Counsel for Children, and is listed in the *Best Lawyers in America* consumer guide for 2001. Mitchell speaks frequently at teaching seminars covering practical divorce advocacy mediation evidence and courtroom trial skills. Mitchell is licensed to practice in Indiana, the U.S. District Court (southern and northern districts) as well as the U.S. Court of Appeals, 7th Circuit.

OGLETREE, DEAKINS, NASH, SMOAK AND STEWART, PC

IN MAY 2000 SEVERAL MEMBERS OF A LARGE Indianapolis general practice law firm's labor relations and employment department took a bold move to better serve their clients. The group broke away from the local firm to join a national firm, resulting in the opening of the Ogletree Deakins office.

"What has happened with accounting firms across the country is beginning with law firms today," said Chuck Baldwin, shareholder with Indianapolis' Ogletree Deakins office. "Our clients need for their lawyers to have a national presence as their companies consolidate operations through mergers and expand their presence across the country, and Indiana is behind the national curve regarding the number of national firms present to serve companies," Baldwin continued. The mid-sized firm is being squeezed out of this market.

Through the Ogletree Deakins office, the lawyers are better able to serve their clients. Since May, the Indianapolis office has established its mark with the firm becoming known as one of the most impressive new offices. It has grown to include 14 lawyers focusing their efforts on labor relations and employment. Backing this office is the bench strength of a much larger firm with a wealth of expertise and resources from coast to coast.

Ogletree Deakins opened its first offices in Atlanta, Georgia and Greenville, South Carolina. The need for representation in the areas of management in labor and employment matters encouraged the firm's expansion. Currently the firm operates 14 offices around the country. It is one of the four largest labor and employment firms in the country. It has been profiled as the most prominent labor relations firm in the U.S. in *The American Lawyer*. Clients range from start-up companies to international corporations, virtually covering every industry.

Ogletree Deakins attorneys have an "insider's view" of many of the agencies with which their clients interact. Included among its lawyers are a former member of the National Labor Relations Board, a former commissioner of the U.S. Equal Employment Opportunity Commission, a former Chief Legal Officer for the U.S. Department of Labor, former Counsel and Special Advisor to the Chairman of the Occupational Safety and Health Review Committee, and several former NLRB attorneys.

As a full-service labor and employment firm, Ogletree Deakins handles litigation, employee benefits, business immigration, construction surety, environmental, and occupational safety and health. Helping clients diminish problems before they become costly legal matters is a main objective for the firm's lawyers. "We encourage clients to be good employers," said Gray Geddie, Managing Shareholder. To that end, the firm holds briefings and seminars helping employers stay on top of current issues in the employment field. "Much of a lawyer's time is spent counseling their clients," he continued.

Unique to labor and employment law firms is Ogletree Governmental Affairs, Inc., a subsidiary of the Ogletree Deakins law firm, located in Washington, D.C. This is a full-service legislative and regulatory affairs consulting firm. These consultants can become part of a client's problem-solving team, work with trade associations, or serve as a client's representative in Washington, D.C.

PLEWS SHADLEY RACHER & BRAUN

PLEWS SHADLEY RACHER & BRAUN WAS FORMED IN 1988 to meet the changing needs of clients which required a firm focused in its practice in environmental law and complex litigation.

"Our niche is complex matters that often require scientific as well as legal understanding. This type of work requires us to stay on top of the latest developments and to work extremely hard to achieve the best possible results for our clients," said George Plews, co-founder of the firm.

"It's our responsibility to analyze and present complicated information to a judge, administrative agency or other decision-maker that will help them truly understand the subject. This is especially true in the area of environmental law, which includes about three-fourths of our practice," Plews added.

Examples of the firm's environmental work include pursuit of permits and defense of agency enforcement actions, prosecution of environmental or other insurance coverage claims, administrative appeals, assisting businesses in cleanups, cost recovery actions, defense and pursuit of toxic tort suits, and defense and management of Superfund claims. A number of the cases the firm has litigated have resulted in landmark appellate decisions, including cases granting broad protection to Indiana insurance policyholders against environmental liabilities, limiting the government's ability to deny permits and changing the law in areas ranging from product liability to administrative procedure.

Plews Shadley Racher & Braun has the largest environmental law practice in Indiana, and its expertise is widely sought. "We advise clients on the environmental aspects of business sales, acquisitions and mergers," said co-founder Sue Shadley. "We provide assistance in the legislative process as well, especially in environmental and insurance matters, and act as counsel for key trade associations."

The firm's diverse client list includes Eli Lilly and Co., Cinergy Corp., Dana Corp., Inland Paperboard and Packaging, and Raybestos Corp. The firm also represented the state of Indiana in litigation against tobacco companies that recently led to recovery of more than $4 billion for the State. It successfully litigated class action suits for consumers seeking recovery of overcharges in adjustable rate mortgages, the first such cases in the nation.

Plews Shadley Racher & Braun has grown from four to 23 attorneys in its Indianapolis office. Two attorneys in its South Bend office, which was established in 1999, serve the needs of clients in northern Indiana. Shadley believes that although the firm has grown and changed, it still has the look and feel of the original.

"Throughout the years, we have preserved the attributes of a small firm," Shadley said. "We have also taken a different approach to some of our working practices to ensure that our clients get the best counsel possible.

"For example, we tend to bring on associates who have been out of law school for at least five years so they already have substantial experience to offer clients. We also like to hire associates with degrees in scientific and technical areas. That strengthens the knowledge base of the entire firm," Shadley said.

"Our practice encompasses the leading edge of the law in areas where legal doctrine, public policy, science, and politics collide. There's always something new and exciting, and our attorneys thrive on the challenge," Plews said.

A History of the Indianapolis Legal Profession

RILEY BENNETT & EGLOFF, LLP

The law firm of Riley Bennett & Egloff began its existence in 1979 in a small office located in the old Merchants Bank Building. Its three attorneys shared a vision of building a respected business and litigation firm through a commitment to providing the highest quality legal services in a timely, result-oriented and cost-effective manner.

That commitment proved to be a recipe for success, resulting in steady and consistent growth for the firm during the ensuing years. Today Riley Bennett & Egloff maintains a comprehensive business and litigation practice, and a staff of 29 attorneys in offices on the 18th floor of the American United Life Insurance Company building. The attorneys of Riley Bennett & Egloff share a common bond of superior academic achievement and the same commitment to excellence that has guided the firm since its inception.

As the firm has grown, so has the breadth of its practice areas. These areas now include business and commercial law (including entity formation, mergers, acquisitions, lender documentation, creditors rights, state and federal regulatory matters and general contractual matters); commercial and other civil litigation (including insurance defense, product liability, environmental liability, toxic tort claims and appellate work); labor and employment law (representing management in employment discrimination claims, labor union matters, wage and hour claims, and the drafting and enforcement of employment agreements and policies); employee benefits law (including the establishment of stock option plans, 401(k) plans, employee stock ownership plans, and other qualified and non-qualified retirement plans, as well as representation in connection with fiduciary matters); real estate and construction law (including project and other contract documentation, zoning variances, and the enforcement of mechanics liens); estate and business succession planning (including trusts, wills, living wills, and family limited partnerships); and intellectual property (including trademarks, copyrights, and internet domain names). The firm provides legal services to local, regional, national and international businesses.

The breadth and diversity of the firm' clients has likewise expanded to include businesses in nearly every industry, including finance, insurance, manufacturing, publishing, data processing, real estate, transportation, wholesale and retail sales, publishing, and health care. Representative clients include: Fifth Third Bank, Provident Bank, Union Federal Savings Bank, the St. Paul Insurance Companies, the Fireman's Fund Insurance Companies, Illinois Farmers Insurance Company, St. Vincent Hospitals, Federal Express, McDonald's Corporation, Duke-Weeks Realty, Hunt Construction Group, Lehigh Portland Cement Company, and the Indianapolis Business Journal.

The attorneys of Riley Bennett & Egloff have always recognized that the provision of legal services is not an end unto itself, and that lawyers provide value to their clients by *solving* problems, not by simply tending to or administering them. Riley Bennett & Egloff heads into the twenty-first century ready and eager to solve its clients' twenty-first century problems, and confident that its commitment to excellence will provide the key to continued success in the years ahead.

ROWE & HAMILTON

Rowe & Hamilton was founded in 1984 by Timothy Rowe, David Hamilton and Tom Austin upon their graduation from Indiana University Law School in Indianapolis. The firm's dedication to defending the rights of the individual has made it a successful member of the Indianapolis legal community.

Located in the historic Victoria Center Building in downtown Indianapolis, Rowe & Hamilton is a firm of four attorneys: Timothy Rowe, David Hamilton, Thomas Robin and Kevin Shepherd. It has remained small by intention, according to partner Timothy Rowe. "We believe that we can go the extra mile for our clients by providing them with personal service. We emphasize direct client-to-attorney contact as a strength of our firm and as the key to building a relationship of trust and respect."

The firm's specialty is personal injury, including premises liability, automobile liability and medical malpractice. Rowe & Hamilton is also expanding its practice into employment law, including discrimination and harrassment, and litigation of nursing home abuse and neglect cases. "Rowe & Hamilton is interested in all areas of the law that protect and reinforce the individual's rights. Our attorneys are not afraid to step into a courtroom and try a case if that action is in the best interest of our client," Rowe said.

Rowe & Hamilton is highly active in both the Indianapolis community and the legal community. The firm participates in an internship program each year in which local high school students who are interested in a career in law spend the summer working in the office and gaining valuable on-the-job experience. As a participant in the annual Indiana Black Expo, Rowe & Hamilton has provided the expertise of an attorney at a mock trial to demonstrate the American judicial system to thousands of Expo attendees. Rowe & Hamilton has also partnered with local television station Fox 59 to sponsor fingerprinting programs that help register and protect the children of Indianapolis.

The firm's attorneys are members of the Marion County Bar Association, Indianapolis Bar Association, Indiana State Bar Assocation, Indiana Trial Lawyers Association, American Bar Association, and the American Trial Lawyers Association. Timothy Rowe currently serves on the board of directors of the Indiana Trial Lawyers Association, has chaired its Young Lawyers Committee and serves on its education committee. He is vice chair of the motor vehicle collision, highway, and premises liability section for the American Trial Lawyers Association and lectures frequently on automobile litigation, soft tissue cases and trial techniques. David Hamilton has served as an officer of the Marion County Bar Association, and, in 1986, made history by becoming the first African-American to serve as a probate commissioner in Marion County.

Rowe & Hamilton began advertising its services on television in 1986, years before most law firms chose this method to communicate with clients. Their advertising is direct, professional and designed to inform individuals of their legal rights. In addition to the Indianapolis office, Rowe & Hamilton also has an office in downtown Anderson. The firm is currently handling prominent cases in Florida and Arkansas.

As the city of Indianapolis has changed and prospered in recent years, so has Rowe & Hamilton. "From our downtown vantage point, we have seen significant progress in Indianapolis since our founding in 1984. We are proud that we have grown with the city and continue to provide the highest quality legal services to all members of the community," Rowe said.

A History of the Indianapolis Legal Profession

RUCKELSHAUS ROLAND KAUTZMAN & HASBROOK

The firm of Ruckelshaus Roland Kautzman & Hasbrook was established in 1895 by John C. Ruckelshaus, grandfather of current partner John C. Ruckelshaus. Throughout the past one hundred and five years, the firm has been a prominent and well-respected member of the Indianapolis legal community.

The firm's principal specialty is the representation of law enforcement officers in such areas as discipline, contract negotiation, defense of criminal charges and defense of civil litigation. Under the leadership of John C. Ruckelshaus, the firm began to establish its reputation in this area of the law in the 1960s and is now nationally recognized as a leader in the field. Ruckelshaus Roland Kautzman & Hasbrook is the only law firm in Indianapolis that offers this level of specialized expertise.

Current partners include John C. Ruckelshaus, Paul G. Roland, William A. Hasbrook, John F. Kautzman, Leo T. Blackwell and M. Elizabeth Bemis. In addition to the emphasis on law enforcement representation, each partner has developed experience and expertise in distinct areas of the law.

John C. Ruckelshaus specializes in law enforcment disciplinary proceedings, law enforcement liability defense and litigation. He has served as general counsel for the Indiana State Fraternal Order of Police and the Professional Firefighters Union of Indiana AFL-CIO since 1967. He was also an Indiana State Senator from 1957 to 1964.

Paul G. Roland concentrates in corporate law, litigation and labor and employment law. He served as an Indiana State Representative and as a member of the Indianapolis Metropolitan Development Commission. He is also currently serving as Vice Consul for Italy in the State of Indiana, a position appointed by Italy's Ministry of Foreign Affairs.

William A. Hasbrook's extensive experience is in personal injury, representing both the Plaintiff and the Defense. He also provides counsel in the areas of wills, trusts and probate and has served as Probate Court Commissioner and Deputy Prosecutor for Marion County.

John F. Kautzman is an experienced civil and criminal litigator who has also served as commissioner/judge pro tempore in the Marion County Circuit Court. He is a contributing author to *Indiana Lawyer* and serves on the Board of Managers of the Indianapolis Bar Association.

Leo T. Blackwell, a retired member of the Indianapolis Police Department, concentrates in contract negotiations, labor law and police associations. His honors include serving as president of the Indianapolis Fraternal Order of Police for five years. M. Elizabeth Bemis, who was named partner in 1998, practices in the areas of domestic relations, personal injury defense and law enforcement discipline.

The firm has had many distinguished partners in its history, including Gerald Reilly, primary author of the Taft Hartley Act; George Craig, former Governor of the State of Indiana; and former Indiana Supreme Court Justice Arch Bobbitt. Bill Ruckelshaus, brother of current partner John C. Ruckelshaus, was a member of the firm until 1968. At that time, he accepted an appointment with the U.S. Department of Justice in Washington, D.C., and went on to serve as acting FBI Director, acting Attorney General and the first director of the Environmental Protection Agency.

"Ruckelshaus Roland Kautzman & Hasbrook will continue to grow in the next decade and will offer additional legal services to meet the needs of our clients," said partner Paul G. Roland.

SOMMER & BARNARD

In 1968, long before the advent of mission statements and strategic plans, six attorneys joined together with one overriding purpose—to practice law at the highest professional standard without sacrificing life outside the office. That year James K. Sommer and his long-time friend and colleague William C. Barnard coined the phrase "Quality life-Quality law" to describe their new firm.

Over the years, as some early partners have left and new partners have come through the ranks or moved from other firms, the firm has not lost sight of its roots. With each new employee, from staff person to attorney, Sommer & Barnard tries to instill the tradition of "quality life-quality law." According to Jim Sommer, maintaining the proper balance between work and life "makes each attorney more effective and helps us to form true partnerships with our clients."

In 1968, the firm was primarily a small litigation boutique. Today, as the firm has topped 50 attorneys, Sommer & Barnard is a complete service business law firm helping businesses and entrepreneurs, throughout Indiana and the nation, formulate, pursue and achieve their goals. The firm's current practice areas include general corporate, litigation, securities, mergers and acquisitions, creditors' rights and bankruptcy law, tax and estate planning, real estate, insurance, labor and employment law, environmental law, governmental affairs, technology transactions and telecommunications and regulatory law. The growth in practice areas developed out of a need to meet the challenges facing the individuals and businesses that the firm represents. Even with all of this growth, Sommer & Barnard has not sacrificed its commitment to "quality life-quality law." The firm continues to provide prompt and expert legal service while at the same time recognizing that there is more to life than practicing law.

Some of the firm's earliest highlights include representing the Indiana Pacers in its antitrust suit against the NBA, which led to the Pacers joining the NBA. The firm also served as lead plaintiff's counsel in the gypsum wallboard antitrust litigation and the plywood antitrust litigation, national cases based in San Francisco and New Orleans respectively. More recently, the firm served as Indiana counsel on behalf of Amoco Corporation in its merger into a wholly-owned subsidiary of BP Oil. At the time, this transaction was the largest industrial merger in the world. In addition, the firm and its attorneys have been instrumental in organizing and chartering one of the nation's first purely internet-based banks, representing the State of Indiana in its litigation against the tobacco industry, serving as special master in the Bridgestone/Firestone multi-district recall litigation, representing over 150 companies in the Seymour Recycling Superfund litigation, one of the first and largest environmental cleanup cases in Indiana history, and representing one of Indiana's largest public retailers in its Chapter 11 bankruptcy.

With each success, Sommer & Barnard's attorneys and other specialists continue the firm's solid reputation for being proactive in solving problems and helping clients. Large or small, friendly or hostile, public or private, Sommer & Barnard is equipped to provide legal counsel and make strategic recommendations for any type of business. As the firm grows, one principle remains constant. Sommer & Barnard's attorneys practice law at the highest level of professionalism while at the same time maintaining a life outside the office. It is a recipe for success, both for our clients and our professionals.

OSBORN HINER & LISHER, P.C.

Osborn, Hiner & Lisher began as Osborn & Hiner. Hiner started his professional life after graduating from Wabash College as a newspaper reporter. He took a commission in the Air Force at the beginning of World War II, and served for a time in a unit commanded by Ronald Reagan.

Because of his newspaper experience, Hiner was asked to serve as the first editor of the state bar journal, which was named *Res Gestae*.

Active in legal ethics matters, Osborn served as a member and then chairman of the Indianapolis and Indiana State Bar Legal Ethics committees. He also chaired the Indiana State Bar committee to study the proposed ABA code of ethics.

John L. Lisher joined the firm a few years after its formation, and remains with the firm today. Hiner died several years ago. Osborn retired and wrote a history book about atrocities during the American-Indian War published by Random House in January, 2001 entitled *The Wild Frontier*.

Currently, Osborn Hiner & Lisher operates with John Lisher and Robert S. O'Dell as partners and two associate lawyers. A concentration of the firm's work involves defending casualty insurance companies and self-insured manufacturers. The firm also works in the areas of personal injury, general civil trial litigation, and product liability.

As the city of Indianapolis has grown throughout the past 27 years, the firm has grown to keep abreast of the changing needs of its clients. The firm prides itself on growing the quality of service provided to its clients and offering lawyers interesting work that stimulates development.

Robert S. O'Dell, left, and John Lisher.

STEPHEN PLOPPER & ASSOCIATES

Within minutes of conversing with Stephen Plopper & Associates one learns that this is a unique law firm. Through a local entrepreneur Plopper began working in Warsaw, Poland in 1983. For 14 years, Plopper worked in Poland, opening a law firm under the name Klineman, Rose and Wolf–Poland in 1991. Then, in 1997, Plopper left the Indianapolis firm he was with to open his own firm. One year later he, along with his Polish partners, purchased the Polish operation, known today as Klineman, Rose and Wolf–Poland.

Plopper spends about 100 days a year in his Polish office. While he concentrates his work, both locally and abroad, on mergers and acquisitions, the Polish firm offers a wide range of legal services to both domestic and multinational clients. The firm represents businesses ranging from large companies to individual entrepreneurs. In cooperation with the Indianapolis office, the firm has a proven record of dealing with cross-border issues. It has created a strong customs specialty and has worked with the Polish Government to draft a new customs law. The firm has also been active with the Polish Government on many other levels including privatization issues, as well as advising the Government itself.

Plopper operates as a solo practitioner from his downtown Indianapolis office, representing venture capital funds and local manufacturing companies. He counts among his accomplishments closing business acquisitions in 12 countries around the world. He is a member of the Bar Association and has led many seminars on the topic of international law.

JOSE D. SALINAS

Although he may not practice in a posh downtown office, Jose D. Salinas knows that he is right where he needs to be to reach his clients. Working as a solo practitioner on Indianapolis' Southeast side, Salinas is easily accessible to the majority of his clients. With a focus on criminal, immigration and administrative legal work, Salinas and his secretary manage a busy office.

Salinas came to Indianapolis in 1994 to attend Indiana University School of Law. Upon graduating, he decided to stay and begin his law practice, which opened in 1997. When he first came to Indianapolis he says he could count the number of authentic Mexican restaurants on one hand. Since that time the Hispanic population has exploded bringing with it many positive rewards in the form of business development as well as challenges in the form of communication for the city.

His arrival in Indianapolis at the right time, Salinas believes, has helped him make a difference and be successful.

Salinas represents a population that needs his attention "I can't imagine sitting in a court room having people decide my fate and not be able to understand what is being said," Salinas commented regarding his work. While the majority of his clients come from the Hispanic community, Salinas is a contracted public defender with Marion County, which helps him expand his reach into the community. He also works with Hamilton County representing its Hispanic population and was appointed by Mayor Bart Peterson to serve on the Marion County Zoning Board II.

RANDALL R. SEVENISH, ESQ.

Randall R. Sevenish, founder of Sevenish Law Firm, P.C., has committed and limited his practice exclusively to accident and injury law. His firm zealously seeks full, fair, and prompt compensation, as the law allows, for injured people. Its goal is to provide superior, professional, and ethical personal injury legal services.

His professional, technical training and life experiences include not only the law, but also law enforcement and martial arts. Mr. Sevenish is a retired Captain from the Marion County Sheriff's Department. Although he obtained his law degree and began practicing personal injury law in 1985, he remained with the MCSD until 1990. He retired with numerous professional credits including, being founder and original commander of the department's SWAT team and being named "Officer of the Year" by the city of Indianapolis. He also received an "Official Proclamation" from the city of Indianapolis by Mayor, William Hudnut III, proclaiming November 8, 1988 "Captain Randall R. Sevenish Day" for "strengthening the community through the professional training of its police officers."

The martial arts have played an important role in his life, so much so that *Indiana Lawyer* published a feature article about his relationship between law and martial arts. Mr. Sevenish, a 6th Degree Black Belt and *Karate Hall of Fame* member, has trained hundreds of students & police and believes that martial arts properly taught can profoundly influence a person's life because it trains you in respect, self-discipline, self-confidence, and believing in yourself without limits.

He believes his life experiences in law enforcement, martial arts & the law, coupled with deep spiritual beliefs, explain his tenacious work ethic and record of "service" to his clients.

A History of the Indianapolis Legal Profession

TABBERT HAHN EARNEST & WEDDLE

FOUNDED IN 1987, TABBERT HAHN EARNEST & WEDDLE, LLP IS A young firm long on experience.

While the firm prides itself on its expertise inside the courtroom, its attorneys share a common vision to successfully resolve disputes before they reach trial.

"From that thinking has evolved a sophisticated group of attorneys who can meet client needs in a variety of specialized areas," said Don A. Tabbert, one of the firm's founders and managing partners. "We all came together at a stage in our individual practices where our experience allows us to provide what our clients need."

Firm members realize one element is crucial to successful legal representation: listening.

"In order for our firm to orchestrate legal strategies that really meet the client's needs, we must determine their goals, objectives, and personal or business concerns," Tabbert said. "The ability to listen allows us to serve current needs, define and plan for future needs and avert the potential for crisis."

Practice Overview

Tabbert Hahn Earnest & Weddle maintains an extensive practice in the healthcare, business, corporate, and real estate arenas as well as a complex litigation practice incorporating both criminal and civil law. Our litigation practice has represented a number of high profile clients. From the healthcare area, a very successful medical malpractice defense has evolved. Additionally, the firm has developed a family law practice and a governmental practice which represents a variety of local and state agencies.

Notable Cases

One of the firm's most notable cases continues to play out: the defense of Vermillion County Hospital against 85 wrongful death claims is the largest medical malpractice claim ever filed against an Indiana healthcare provider. Former nurse Orville Lynn Majors, called one of history's most prolific serial killers by the media, was convicted in 1999 for killing six patients. During the investigation, he was linked to 124 more deaths that occurred in the hospital over a 13-month period.

In the governmental arena, the firm handled the very complicated and competitive licensing of the state's first river boat casino license in its representation of Trump Casino on Lake Michigan, in Gary, Indiana. The firm continues to support Mr. Trump's interest in Indiana as well as Bally Entertainment and several other gaming related companies.

Future Plans

While firm members plan to grow their healthcare practice, one area they will focus on in the coming years is the governmental arena. "Government is trying to connect more with people's lives, while at the same time, evolving into a more efficient operation," partner Robert Weddle said. "Government's role in privatizing departments brings many more legal issues to tackle."

Community Involvement

The firm's 14 attorneys are vigorous supporters in both dollars and hours donated to area charities. The firm as a whole has been a longtime supporter of the Indiana University School of Law's Bloomington and Indianapolis campuses and their respective programs. The firm gave generously to the capital campaign for the Indianapolis School's new building completed in 2001. Other agencies which benefit from the firms support include the Indiana Bar Foundation and the Indianapolis Bar Foundation, WFYI FM 90.1, Wheeler Mission, YMCA at the Athenaeum, and the Washington Township Schools Foundation.

Founding Members

Don A. Tabbert, an I.U. School of Law graduate was admitted to the bar in 1953 and is licensed to practice before all Indiana State and Federal courts as well as the U.S. Court of Appeals for the Seventh Circuit, U.S. Tax Court for the Southern District of Indiana and U.S. Supreme Court. Mr. Tabbert was a United States District Attorney with the Southern District of Indiana.

Gregory F. Hahn, also a graduate of the I.U. School of Law, was admitted to the bar in 1974 and licensed to practice in Indiana and U.S. District Court, Southern and Northern District of Indiana, the U.S. Court of Appeals, Seventh Circuit. He is a member of the Indianapolis, Indiana State, and American Bar Associations, and the American Association of Gaming Lawyers and several local private and public boards of directors.

Lante K. Earnest, an I.U. School of Law graduate was admitted to the bar in 1973 in Indiana and is licensed to practice in Indiana, U.S. District Court, Northern and Southern Districts of Indiana and U.S. Court of Appeals, Seventh Circuit. He is active in a variety of activities with IUPUI and the Indianapolis Bar Foundation and serves on Natural Resources and Heritage Trust Foundations.

Robert G. Weddle, a *cum laude* graduate of I.U. School of Law, was admitted to the bar in 1972 and is licensed to practice in Indiana, U.S. District Court, Northern and Southern Districts of Indiana and U.S. Court of Appeals, Seventh Circuit. He has authored several articles on trial tactics and procedure and frequently lectures on those topics.

A History of the Indianapolis Legal Profession 201

SOLOMON & SOLOMON

WORKING ALONG SIDE HIS FATHER FOR FIVE YEARS PROVIDED MARTIN Solomon with a thorough understanding of both working with clients and managing a law practice. Growing up in Albany, New York, Martin Solomon and his brother Mitchell were the sons of a well-respected area lawyer, who in 1947 was appointed by President Truman to be a Federal Judge. Upon his retirement in 1982, Judge Solomon was one of the longest serving Federal Judges in the nation.

In 1984 Martin Solomon journeyed to Indianapolis to visit some friends, and he just never left. He opened his solo practice and began representing clients on criminal defense and personal injury cases. His reputation as an excellent attorney circulated and his client list grew simply through referrals. Three years later in 1987, Mr. Solomon's brother, Mitchell, joined him in Indianapolis and the two formed a partnership that continues today.

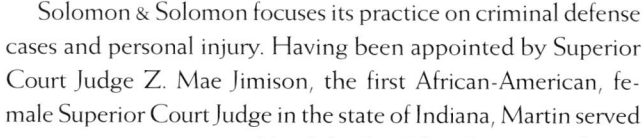

Solomon & Solomon focuses its practice on criminal defense cases and personal injury. Having been appointed by Superior Court Judge Z. Mae Jimison, the first African-American, female Superior Court Judge in the state of Indiana, Martin served as a public defender. After three years, he resigned his position to devote more time to his private practice.

A member of the Federal Criminal Justice Act Panel since 1984, Mr. Solomon has represented clients in cases ranging from murder to the Federal "Getto Boys" drug ring to the winner of $89.3 million in the Powerball lotto.

Both Martin and Mitchell are members of the Indianapolis and Indiana State Bar Associations. Martin is also a member of the National Association of Criminal Defense Attorneys, serves as a judge pro-tem, and is active within the community.

STEVEN A. SPENCE

AN ATTORNEY-MEDIATOR, STEVEN SPENCE IS founder of The Mediation Alternative. He is actively engaged in promoting the use of mediation throughout Indiana as a preferred means for resolving both civil and domestic disputes.

With more than 20 years experience as a litigator in the areas of civil, domestic, and criminal litigation, Mr. Spence has come to believe that mediation can, in most cases, help minimize the cost and risk involved in litigation. In 1993 Mr. Spence began shifting his practice from litigation to mediation. Since January 2000, he has devoted his entire practice to mediation and arbitration.

Mr. Spence is a member of the Board of Directors of the Indiana Association of Mediators (IAM), the largest state-wide mediation organization dedicated to promoting mediation in Indiana. He is a past president of the organization, a member of SPIDR, and the ADR section of the Indiana State Bar Association.

Mr. Spence provides a range of alternative dispute resolution services including arbitration and mediation of personal injury, business, contract, domestic, real estate, and ADA disputes. In 1998, as part of his domestic mediation practice, Mr. Spence was instrumental, in conjunction with the Marion County Prosecutor's Office, in developing the Title IV-D pilot program. The program assists battling couples in IV-D court resolve child-related disputes through mediation and thereby avoid a lengthy court battle. The program has enjoyed an 80% success rate.

Mr. Spence was the first mediator in Indianapolis to put his calendar of available dates on the internet to allow disputing parties to easily determine dates for mediation. Mr. Spence prides himself in successfully meeting the arbitration/mediation needs of the general public and the legal community in a fast, efficient and cost effective manner. Mr. Spence is positioned to assist in resolving through mediation or arbitration whatever disputes may arise.

WALLACK SOMERS & HAAS

"IF WHAT YOU DO AFFECTS OR IS AFFECTED BY COMMERCIAL REAL ESTATE, then we are the attorneys to consult," explains Barry Wallack, the managing partner of the six attorneys who comprise Wallack Somers & Haas, a real estate boutique firm located in the heart of Indianapolis.

With over 75 years of combined real estate experience, Barry Wallack, Michael Wallack, George Somers, and Karl Haas played a lead role in a great many of the real estate projects that have shaped Indianapolis over the last twenty years, including the development of Circle Centre Mall, Deer Creek Music Center, and Conseco Fieldhouse as well as the renovation of Glendale Mall, the Murat Centre, and the Naval Air Warfare Center.

The firm's attorneys have represented numerous well-known retail, office, industrial and apartment developers, as well as the institutional owners of many of Indianapolis' prominent properties. The firm does not restrict itself solely to Indianapolis, however, and has recently assisted clients in transactions throughout the greater Midwest, Florida, and Texas.

Each of the attorneys at Wallack Somers & Haas brings to their firm the knowledge and experience gained from working at larger firms. Barry and Michael Wallack were previously with Klineman Rose Wolf & Wallack, where Barry was the managing partner, while George Somers and Karl Haas were both partners with Baker & Daniels.

Wallack Somers & Haas clearly recognizes the trend in today's legal market: either expand to be a regional "megafirm" or provide concentrated legal services as a boutique. Each of the attorneys at Wallack Somers & Haas made the choice to leave a larger firm for the advantages of the small boutique firm. Specifically, they enjoy the close personal contact with their clients, and their clients like knowing that one of the principals always will be directly available. The firm strives to combine a "small firm's attention to the client's needs and interests and the sophistication and experience of a large firm."

Wallack Somers & Haas' clients also appreciate that the attorneys approach problems from the client's point of view. "We understand the risks inherent in development, and help clients navigate the most direct route around those risks. We recognize that substantial assets are at stake, and we work as a team with our clients to focus on the bottom line," explains George Somers. "From the lender's point of view, it helps to hire a firm that understands the risk-takers because they are the borrowers," explains Michael Wallack, "Lenders also are trying to be responsive to their borrowers, so having an attorney understand what the other side needs is tremendously useful."

By focusing on what they do best, the firm is also free to guide their clients in the best direction for any additional legal assistance. "We can help clients find the best counsel to assist in other matters that arise. This works well for all involved. For commercial real estate, talk to us. If it's something else, then we can guide you to the right firm or attorney who best can suit your particular needs," says Karl Haas.

In short, this new boutique firm is confident of its role in the fast changing legal environment and of its value to the commercial real estate community.

A History of the Indianapolis Legal Profession

WILSON KEHOE & WININGHAM

For 30 years Wilson Kehoe & Winingham has been dedicated to representing plaintiffs who are personal injury or wrongful death victims of aviation and vehicle accidents, product liability situations, fires and explosions, and medical malpractice. The depth of experience of the firm's three partners—Harry Wilson, Bruce Kehoe, and Bill Winingham—is complemented by an expert support staff, including a full-time medical doctor and nurse who provide medical expertise in serious injury cases. This experience, coupled with a record of success, has resulted in the firm receiving the highest rating available—the Martindale-Hubbell AV rating.

With seven lawyers and a support staff of 35, Wilson Kehoe & Winingham has the capability to bring cases to life for the jury when necessary. Using demonstrative evidence, such as a semi tractor-trailer cab or even a cockpit of an airplane, in court has become a trademark for the firm.

Through extensive discovery, computer graphic animation of crashes and explosions, and use of expert witnesses, the firm has successfully represented victims in many well-known cases such as a midair collision over Greenwood, Indiana, that resulted in the deaths of several prominent Indianapolis civic leaders and caused serious burns to others. When a young driver suffered severe brain damage from colliding at night with a flatbed trailer not properly equipped with lights and reflective tape, Bruce Kehoe used the firm's resources to demonstrate how the accident could have been avoided. (Retro-reflective taping has since been mandated for use on all such tractor-trailer rigs.) On a day when the Indianapolis 500 turned deadly for one spectator, Bill Winingham's successful efforts to recover damages for the victim's widow included nearly 40 depositions of engineers, race car drivers, and racing officials, including depositions in Europe of the race car manufacturer. The firm set National Precedent when, on behalf of his client, Harry Wilson successfully sued the United States government for failing to warn an airplane pilot carrying USAC officials of dangerous weather conditions ahead, resulting in the crash of the plane and the death of five people.

Harry Wilson's background as a former Air Force pilot and mechanical engineer has allowed him to be successful in pursuing aviation and product liability claims. Harry is also a member of the Indiana Trial Lawyers Association, and the Lawyers-Pilots Bar Association. He was the Indiana Trial Lawyers Association's 1990 Trial Lawyer of the Year.

Bruce Kehoe began his professional career as a registered physical therapist, which helps him form a unique perspective on relating the law to the practice of medicine and the lives of seriously injured people. In addition to his medical knowledge, Bruce also is a pilot and works on the aviation cases. Bruce is on the Indiana Trial Lawyers Association's Board of Directors. He often lectures on issues of medical malpractice and personal injury litigation.

As a former federal and state court prosecutor, Bill Winingham gained experience in taking depositions and trying lawsuits in the Marion County Prosecutor's and U.S. Attorney's Offices. Bill focuses on product liability matters, fire/explosion cases, and motor vehicle accidents. He served as liaison counsel in the nationwide multi-district litigation against Bridgestone/Firestone and Ford Motor Company. He is also on the Indiana Trial Lawyers Association's Board of Directors.

Partners of Wilson Kehoe & Winingham, left to right, Bruce Kehoe, Harry Wilson, and Bill Winingham.

WOODARD, EMHARDT, NAUGHTON, MORIARTY & McNETT

After spending most of his 63-year career in the relatively arcane practice of intellectual property law, Harold Woodard sees a promising future for people who choose the same path he did. That and the $500 scholarship he received to attend Harvard College in 1929, may explain why he has given so many scholarships to aspiring young attorneys over the years. Woodard went on to graduate from Harvard Law School in 1936. Ten years later, he joined the firm now known as Woodard, Emhardt, Naughton, Moriarty & McNett, which limits its practice to an area that many attorneys gladly avoid.

"About 20 to 25 years ago, we were one of only three firms in town that concentrated on intellectual property law," Woodard said. "When the other firms merged with larger general practices, we wondered if we should be doing the same." But a few years later, Woodard said the firm doubled in size, partly because of referrals it received from general practice lawyers who weren't worried about losing clients to their highly-specialized peers at Woodard, Emhardt, Naughton, Moriarty & McNett.

As one of the few remaining Indianapolis law firms that restricts its practice to intellectual property, Woodard expects the growth of technology and information to increase demand for the firm's unusual breed of attorneys, each of whom also has an advanced degree in science or engineering. Some members of the firm also have technical work experience in industry. Their clients come from all over the world, drawn by the firm's expertise in handling everything from intellectual property litigation to lengthy patent applications.

Woodard became the third partner to manage the firm founded in 1879 by Charles Jacobs—a man with remarkably broad interests beyond his law practice. By the time he died at age 54, Jacobs had also been a newspaper correspondent, astronomer, composer, lyricist, and teacher. Among his gifts to the community was his role in establishing two law schools where he also taught classes.

Jacobs' teaching tradition has continued within the firm. Harold Woodard served as an adjunct professor of patent, trademark and copyright law at the Indiana University School of Law-Indianapolis from 1957 to 1988 and was followed by Thomas Q. Henry, former President of The Indianapolis Bar Association. Joseph Naughton, who has been a member of the firm since 1960, served as an adjunct professor at the Indiana University School of Law-Bloomington and has been succeeded by Daniel J. Lueders. The firm's attorneys also maintain an active presence in Indianapolis civic and professional affairs, serving on the boards of numerous organizations.

Partners of Woodard, Emhardt, Naughton, Moriarty & McNett, seated left to right, C. David Emhardt and Harold R. Woodard; standing left to right, Thomas Q. Henry, John C. McNett, Jack V. Moriarty and Joseph A. Naughton, Jr.

With a staff of 45 to 50 attorneys, Woodard, Emhardt, Naughton, Moriarty & McNett is managed more by consensus than not, said David Emhardt, a partner who serves as its unofficial leader. "As we've gotten bigger, we've questioned whether running things by committee is still right for us, but that's our current style and it's one that's given us steady growth and a harmonious atmosphere that still allows us to serve our clients very well."

A History of the Indianapolis Legal Profession

YORK SCHRAGER BAXTER JAMES & ROSE

When you walk through the door at YSBJ&R, you are immediately greeted by a massive bronze eagle statue and artwork featuring the eagle. The firm's founder, Robert W. York, says that the eagles provide constant reminders to us "of the freedoms we enjoy and that as lawyers we must continue to serve as both the shield and the sword protecting and fighting for these freedoms."

The law firm of York Schrager Baxter James & Rose, located on the Northeast side of Indianapolis, was founded under the name of Robert W. York & Associates in 1984. When Mr. York began private practice in 1973, he had already become a seasoned trial lawyer as an intern deputy prosecutor in the felony courts of Marion County. His reputation as a thoroughly prepared and effective court room lawyer led to his appointment as an Indiana Administrative Law Judge for the next ten years, during which time he also maintained a private practice. In 1985, Edward F. Schrager, a former deputy prosecutor for Monroe and Greene counties and the son of South Bend, Indiana lawyer, Bernard Schrager, moved his private practice to Indianapolis and became a member of the firm. In 1987, Arthur R. Baxter, Jr., grandson of former Marion Circuit Court Judge, John L. Niblack, joined the firm. In 1990 the law firm's name became York, Schrager & Baxter. In 1994, attorneys Robert G. James, his son, Robert G. James, Jr., and Cynthia S. Rose, a registered nurse and attorney, joined the firm and the name of the firm became York Schrager Baxter James & Rose. Today, the firm's principals are: Robert W. York; Edward F. Schrager; Arthur R. Baxter, Jr.; Robert G. James, Jr.; Cynthia S. Rose and Cynthia A. Marcus.

A massive bronze eagle statue greets visitors to the offices of York Schrager Baxter James & Rose.

"Our firm was founded on the principles of providing ethical and high quality legal services to people from all walks of life. We have built our firm on a reputation for integrity and vigorous representation in virtually every area of the law. The firm's size allows us to interact one on one with each other and with our clients. We never want our clients to feel that they become simply a number. Instead, our philosophy is that when clients come to the firm once for legal help, they will want to return for all their legal needs and be proud to refer us to their friends and neighbors," stated Mr. York.

When York founded the firm, the lawyers and staff shared less than 600 square feet of office space. Today the firm's offices include space of more than 5,000 square feet devoted to providing professional and comfortable surroundings to the firms' members and clients. York Schrager Baxter James & Rose has been awarded the highest rating of "A/V" by the Martindale-Hubble National Lawyers Rating Service.

The law firm of York Schrager Baxter James & Rose believes that its uniqueness is formed by the varied backgrounds of its lawyers. With experience as judges, authors, business owners, registered nurses, teachers, prosecutors, insurance adjusters, and military officers, the lawyers use this wealth of work and personal life experiences to work together as a team to solve the real life problems of all its clients. The firm also takes seriously its involvement in the community with its lawyers serving on community boards ranging from the Humane Society to the Library Board. They also contribute their time and resources to numerous service organizations, home owner's associations, youth sport teams and charitable groups.

The firm's lawyers focus their individual practices on particular areas of experience. The firm has lawyers experienced in trying cases to the court or jury; lawyers who have an emphasis in personal injury and insurance law; lawyers who practice family law, including adoption, guardianships and juvenile matters; lawyers who practice in the area of trusts, estate planning, and elder law; lawyers who use their registered nursing experience in matters involving health care disputes; lawyers representing those charged with a crime in either federal or state court; lawyers experienced in corporate and business matters; lawyers who draft, interpret and help enforce contracts; and, lawyers experienced in representing persons on general legal matters. Attorneys at YSBJ&R are members of local, state and national bar associations and belong to numerous trial lawyer associations and other professional associations.

York Schrager Baxter James & Rose founder Robert W. York.

Robert W. York, a native of Fort Wayne, Indiana, obtained his Bachelor of Science degree from Indiana University and in 1973 earned his Doctor of Jurisprudence Degree, *cum laude*, from the Indiana University School of Law, Indianapolis, Indiana. He has extensive court and jury trial experience and is also frequently appointed as Special Judge to preside over major felony criminal cases. Mr. York devotes his practice to trying civil law suits in courts throughout Indiana. He is admitted to the bar of the United States Supreme Court and all of the courts in Indiana. He is also a recognized author in a number of legal publications and the former long-time editor of *Verdict Magazine*, a publication distributed to all Indiana courts and trial lawyers. He is a past president of the Indiana Trial Lawyers Association, an officer since 1993 and a member of it's Board of Directors since 1983. He is featured in the Bar Register of Preeminent Lawyers, is designated as Senior Counsel by the American College of Barristers and is a Life Member, National Registry of Who's Who. Mr. York is also certified by the United States Hockey Association as a Master Coach.

Edward F. Schrager, a native of South Bend, Indiana, attended Columbia University, New York and received his B.A. degree, *cum laude*, from Indiana University. In 1980 he received his Doctor of Jurisprudence degree from Indiana University School of Law, Bloomington, Indiana. During his four years as Deputy Prosecuting Attorney, Mr. Schrager prosecuted violent crime and major narcotic cases. Today, he is primarily involved in litigation with an emphasis on federal criminal and civil cases. He also handles personal injury, all aspects of family law, and represents several corporations of substantial net worth. He is admitted to the bar of the United States Supreme Court and all of the courts in Indiana. In 2000 he was appointed to serve on the Federal Judicial Merit Selection Panel.

Arthur R. Baxter, Jr., an Indianapolis native, received his B.A. degree from Vassar College, Poughkeepsie, NY, and his

Doctor of Jurisprudence from Indiana University School of Law, Indianapolis, Indiana in 1986. While attending the Indiana University School of Law, he served as Associate Editor of the Indiana Law Review. He has represented hundreds of injured people, and has handled a variety of employment law matters. He is admitted to the bar of the United States Supreme Court and all of the courts in Indiana. He is a contributing author to *Verdict* Magazine. He advises numerous business entities and is regularly engaged in complex commercial and business litigation matters. Mr. Baxter is also a member of the Millersville Lodge 126 and the Ancient Accepted Scottish Rite.

Robert G. James, Jr., a native of Hamilton County, Indiana, received his B.A. degree from DePauw University, Greencastle, Indiana. In 1992, he received his Doctor of Jurisprudence from Indiana University School of Law, Indianapolis, Indiana. Prior to receiving his law degree, he worked for eight years for Farm Bureau Insurance. Mr. James' legal practice focuses on personal injury and insurance contract dispute. His many years of claims adjusting experience and his subsequent personal injury law experience assist him in optimizing recovery for his clients. He is admitted to the bar of all of the courts in Indiana. Mr. James is also active with numerous Masonic organizations and is currently the incoming Commander-in-Chief of the Scottish Rite Valley of Indianapolis and Marshal of Murat Temple, Indianapolis. He is an officer in the Red Cross of Constantine and Parliamentarian of ROJ Court 15.

Cynthia S. Rose, a native of Hastings, Nebraska, received her B.S. degree from the University of Nebraska, her Master of Nursing Degree at the University of Illinois, Chicago, Illinois, and her Doctor of Jurisprudence from the Indiana University School of Law, Indianapolis, Indiana, in 1988. She began her professional career as a registered nurse and practiced nursing for 13 years throughout the Midwest. Ms. Rose then attended law school and obtained her law degree. She has been practicing law since 1989. The combination of nursing and law is particularly advantageous to her and her clients in cases involving injury and medical malpractice. She is admitted to the bar of all of the courts in Indiana. Ms. Rose is a member of the American Association of Nurse Attorneys. Having once specialized in cardiovascular nursing, she frequently speaks to groups of nurses, physicians, and EMT's about legal matters involving health care.

Cynthia A. Marcus, a native of Rockford, Michigan, received her B. S. degree from Ball State University, Muncie, Indiana, and her Doctor of Jurisprudence Degree from Indiana University School of Law, Indianapolis, Indiana, in 1994. She began her professional career as a registered nurse and served as a Captain in the United States Army. These experiences allow her to bring a special expertise to the area of law involving personal injuries suffered by those who have been injured through negligence of another. The areas in which she represents injured people include medical malpractice, car accidents, and injury by unsafe products. Ms. Marcus also represents individuals in military law matters, family disputes, including divorce, juvenile law, child support, visitation, and adoption. She is admitted to the bar of all of the courts in Indiana. Ms. Marcus is a member of several professional organizations including the Sigma Theta Tau and the American Association of Nurse Attorneys.

YOSHA KRAHULIK & LEVY

Civil and personal injury lawyers Louis "Buddy" Yosha, Jon D. Krahulik & William Levy pack the experience and influence of a large firm into the size of a small and flexible practice of 10 lawyers. While the firm has evolved over the years, how the lawyers try cases remains largely the same.

"One of the basic tenants of the personal injury practice is to do all that you should do to maximize your client's recovery," said Jon Krahulik, a partner with Yosha Krahulik & Levy since 1994. "The areas in which we practice have changed and evolved but how we practice and how we treat our clients goes unchanged."

In a legal career spanning more than three decades, Buddy Yosha has practiced with and mentored some of the states brightest lawyers. Many of them have gone on to create their own successful practices and law firms. A prolific writer in state and national legal journals, Yosha has been written about as well. *Fortune, Cosmopolitan, The Washington Post* and *The Wall Street Journal* have all reported on Yosha's savvy trial tactics.

"From the beginning of my career I have just worked really hard and it's paid off for me," recalled Yosha, a 1963 graduate of Indiana University School of Law-Bloomington. "I've been successful, but I've also been blessed to work with great lawyers and who bring great cases and great clients."

Yosha is well known for his trial preparation skills —described by those who practice with him and against him as "meticulous" and "painstaking." Krahulik, on the other hand, has admittedly the opposite approach to a trial. "I'm a little more laid back in how I approach a trial and a jury, but that reaps rewards for our clients because we are a great team in the courtroom."

While each handles their own caseload, Yosha and Krahulik routinely team up when the stakes are the highest.

"Jon, as a former Indiana Supreme Court Justice, knows so much about the law and he sees formations in the law because he has operated from above the fray," Yosha said. "He brings with him into the courtroom a confidence that our clients and, ultimately the jury, really pick up on. His best attribute is how well he can summarize the complex points we are trying to make and help the jury understand."

With so many years of practice among the three partners, there are several unique and important cases. In *Schmidt vs. Alrelco Inc.* Yosha and Krahulik argued their client was injured seriously as a result of a fall because of a clean-up crew's work before the customer areas were closed. Yosha and Krahulik proved the Alrelco-managed National Car Rental branch had assigned the crew to cleanup an hour early in order to avoid paying overtime. The firm's persuasion of the jury resulted in a $5.5 million verdict for their client, which was the largest of its kind in Indiana.

While the firm will stay rooted in its personal injury and professional negligence practice, Krahulik said the firm plans to expand deeper into medical malpractice as well as employment litigation. The Krahulik name will likely be with the firm

Partners of Yosha Krahulik & Levy, left to right, Jon D. Krahulik, William Levy, Louis "Buddy" Yosha.

a long time as Jon is currently joined by David, his oldest son and, after graduation from law school next year, by Samuel, his youngest son.

William Levy, who, like Krahulik, graduated from I.U. School of Law-Indianapolis, has maintained a highly successful practice over the last 35 years. A former prosecutor, public defender and Municipal Court Judge, he has tried over 100 jury trails both as a sole practitioner and as a partner in the firm. His current area of emphasis is worker's compensation, where much of his work has helped define the definition of "disability" in Indiana law.

With a professional staff and the drive to expand into new areas of the law, as well as the perspective on serving on the bench, Yosha Krahulik and Levy exists as a rare bird on the state's legal landscape.

VAN VALER LAW FIRM

ORIGINALLY LOCATED IN DOWNTOWN Indianapolis, the Van Valer Law Firm was founded in 1963 as Williams Dixon & Van Valer. In 1967 the firm relocated to the heart of old downtown Greenwood. Today the firm has three principal lawyers: Joe N. Van Valer, Joyce A. Neis, and Tom Vander Luitgaren.

The firm began as a general practice firm, developed an emphasis on criminal work in the late 1960s and early 1970s. Through the years, the firm discontinued its criminal work to focus on business transactions and real estate law, including planning and zoning. Ms. Neis has developed additional areas of practice in domestic relations, school law, and business litigation. Mr. Vander Luitgaren has added emphasis to general litigation and estate planning.

Van Valer Law Firm can be found in the heart of downtown Greenwood at Main and Madison in a building built in 1860, which is noted on the National Historic Register.

Mr. Van Valer served as a member of the Board of Directors of the Home Warranty Corporation of Washington D.C. for more than five years, developing experience in the area of Residential Warranties. He is a noted lecturer on the topics of implied warranties and construction contracts.

Mr. Van Valer served on the National Bank of Greenwood's Board of Directors and was general counsel for more than 15 years until the National City Corporation acquired the bank in the early 1990s.

Collectively, the firm has participated in the creation of more than 4000 residential home sites and many commercial and industrial projects in northern Johnson County and served as general counsel to the Greenwood Community School Corporation for the last 23 years.

All members of the firm are members of the American, Indiana, Indianapolis, and Johnson County Bar Associations. They are active in the local Chamber of Commerce, Leadership Johnson County, and other community associations.

WILLIAM A. WADDICK

WILLIAM A. WADDICK HAS BEEN PRACTICING LAW IN THE INDIANAPOLIS community for more than 39 years. After being admitted to practice in the state of Indiana and the Federal Court in 1961, Mr. Waddick joined the law firm of Kunz and Kunz where he became a partner and practiced for 33 years. His practice focused on litigation in many areas. In 1993, Mr. Waddick began practicing on his own and opened The Waddick Law Firm, P.C. His office is located in the Keystone at the Crossing area. His areas of expertise include personal injury, wrongful death claims, and small business representation.

Mr. Waddick is a member of the Indiana Trial Lawyers Association, American Trial Lawyers Association, Indiana State Bar Association, and the Indianapolis Bar Association. He is listed in *Who's Who in the United States*, *Strathmore's Who's Who*, *Who's Who in the Midwest*, *Notable Americans*, and *Who's Who in American Law*.

Although he was born in Chicago, Illinois, Mr. Waddick grew up in Indianapolis. He graduated from Cathedral High School and attended St. Xavier University in Cincinnati, Ohio before enlisting in the United States Air Force. After spending four years in the Air Force, Mr. Waddick attended the University of Notre Dame, graduating cum laude in commerce in 1957. He attended Indiana University School of Law and graduated with a J.D. in 1961.

Having experience in working both in a law firm and a solo practice, Mr. Waddick plans to continue serving his clients as a solo practitioner. Assisting Mr. Waddick in his practice are his administrative assistant and a paralegal.

LAW IN AMERICA'S
CROSSROADS

FRIENDS OF THE BAR

THE CORPORATIONS WITHIN A city's boundaries often influence the legal profession and the growth of that city, and its surrounding communities. This holds true for the city of Indianapolis and the growth and development of its legal activity. Included within this chapter are profiles of many of the city's prominent businesses and their legal departments. Representation of companies ranging from pharmaceuticals to agriculture, from financial institutes to real estate, from marketing to medical devices has impacted the legal profession and the community through the years.

Reviewing these corporate profiles reveals the breadth of legal activity companies may include. While the arena in which these companies operate is also highlighted, the focus of these profiles was upon their legal departments. As the legal profession continues subdividing into specialties, so too do legal departments within the city's most prominent businesses. Legal work within a corporate setting may include working on general corporate law, securities and anti-trust law, mergers and acquisitions, real estate law, intellectual property law, health care law, employment contracts, and insurance law. Many of the corporations profiled in this book carry their work outside the city limits as well as the country's boundaries. It is often through the city's corporations and their worldwide reach that outside influences are brought into the local picture.

We gratefully acknowledge the participation of these "Friends of the Bar" for sharing their stories for publication.

The old Marion County Courthouse was torn down in 1870, and this new, much larger structure took its place in 1876.

A History of the Indianapolis Legal Profession   211

CMG WORLDWIDE

CMG WORLDWIDE IS THE BUSINESS AGENT FOR OVER 200 OF THE world's most sought after and recognizable celebrities, including: entertainment giants Marilyn Monroe, James Dean and Sophia Loren; sports legends Babe Ruth, Jackie Robinson and Vince Lombardi; musical entities Chuck Berry and Buddy Holly; and historical figures Princess Diana and Malcolm X. Chairman and CEO Mark Roesler has successfully positioned his 20-year-old marketing and management company as the dominant force in the evolving intellectual property arena. Headquartered in Indianapolis, CMG has additional offices in Los Angeles and Rio de Janeiro.

Roesler is internationally recognized as the foremost authority on intellectual property rights involving celebrities, credited with helping to establish guidelines that delegate the control of a celebrity's image or likeness. He continues to make history with numerous legal battles that have shaped the emerging area of intellectual property law. In 1988, Roesler took the field against Major League Baseball and earned the right for retired players to be shown in their team uniforms while endorsing a product or service. In 1992, he battled Warner Bros., who claimed ownership of the lucrative merchandising and endorsement rights to James Dean since the star was under contract with them when he died. Roesler maintained Dean's family possessed those rights, and the courts agreed. Countless stars and their estates have since used the landmark case to effectively protect and market their names and likenesses.

CMG Worldwide's client roster boasts many of the world's greatest legends, left to right, Marilyn Monroe, James Dean, Babe Ruth, Princess Diana and Sophia Loren.

Roesler's 1993 high profile legal battle with Malcolm X director Spike Lee established that Malcolm X's widow, Betty Shabazz, controlled the rights to the "X" used in association with her husband. Lee was ordered to pay Shabazz a licensing fee. In 1994, Roesler helped pass Indiana's Right of Publicity Statute, which is regarded worldwide as the most progressive and celebrity friendly. The Statute protects the image and likeness of a famous personality for 100 years, and is the model for states looking to enact or amend Right of Publicity legislation, including California, Illinois, Washington and Ohio.

From Hugh Hefner to Muhammad Ali, Roesler is utilized by celebrities as an advisor and expert witness. At the 1997 O.J. Simpson civil trial, he received international acclaim as the expert whose testimony brought some justice to the families of Nicole Brown Simpson and Ronald Goldman. Roesler definitively established Simpson's future worth as $25 million, and his credibility resulted in the jury's award of that exact amount. Although Simpson filed an appeal to reduce damages, the decision was upheld in January 2001, and Roesler's testimony once again deemed a fair and accurate assessment.

Currently, the evolution of the World Wide Web has CMG's lawyers extremely busy. They constantly fight, and consistently win, battles with cyber squatters who misappropriate the names and images of their clients on the Internet. CMG has retained numerous domain names for their clients, including MarilynMonroe.com, BabeRuth.com and PrincessDiana.com, and are at the forefront in the removal of pornography on Web sites for clients such as Sophia Loren and the estate of Princess Diana.

ELI LILLY AND COMPANY

In its 125-year history, Eli Lilly and Company has played an active role in the development and progression of Indianapolis both through its employment opportunities and its civic undertakings. As the company's product lines expanded, so did its legal needs.

In 1915, the company generated enough legal work to justify making a part-time arrangement with a local lawyer. Lilly hired George L. Denny to spend an hour or two each day taking care of routine legal matters, except patent issues. Over the course of 20 years, Denny examined real estate titles, handled product liability claims, and advised the company on taxation, insurance and labeling.

The growth of the government between 1915 and 1936 necessitated additional staff to address Lilly's legal needs. In 1936, the company established a full-time legal department, headed by Walton M. "Sam" Wheeler, Jr. A graduate of Purdue University and Harvard Law School, Wheeler was the company's first general counsel.

Today the legal department has grown to 120 lawyers located throughout the world. General counsel is Rebecca Kendall, who began her career at Lilly in 1975 as an attorney for Elanco. She has held several positions with Lilly, including attorney for environmental affairs, for industrial relations and as secretary and general counsel for Elanco and later for the pharmaceutical division. She was named senior vice president and general counsel in 1998.

Her career is illustrative of the uniquely broad range of opportunities available to attorneys who work at Lilly. "The in-house counsel are business partners with the company," said Kendall, and thus provide insight at multiple levels.

Lilly lawyers also enjoy the unique advantage of exploring career opportunities that might not even be in the legal division. Many attorneys have discovered new ways to employ their skills in an aspect of the business they didn't know existed when they came on board to practice law. "You're not locked in here," says Kendall. "There aren't many places like Lilly, where you can change careers without changing companies. This is a distinctive characteristic of ours."

With operations around the world, Lilly also believes it's developmentally important that members of the legal department gain a global aspect of the company. From that perspective, the company recruits for the department around the world as well as offering possible placement for Indiana-based attorneys to work overseas. There is a great need of understanding the legal aspect of the business in all countries in which the company has a presence.

Lilly prides itself in its progressiveness with recruiting employees and the company has been recognized for its efforts in recruiting minorities. Currently 14 percent of the legal department in the United States are minorities and 32 percent are women. In addition, Lilly is beginning a new program in partnership with a local law firm for minority internships. Summer interns will spend half of their time exploring the corporate perspective of the legal world by working in the Lilly legal department, and the other half experiencing a law firm perspective.

A History of the Indianapolis Legal Profession

DOW AGROSCIENCES

With a mission of "delivering innovative technology that exceeds market needs and improves the quality of life of the world's growing population," Dow AgroSciences develops products that assist in crop protection, pest control, aid food production worldwide, and expand agricultural resources.

The Dow Chemical Company, headquartered in Midland, Michigan, has been in the agrochemical business for 95 years. In 1989, Dow formed a joint venture named DowElanco with the Plant Science business of Eli Lilly and Company. Bringing together expertise from both companies, the law department was formed under the direction of Dale Lewis, General Counsel. Lewis, an Eli Lilly and Company employee remained in this position until 1994. Lou Pribila, a Dow Chemical employee, relocated to Indianapolis to become General Counsel for the next three years. The current General Counsel for the company is Bill Wales who transferred from DowBrands, the consumer products subsidiary of The Dow Chemical Company.

In 1997 The Dow Chemical Company acquired Lilly's remaining interest in DowElanco and in 1998 the new wholly owned subsidiary was renamed Dow AgroSciences. With operations around the world, the law department at Dow AgroSciences, with the help of Dow lawyers, handles a broad range of legal issues in terms of geographical scope and subject matter.

"One of the biggest advantages of working in the corporate setting is the direct contact with clients," said Bill Wales, Vice President, Secretary and General Counsel for Dow AgroSciences. As the company continues expanding in both the agrochemical and biotechnology fields, the law department at Dow AgroSciences is presented with challenging opportunities.

GUIDANT CORPORATION

Guidant Corporation is a global company that designs, develops, manufactures, and markets a broad range of innovative therapeutic medical technologies for the treatment of cardiovascular and vascular disease. It was formed in 1994 as a split-off from Eli Lilly and Company.

Guidant's first General Counsel was J. B. King. He retired from Lilly to become general counsel for Guidant where he remained until the year 2000. John Jenkins, another former Lilly lawyer, then took over the position in October, 2000.

Currently Guidant's legal department includes 24 attorneys. Five attorneys operate out of the company's corporate headquarters in downtown Indianapolis. The remaining attorneys are distributed between the company's three business units in California, one unit in St. Paul, Minnesota, as well as the company's operations in Japan and Belgium. About one-third of Guidant's attorneys are intellectual property specialists. Lawyers working for Guidant may have the opportunity to work in a variety of areas within the law and around the world.

The company encourages its attorneys to expand their legal horizons while learning new aspects of the company's business.

Working within the company's legal department lawyers get involved in a wide breadth of subject matters. The intellectual property attorneys may find themselves negotiating a licensing agreement or managing complex patent litigation while the general attorneys may be handling a corporate acquisition, securities filing or FDA regulatory matter. Whatever the task, the rewards are many, but none greater than the realization that their work is helping to save lives.

214 Law in America's Crossroads

INDIANAPOLIS LIFE INSURANCE COMPANY

INDIANAPOLIS LIFE INSURANCE COMPANY HAS BEEN A PART OF INDIAnapolis since 1905. One of the five founders of the company Ed Raub, served as its first general counsel and later became president of the company. In 1935 the company engaged Newell Munson as Assistant Counsel. He later became General Counsel, serving until 1955 when he left to become president of Associates Life Insurance Company.

Andrew C. Emerson joined the Company as General Counsel in 1958. Until 1970 when Angelo Kostas joined the company, Emerson was the only member of the legal department. The department grew and in 1980 Margaret McKinney joined the company, becoming General Counsel when Emerson retired in 1996. McKinney was instrumental in the legal work related to the securities business, including forming a registered broker dealer subsidiary. Currently, Janis B. Funk, serving as the Vice President Law and Chief Compliance Officer, manages the department. Richard Freije joined the company in 2000 as Senior Vice President, Chief Administrative and Legal Officer. The company has attorneys working in a variety of other capacities, including Larry R. Prible, President and CEO of the Company.

Department members serve the profession and the community through their associations. Emerson served as Chairman of the Insurance Committee of the Indiana State Bar Association for 17 years and as a member of the board of managers of the Indiana and Indianapolis Bar Associations. Emerson was also the Association of Indiana Life Insurance Companies (AILIC) secretary for 25 years. Funk has served as a member of the board of managers of the Indianapolis Bar Associations and is a fellow of the Indiana State Bar Association and the Indianapolis Bar Foundation.

STEWART TITLE

THE HISTORY OF STEWART TITLE GOES BACK TO Galveston, Texas. In 1893, Maco Stewart, at the age of 22, launched a title abstract business, which has grown into what is now Stewart Title. Back in those days, land titles were handled through attorneys. Maco followed in his father's footsteps and practiced law. His brother, Clegg Stewart, a partner in the law practice, moved to Beaumont, Texas to expand the firm. Unfortunately Clegg died in 1902. The other Stewart brother, Minor, also joined the firm. W. C. Morris joined Maco Stewart Law and Land Title Office in 1897, and married Maco's sister. W. C. Morris ultimately became executive vice president of Stewart Title Guaranty Company and president of Stewart Title Company.

Beginning in 1910, Stewart expanded outside of Galveston, Texas. Maco Stewart passed away in 1938 and W. C. Morris and Maco Stewart, Jr. continued expanding the company until they

Carloss Morris, Malcolm Morris, Stewart Morris, Jr., and Stewart Morris stand in front the company headquarters.

both passed away in 1950. The company flourished operating under the leadership of Morris' sons: Carloss and Stewart Morris.

In 1956, under the direction of Stewart Morris, the company expanded outside Texas. It has insured land in Indianapolis and Indiana since 1975. By 1995, the number of issuing offices exceeded 3,500 in all 50 states, the District of Columbia, Canada, and abroad. A passing of the leadership baton occurred again in 1991 when Malcolm Morris became president of Stewart Title Guaranty Company for underwriting and Stewart Morris, Jr. became president of Stewart Title Company for title operations, technology, and real estate information companies.

Today, the Stewart family of companies offers products and services geared toward automating the title office and accelerating growth in the real estate information business.

HOOSIER LOTTERY

ON NOVEMBER 8, 1988 INDIANA VOTERS approved a lottery referendum by a strong majority—62 percent. On May 3, 1989, the Indiana General Assembly passed the Lottery Act and, a week later, Governor Evan Bayh signed the Lottery Act into law. The Governor appointed the first lottery director and the five-member lottery commission within the next two months.

Three months after the creation of the first commission, the Hoosier Lottery was in full operation; Instant, or scratch-off, ticket sales began on October 13, 1989. Six months later, the Lottery launched its first on-line game, Lotto Cash. By the end of 1991, the Hoosier Lottery topped $1 billion in sales. Since inception, the state has received approximately $1.9 billion in lottery profits.

Although the Lottery is a quasi-state agency, the Lottery's mission, as mandated by the General Assembly, is to raise substantial revenue for the people of Indiana while maintaining the dignity and integrity of the state. Thus, the Lottery operates in an entrepreneurial manner, subject to the statutorial guidance of the legislature. The legal department of the Lottery acts similarly to that in any multimillion-dollar corporation. The Lottery seeks legal advice and representation from both in-house counsel and from outside firms.

In-house counsel faces the variety of legal questions that would be expected from any $600 million corporation that combines 220 employees, 4,500 outside vendors, and millions of dollars in prizes and contracts. The gamut of issues ranges from the definitions of trade secrets and public records to complicated EEOC actions, contract matters and employment law. When necessary, outside counsel has been sought for assistance with litigation.

In the history of the Lottery, only two of the directors have not been lawyers, and the Lottery currently has four lawyers on its staff. John Ross became director of the Lottery in January 2001. Prior to his appointment, he served for three and one half years as the Lottery's deputy director and chief counsel. Janna Shisler has served as general counsel for the Lottery for more than eight years. The two remaining lawyers primarily use their legal training indirectly. Communications Director, Colleen O'Brien, is responsible for publications, Web site communications and communications on behalf of the director. Director of Administration, Norman Aranda, is responsible for administrative functions, procurement and facilities management.

The Lottery's attorney's are all members of the local and state bar associations and are active in continuing legal education programs.

IU SCHOOL OF LAW–INDIANAPOLIS

THE IU SCHOOL OF LAW-INDIANAPOLIS TRACES ITS ORIGINS TO THE late nineteenth century when the first of its private predecessor schools, the Indiana Law School, began operating in 1894. A full-time day school, the Indiana Law School was part of a newly-formed University of Indianapolis that also included Butler University, the Medical College of Indiana and the Indiana Dental School. All three professional schools later became part of Indiana University. Among the first trustees of the school were former United States President, Benjamin Harrison, and Indiana industrialist, Eli Lilly.

In 1898 a second predecessor school, the Indianapolis College of Law, was founded, offering a two-year evening program. This school, located in the Pythian Building in downtown Indianapolis, was advertised in 1906 as "known everywhere for its successful graduates," and boasted tuition of $10 per term. A few years later, another evening school, the American Central Law School, was established. In 1914, these two evening schools merged to become the Benjamin Harrison Law School, and in 1936 this school and the Indiana Law School merged, taking the name of the latter, and offering both day and evening programs.

In 1944, the Indiana Law School became affiliated with Indiana University, becoming the Indianapolis Division of the IU School of Law. Beginning the following year, the school was housed in the Maennerchor Building, an architectural landmark in Indianapolis. The school gained autonomy in 1968, becoming the Indiana University School of Law-Indianapolis, the largest law school in Indiana and the only law school in the state to offer both full and part-time programs. It moved into a new building at 735 West New York Street in 1970. The school was housed in that facility until its move to Lawrence W. Inlow Hall, located at 530 West New York Street, in May 2001.

Faculty members have studied at law schools throughout the United States. Many hold advanced degrees beyond the J.D. and are widely published in scholarly journals. They also have authored, co-authored or co-edited books. In terms of curriculum, the late 1980s and early 1990s saw emphasis placed on developing the school's clinical programs, expanding them to include the current opportunities in the civil practice, criminal defense and disability clinics. The 1980s and 1990s also saw the development of research institutes such as the Center for Law and Health, the Program on Law and State Government, and the Program in International Human Rights Law. Additionally, the international course offerings were expanded during this period to include the China Summer Program, The European Law Summer Program and International Human Rights Law summer internships offered throughout the world.

The number of internships available to students in state and federal courts, and also in state offices increased dramatically in the late 1990s. The school now offers a variety of court internships, as well as interning opportunities in eighteen state government offices. Additionally, four joint degree programs are now available in cooperation with the IU Schools of Business, Public and Environmental Affairs and Medicine. The programs combine the J.D. with a Master of Business Administration (M.B.A.), a Master of Public Affairs (M.P.A.), a Master of Science in Health Administration (M.H.A.) and a Master of Public Health (M.P.H.).

Currently, there are 28 active student organizations at the school, including the Student Bar Association, the Black Law Student Association, the Hispanic Law Society, the Asian Law Student Association, the Women's Caucus, and the Sports and Entertainment Law Society, just to name a few. The school's Moot Court and Client Counseling teams also have been quite successful and a Trial Advocacy team was established in 2000. Two law reviews, the Indiana Law Review and the Indiana International and Comparative Law Review afford students opportunities for legal research, writing and editing. They also participate actively in the school's Pro Bono Program and have volunteered thousands of hours to non-profit organizations in the Indianapolis community. For example, through the Volunteer Income Tax Assistance (VITA) program, every year students help hundreds of non-native English speakers with their tax forms. They have also volunteered their help with Teen Court, and served in guardian ad litem positions for abused and neglected children.

Since 1995, the school has sponsored an annual Distinguished Visitor Series, bringing a variety of prominent legal scholars, practitioners and judges to the school for lectures on timely topics of interest to students and alumni. The school also has sponsored a successful continuing legal education program, providing low-cost CLE for alumni and local members of the bar, while allowing faculty members to showcase recent research and scholarship.

The IU School of Law-Indianapolis has become an integral part of the Indianapolis community. The school looks toward a bright future, where the ties to business, government and the legal community are further strengthened, expanding opportunities for the next generation of IU-Indianapolis graduates.

UNION FEDERAL TRUST AND PRIVATE BANKING

As an example of Union Federal Bank's commitment to developing new products and services, the bank established a Trust and Private Banking Department in 1993. By the year 2000, the department had grown to more than $1.3 billion. Every day the experienced staff works to expand an already substantial client roster that includes clients like the American Legion and The Masonic Home.

The trust department serves as a Trustee for clients' assets, offers investment advisory services, and assists clients with tax and estate planning. Private banking serves clients with major assets in the bank's care. The combined department provides personal banking services to these clients, including traveling to their homes or place of business to handle financial needs.

George A. Buskirk Jr., a 34-year veteran of banking with trust experience, heads the department. Mr. Buskirk joined Union Federal in 1993 because he holds firm to the belief that customers are best served by people with whom they live and work. He is a member of the Indianapolis Bar Association. Since 1972 he has served the Bar Association in a variety of positions including serving as its president in 1996. Connie Allman works along side Mr. Buskirk. She is a member of the Paralegal Section of the Indianapolis Bar Association.

With a theme of providing quality customer service, the Trust and Private Banking Department has received a national rating of greater than 10 for the past several years. The department focuses on serving local clients, professionals, and institutions that enjoy the security of having their assets held in the community in which they live and work. Clients of the Trust and Private Banking Department enjoy the benefits of having local advisors able to offer expert opinions on their legal needs regarding their finances.

Union Federal Bank, one of the largest Indiana-owned and operated financial institutions, is a subsidiary of the Waterfield Group of Companies. Union Federal lineage can be traced back to 1887 when its parent institution was founded. The institution converted to a federal savings and loan in 1937. In September of 1984 Waterfield Mortgage Company acquired Union Federal Savings and Loan. This union created a strong, aggressive financial institution that welcomes progressive banking to best support and serve its clients.

The Trust and Private Banking Department plans to continue leaving an impression on the Indianapolis community by serving its clients with a high level of customer service throughout central Indiana. The institution plans to continue its specialized work in the trust and private banking area with residents and professionals who want their assets and advisors to remain grounded in central Indiana.

Law in America's Crossroads

Past Presidents of the Indianapolis Bar Associaton

Bibliography

Index

Acknowledgments

LAW IN AMERICA'S CROSSROADS

PAST PRESIDENTS INDIANAPOLIS BAR ASSOCIATION

1999 C. Joseph Russell	1987 James S. Kirsch	1975 Keith C. Reese	1963 Charles D. Babcock
1998 Phil Isenbarger	1986 Robert F. Zoccola	1974 Douglass R. Shortridge	1962 Earl A. Kightlinger
1997 George A. Buskirk Jr.	1985 Michael R. Maine	1973 Karl J. Stipher	1961 John W. Houghton
1996 Neil E. Shook	1984 D. William Cramer	1972 William J. Wood	1960 Gustav H. Dongus
1995 Harry V. Huffman	1983 Eugene E. Henn	1971 Kenneth Foster	1959 Floyd R. Mannon
1994 Thomas L. Davis	1982 G. Weldon Johnson	1970 Philip S. Kappes	1958 David M. Lewis
1993 Kristin G. Fruehwald	1981 Donald L. Jackson	1969 John M. Kitchen	1957 Howard P. Travis
1992 Robert C. Hagemier	1980 Raymond Good	1968 Paul H. Buchanan Jr.	1956 Elbert Gilliom
1991 Thomas Q. Henry	1979 F. Boyd Hovde	1967 C. Wendell Martin	1955 Irving M. Fauvre
1990 Donald W. Buttrey	1978 Joseph N. Myers	1966 Ben J. Weaver	1954 John K. Ruckleshaus
1989 Mary Y. Marsh	1977 F. Emerson Boyd	1965 Francis M. Hughes	1953 Paul N. Rowe
1988 S. R. "Chic" Born	1976 Howard S. Young	1964 Charles B. Feibleman	1952 Herman W. Kothe

1951 Floyd W. Burns	1932 Paul G. Davis	1913 Ernest R. Keith	1896 Samuel O. Pickens
1950 Charles C. Baker	1931 Howard S. Young	1912 Cassius C. Shirley	1895 Henry Clay Allen
1949 Herbert E. Wilson	1930 William L. Taylor	1911 William A. Pickens	1894 Roscoe O. Hawkins
1948 Alan W. Boyd	1929 Michael E. Foley	1910 Charles Martindale	1893 Silas M. Shepard
1947 William H. Wemmer	1928 Emsley W. Johnson	1909 Albert Baker	1892 Charles W. Smith
1946 Theodore L. Locke	1927 Samuel Ashby	1908 James P. Baker	1891 William A. Ketcham
1945 Jeremiah L. Cadick	1926 James J. Ogden	1907 Merrill Moores	1890 Addison C. Harris
1944 Harvey B. Hartsock	1925 Lawrence B. Davis	1907 Lawson M. Harvey	1889 Thomas L. Sullivan
1943 Harvey A. Graybill	1924 Charles E. Cox	1906 John E. Scott	1888 Solomon Claypool
1942 B. Howard Caughran	1923 Earl R. Conder	1905 John B. Elamn	1887 Ferdinand Winter
1941 Fred C. Gause	1922 Lewis A. Coleman	1904 Daniel W. Howe	1886 Livingston Howland
1940 Samuel Dowden	1921 Larz A. Whitcomb	1903 Nathan Morris	1885 William H. H. Miller
1939 Clarence F. Merrell	1920 William P. Kappes	1903 Lewis Newberger	1884 William H. H. Miller
1938 Thomas D. Stevenson	1919 Henry H. Hornbrook	1902 Alexander C. Ayers	1883 Addison C. Harris
1937 Russell Wilson	1918 Aquilla Q. Jones	1901 Ovid B. Jameson	1882 Myron B. Williams
1936 Hubert Hickam	1917 Elmer E. Stevenson	1900 John S. Duncan	1881 Horatio C. Newcomb
1935 Carl Wilde	1916 James W. Fesler	1899 Lewis C. Walker	1880 Horatio C. Newcomb
1934 Frank C. Dailey	1915 Charles Remster	1898 Charles A. Dryer	1879 Oscar B. Hord
1933 Homer Elliott	1914 Charles W. Moores	1897 Edward Daniels	1878 Napoleon B. Taylor

A History of the Indianapolis Legal Profession

BIBLIOGRAPHY

PUBLICATIONS

Baker, Judge John G. "The History of the Indiana Trial Court System and Attempts at Renovation," 30 Ind.L.Rev. 233

Baltzell, Robert C. Collection. Indiana State Library

Barteau, Betty. "Thirty Years of the Journey of Indiana's Women Judges 1964-1994," 30 Ind.L.Rev. 43.

"Bridging the Gap to Justice: The Indiana Pro Bono Commission," *Indiana Lawyer*, April 11, 2001.

Brokenburr, Robert Lee Collection. Indiana Historical Society

Barnes, Hickam, Pantzer and Boyd (The First Twenty-Five Years): Friday the Thirteenth of September 1940 (Author Unknown)

Bodenhamer, David J. *Crime and Criminal Justice in Antebellum Indiana*. Indiana University, 1977.

Bodenhamer, David J. and Barrows, Robert G., editors. *The Encyclopedia of Indianapolis*. Bloomington and Indianapolis: Indiana University Press, 1994.

Buchanan, Paul H. Jr., "A Confrontation with the Fix," *The Indianapolis Lawyer*, January, 1989.

Buchanan, Paul H. Jr., "Lawyers are Peacemakers," *The Spotlight*, February 2, 2000.

Dillin, S. Hugh. "The Origin and Development of the Indiana Bar Examination," 30 In.L.Rev. 391.

Dunn, Jacob P. *Greater Indianapolis: The History, the Industries, the Institutions and the People of a City of Homes*, 2 vols. Chicago: Lewis Publishing Company, 1922.

Emerson, Daniel C. "This veteran lawyer left lasting mark on the city," *The Indianapolis Star*, February 22, 2001.

Garrison, J. Gregory and Roberts, Randy. *Heavy Justice: The Trial of Mike Tyson*. Fayetteville: The University of Arkansas Press, 2000.

Geib, George and Geib, Miriam. *Indianapolis First*. Indianapolis: Indianapolis Chamber of Commerce, 1990.

Geib, George W. *Indianapolis: Hoosiers' Circle City*. Tulsa, OK: Continental Heritage Press, Inc. 1981.

Holliday, John Hampden. *Indianapolis and the Civil War*. Indianapolis: Indianapolis Society of Indiana Pioneers. 1972.

Holloway, W.R. Indianapolis: *A Historical and Statistical Sketch of the Railroad City*. Indianapolis: Indianapolis Journal Printing Company, 1870.

Honored to Serve, Indiana Judicial Service Report, 1999.

Ice, Harry T. *History of a Hoosier Law Firm: Ice Miller Donadio & Ryan and its Predecessors, 1910-1980*. Indianapolis: Harry T. Ice, 1980.

Indianapolis Bar Association Collection. Indiana Historical Society.

Leary, Edward A. *Indianapolis: A Pictorial History*. Virginia Beach: The Donning Company, 1980.

Leary, Edward A. Indianapolis: *The Story of a City*. Indianapolis. The Bobbs-Merrill Company Inc., 1971.

Lutholtz, M. William. Grand Dragon: D.C. Stephenson and the Ku Klux Klan in Indiana. West Lafayette: Purdue University Press, 1991.

"Milestones, 2000." *Indianapolis Business Journal*.

Monks, Leander. Courts and Lawyers of Indiana. Indianapolis, 1895.

Niblack, John Lewis. *The Life and Times of a Hoosier Judge*, 1973.

Nolan, Jeannette Covert. *Hoosier City*. New York: Julian Messner, Inc., 1943.

Radcliff, William Franklin. *Sherman Mionton: Indiana's Supreme Court Justice*. Indianapolis: Guild Press of Indiana, 1996.

Rowe, Paul N. *Baker & Daniels: Founded 1863*.

Scanlon, Thomas M. *Early History of the Firm* (Barnes, Hickam, Pantzer & Boyd).

Schwartz, Bernard. *The Law in America*. New York: American Heritage Publishing Co. Inc., 1974.

Senior Lawyers Project Collection, 1968-1991. Indiana Historical Society.

Sharp, William T. *The Establishment and Development of the Municipal Court of Marion County, 1925-1969*. MA, History Thesis, Butler University, February 10, 1994.

Sievers, Harry J. *Benjamin Harrison*, 3 vols. Chicago: Henry Regnery Company, 1952.

Smith, Oliver H. *Early Indiana Trials*. Cincinnati, 1858.

Sulgrove, B. R. *History of Indianapolis and Marion County*. Philadelphia: L. H. Everts and Company, 1884.

Staton, Judge Robert H. and Hicklin, Gina M. "The History of the Court of Appeals in Indiana," 30 Ind.L.Rev. 203

Steckler, William E., Oral Interview with Senior District Judge, November 24-25, 1987.

Taylor, Charles W. *Biographical Sketches and Review of the Bench and Bar of Indiana*. Indianapolis, 1895.

Thornbrough, Gayle and Riker, Dorothy, editors. *The Diary of Calvin Fletcher*, 4 vols. Indianapolis: The Indianapolis Historical Society, 1975.

Thornbrough, Emma Lou, "The Indianapolis School Busing Case," *We the People: Indiana and the United States Constitution*. Indianapolis: Indiana Historical Society, 1987.

Thornbrough, Emma Lou. *The Indianapolis Story: School Segregation and Desegregation in a Northern City*. Indiana Historical Society (unpublished manuscript).

Visitors Guide to the United States Court House, Indianapolis, Indiana and the United States District Court for the Southern District of Indiana, November 2000.

Withered, Jerome L. *Hoosier Justice: A History of the Supreme Court of Indiana*. Indianapolis: Supreme Court of Indiana, 1998.

Woodard, Harold R. *A Firm Foundation: The First One Hundred Years, 1879-1979—Woodard, Weikart, Emhardt & Naughton*. Indianapolis: Harold R. Woodard, 1979.

PERSONAL INTERVIEWS

Born, S.R. "Chic", Former President, Indianapolis Bar Association

Buchanan, The Hon. Paul H. Jr., Indiana Court of Appeals, Ret.

Dickson, The Hon. Brent E., Indiana Supreme Court

Endsley, The Hon. Patrick, Magistrate, United States District Court, Southern District of Indiana, Ret.

Felton, Rosie, Executive Director, Indianapolis Bar Association, Ret.

Given, The Hon. Richard M., Chief Justice, Indiana Supreme Court, Ret.

Houghton, John

Kite, Donald Sr.

McCarty, Virginia Dill

Metzger, Norman, Executive Director, Legal Services Organization of Indiana

Moss, John Jr.

Nolan, Alan T.

Sullivan, Patrick D., Indiana Court of Appeals

Woodard, Harold R.

PERSONAL CORRESPONDENCE

Prof. William F. Harvey, Former Dean, Indiana University School of Law at Indianapolis

INDEX

NOTE: **Bold** page numbers refer to pictures and captions.

Autocephalous Greek Orthodox Church of Cyprus v. Goldberg, 134-35

Bail bond system, reform of, in 1970s, 136
Bailey, Robert L., 78
Baker & Daniels, 94
Baltzell, Robert C., 96-97, 102-103
Bamberger & Feibleman, 94
Barker, Sarah E., 132
Barnes and Thornburg, 104
Barteau, Betty S., 133
Barton, John J., 122
Bell, Joseph E., 75
Benjamin Harrison School of Law, 80, 98-99
Bingham, James, 78
Bingham, Joseph J., 36
Blackford, Isaac, 21, **22**, 29, 150
Blackford Reports, 21, **22**
Blair, Solomon, 52
Bloomfield, Lot, 14
Bose, Lewis C., **123**, 125, 126, 127
Branifan, Richard, **131**
Bridge, John, Jr., **17**
Brokenburr, Robert L., 74, 110-111, **114**
Brooks, Gene Edward, 132
Buchanan, Paul H., Jr., 116, 117, 151
Butler, Benjamin, 45

Butler, John W., 81
Butler, Ovid, 28, 29
Butler, Susan W., 81
Butler University, 28

Carmichael, Hoagy, 78-79
Carr, John W., 14
Caven, John, 38, 57-59
City-County Building, 69, 70, **107**
City Hall (1909), 68-69
Civil liberties, in Civil War, 39-47
Civil War: Indianapolis during, 32-36; consequences of, for city, 36-38, 53; and "Treason Trials," 39-47
Clark, Charles, **114**
Coburn, John, 30-31
Coleman, Lewis A., 101, 151
Coleman, Robert, 101
Columbia Conserve Co., 91-93
Conn, Harriette B., 115
Cordingly, Antoinette A., 133
Court cases, sensational, in 1970s, 136-37
Courthouses: first (1825), 14; federal, **100**, 103. *See also* names, e.g., Marion County Courthouse
Courts: at city's founding, 11-12; in settlement times, 15, **16**, 19, 22; reorganization of, at mid-century, 27; and creation of superior court system, 52; of appeal, 1920s, 102. *See also* courts by name, e.g., Indiana Supreme Court

Cramer, William D., 117
Crispus Attucks High School, **84**
Curry, Hiram M., 14

Daily, Thomas A., 100
Denny, Caleb S., 59-60
Denny, George L., 80-81
Dillin, S. Hugh, **98**, 121, 126, 128
Dillon, John J., 113
Donadio, James, 79
Drummond, Thomas, 56
Dumont, Ebenezer, 34, 37
Duvall, John, 84

Eaglesfield, Bessie, 51, 132, 151
Elections: of 1860, 32
Eli Lilly. *See* Lilly, Eli
Elliott, Byron K., 55
Elliott Wale & Jewett, 94
Emerson, Daniel C., 127
Endsley, J. Patrick, **116**, 151
English, William Eastin, 53
English, William H., 53
Ex parte Milligan, 39-47
Ex parte Quirin, 46-47

Fairbanks, Charles W., 54, 56-57, 73-74
Felt, Edward Webster, 100
Felton, Rosie, 134, 135, 136
Field, David Dudley, 45
Fishback, William, 55
Fitch, Graham, 32

Fletcher, Calvin, 10, 14-15, 23, 25-26, 28, 31
Fletcher Trust Building, **95**
Foote, Obed, 10, 14, 15, 22
Forney, William, 80
Fortune, William, 61
Foster, Kenneth, 134
Freeman, John, 29-30

Garfield, James A., 45
Gifford, Patrick L., 133
Givan, Richard M., 82, 130, 146
Givin, Clinton H., 82
Givan, Richard, 82, 130, 131
Goldsmith, Stephen, 142
Grabill, Harvey A., 105
Gregg, Harvey, 14
Gresham, Walter O., 56
Grow, Patricia Orloff, 150

Harrison, Benjamin: 38, 53, 54, 62-63
Harvey, William F., 98, 99
Hendricks, Thomas A. 32, **38**, 56
Hill, James T. V., 51, 115
Holman, Jesse L., 21, 29
Holmes, Ira, 80
Holtzman & Coleman, 101
Houghton, John, 104-105, 111, 151

Ice, Harry T., **94**, 118, 149
Ice Miller, 94, 105, 118, 121, 148
Indiana Civil Liberties Union, 118-19
Indiana Court of Appeals, 146-47, and 1970s controversy over rules for removal of judges, 129, 132
Indiana Law Journal, 55
Indiana Supreme Court: 21, 146; merit system created for, 129; and admission to law practice, 129
Indiana University Medical Center, 91
Indiana University School of Law, Indianapolis, 54-55, 99, **140**
Indianapolis: founding of, 8; establishment as state capital, 8, 10, 12, 18, 20; early days in, 10-11; platted, 13; transportation routes to, 18; frontier society in, 18; incorporation of, 22; growth of, in 1830s, 22-23; canal speculation in, 22-23; antebellum economy of, 24-25; coming of railroads to, 25; demographics of, 1840s-1850s, 31; charter received by, 26; mobility in, during early 19th century, 26-27; blacks in, during antebellum years, 29; slavery as legal issue in, 29-31; and the Civil War, 32-36; "Treason Trials" in, 39-47; as modernizing metropolis, 48-49; demographic of, 1860s-70s, 49-52; postwar commercial activity in, 52-53; at end of 19th c., 61; physical development of, in early 20th c., 64, 67-70; and the automobile, 64-67; early 20th c. labor relations in, 74-75; in World War I, 76-77; selected as national headquarters of American legion, 77; racial and religious hatred in, in 1920s, 82-86; during Great Depression, 88-93; in World War II, 103-105; postwar development of, 106-109; 1950s gambling cases in, 119; State Fairgrounds Coliseum explosion in, 120-21; in the 1960s, 122-25; suburbanization of, 124; and unified government, 125-28; and Mass Transportation Authority lawsuit, 1967, 130-31; in 1992-2000, 138-42
Indianapolis Bar Association: formed, 58-59; and World War I, 76-77; growth of, by 1920, 78; promotes criminal law reforms, 81; postwar expansion of, 109-13; sponsors postwar refresher course, 109; launches Legal Aid Society, 109; institutes referral system, 109; creates placement committee, 111; desegregates, 111; and divorce cases controversy, 111-13; and 1960 fee schedule controversy, 111-12; and mounting case loads, 113; admission of women to, 113-15; leads municipal court reforms, 117; expands services in 1970s-80s, 134-36, participates in children's protection services, 135-36
Indianapolis Bar Foundation, 150
Indianapolis City Hall, 108
Inman, Ephraim, 80, 85

Jackson, Edward, 82, 84
Jacobs, Andrew, Sr., 129, 132
Jennings, Jonathan, 8
Jimison, Z. Mae, 133
John Birch Society, 117
Judah, John M., 76
Julian, George Washington, 48
Juvenile Court, 70-71

Kennington, Robert E., 76
Kern, John W., 103
Kern, John Worth, Sr., 74
Kissler, George, **114**
Knefler, Frederick, 34, 37-38
Ku Klux Klan, **81**, 82-85, 86
Kuykendall, Rufus, 111, **112**

Lane, Henry, 32
Law firms. *See* firm by name
Law, practice of: in settlement times, 15, 16-18, 19; in antebellum years, 24; in mid-19th century, 23, 24; requirements for, in mid 19th century, 27; by early 1960s, 113; specialization in, 148, 149, 150; organization of, in early 21st century, 149
Lawyers: roles of in civic improvements, 23; education of, 28, 54-55; admission of blacks to, 50-51; admission of women to, 51-52, 55; and Panic of 1873, 55-56; and late 19th c. commercial activity, 53; qualifications of, 1925, 80-81; and Great Depression, 94-95; establishment of bar examination for, 96-98; education of, in 1930s, 98-99; during World War II, 104-105; role in unified government, 125; women 132-33; and rise of marketing, 140, 148-49; mounting caseloads of, 146-47; and pro bono responsibilities, 147-

48; and societal changes in late 20th c., 150-151
Lawton, Stan, 121
League of Women Voters, 80
Leach, Antoinette D., 51, 151
Legal Services Organization, 142-46
Likens, Syliva Marie murder case, 121
Lilly, Eli, **52**, 53, 54, 90, 139
Lincoln, Abraham, 32, 33-34, 36, 40
Lockfield Gardens, 90, **92**
Lugar, Richard, **124**, 125

Mance, Mercer M., 111, **112**
Marion County: organization of, 12; first county court of, 14; redistricting of judicial circuits and 22; Municipal Court of, 116-17, 136; last hanging in, 96-97
Marion County Bar Association, 115-16
Marion County Courthouse, 49, 68, **69**, **107**, 108
Marion County Lawyers Club, 78
Marston, Frederick E., 94
Marston Ross McCord & Clifford, 94, 95, 105, 149
McCallister, Fred, 80, 100
McCarty, Virginia Dill, **113**, 133, 151
McDonald, David, 54
McDonald's Treatise, 54
McIllvaine, James, 11
McMaster, John L., 59
Merrill, Samuel, **9**, 18, 29, 31
Miller, Merle, 118
Milligan, Lambdin P., 36, 42
Mitchell, James L., 57
Morris, Morris, 20
Morton, Oliver P., 32, 33, 34, 35, 38, 42, 51
Moss, John, Jr., 127, 128, 151
Murray, Raymond, F., 81

Newcomb, Horatio Cooley, 26, 52
Niblack, John Lewis, 80, 82, 84-85, 94-95, 117
Noble, James, 14, 17
Nolan, Alan T., 111, **112**, 118, 151

Noland, James Ellsworth, 132

Perkins, Samuel E., 28, 31
Pickens, Davidson, Gause & Pickens, 94
Police Court, 70
Public defender system, 146-47

Ransom, Freemon B., 74
Ransom, Willard B., **114**
Rand, Frederick, 52
Rappaport, Phillip, 49
Rariden, James, 14, 17
Ray, James B., **17**, 18
Rehnquist, William, 39-47
Remy, William H., 80, 81, 82, 86
Richardson, Henry J., Jr., **114**
Riley, James Whitcomb, 61
Rohback, James, 80

Sanders, Fred, 143
Scanlon, Thomas M., 105
Scott, James, 21
Scottish Rite Cathedral, **68**
Shank, Lew, **82**, 84
Sharp, William, 117, 136
Shields, Vivian Sue, 132
Shoup, Francis A., 34
Smith, Asa J., 86-87
Smith, Caleb Blood, 32, 37
Smith, Oliver H., 14, 19, 23
Snow, Margaret Butler, 81
Soldiers and Sailors Monument, **50**
Speed, James, 45
Stark, Wetzel & Co., 90
Steckler, William E., 96, 97, 146
Stephenson, David Curtis, 82, **83**, 85, 86
Stokely-Van Camp Co., 91
Stubbs, George W., 70, **71**, 73, 151
Sullivan, Jeremiah, 8, **10**
Sullivan, Patrick D., **131**, 146, 151
Sullivan, Thomas L., 60

Taylor, William T., 81
Temperance: history of, in 19th century, 31

Test, Charles H., 19
Thornton, W. W., 67
Tinder, John, Sr., 119
Tyson, Mike (convicted rapist), 144-45

U.S. District Court, 22, 81, 102, 119-20, 132
Union Station, **109**
United States v. Board of School Commissioners, 126-28

Vigilantes, 28

Wallace, Lew, 29, 34, 37, 52, 151
Ward, John Preston, 128
Weaver, Ben, 109
Wetter, Paul, 100
Whitcomb, James, 14
White, Dan, 100
Wick, Daniel B., 14
Wick, William, 14, 15
Wilmuth, Delbert O., 100
Woodard, Harold R., 95, 149

LAW IN AMERICA'S
CROSSROADS

INDEX TO FIRM HISTORIES

Baker & Daniels	157
Barnes & Thornburg	160
Bingham Summers	158
Bose McKinney & Evans LLP	161
Brattain & Minnix	166
Campbell Kyle Proffitt	162
Cline Farrell Christie Lee & Caress	166
Conour Doehrman	163
Coots, Henke & Wheeler	164
Doyle, Wright & Dean-Webster, LLP	167
Dale & Eke	165
Dann Pecar Newman & Kleiman, PC	168
Feiwell & Hannoy, P.C.	169
Findling Garau Germano & Pennington, P.C.	167
Foley & Pool, LLP	170
Frank & Kraft, P.C.	171
Hackman Hulett & Cracraft, LLP	172
Charles Hankey Law Office	182
Harrison and Moberly	173
Henderson Daily	174
Hollingsworth & Associates	182
Hovde Law Firm	175
Ice Miller	176
Indianapolis Bar Association	154
Kiefer & McGoff	183
Kightlinger & Gray, LLP	178
Knowles & Associates, LLC	179
Kortepeter McPherson Hux Freihofer & Minton	183
Krieg DeVault Alexander & Capehart, LLP	180
Ladendorf & Ladendorf	188
Lee Burns & Cossell, LLP	188
Lamberti & Grow	184
Lewis & Wagner	185
Diane L. Liptack, P.C.	189
Locke Reynolds LLP	186
Lowe Gray Steele & Darko, LLP	187

Maddox Koeller Hargett & Caruso	189
McNamar, Fearnow & McSharar, P.C.	190
Gloria K. Mitchell	191
Ogletree, Deakins, Nash, Smoak and Stewart, PC	192
Osborn Hiner & Lisher, P.C.	198
Plews Shadley Racher & Braun	193
Stephen Plopper & Associates	198
Riley Bennett & Egloff, LLP	194
Rowe & Hamilton	195
Ruckelshaus Roland Kautzman & Hasbrook	196
Jose D. Salinas	199
Randall R. Sevenish, Esq.	199
Solomon & Solomon	202
Sommer & Barnard	197
Steven A. Spence	202
Tabbert Hahn Earnest & Weddle	200
Van Valer Law Firm	210
William A. Waddick	210
Wallack Somers & Haas	203
Wilson Kehoe & Winingham	204
Woodard, Emhardt, Naughton, Moriarty & McNett	205
York Schrager Baxter James & Rose	206
Yosha Krahulik & Levy	209

FRIENDS OF THE BAR

CMG Worldwide	212
Dow AgroSciences	214
Eli Lilly and Company	213
Guidant Corporation	214
Hoosier Lottery	216
IU School of Law-Indianapolis	217
Indianapolis Life Insurance Company	215
Stewart Title	215
Union Federal Trust and Private Banking	218

A History of the Indianapolis Legal Profession

LAW IN AMERICA'S
CROSSROADS

ACKNOWLEDGMENTS

ALICIA DEAN CARLSON IS AN AWARD-WINNING, INDIANAPOLIS-BASED writer and a former newspaper reporter for the *Elkhart Truth* and the *Indianapolis Business Journal*. Her articles have appeared in the *Indianapolis Star, Indianapolis Monthly, Indianapolis Woman* and the alumni magazine of the IU School of Law-Indianapolis. Carlson edits an annual publication, *NEXT: Life After High School in Indiana, GRAD*, a magazine for college juniors and seniors, and *The Ribbon*, quarterly newsletter of the breast cancer support group Y-ME of Central Indiana. A graduate of Indiana University-Bloomington, Carlson and her husband, Jim, are raising two daughters in the city's historic Butler-Tarkington neighborhood.

WRITER AND JOURNALIST SANDRA B. CLINE IS THE AUTHOR OF one previous historical reference, *The Great Theatre*, and co-editor of another, *Zionsville: The First One Hundred Years*. The former editor and publisher of the *Zionsville Times Sentinel*, she was the first woman to serve as president of the Hoosier State Press Association. She has been honored by the National Newspaper Association, Inland Press Association, Hoosier State Press Association and Women in Communications. Cline's work appears in a variety of local and regional publications, and she serves as contributing editor of *The Indiana Publisher*. She holds both master's and bachelor's degrees from St. Mary-of-the-Woods College, and resides in Carmel with her husband, attorney/arbitrator Stephen C. Cline.

THE AUTHORS WOULD LIKE TO ACKNOWLEDGE THE VALUABLE insight and contributions of many individuals. George Geib, professor of history at Butler University, kindly read and commented on drafts of the first few chapters of the book, as did Ray E. Boomhower, managing editor of *Traces of Indiana and Midwestern History*. Sources of both inspiration and friendly advice included Indiana Supreme Court Justice Brent E. Dickson, Indiana Court of Appeals Judge Patrick D. Sullivan, former Marion Superior Court Judge John C. Christ, former Indianapolis Bar Association President S. R. "Chic" Born, and former U.S. District Court Clerk Donald Kite Sr. We are grateful to staff at the Indiana Historical Society Library, the Indiana State Library and the Indianapolis Public Library for their courteous and knowledgeable service. On a personal note, much credit belongs to the authors' families for their enduring patience, enthusiasm and support—especially husbands Jim Carlson and Stephen C. Cline (who also served as a boundless resource and a tireless editor).

THE PUBLISHERS WOULD LIKE TO THANK THE FOLLOWING SOURCES for granting permission to reproduce pictures from their collections in this book:

INDIANA HISTORICAL SOCIETY: pages 1, 6-7, 9, 10 (above left and right), 11 (below), 15, 16 (above), 18, 24-25, 26, 27, 31, 33, 35, 38 (left), 43, 44, 46, 48-49, 50 (above), 51, 53, 58, 60, 60-61, 61 (above), 63, 66 (both), 67, 68, 69 (above), 70, 72-73, 75 (both), 77, 79 (above), 81, 82 (below), 84, 85, 89, 90, 91 (both), 92 (both), 93 (both), 95, 100, 103, 104, 107, 108, 110, 112 (above), 114 (both), 115, 120, 211.

INDIANA STATE LIBRARY: pages 2-3, 4-5, 10 (below), 11 (above), 12, 13, 16 (below), 17 (all), 19, 20, 21, 22, 23, 30, 32, 34, 36, 37, 38 (right), 51 (below), 56, 57, 61 (below), 64, 65, 69 (below), 71, 74, 76, 78, 80, 82 (above), 86, 87, 94 (below), 97, 98, 101, 109, 118, 124, 152-153.

INDIANA STATE ARCHIVES, INDIANA COMMISSION ON PUBLIC RECORDS: 83, 113 (above), 131 (above), 145.

INDIANA UNIVERSITY ARCHIVES: 54.